RAIN OF ASH

Rain of Ash

ROMA, JEWS, AND THE HOLOCAUST

ARI JOSKOWICZ

Dek, Feb. 1, 2024

for Robin

A. Joy

PRINCETON UNIVERSITY PRESS

PRINCETON & OXFORD

Published by Princeton University Press
41 William Street, Princeton, New Jersey 08540
99 Banbury Road, Oxford OX2 6JX

press.princeton.edu

All Rights Reserved

Library of Congress Cataloging-in-Publication Data
Names: Joskowicz, Ari, author.
Title: Rain of ash : Roma, Jews, and the Holocaust / Ari Joskowicz.
Other titles: Roma, Jews, and the Holocaust
Description: Princeton : Princeton University Press, 2023. | Includes bibliographical references and index.
Identifiers: LCCN 2022037764 (print) | LCCN 2022037765 (ebook) | ISBN 9780691244044 (hardback) | ISBN 9780691244037 (ebook)
Subjects: LCSH: Romani Genocide, 1939–1945. | World War, 1939–1945—Atrocities. | Holocaust, Jewish (1939–1945) | Romanies—Nazi persecution—Historiography. | Romani Genocide, 1939–1945—Historiography. | BISAC: HISTORY / Modern / 20th Century / Holocaust | POLITICAL SCIENCE / Genocide & War Crimes
Classification: LCC D804.5.G85 J67 2023 (print) | LCC D804.5.G85 (ebook) | DDC 940.53/1808991497—dc23/eng/20220809
LC record available at https://lccn.loc.gov/2022037764
LC ebook record available at https://lccn.loc.gov/2022037765

British Library Cataloging-in-Publication Data is available

Editorial: Priya Nelson, Barbara Shi, and Emma Wagh
Production Editorial: Nathan Carr
Jacket/Cover Design: Katie Osborne
Production: Danielle Amatucci
Publicity: Alyssa Sanford and Charlotte Coyne
Copyeditor: Lachlan Brooks

This book has been composed in Arno

Printed on acid-free paper. ∞

Printed in the United States of America

10 9 8 7 6 5 4 3 2 1

To my grandparents

CONTENTS

PREFACE

FOR MUCH OF my childhood, my four grandparents came to our house on Sundays. Sometimes, as we sat around my family's large dining table with coffee and cake in the afternoon, they would speak about the dark times. Their stories of the calamities they suffered in ghettos and concentration camps came without explanation because they told them to each other, Jewish survivor to Jewish survivor. I grew up as a Jew in Vienna in the 1980s at a moment of intense debate about Austrian complicity in Nazi crimes, so these stories made intuitive sense to me as accounts of our family's and community's origins. Yet, their details were lost on me. Although my grandparents came from different places and backgrounds and faced violence at the hands of different perpetrators, the traumatic episodes they lived through blurred into a single story of gruesome things that happened in unnamed camps. Familiar with the general narrative of the Holocaust but unable to distinguish between labor and extermination camps or between German and Romanian killers, I had little sense of chronology or causality. Without historical context or an analytical framework, I remember the sentiment but not the content of most of their stories. With my grandparents long gone, deprived of the opportunity to ask them about their lives, I feel the lesson of these Sunday afternoons keenly: empathy without knowledge is fleeting.

Many scholars have written in recent decades about the complicated relationship between history and memory, noting how the formal study of the past can either challenge or reinforce individuals' recollections. My experience of my grandparents' accounts reflects both patterns. On the one hand, information I have gleaned from academic books and historical documents contradicts some of the stories my grandparents told. Yet the process of researching the Holocaust has also opened up new personal, emotional, and ethical dimensions of my family's narratives. Seemingly dry and impersonal information, such as administrative records, chronologies of events, and statistics, has helped me grasp the depth of their losses and the complexities of their experiences. My grandmother's story of survival during the war acquired special meaning for me after one encounter with a compilation of names and numbers a few years back. Perusing a *Book of Remembrance* with the names of German, Austrian, and Czech Jews whom the Nazis had deported to the Baltic countries, I found my grandmother listed among those forced onto a train that departed Vienna's Aspang rail station for Riga on January 26, 1942. Of the 1,001 Jews on the transport that day, only 31 lived to see liberation. The sheer improbability of my grandmother's survival suddenly became clear to me, lending new weight to her accounts.

My grandparents' conversations about camps—whose names I could not recall—also conveyed a different kind of knowledge. My most vivid memory is not a particular story my grandparents related but the shame I felt about my own contribution to one such discussion. I must have been around ten when my paternal grandmother, Rosi, was speaking of the dangers that awaited inmates who tried to communicate between blocks in a concentration camp. Curious to understand why they had not resisted, I inquired whether barbed wire had divided the barracks. After she said no, I started wondering aloud why she and her fellow prisoners had not snuck into each other's blocks. I still remember the blank stares and embarrassed silence in the room before they returned to their conversation. I understood immediately that they considered my question thoughtless—a reflection of my youth and the fact that I had learned about violence only from Hollywood action movies. These moments of painful miscommunication contained their own essential lessons. Knowing what to say, what to ask, and when to remain silent allows us to strengthen familial and communal bonds of trust and understanding.

I see my students experience something similar as they are socialized into the academic community, sometimes learning about "good" questions by watching others ask theirs, sometimes learning by trial and (humiliating) error. In the process, they also realize that the questions that prevail in one community can appear inappropriate in another. In recent decades, scholars of the Holocaust have turned their attention to experiences of sexual violence during the war, for example. I cannot begin to imagine what my grandparents' reaction would have been if someone had raised the topic at a family gathering. Yet the scholarly community has long had its own taboos, which were not necessarily shared by their historical subjects. After the war, many survivors felt comfortable talking about their desire for revenge, even as historians were largely unwilling to broach such themes.

As I reflect on my own process of learning new questions, I suspect that the issues I raise in the following pages represent a departure from what my grandparents would have considered sensible topics. In this book, I explore the relations between Jewish and Romani victims of Nazism during the Holocaust as well as their attempts to come to terms with their parallel fates ever since. These relations were often distant, unequal, and full of hurtful misunderstandings. I do not know what my grandparents thought of Roma because I cannot recall anyone speaking of them on those Sunday afternoons. The people they would have called "Gypsies" simply never came up. I cannot say whether my grandparents did not talk about them because they did not encounter Roma in the years of persecution and destruction, or whether they lacked a framework within which to remember and convey these experiences. Did they lack words, chronologies, and connections that would have given meaning to any interactions they might have had with Roma?

Whatever the answer, their silence on this topic was not unusual. Despite the fact that Jews played an outsized role in the struggle to recognize and conserve stories of Romani suffering during the war, most Jews, including Jewish Holocaust survivors such as my grandparents, expressed little interest in the topic. The same can be said of my other communities, scholars of the Jewish past and of the Holocaust. While historians of the Holocaust have started to deal with the Romani genocide, they have mostly studied the actions of the perpetrators, rather than the lives of their Romani victims. This largely comes down to a problem of expertise and method, as I have experienced myself. Wading into the field of Romani history has thrust me into the position of student once again. In the process, my background as a Jew and a scholar of Jewish history has been both an opportunity and an obstacle.

Over the years, many Jewish scholars have written books about the Holocaust based on the lives of their ancestors. This is not one of them. My grandparents will not appear again in the following pages because this is a book about the stories they never told.

RAIN OF ASH

Introduction

Jews and Roma in the Shadow of Genocide

Encamped Gypsies from Lithuania and Poland,
You bearded men, daughters like black earth,
Berlin ordered all of you killed,
Slaughtering a forest with song and laughter.
Together with the Jews they burned you,
For both, the earth ripped apart in ritual mourning,
A rain of ash purified the bones,
A rain of ash over Mother Vilija.
And your wagons, muddy and rotten,
Encamped Gypsies from Lithuania and Poland.

Pushkin revealed your splendor, your wandering.
His heart drummed within your bandura.
Will another memorialize the Gypsy extermination in song,
With the same melodious heroism?
Unless the nightingale will, the only elegist
That accompanied you to the snake pits.
The willow crowns darkly bend,
And absorb you into their green thoughts.
O tribe of honored poets above all!
It may be that Petro has remained the last of you.

AVROM SUTZKEVER, "ENCAMPED GYPSIES"
("TABOREN ZIGEINER")[1]

WORLD WAR TWO inextricably linked Romani and Jewish history. Across Europe, Jews and Roma died together at the hands of the same murderers, often in the very same places. Yet the world did not register and acknowledge their destruction equally. In the years and decades that followed, Jews managed to have their accounts of persecution heard and documented. Roma, by contrast, struggled to gain recognition of everything they had suffered and lost.

It was this realization that compelled Avrom Sutzkever, the most famous Yiddish poet of the great Jewish calamity, to write about the Romani Holocaust. Who would tell the story of the Roma's wartime slaughter, he wondered, and how should their lesser-known mass murder be remembered? Sutzkever's poem "Encamped Gypsies," composed in Moscow and Paris between 1945 and 1947, raised these questions when few considered them. It conjures a shared native land whose soil mourns its children by tearing itself up, much as Jews mourn their dead by ritually tearing their clothing. Sutzkever's poem also invokes those whom he believed were most able to portray Romani life: either Roma themselves, or non-Romani writers such as the Russian author Alexander Pushkin, who penned a famous epic poem about "Gypsies" in the 1820s. Yet, Sutzkever suggested, the Roma had all but disappeared, and there was no new Pushkin in sight. The task of memorializing the Romani victims was left only to the melodious but wordless nightingale—and perhaps to the Jewish author himself.

Sutzkever wrote in Yiddish, the language of beleaguered survivors who had just lost everything. During these years, his Jewish readers struggled to come to terms with the murder of their families and the unprecedented scale of the genocidal campaign that had been leveled against them; they sought to honor the dead and to indict the murderers while finding ways to move on. It is hardly surprising that most Jews under these conditions did not share Sutzkever's point of view and felt no moral imperative to discuss the fate of people many of them hardly knew. We should not presume that people who have experienced oppression or persecution will necessarily have a greater capacity to hear others' stories of suffering or to feel connected to other victims.

What would Sutzkever have found if he had sought out the people he depicted as having vanished? He might have read the 1946 account of the Latvian Rom Vania Kochanowski about the murder of Roma not far from Sutzkever's native city of Vilna (Vilnius), or learned songs such as "Aušvicate hi kher báro" ("In Auschwitz There is a Large House"), sung by Romanies in Auschwitz and still performed in different versions today.[2] He might have also discovered Roma who compared their own experiences to that of Jews, such as Rudolf Braidić, a

Yugoslav circus performer who in 1948 sought support for himself and his family from the International Refugee Organization. Describing his experiences under fascism, Braidić explained that the Italians "wanted to send me to Croatia, with the family, but I refused to go," since "for us, GYPSEY, was very dangerous to go there, same as to Jews."[3] Across the Cold War West, which boasted some of the most effective infrastructure to document and study the Nazi genocides, many Roma sought to bring attention to their suffering by likening their fate to the better-known persecution of Jews. Whether they claimed monetary compensation, new residency status, or protection from discrimination, Romani survivors regularly drew parallels to Jews' experiences during the war.

Braidić's appeal has no equivalent in Jewish files, just as Sutzkever's poem has none in Romani sources. This is not a matter of genre—Roma authored poetry and Jews submitted judicial appeals. Instead, the difference has to do with the way Jewish and Romani experiences of World War Two have been collected and recounted. Some Jews conceded that "Gypsies suffered like us," while Roma routinely claimed, "we suffered like the Jews." "We suffered like them" and "they suffered like us" might sound similar enough, yet they emerge from very unequal positions. This book is about this unequal relationship and the profound consequences it has for our understanding of the Holocaust and its aftermath.

———

Long before the Nazis targeted both groups, Jews and Roma faced similar stereotypes.[4] For much of the modern period, members of each group appeared in European sources as alien and rootless.[5] The idiom of ethnic nationalism that took hold in nineteenth-century Central and Eastern Europe raised the stakes of these negative portrayals for both groups. Nationalists in European countries with the largest Romani and Jewish populations envisioned the transformation of dynastic states into polities that would represent groups of descent, united by spiritual characteristics and embodied in culture, language, religion, and blood relations. The language of national self-determination easily translated into the notion that Jews and Roma were outsiders, or, at best, mere guests.[6] Proponents of such visions also articulated their sense of Jews' and Romanies' innate differences in physiological terms that increasingly found elaboration in the language of racial science after the late nineteenth century.[7]

These similarities notwithstanding, the differences in the ways outsiders perceived Roma and Jews were just as crucial to their entangled histories.

Political leaders, state bureaucrats, and ordinary citizens often imagined "Gypsies" at the bottom of the social ladder while fearing what they perceived as Jews' power, whether as radicalized poor immigrants or a cabal of influential elites. Neither the denunciations of Jewish finance capital nor fears about "Judeo-Bolshevism" had equivalents in anti-Romani campaigns.[8] As a result, antisemites viewed Jews as a political threat worthy of the creation of entire movements dedicated to anti-Jewish activism, while xenophobic Europeans tended to portray Roma as a social problem to be dealt with inconspicuously by security forces and local authorities.[9]

Differences—more than the similarities—also came to characterize Romani and Jewish self-descriptions, their perceptions of each other, and the divergent resources they had at their disposal as they sought to respond to their marginalization. Jews lived disproportionally in the urban core, whether in large cities, mid-sized towns, or small villages, whereas Roma were often relegated to the urban periphery or rural areas.[10] Roma also tended to have low rates of literacy, whereas Jews were among the most literate groups in Europe.[11] In some cases, Romani and Eastern European Jewish migrants to countries farther west looked similar to outsiders: bureaucrats often treated both with disdain and suspicion, for example.[12] Yet, by the second half of the nineteenth century, even indigent and disenfranchised Jews were able to participate in robust political movements that represented them while also drawing on the support of Jewish philanthropic organizations, opportunities that were largely unavailable to Roma.[13]

Interconnected local and transnational networks of Jews found support in a highly literate, economically mobile, urban population, including in small towns. Jews' ability to draw on professional nongovernmental associations that transcended individual communities, and the absence of similar organizing among Roma, changed each group's ability to react to persecution, aid migration, and commemorate events. While ethnic nationalism and biological racism increasingly inspired the exclusion of Jews and Roma on similar grounds, with the rise of modern politics, Jewish and Romani lives diverged more than ever. Members of each group connected differently to those with political power, followed different routes of economic advancement, and found that they had unequal opportunities to assert themselves individually and as groups throughout the nineteenth century.

These disparities in resources and forms of self-organization also hint at the ways the two groups related to each other. Underlying many discussions of marginality are spatial metaphors about insiders and outsiders.[14] Like depictions of state territories on a map, imagining insiders and outsiders requires only two dimensions. There are those who reside inside the ethno-national circle of unchallenged membership in the state, nation, or society, and those who do not belong there. Most commentators who rightly point to Jews and Roma as targets of nationalist ire think in these implicitly horizontal terms.

Yet, political mobilization against Jews and Roma, as well as their views of each other, also relied on assumptions about economic and social prestige in society. Sizing each other up from a distance on the street, trading with each other at the marketplace, considering possible romantic or sexual liaisons, Jews and Roma also measured their relative social standing in hierarchical terms, as people on the top and at the bottom of society. For many Roma and Jews, the vertical aspect of their relationship was paramount in defining their sense of each other.

The compensation claims of the Hamburg lawyer and businessman Edgar Behr illustrate this tendency to think of the world in terms of hierarchies and status. The Nazi regime had identified Behr as a half-Jew, since his father—the owner of the major import firm Ribeco—was Jewish. After managing to remain employed and free for most of the war, the Nazi regime drafted him into a forced labor battalion in September 1944. Some years after the war, in 1952, he requested compensation for his seven months of slave labor. To buttress his claims he explained how the work felt demeaning to him: "I experienced the shared work with Gypsies and prisoners as particularly discriminating."[15] Other Jewish witnesses may have been less blunt but still managed to communicate that they considered being placed next to "Gypsies" an affront to their dignity.[16] Such individuals presumably believed that both officials and the wider public would understand their sentiments—a rational assumption given the pervasive anti-Romani prejudice that persists into the present.

Romani testimonies also sometimes express expectations of vertical hierarchies in interactions with Jews. The interviews that the sociologist Gabrielle Tyrnauer collected for the Fortunoff archive in 1991 are typical in this regard. Producing the first large set of audiovisual recordings with Romani survivors for a major archive, Tyrnauer purposefully highlighted her own identity as a Jew to help her interlocutors open up. In turn, these Romani survivors repeatedly appealed to connections they believed the Canadian scholar might have as a Jew to sway the German government on their behalf.[17] The result is that her interviews on the Holocaust illustrate conflicting ideas about political influence among Jewish academics and their Romani interlocutors. While Tyrnauer tried to relate to her Romani interviewees as fellow outsiders, they often treated her as someone with a fundamentally different role in society—in other words, as a Jew with power.

Of course, status is not stable. It gets renegotiated in each new social or political context. Individual Romanies and their families might have a respected role in the local economy or acquire wealth, just as indigent Jews might encounter scorn and social ostracism. Yet in new encounters with people they could not easily place, members of each group frequently made assumptions about each other's status, reflecting the prejudices of their environment. The sense that Jews and Roma had different social and economic opportunities dominated relations between members of the two groups before, during, and after the Holocaust—even as the shared language of fighting exclusion (horizontally) eventually became central to commemorative efforts.

Measures targeting Roma and Jews also differed in how publicly they were set in motion, complicating the attempts of sympathetic members of both communities to document and discuss their persecution together. In most contexts, Roma experienced what I would call silent persecution—the kind of targeting that takes place at the level of experts and in local decisions that often leave few traces. By the end of the nineteenth century, their exclusion took its force from the power of administrators to decide that certain Romani individuals or collectives were not entitled to citizenship or legal protections.[18] Such decisions met with limited objections. Even those who otherwise proudly upheld constitutional rights—including members of liberal parties and Social Democrats—rarely took exception when administrators decided to exclude "Gypsies" from the right to move across borders in spite of valid identity papers or to detain them as suspicious enemies during wartime.[19] To most observers, the surveillance of Romani populations and limitations on their movement and freedom of occupation seemed reasonable. This racism toward "Gypsies," which few Jews publicly objected to in the prewar era, also motivated and facilitated anti-Romani measures during Nazi rule.[20] The Nazis and their allies rarely campaigned with explicitly anti-Romani messages and left local actors a good deal of leeway in determining who qualified as a "Gypsy" for persecution measures.[21] These decisions, therefore, left a considerably smaller paper trail than the extended debates over the identification, exclusion, and removal of Jews during Nazi rule.

Roma were only one among many groups facing such silent persecution, of course, and many Jews faced similar injustices. For example, Roma and Jews were equally the subject of refugee panics that led to new registration practices and changes to citizenship laws in the late nineteenth and early twentieth centuries.[22] Such measures caused deep disruptions to the lives of many Roma and Jews and forced them to suffer abuses by local administrators.

However, anti-Jewish activities both before and during World War Two were distinct from anti-Romani policies in so far as they were more likely to produce substantial political noise as well as a substantial paper trail. Parliaments discussed anti-"Gypsy" legislation, but these deliberations largely produced a consensus that transcended left-right divisions. By contrast, legislative debates on Jews were contentious and offered politicians an opportunity to clarify their positions on major social and political issues. In the first two years of the French Revolution, the National Assembly dedicated no less than thirty-two parliamentary sessions to the subject of whether to give Jews—who constituted less than one percent of the population—citizens' rights.[23] One estimate claims that around 2,500 works on Jewish emancipation appeared in German lands between 1815 and 1850.[24] Such disproportionate attention to the rights and actions of a small minority only grew by the late nineteenth century, when parties on the right made the threat of Jews, Jewish money, and Jewish liberalism a signature theme.[25] Unlike much of the discrimination that was quietly leveled against Roma, with little debate, anti-Jewish sentiment was something people mulled over publicly and vocally—and also something that Jews opposed with just as much debate and ink. The challenge is to think of these dimensions—the relative silence or noise accompanying persecution and the traces it left—without creating hierarchies of suffering.

———

Comparisons between the experiences of Jews and Roma have their own checkered history. Even as their differences shaped relations between members of each group in palpable ways, attempts to compare them created new inequalities. This dynamic was evident in a legal case from 1952, when a German appeals court weighed whether a Romani family would receive monetary compensation for their persecution under Nazism. The family's trial was one of a series of proceedings that concerned the deportation of German Sinti and Roma to Nazi-occupied Poland in May 1940, an event which many state offices did not consider racial persecution as defined under state law.[26] To evaluate the Romani applicants' claim, the court looked closely at the intentions of Nazi officials and the conditions that the Romani deportees had experienced, comparing them to the conditions Jews had faced. In their interpretation of deportation policies, the judges took Nazi administrators at their word: following the reasons provided in the relevant decrees, they argued that the deportations were necessary military and police measures and thus not a form of racial persecution. The comparisons they drew to the suffering of Jews were equally damning. The judges wanted to know about markings on prison uniforms, the existence of barbed wire fences, and whether the Nazis split up families. They concluded that none of the experiences of the Romani claimants counted as persecution "when we use Jewish fellow citizens as a comparison." Whereas "Jewish families were torn apart mercilessly," the "Gypsies" stayed together; whereas "all Jewish inmates of ghettos were shot," the Nazis had not extended the same treatment to "Gypsies." Remarking on the fate of the Romani claimant's family when they lived briefly on the territory of the former Jewish ghetto in the Polish city of Siedlce, the court noted that the situation of Sinti and Roma improved when they gained additional resources after the murder of Siedlce's Jewish population. In light of these differences, and without written evidence from the Nazis that they intended their measures as racial persecution, the court decided to reject these Romani survivors' compensation claims.[27]

This judgment reminds us that comparisons between the experiences of victims are not academic matters. They have real-life consequences for victims and their families, as well as for those who identify as members of the larger group. Their claims to compensation as individuals and to historical redress for the group, even after the death of the victims, depends on their inclusion in capricious categories. Undoubtedly, some comparisons are unavoidable. As humans, we understand events in relative terms. This was true for the victims of Nazism who compared their situation to previous policies against their group and policies enacted against others at the same time. It is equally true for administrators and historians who seek to gather similar events into categories that allow them to make sense of a chaotic reality. Administrators sometimes needed to figure out whether a person's particular fate counted as "racial persecution" as defined by law and legal precedent, much as historians have often sought to determine which cases of mass murder qualify as "genocide." Such disputes often come down to empirical questions: What were the intentions of policy makers? Did they intend to kill all members of a group or was their approach more arbitrary? Did certain individuals suffer more or less than others?

The history of such comparisons should make us suspicious of the very questions that have spurred them. Scholarly debates on the murder of Europe's Romani population show just how unproductive these questions can be. For decades, historians and activists fought over the degree of similarity between the Nazi genocides of Jews and Roma. These conflicts have seen multiple itera- tions, often accompanied by recriminations from everyone involved that members of the other side were arguing in bad faith. In the 1980s and 1990s, Yehuda Bauer, one of the most senior historians of the Holocaust, emphasized in several essays that the mass murder of Roma was neither pursued as fer- vently nor as systematically as that against Jews. Opposing his view, the histo- rian Sybil Milton argued that the crucial similarity consisted of collective de- portations and murder due to heredity.[28] A few years later, these conflicts continued in a heated exchange between Bauer and the Romani civil rights leader Romani Rose.[29] Many others have also sought to take on the question of genocide, focusing on intent: together with Yehuda Bauer, Gilad Margalit and Guenther Lewy have claimed that the Nazis did not have a plan for the murder of all Roma, whereas Ian Hancock, Anton Weiss-Wendt, and a host of recent scholars emphasize the dynamic nature of Nazi intentions that corrobo- rate an evolving desire for universal extermination.[30]

Yet, these scholarly debates do not address how we should determine the relevant criteria for such comparisons. Like the administrators and the judges of the past, who tested whether a predefined category of "racial persecution" fit the history of the Romani survivors who stood before them, historians and activists in these debates tend to emphasize their detachment. As Weiss- Wendt puts it in his discussion of the murder of the Roma, he believes that the key term must be "genocide" because it offers "emotionally neutral scholarly terminology."[31] But this attempt to invoke scholarly neutrality clashes with the reality of genocide as a "normative action-oriented concept."[32] The use of the term aims at moral condemnation that allows for political intervention or ju- dicial action and focuses on the collective intent of the perpetrators. In most societies, including Nazi Europe, where the state and other parts of society interacted to carry out mass violence, this means scholars must reduce the actions of many to a single idea or ideology. This tends to work better for the loud persecution experienced by Jews than for the relatively silent persecution experienced by Romanies. It is also dubious whether we can avert future geno- cidal violence—a frequent claim made by scholars of genocide—if compari- sons lead us to rank the loud persecution that leaves more traces above the silent persecution that eludes casual political observation. Looking at both in their distinctiveness, we might wonder: how do we know that administrative persecution is not the more urgent subject to study, especially in an age of algorithm-driven policing and the expansive use of digital surveillance?[33] In short, there is nothing neutral about the category of genocide, whether in scholarly, emotional, or political terms.

The mere fact that these comparisons have psychological, financial, and political stakes does not mean that the categories are biased. It does force us to come up with good explanations for choosing one criterion over another, however. There is no sensible way of adjudicating which questions are correct in the form that these debates usually take place. What we can find are categories that work better for one or the other case, or categories that allow us to make relevant and novel arguments. To do this, it is useful to consider how we come to know different instances of persecution and genocide. If we fail to reflect on how people left traces of past injustices and how these traces are passed down to us, we will easily reproduce the injustices of the past, as the postwar German court did when it took the explanations given in official Nazi orders at face value. With this aim in mind, I remain acutely aware that even the limited comparison that I have proposed here between silent and loud persecution could be understood as establishing a hierarchy between them. How to avoid this?

This book, which is in part an attempt to answer that fundamental question, pursues a relational history. Historians looking at relations between groups often concede that there is no relational history without comparisons first.[34] If we cannot distinguish between Jews and Roma, we cannot write the history of their interactions. Yet, in dealing with entangled histories, the opposite is also true. It is impossible to compare these mass killings unless we first grasp how interconnected experiences, records, historical categories, and methods of collecting and disseminating information have determined what we know about each genocide. This is not the same as a history of people who share intimacy, familiarity, or cultural worlds. Instead, Jews and Roma have become inextricably connected by proximate experiences, overlapping archival labor, and comparative perceptions of their fates.

———

The first permanent exhibition on the Romani Holocaust that opened in 1997 in Heidelberg, Germany, welcomes visitors with a large sign that declares: "The genocide against the Sinti and Roma was executed with the same motive of racial hatred, with the same intention and the same will to systematically and definitively exterminate as the genocide against the Jews." An identical sentence appears at the entrance of the Romani exhibit at the Auschwitz Museum and was also proposed, at an early stage, as an inscription for Berlin's Monument to the

Murdered Sinti and Roma of Europe.[35] As suggested by prominent displays of this quote, which is derived from a speech by German president Roman Herzog (1994–99), the Jewish Holocaust has long played a central role in explanations of the Nazi persecution and mass murder of Romanies.[36] At nearly every location where Romani representatives have chosen to create museums, monuments, and archives dedicated to their history, a Jewish museum, monument, or archive already exists. What is more, Jewish Holocaust institutions have become principal sites for knowledge production about Roma. Take, for example, the case of the University of Southern California (USC) Shoah Foundation: the foundation's 406 interviews with Romani survivors—which exist alongside over 50,000 interviews with Jewish survivors—makes its collection the largest repository of audiovisual testimony on the Romani Holocaust. Scholars interested in hearing the voices of Romani survivors often have little choice but to consult archives originally built to store the testimonies of Jews.

What does it mean for members of one minority group to control a large part of the archives and, thus, the history, of another? This may sound like an abstract problem, but to those who care about the Romani genocide, this was and remains a fundamental question with practical implications. Anyone who enters a Holocaust archive and searches for the words "Gypsies," "Roma" and related terms in the catalog, will first encounter the mass of Jewish testimonies that mention Romani victims rather than the (many fewer) testimonies of Roma themselves. Romani history is thus filtered through Jewish history.

Grappling with this fact while writing an integrated account of the racialized victims of the Nazi regime requires breaking down the conventional barrier in scholarship between what happened during the Holocaust and how it has been represented ever since. Many decades ago, when the field was still in its infancy, Saul Friedländer challenged this boundary in his book *Reflections on Nazism*.[37] In that work, Friedländer demonstrated the uncanny resemblance between Nazi depictions of violence as a melodramatic story of heroism, sacrifice, and apocalypticism and later representations of the Nazis' murderous policies, reminding his readers that we are prone to misread history if we ignore the connections between wartime and postwar accounts.[38]

The division between the history of the Holocaust and its aftermath in thought and representation becomes particularly unconvincing in light of the sources we use. Many foundational documents of Holocaust scholarship came to historians' attention thanks to the postwar prosecutors who collected them. This process began with the Nuremberg trials—the high-profile proceedings in the International Military Tribunal of 1945–46 and subsequent trials under the auspices of the US—when prosecutors published twenty-seven volumes of evidence to supplement forty-two volumes of trial records.[39] Indeed, courts not only assembled but also produced evidence when they compelled witnesses to give depositions. Many of the most prominent books about the Holocaust could not have been written without these judicial efforts to amass documents and statements from perpetrators, victims, and everyone in between.[40] Legal and historical interpretations from the postwar period—and not merely sources "from the time"—have thus determined what we know about people's experiences of Nazism.

Conversely, state documentation produced during the 1930s and 1940s has inevitably influenced both the unfolding and interpretation of history ever since. This includes the biased perspectives that perpetrators injected into their documentation, which postwar courts often took at face value when they adjudicated claims by Romani victims. Neglecting basic rules of historical source critique, they often accepted Nazi characterizations of Roma as "asocial," for example, treating this claim as a reasonable administrative motive for lawful persecution and ignoring its underlying racialization of an entire population. Other cases are less clear-cut but equally salient. Even the most sophisticated interpreters consistently rely on state documentation that purposefully conceals information—whether for administrative reasons or due to the interpretive limitations of its original authors.

Sources produced by victims, from Jewish newspapers to the earliest testimonies of mass killings smuggled out of Nazi-occupied Europe, present similar challenges. Their blind spots become evident, for example, in Jewish commentators' silence about the new detention facilities that German municipalities had already built for "Gypsies" on the outskirts of cities starting in the mid-1930s. Jewish observers at the time proved no more likely than their non-Jewish contemporaries to register the fundamental injustice of the forced removal of German Sinti and Roma to surveilled living quarters. Nor do they appear to have been any more insightful than others about the ways in which these institutions were laying the groundwork for more radical persecution. Postwar scholars—including survivor historians—similarly elided mention of this step in the development of a genocidal state infrastructure. In Romani history, as in the history of other groups whose marginalization has long appeared self-evident to their neighbors, these oversights result in a skewed view of the past that never reveals just how skewed it is.

The history I seek to tell in this book requires that we return to the very moments in which our sources came into being. One of the most influential descriptions of this imperative comes from Haitian anthropologist Michel-Rolph Trouillot, who argued that the complexity of history only becomes fully apparent once we have traced our story all the way back to its earliest articulations as well as to the original formation of our archives.[41] Taking this approach not only reminds us to reflect on the various circumstances that compelled the creation of each source and collection but also to recognize that history and memory are not discrete phenomena. The case of shared Romani and Jewish archives similarly necessitates a return to the Nazi period, when perpetrators, victims, and various others created the first and most substantial holdings in the field. "Memories" of the Holocaust were formed long before the war's end in 1945.

———

In many respects this book is not about "memory" as it is commonly understood but rather about the production of knowledge. This means, first, paying attention to the ways different entities register, collect, and make available traces of the past. New archives founded since World War Two to commemorate genocide and mass violence are pivotal in this regard. Holocaust and genocide archives are among the best-organized alternatives to the large, centralized collections of bureaucratic records—the traditional state archives—that emerged in Europe in the seventeenth and eighteenth centuries.[42]

They also offer another model for acquiring and grouping records and for making them available. Non-state collecting, including initiatives by private individuals, ethnographic societies, or local historical associations, initially focused on material ignored by well-funded state archives.[43] This changed with the Holocaust. The destruction of Jewish communities across Nazi-dominated Europe and the greater availability of microfilming and other reproduction methods led to the proliferation of new taxonomies of collecting, whereby archivists selectively copied official documents based on their significance for Jewish history.[44]

Archives documenting Nazi persecution of the Jews were at the forefront of this shift. The two largest—Yad Vashem and the United States Holocaust Memorial Museum—became vast repositories of recontextualized state documents, as well as testimony collections that they both produced themselves and incorporated from outside projects. Such institutions often collaborate with and build on the work of smaller institutions that preceded them, including the Wiener Library in London, the Jewish Historical Institute in Warsaw, the Ghetto Fighters' House in northern Israel, and the Center for Contemporary Jewish Documentation/ Mémorial de la Shoah in Paris. Many other institutions that were created to deal with Nazi crimes and antifascist resistance in a single state, such as the Netherlands Institute for War Documentation or the Documentation Center of Austrian Resistance, pivoted to collect broadly on issues of genocide. Together these repositories of knowledge are nodes in a transnational network that has allowed for the massive duplication of documents through microfilm and digitization. Today the combined resources of these institutions match those of traditional state archives in the role they play in supporting Holocaust scholarship.

In recent years historians have grown increasingly attuned to finding submerged voices in the archives of the powerful. Many scholars have mined colonial and police archives for evidence of the anxieties and biases of the powerful bureaucrats who created them.[45] Yet they have rarely used the same methods to interrogate archives of powerlessness, including the many centers dedicated to documenting Jews' experiences of the Holocaust. The histories of these collections are complex: built by a minority that was increasingly recognized and empowered in the decades after the war, they tell the history of Jews' radical subjugation and powerlessness under Nazism. Yet their holdings do not merely record the experiences of the people they were meant to empower. Hidden within them we can find other silenced experiences that disclose relations between different victim groups. Moving beyond the binary of archives created by the powerful and those of the powerless, we can see how Jewish archivists, activists, and scholars concerned with registering Jewish victimhood inadvertently wove the history of another group of victims into the fabric of Jewish history.

———

The developments that made Jewish archives centers for the creation of new information on Romani history reveal the roles that funding, networks, expertise, and time-consuming labor play in the production of historical knowledge. There are disadvantages to using the metaphor of memory to understand how societies deal with their past. Chief among them is the fact that, for individuals, memory comes for free, while collective memory requires resources.

How much did it cost to know about Jews' lives and deaths in Auschwitz-Birkenau? How much to understand the fate of Romanies there? These questions might seem trivial, but traces of the expenditures required to produce historical information appear everywhere. The Nuremberg trial records that form the bedrock of all source work in the field resulted from the efforts of dozens of experts who in turn worked for a massive legal and military bureaucracy. With many of the original wartime documents largely out of reach in archives of the Soviet Union and other communist states, prosecutors— primarily in West Germany—relied on these published collections. Yet, retrieving pertinent historical information remained a challenge that required extensive money, time, and networking skills. Well into the 1980s, entire teams of investigators continued to use all of their connections simply to locate original documents or discover basic facts about the Holocaust in academic books and journals.

The 1987–91 trial of the Auschwitz SS man Ernst August König for crimes committed in Auschwitz's "Gypsy camp" is a case in point. By this moment German courts had decided on hundreds of similar cases and could rely on the expertise of a central coordinating body, founded in 1958, for all investigations of Nazi crimes.[46] To assure König's conviction, Hans-Joachim Röseler, a senior public prosecutor from Cologne, worked with a police officer named Matyssek to establish simple information about Birkenau and its Romani prisoners that they would need to build their case. It took the two men over a year to realize that the registry books from the "Gypsy camp" survived, allowing them to prove when witnesses arrived in Auschwitz and when victims died. Even after they learned of these documents, however, they struggled to locate a copy. The Auschwitz Museum, which held the originals of the registry books, did not respond to their requests in a timely manner, requiring German investigators to use survivors as intercessors who promised to lobby the museum's director personally.[47] Eventually, Hamburg prosecutors informed Röseler that another institution, the International Tracing Service operated by the Red Cross, had a microfilm copy.[48] Although Röseler and Matyssek appear in court documents as well-meaning and sophisticated investigators, it took them months to identify and acquire material that is now available as a published book at most research libraries.[49] Accumulating testimonies was even more cumbersome. To interrogate three witnesses in three southern German cities, Röseler and Matyssek drove fifty hours and approximately 930 miles together in mid-December 1985.[50] Collective and institutional "memory" work requires a serious investment of resources, and these investments determine what reaches us.

The internet often seems to resolve such issues, and yet this is only the most recent chapter in the economic history of information processing and retrieval, rather than its conclusion. Undergraduate students in my Holocaust course compile bibliographies on specialized subjects and locate each text in a day using digital resources, whereas previously scholars commonly needed months to get ahold of a single article. But the current availability of sources is the result of labor done out of sight, including the expensive original digitization of catalogs and collections. Such labor is paid indirectly through taxes, fees, endowment incomes, and—in the case of general search engines—the sale of aggregate user data. Even as the price of knowledge production and dissemination changes, the disadvantages of limited resources have persisted. The familiar gatekeepers who decide on the content of scholarly training, research funding, or professional certification are now joined by those who select what gets digitized first or control popular websites and podcasts. It has simply become harder to pinpoint exactly who makes these decisions.

Examining financial resources in the context of genocide memorialization may seem an uncomfortable choice given that some critics—and many dedicated antisemites—have accused Jews of cynically profiting from Holocaust memory.[51] It is perhaps for this reason that scholars have resisted studying the mechanics of the funding that has supported and continues to support new Holocaust research. Yet, there need be no contradiction between caring deeply about the Holocaust and recognizing the importance of funding research on the subject. Understanding the history of the financial and institutional scaffolding that sustains the field of Holocaust Studies is especially important in the context of this book, which explores the relations between one group (Jews), which has historically had greater resources than another (Roma). Without understanding the economy of knowledge production about the Jewish Holocaust we cannot start to come to terms with the Romani Holocaust or the relationship between the two groups. The ethical and epistemological challenges that emerge from these parallel genocides come into view only when we add to our familiar moral vocabulary of "recognizing others" and "hearing silenced voices" less familiar formulas, such as "investing in knowing" about others. The voices of the past may be preserved in poems, songs, and petitions, but they reach us increasingly through digitization initiatives, research grants, and websites that make them available to scholars and the broader public.

———

Disparities in documentation reflect the unequal status of Roma and Jews almost everywhere they have lived in recent centuries. Most works on these two groups begin with introductions that illustrate one element of this imbalance: scholars presume that readers know who Jews are, but not Roma.

Beginning with book and article titles, scholars make choices about naming their subjects in Romani history that rarely arise in Jewish history. Should they choose the term "Gypsies," the designation used in most historical sources, but which most people to whom the term applies understand to be insulting? Or do they choose one of many self-designations that exist, such as Roma? Each decision raises new methodological challenges. Those who retain the appellation "Gypsy" argue that it is inaccurate to translate the term into our current ethnicized language because the term shifted over time from an administrative category with a strong social component to one with clear ethnic and racial dimensions. From the seventeenth to the nineteenth century, European administrators usually used the word "Gypsies" to refer to a variety of people who roamed the streets and whom they suspected of engaging in criminal behavior.[52] In some ways, this broader meaning informed the Nazi persecution of Yenish, non-Romani travelers in central Europe, and has remained politically important in other contexts such as the United Kingdom, where Romani and Traveller communities have combined forces for political self-organization.[53]

At the same time, many scholars and Romani representatives argue that those who treat Roma as a figment of state officials' imaginations silence their history in the process.[54] They insist that scholars write the history of Roma like that of any ethnic group with its own customs, practices, and linguistic traditions, even if their centuries-long marginalization makes it difficult to find their lives in historical sources. These reasonable demands for a national history—no more constructed or hazy than all other national histories—pose challenges for historians who do not wish to racialize the individuals and groups they encounter in official sources. It takes much effort and some informed speculation to claim that a "Gypsy" in a legal document from the seventeenth or eighteenth century was Romani.[55] Administrators in the past shared this challenge: they often did not agree on who was a "Gypsy" and found it difficult to count them through a census or civil registry. Roma also had few incentives to register themselves as "Gypsies" or under equivalent categories, which tended to have only disadvantages.[56]

Using an ethnic lens brings its own problems. Among these is the risk of giving the impression that Roma constitute a homogeneous group when, in fact, Europe's Romani population hails from diverse communities whose relations were often tenuous and who likely only started to conceive of themselves as part of a larger ethnic whole in the course of the twentieth century—if they did at all. Historically, Roma adhered to different religious traditions—being predominantly Catholic (and sometimes Protestant) in Western Europe, Christian

Orthodox in Eastern Europe and Russia, and Muslim in certain parts of South-eastern Europe, Turkey, and the Middle East—although such divisions have recently begun to blur as growing numbers of Romanies around the world have turned to Pentecostalism. In different contexts, Roma have spoken mutually unintelligible varieties of Romani or indeed no Romani language at all, and they may have understood members of other Romani groups as following related traditions but still frowned on intermarriage with them. By the modern era, the majority of Roma in Central, Eastern and Southeastern Europe spent most or all of the year in one home, while many Western European Romanies traveled for longer periods. Romani groups and individuals also differ widely in their approach to commemorating their dead and past violence against them.[57] When scholars treat this diversity of people as a single group, they often highlight Romani groups' shared origins following their migrations from India to Europe in the Middle Ages. Though linguistic research supports assertions of the shared ancestry of Romani speakers, such perspectives have only relatively recently begun to come to the forefront of the ways that Roma think about and organize themselves. It was largely their shared desire to protect their rights and traditions in the face of societies that continued to constrain their freedoms as well as their shared experience of calamity that increasingly united Roma across Europe and the globe.[58]

Romanies' earliest attempts to organize politically in the interwar period showcase the diversity of Romani constituencies even as they sought to unify them. Across interwar Eastern and Southeastern Europe, Roma established small organizations to represent them vis-à-vis the authorities and to further the education and social standing of fellow Roma. Some of these efforts were local, such as the Romani mutual aid society that formed in the Yugoslav capital of Belgrade, or limited to representatives of one occupation, as with the interwar Hungarian unions of "Gypsy musicians."[59] Other associations, such as those in Romania and the early Soviet Union, aspired to speak for all Roma in a single country.[60] Yet, these short-lived efforts by individuals often clashed with the self-perception of many Roma who identified the leaders of these organizations as speaking for only a particular Romani subgroup. Although these organizations sometimes reported in their newsletters and newspapers about "Gypsies" elsewhere, their focus was not on forging transnational alliances. Ideas about Roma as Europe's largest ethnic minority or as a global diaspora have existed as compelling motifs of common mobilization and political lobbying only since the second half of the twentieth century.[61]

The genocide of Roma during World War Two—and attempts to understand their murder as similar and related to the mass murder of Jews—played a central role in this shifting perception.[62] Since the 1960s, documentation, lobbying, and history writing among Romani scholars and activists as well as their allies has encouraged a view of Roma as a transnational minority. Perhaps not surprisingly, a sense of unity among Roma is strongest wherever politics matters most—for example in the Romani youth movement described in chapter 6—even when it is not a lived reality for all Roma.

Despite all this, I am convinced that the insights gained by framing their history in the twentieth and twenty-first centuries with terms such as "Roma" outweigh the costs. We can remain aware of the diversity of experiences, traditions, and outlooks among different communities and yet speak of the pressures, opportunities, and situations that many Roma have shared, and continue to share. This approach also makes it easier to think in terms of a relational history with another group—Jews—whose members are not asked to prove their shared history.

This is not to suggest that the idea of Jewish unity has remained uncontested. Jews regularly reject each other's claims to Jewishness, look down on coreligionists who are different from them, and obsess over tensions between religious, nationalist, and non-normative definitions of Judaism. Yet anyone who ventures into both fields will be struck by the level of agreement between scholars and laypeople about the subjects of Jewish history when compared to the contentiousness of the topic in most Romani Studies settings.

The choices I make in this book reflect the semantic peculiarities of transnational Romani history. For the most part, I will speak of Roma and sometimes of Romanies. The former is the most common term, while the latter is a chiefly British usage but has the advantage of being more inclusive than the alternatives. It is generally understood to encompass numerous subgroups ranging from Romanian Kalderash to British Romanichals, including German Sinti, who often reject Roma as an umbrella term. The term Romanies also mirrors the adjective Romani, which is universally accepted in all English usage.[63] When I was certain that the vast majority of individuals in a particular situation would have identified as Sinti, the preferred name of Romani groups in German and adjacent lands, I have used that term, or the compound Sinti and Roma.[64] Eschewing a single term not only allows for stylistic variety but also recognizes the lexical diversity that characterizes Romani Studies. This is something Jewish Studies does not offer. Historical alternatives once employed to refer to Jews—Israelites, people of the Mosaic persuasion, Hebrews—have been deemed obsolete for good reason.

As is true of the Nazi genocide of Jews, survivors and commentators have used a variety of terms to speak of the Nazi genocide of Roma. Survivors sometimes used concrete descriptions—such as speaking of "when we were deported to the Bug," an expression common among Romanian Roma referring to their deportation to Transnistria, in Romanian-occupied Ukraine, near the Bug River. With time, activists and scholars sought a single term that might capture the targeting of Roma across Europe in unambiguous ways, parallel to the word "Shoah" for the Jewish Holocaust. The best-known of these names is Porrajmos, coined in the early 1990s by the Romani linguist and US-based activist Ian Hancock.[65] While the term is now commonly used by non-Romani academics, it has fallen out of favor among many Romani representatives because of its troubling connotations: the term translates not only as the "devouring" but also has sexual undertones and can be metaphorically understood to refer to sexual violence.[66] Another scholar, Marcel Courthiade, championed the alternative term Samudaripen (a Romani word for mass killing). Although many Romani activists prefer this term, it has been slow to catch on. I have decided to refer to the Romani Holocaust both because it is broadly legible and to emphasize its simultaneity with the Jewish Holocaust. No doubt, the term Holocaust has its own problems. Critics will note that its origins are in a Greek term for a sacred burnt offering, implying inappropriately that the victims of genocide might be seen as the equivalent of a divine sacrifice.[67] Other scholars emphasize that the term has a long secular use to describe a major atrocity rather than genocide specifically—a use illustrated by some of the actors in this book.[68] Irrespective of its etymology, the term remains the most widely understood, and—more importantly—its inadequacies apply equally to both of the cases discussed here.[69] Ultimately, referring to both the Romani and Jewish Holocausts allows me to underline a central point of this book: that an integrated history of the Nazi genocide and its aftermath requires an adequate treatment of both calamities as connected events.

———

In the immediate wake of the war, Avrom Sutzkever wrote about the Romani genocide as a crime without witnesses that required an epic and poetic response. Over the past decades, we have become weary of the "melodious heroism" that he prescribed as the remedy. We have also come to understand that there were, in fact, many witnesses as well as textual and material traces to the decimation of Europe's Romanies. To take up his challenge today involves pausing to think about what makes it possible for us to speak of the suffering of others. This requires us to remain attuned to Sutzkever's appeal to our empathic and imaginative faculties but also to the politics, technologies, and economies of knowing.

Tracing the relationship between Roma and Jews from Nazi camps and killing sites to the archives that contain documentation of Nazi crimes, this book offers an alternative history of episodes that scholars have primarily analyzed through a Jewish lens. Starting with the victims' fate under Nazism, their early struggles to rebuild shattered lives, and their first attempts to document injustice and seek redress in courts, it ends with the rise of a new memorial culture, and the politicization of memory in debates over colonialism and Zionism. Rethinking these moments as formative for the history of Jews and Roma alike not only unsettles received narratives about the Holocaust but also probes the very means by which those narratives have come down to us.

I wrote this book as members of a new generation of Roma and Jews engage in an intimate dialogue about the past, minority politics and the state of Israel that would have been unthinkable in the early postwar years. This study of the unlikely trajectory from the incomprehension of the suffering of the other to shared archives, activism, and lobbying offers a new integrated history of Nazis' racialized victims. Itself a product of the burgeoning Romani-Jewish engagement that it describes, it is also an attempt to inspire a new dialogue about the opportunities and challenges of such unequal alliances.

1

Roma and Jews in Nazi Europe

IN NOVEMBER 1966, a German prosecutor asked Konrad Reinhard to recall the time he had spent imprisoned in Auschwitz-Birkenau. Reinhard had been working as a musician at a café in the German city of Essen when the police arrested him with his wife and three children and deported them as "Gypsies" to the camp.[1] In Birkenau, he played in the orchestra and was subsequently assigned various duties, including a labor detail charged with upkeep of the camp and another that built sewage lines. Reinhard's access to different parts of the sprawling compound made him a promising witness. Prosecutors hoped that he might have observed SS men mistreating Jews at the ramp where Hungary's Jews arrived beginning in spring 1944. Reinhard could not identify any of the suspects involved in the selection process but did have something to say about the mass murder of Jews:

> I wanted to figure out and to know what is happening to us and the others who have been deported with us. Then at some point during my time in the camp I was able to see how arriving transports were brought to the gassing bunker. After some time, I realized that these were mostly Hungarian Jews. I noticed it due to their clothes, the bread they threw away, the goose lard in bottles, and the money [we] found. I understand the Hungarian language, so I was able to recognize these objects as originating in Hungary.[2]

Reinhard described one of the largest killing operations of the Jewish Holocaust: the deportation of approximately 380,000 Hungarian Jews to Auschwitz-Birkenau between May and July 1944 and the murder of the vast majority of them upon arrival.[3] Like many Sinti and Roma who lived and worked close to the infamous ramp, he had an intimate understanding of what was going to happen to these new arrivals. Yet, his interactions with them were largely indirect. He gave no indication that he was able to communicate with the Jews who were about to be killed and instead recalled his quest to deduce their origins from material clues, explaining his detective work as part of his desire to understand his own situation in the camp. Reinhard's is a report about distinct yet intertwined fates, separated by physical barriers and observed from a distance. It is also the type of observation that prosecutors found useless as evidence but that could be profoundly meaningful to victims themselves.

Interactions like those reported by Reinhard took place across Nazi-controlled Europe as a result of the related development of Nazi genocidal policies against both groups. The Nazis sought to redefine the state as the political container for their *Volksgemeinschaft*, a national community based on biological-ethnic coherence. To achieve that vision, they made it their mission to remove from society Jews, Sinti and Roma; people deemed asocial, feeble-minded, or hereditarily ill; and children of partial African descent.[4] Each of these groups had different histories of marginalization. Different actors and institutions also called for and carried out their persecution early on. Whereas early measures against Jews often came from the upper echelons of the state and Nazi party stalwarts, municipalities and the police were the main drivers of new anti-Romani measures. Even when members of both groups faced assaults on a local level, these occurred at different times and in different locations. Although both Roma and Jews saw their situation rapidly deteriorate, their concrete experiences before the outbreak of World War Two were frequently different.

The persecution of Roma and Jews increasingly converged as measures became more lethal following the outbreak of the war. By 1940, Nazi Germany experimented for the first time with the deportation of both Roma and Jews to occupied Poland. Parallel to the short-lived plan to establish a "Jewish reservation" around the Polish town of Nisko, the Nazis deported the first group of 2,500 German Sinti and Roma to the region in May 1940.[5] While the Nazis started concentrating Jews in ghettos in occupied Poland, they also radicalized measures against Romani populations—limiting the movement of Sinti and Roma in Germany and deporting the first Romanies to Jewish ghettos. The final turn to mass murder following the Axis invasion of the Soviet Union increasingly led to similar policies toward Jews and Roma in increasingly proximate locations. In the late summer and fall of 1941, special killing squads— the *Einsatzgruppen*—supported by local units and other German formations, started the mass shooting of Jews as well as Roma in the occupied Soviet Union.[6] The Nazis also murdered Romani victims in concentration and death camps where they interned, exploited, and murdered Jews; Croatian authorities systematically killed Roma and Jews—as well as Serbs—in the same camp (Jasenovac), while the Romanian state deported both Jews and Roma to camps and ghettos in occupied Ukrainian territory.[7]

These policies made Roma and Jews observers of each other's demise in various locations across Europe. Often these interactions occurred in spaces conceived first or primarily for the persecution of Jews. This included ghettos, labor camps, transit camps, sites of mass shootings, concentration camps with mostly Jewish prisoners, and others that filled up with racial persecutees toward the end of the war. In some of these encounters, Roma and Jews competed for resources or were forced to manage each other's labor or very lives; in others, Jews and Roma had opportunities to cooperate, as when they joined together in smuggling operations. Yet, more often than not, Romani and Jewish victims found themselves in the situation that Reinhard describes: seeing and hearing each other from a distance, or handling each other's property or corpses.

Scholars and commentators who compare the experiences of both groups tend to ignore what lies hidden in plain sight: Roma and Jews experienced their persecution next to each other. Survivor testimonies and accounts demonstrate the chasm that separated many victims from one another but also the deep impressions that interactions across the (often metaphorical) barbed wire fence could leave. These interactions shaped the earliest testimonies we have, created when the victims themselves first sought to make sense of the violence they had faced. It would also subsequently shape Holocaust Studies and determine what the world came to know about the Romani genocide as reports of the mass murder of Roma emerged collaterally within Jewish attempts to tell the history of the mass murder of Jews.

Early Interactions

From the vantage point of the present, parallels between the treatment of Roma and Jews seem obvious. Yet evidence suggests that members of each group rarely saw things this way in the early years of the Nazi state. While the approximately 20,000 to 30,000 Sinti and Roma who lived in interwar Germany left insufficient traces for us to determine with any certainty how they understood the policies aimed at the country's much larger population of approximately 500,000 Jews, the regime's antisemitism was surely impossible to miss.[8] In some postwar accounts, Romani survivors recalled moments when Jews warned them of impending darker times, while others say they fled,

fearing that anti-Jewish measures might also target them.[9] Yet we should approach these statements with caution. Testimonies given after liberation do
not offer simple keys to reconstructing the attitudes of Jews and Roma toward
each other's early persecution. By the war's end, many witnesses understood
the similarities between the killings of both groups and thus retrospectively
identified early measures as parallel tracks leading to more radical violence. In
the immediate years after the Nazis took control of the state, however, neither
Roma nor Jews in Germany could have known that they might one day end
up next to each other in camps or facing shooting squads.

There is also little indication that Jews or members of political groups targeted by the regime paid close attention to the persecution of German Sinti
and Roma in the 1930s.[10] Reading Jewish sources—and histories of the Holocaust that draw on these sources—one would not know that Roma lived
through new forms of internment before Jews did. In fact, as early as 1935 municipal authorities in Cologne began moving Roma to camps. These efforts
accelerated around the 1936 Berlin Olympics, when authorities decided that
the removal of "Gypsies" from urban centers would help Germany manage its
international reputation.[11] By the end of 1936, Berlin, Frankfurt am Main, Düsseldorf, Essen, Dortmund, Gelsenkirchen, and other municipalities operated
policed camps for "Gypsies."[12] This confinement of Sinti and Roma to particular living areas allowed the authorities to surveil, register, and more effectively categorize them, eventually facilitating authorities' ability to deport
them to concentration camps.[13]

If and when German Jews noticed these attempts to isolate German Romanies, they likely perceived them much as other Europeans did, as extensions
of long-standing policies toward unwanted populations by welfare authorities,
municipalities, and state security forces. Given the long history of anti-Romani
policing in Europe, arresting "Gypsies" as asocials might have seemed like
business as usual, whereas boycotting Jewish stores seemed like a radical departure. Being treated like a "Gypsy"—"behandelt wie a zigeiner," as the historian Simon Dubnow put it to describe the abuse of Jews in nineteenth-
century Romania—was certainly an ominous sign.[14] Yet there was little reason
for German Jews to think they would end up in a "Gypsy camp" on the outskirts of German cities.[15] Most Jews viewed themselves as people who occupied a fundamentally different place in society than did the Sinti and Roma in
their environment. Under these circumstances, it is not surprising that
"Gypsy" camps did not show up in early Holocaust histories: the first generation of survivor historians did not understand them as part of their story.[16]

In the prewar years, some Jews even found solace in comparing their position to that of Romanies. The Jewish lawyer Fritz Goldschmidt, whom the Nazis removed from his position as a judge in Berlin, reported on how he invoked the distinct treatment of Jews and Roma in lectures to Jews in Nazi Germany to "strengthen his listeners' power to resist."[17] Playing on Friedrich Nietzsche's claim that people despise those beneath them but only hate those equal to or above them, he argued that the Nazis only hated Jews because they implicitly respected them. This was different than the attitude toward "Gypsies" that he had observed in Berlin-Weissensee, where he had served as a judge, Goldschmidt explained: Germans looked down on them as useless "vagabonds" of too little consequence to spur an "organized anti-Gypsy movement."[18] Jews could thus take pride in being hated rather than despised.[19]

Certainly, there were moments when Jewish journalists noticed that the Nazis included "Gypsies" as well as other groups in decrees targeting Jews. For instance, various Jewish papers reported on statements by German Minister of the Interior Wilhelm Frick and others in late 1935 that the Nuremberg laws would define not only Jews but also "Gypsies" and "Negroes" as second-class citizens.[20] Such reports made clear that Jews were being put in a category with other "unwanted" groups that different states had previously excluded from legal protections. Yet, there is little indication that this prompted German Jews to inquire about the fate of these other groups. The general silence of German-Jewish newspapers on this subject might be attributed to their attempts to avoid statements that could provoke the Nazi state, but it is telling that reports of measures that simultaneously affected Jews and other groups elicited limited responses from the Jewish press in other countries as well.[21]

At the time, Jewish journalists' comments about "Gypsies" dealt with Roma as a threat rather than as fellow victims. In the summer of 1937, the Jewish Telegraphic Agency (JTA), a wire service based in New York serving Jewish newspapers in the US and abroad, ran a story about attempts by the extreme right-wing Romanian National Christian Party (1935–38) to coopt Romani organizations and mobilize them as voters.[22] According to the article, the party's daily *Ţara Noastră* (Our Country) published a Romani-language edition saturated with antisemitic propaganda in anticipation of upcoming elections.[23] As the JTA piece highlighted, Romani representatives who sought to promote "Gypsy music" by campaigning for the prohibition of Jewish musicians were open to the propaganda.[24] Jewish German-language papers picked up the theme as well, noting how some "Gypsies" had apparently joined the ranks of their enemies.[25] While these reports reflect Jews' sense of their social distance from Roma, there is no indication that they exacerbated tensions between the groups in any palpable way. The choices of a marginal group living farther east were a curiosity, perhaps a sign of the sad ubiquity of antisemitic politics, but hardly an immediate cause for alarm.

Forced Labor Camp Bełżec: The First Camp for Jews and Roma

Jews and Roma could ignore how Nazi policies targeted both groups as long as they experienced persecution in separate spaces. Initially the Nazis detained some members of each group in the same concentration camps, but neither Jews nor Roma were originally the main target of arrests. Even when larger numbers of Roma and Jews ended up in concentration camps—Roma following a police campaign targeting the "work-shy" in June 1938 and Jews following Kristallnacht in November 1938—they nevertheless found themselves in facilities that had first been established for the incarceration of other groups.[26] Camps like Dachau were part of a repression apparatus aimed at various people who did not fit the Nazi vision of their authoritarian and racist new order but more than anything targeted political opponents. The camps of the mid-1930s conformed to the depiction of the concentration camp universe in historical scholarship of the late 1940s and 1950s: they were sites of totalitarian terror where racial persecution was one story among many.[27]

This changed after the invasion of Poland in September 1939, when the Nazis and, later, their allies created detention facilities, and eventually extermination camps, for both racially persecuted groups. One of the first places of persecution where Roma and Jews fully engaged with each other's presence was Forced Labor Camp Bełżec, which opened in 1940. Here, in a camp largely forgotten due to the prominence of the extermination camp of the same name later established in the same location, Jews and Roma were for the first time interned next to each other in spaces created solely for them.[28] Many of the patterns established there would remain relevant over the course of the Holocaust.

Although Romanies and Jews found themselves in Bełżec under similar conditions, the reasons for and circumstances of their deportations differed dramatically. Jews who ended up in Bełżec and the large complex of connected camps were men requisitioned for labor. They were there because Odilo Globocnik, the district's SS and Police Leader who later became the main architect of the death camps, saw an opportunity to expand his influence by establishing a new type of exploitative detention facility.[29] For one summer building season, these Jewish men from Lublin and other Jewish ghettos had to dig anti-tank trenches along the German-Soviet armistice line, a project that turned out to have no military or other value.[30]

Jews arrived as unrelated men in Bełżec, whereas Nazis deported extended networks of Romani families from Germany to the camp. The different agencies that initiated and enacted measures for both groups had different priorities. Unlike the Jews, whom the authorities imprisoned because of an imagined need for their labor, Sinti families found themselves in Bełżec because the Nazis had decided to expel them from Germany. Reinhardt Heydrich and others within the newly established central office overseeing much of the state's security apparatus, the Reichssicherheitshauptamt, demanded the removal of "Gypsies" together with other unwanted persons to occupied Poland in late 1939. First slowed by Nazi experts who preferred sterilization policies, they were able to follow through with their plans once the army requested the removal of "Gypsies" in preparation for an attack on the Western Front. Heinrich Himmler, as head of the SS and the police, ordered the deportation of 2,500 "Gypsies" in family units to the General Government in occupied Poland on April 27, 1940.[31] The regime confined many of those detained—some 1,140 Sinti mostly from Hamburg—in Bełżec. They arrived before the Jewish men for whom Globocnik had established the camp.[32] These Romani families spent six weeks in the camp before authorities in the General Government removed them to other locations. They were long gone from the camp by August 1940, when the Nazis requisitioned and rounded up over 10,000 Jewish men in various ghettos and sent them to Bełżec and connected neighboring camps.

The third group deported to Bełżec consisted of Polish Roma, many from Zamość. Like German Sinti, they arrived as families.[33] While they might have shared the designation "Gypsies" with German deportees, these two groups stayed in separate areas on the same floor of a large industrial barn and had limited contact.[34] This became clear in investigations after the war, when German authorities sought to prosecute the camp's commander for killing a Polish Rom.[35] The German Sinti they interviewed could name dozens of individuals from families deported from their part of the country, but they seemed hard pressed to remember any Polish Roma.[36] These depositions remind us of the diversity of Romani communities, even as they became targets of similar anti-"Gypsy" measures—a diversity that was largely lost on the Jewish prisoners who left testimonies.

Both Polish Jews and German Sinti reported that the Jewish men and the Romani families interned at Bełżec almost invariably experienced each other from a distance. The Nazis had housed Jews in the same large building but on a different floor than Sinti and Roma. This simultaneous proximity and separation would characterize their confinement in other locations as well, including in many ghettos and camps where the Nazis found it useful to segregate populations based on categories they devised. Such spatial arrangements, often supported by distinctive symbols on uniforms, allowed for easier differential treatment and collective punishment.[37] Segregation would continue in most other camps, with separate barracks for Romani and Jewish prisoners. In Bełżec, Roma and Jews seem to have been almost entirely isolated, even beyond their living quarters. German and Polish Romani men worked next to Jewish men digging anti-tank trenches, but later accounts suggest that they were separated into distinct labor gangs and that communication between them was infrequent.[38]

Given their separation and lack of communication, Romani and Jewish testimonies from Bełżec—as well as similar sites of confinement—tend to mention members of the other group primarily to make a point about their own experiences. Encountering each other for the first time in camps with no other prisoner groups, the presence of the other helped Jews and Roma gauge their relative position within the camp and narrate their impressions later.[39] We see this in testimonies from Jewish victims of Labor Camp Bełżec, such as when a survivor told an interviewer in 1998 that he had heard from other Jews that 28,000 Roma had been murdered there before his arrival.[40] This Jewish survivor's (historically inaccurate) statements about Romani inmates allowed him to explain how desperate the situation was for everyone, including Jewish inmates.

In comparison, some Romani survivors referenced Jews to convey the specific suffering Sinti and Roma faced because of their imprisonment with other family members. These testimonies diverge from many accounts of Jews in Auschwitz, who recalled feeling jealous when they saw Roma in a camp with their families, since they had been forcibly separated from their own relatives and often knew or feared that their loved ones had been murdered. In Bełżec, by contrast, there could be no doubt that deportation as a family was a disadvantage. Whereas Jewish men held out the hope of seeing their relatives again once their labor deployment ended, Romani men and women often witnessed their children perish in front of them.[41] Unlike Jews, Roma in the camp also had to deal with the humiliation that came with suffering alongside their closest kin. Sexual violence, and witnessing it as a community, scarred families and undermined communal structures.[42]

Another testimony of a Bełżec survivor points to the lasting trauma of seeing children die while referencing some of the rare—and fraught—interactions between the two prisoner groups. In the context of a criminal complaint that Helmut Rose, a German Sinto, filed in February 1965 against police agents who arrested him and his family in Hamburg, he spoke to prosecutors about his experiences in Bełżec. Rose described small children who died due to insufficient food provisions and were subsequently buried close to the improvised latrines at the site. "The Jews received the order to take the dying children from their mothers and carry them to the pit. This way some children who were still alive were thrown into the pit and covered with sand," he recounted.[43] It is impossible to assess the veracity of these claims. They did not appear in the testimonies of other Sinti survivors during a larger investigation into the killing of Romanies at the Bełżec camp that began one year later.[44] Yet we can understand them as an expression of grief about the uncertain circumstances of Romani children's deaths in the camp and of the lingering suspicions between Jews and Romanies.[45]

While Bełżec marked a new phase in the entangled persecution of Roma and Jews, this still largely entailed watching the suffering of others from a distance. Each group remained in its section under different conditions. Experientially, there was not one camp but three: two camps for Romani families (one German and one Polish) and another for Jewish men. This pattern of adjacent imprisonment would soon unfold across Europe. Postwar archives later combined the memories of Jews and Roma under a single index term while activists and historians framed their fate as a single narrative of racial persecution and genocide. Yet the accounts of Romani and Jewish survivors themselves suggest that they were mostly proximate strangers.

Images of Romanies

Even during the period of intensifying persecution, Jews mostly encountered Roma as symbols. Because Jews were often first detained in places where they did not meet Roma, it was easy for them to retain their previous views of "Gypsies" as cultural tropes. The letters of Etty Hillesum, a well-known diarist of the Holocaust in the Netherlands, offer one such example. Hillesum left us her impressions of Westerbork, a camp intended exclusively for Jews—first as a site established by the Dutch government to detain Jewish refugees from

Germany and Austria and later as a transit camp for Jews earmarked for deportation to concentration and death camps. In her wartime writings, the term "Gypsy" appears regularly but never in relation to any real Roma. Instead, the term indicates something either exotic and enticing—she refers to having a "Gypsy dress"—or dire, as in her statement: "It is certainly not very pretty here: a Gypsy life, poverty, mud."[46] In another letter from 1943, Hillesum described the poor hygiene situation in the transit camp Westerbork, explaining, "Father complains bitterly that he is the biggest Gypsy in Westerbork; he doesn't see that everyone else is in the same boat."[47] For a middle-class Dutch Jewish woman, the daughter of a classical philologist, "Gypsies" were a figure of speech, a metonym for deprivation, squalor, or, at times, romanticized exoticism. When Hillesum's father allegedly called himself "the biggest Gypsy in Westerbork," there were indeed no Romani deportees in the camp.[48] That changed on May 16, 1944, when Dutch police arrested 309 people identified as "Gypsies" from across the Netherlands and interned them at Westerbork for three days and nights in a separate barrack.[49] From this group, the Germans released sixty-four individuals for various reasons and deported the rest on a train to Auschwitz on May 19, 1944. Only late in the war and during brief moments did Jews encounter Roma in transit camps such as Westerbork in the Netherlands or Mechelen/Malines in Belgium. Failing such concrete contacts, Western European Jews continued to speak about "Gypsies" in metaphorical terms rather than as real people.[50]

Jews in Central and Eastern Europe shared a similar repertoire of stereotypes. When Avrom Sutzkever wrote his poem on the murdered Roma of Lithuania and Poland after the war, he was inevitably responding to popular Jewish literary and oral traditions that depicted "Gypsies" as unburdened by the constraints of bourgeois life. These ideas transcended milieus and traveled across continents. Young Jews from eastern European immigrant families in the United States celebrated something they called "Gypsy evenings" and played "Gypsy Tavern" in their camp retreats in the summer of 1939.[51] It is not clear what exactly these Jewish teenagers did on such occasions, but they likely tapped into the pervasive notion of "Gypsies" as untamed outsiders whose exotic nature conjured sympathetic if comical images.[52] Their peers in Poland had recourse to similar forms of entertainment: during the same final summer before the war, a cinema in Grodno advertised performances of rousing "Gypsy melodies" and songs in the Yiddish press.[53]

Yiddish novels also regularly portrayed "Gypsies" in racialized terms, as alluring yet potentially deviant figures.[54] This was true across the artistic and

FIGURE 1.1. Yankev Mitler, "Zigeiner" illustration from Shneur
Vaserman's Yiddish children's book *Shvebelekh: Kinder-lider un
poemes* (1938), p. 50.

political spectrum, from collections of folk stories to the expressionist novels of the communist Yiddish poet Meir Wiener, who wrote of mysterious
"Gypsies" who were "really black, like the devil."[55] A 1937 illustrated Yiddish
children's book included a poem on "Gypsies": "[T]he father has black eyes/
the mother has black eyes/ and the children, the little ones/ have eyes like
black flames" (see Figure 1.1).[56] Even texts that showed some understanding
of Romani culture tended to retain ambivalent images of a group they depicted as both menacing and impressive, albeit often for humorous purposes. A book of stories by the Orthodox Yiddishist Eliezer Shindler explained that Rom means "human" in "Gypsy language," yet introduced this
fact in a comedy about two "Gypsies" competing over who could steal more
effectively.[57]

One of the rare voices to challenge these stereotypes successfully was Shim-shon Kahan, a friend of Sutzkever and a fellow member of his literary circles in 1930s Vilna.[58] Kahan lived with Lithuanian Roma, learned Romani, and translated some of their songs. By depicting the poverty and discrimination they faced, Kahan resisted portraying Roma merely as free people who sing of love and live in the woods. In a poem entitled "Lithuanian Gypsies", he warned his Jewish readers against treating Roma with disdain. "You speak of them, you curse them, you spit," he wrote before conjuring a vision of a new and better world, where "Gypsies will unite with the people of this earth" and demand a "Gypsy republic."[59]

It is doubtful that Kahan's writings had much of an effect on the views his coreligionists held about Roma.[60] Even at times of accelerated persecution, Jewish artists continued to use the allure of all things "Gypsy" to advertise their music with little sense of the kind of political alliance Kahan had envisioned. A poster produced for a "Great Festival of Gypsy Romances" in the Warsaw Ghetto on February 6, 1941 exemplifies Jews' continued participation in a long tradition of romanticizing Europe's Romani populations (Figure 1.2).[61] The concert featured the violinist Artur Gold, the pianist Władysław Szpilman, whose memoir served as the basis of the film "The Pianist," and the violinist and jazz musician Arkadi Flato. Drawing on entrenched ideas conflating Roma with pleasure and debauchery, Flato soon opened his own restaurant in the Warsaw Ghetto by the name of Gypsy Tavern (*Cyganska Tawerna*).[62]

The most famous song about "Gypsies" to emerge in Nazi ghettos illustrates just how powerful such templates continued to be: "Zigeiner lid" or "Gypsy song," written and composed by David Beigelman.[63] Beigelman, a popular Yiddish violinist and composer, was in the Łódź ghetto when the Nazis deported over 5,000 Austrian Roma there. Using his medium of choice, Beigelman sought to explain their fate to his largely Jewish audiences. His song describes "Gypsies" who "live like no other, suffering pain, and hunger too," while its principal Romani character "broods" and "strings his guitar" in a night that is dark "like blackest coal." The powerful lyrics express sympathy, yet the images of the brooding Gypsy at night remain trapped in the racialized color schemes and emotional range that most European Jewish listeners would have associated with Roma. They also convey pain in ways that did not require knowledge of the Romani genocide and could be consumed alongside older Yiddish songs after the war without much deep thought about its subject.

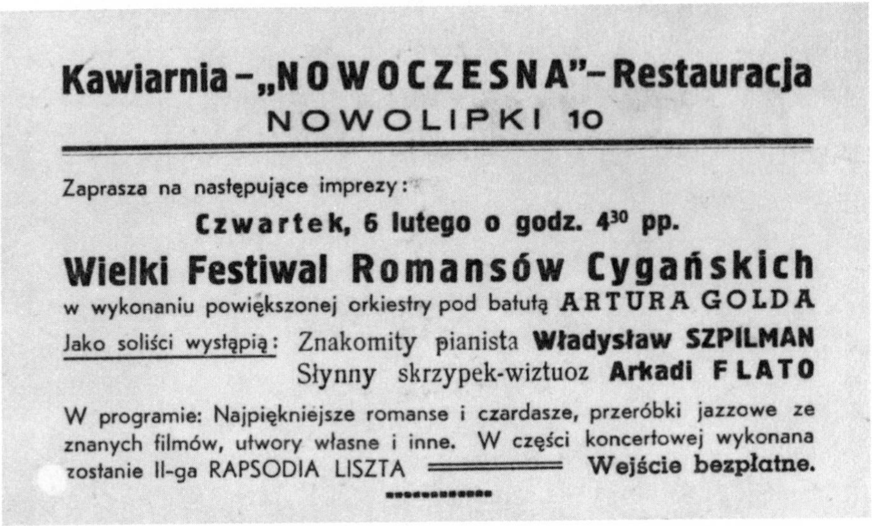

Kawiarnia –„NOWOCZESNA"– Restauracja
N O W O L I P K I 10

Zaprasza na następujące imprezy:
Czwartek, 6 lutego o godz. 4³⁰ pp.
Wielki Festiwal Romansów Cygańskich
w wykonaniu powiększonej orkiestry pod batutą ARTURA GOLDA
Jako soliści wystąpią: Znakomity pianista **Władysław SZPILMAN**
Słynny skrzypek-wiztuoz **Arkadi FLATO**

W programie: Najpiękniejsze romanse i czardasze, przeróbki jazzowe ze
znanych filmów, utwory własne i inne. W części koncertowej wykonana
zostanie II-ga RAPSODIA LISZTA ========= **Wejście bezpłatne.**

FIGURE 1.2. Poster advertising a "Great Festival of Gypsy Romances" at the
coffee house and restaurant Nowoczesna, Warsaw Ghetto, 1941. From the collections of the E. Ringelblum Jewish Historical Institute, Oneg Shabbat Archive,
ZIH—833.

Seeing, Hearing, Smelling Each Other

The reality of persecution and death ultimately challenged Jews' received images of "Gypsies," transforming them from static tropes into embodied beings.
Roma, too, increasingly encountered Jews as real people who suffered and died
within their view. Camps and killing sites were never completely separated,
even where the Nazis intended them to be. Suffering and death thus created
sensory experiences that victims found hard to ignore. In places such as
Auschwitz-Birkenau, section BIIe—the "Gypsy camp" or "Gypsy family
camp"—was located within the Nazis' geography of death such that Roma
became direct witnesses to the destruction of European Jewry. Their camp was
close to the ramp used after May 1944 for arriving deportation trains. Although
they could not easily observe the unloading of trains, Romani prisoners, like
Konrad Reinhard, managed to glimpse some part of the selection and destruction process. This included seeing the SS driving Jewish deportees who were
too fragile to walk to the gas chamber.[64] Many testimonies that have emerged
from legal settings tend to emphasize sight, or seeing, because prosecutors
needed visual confirmation from eyewitnesses for convictions. Even in these
testimonies, accounts of smell nevertheless sometimes appear. While it was

possible to avert their eyes from the organization of death at the ramp and the road to the crematoria, the stench when the SS ordered the corpses of murdered Jews incinerated was inescapable.

Jewish testimonies of Romani suffering often dwell on the visual, the dominant sense of the testimony genre, but emphasize auditory aspects just as often. Breaking the familiar association of "Gypsies" with music, these testimonies are largely about Jews hearing Roma screaming. In a 1995 video testimony, Manya Altman, a Polish-Jewish survivor, addressed the fate of the over 5,000 Roma from the Austrian Burgenland whom the Nazis had deported to a fenced-off part of the Jewish ghetto in Łodz.[65] Altman never saw the Roma who stayed nearby in a few blocks of segregated buildings, but explained that the "Gypsies" kept her awake at night. Asked about witnessing their murder, she answered instead with the reason she could not sleep: "We heard the screams."[66] Many other Jews who lived in the parts of the Jewish ghetto nearest to the Romani ghetto gave similar testimony, with one witness emphasizing over and over how their "screams of death" were "out of the ordinary."[67] Unable to see into the separate ghetto established for Roma, most Jewish ghetto inhabitants could only speculate as to precisely what was befalling their Romani neighbors.[68]

Jews left similar recollections of the dreadful sounds of anguish during the liquidation of the subcamp for Sinti and Roma in Auschwitz-Birkenau on the night of August 2, 1944. For many Jews, the murder of over four thousand remaining inmates of the "Gypsy camp" came as a shock.[69] Since the SS forced all prisoners to stay in their blocks, there were few eyewitnesses, but many who heard what transpired. Among the Jews who spoke about the event, nearly everyone reported on the screams, attributing them to the brutality of the SS and the will of Romanies to resist. Testimonies of these events proved useless for legal purposes because they demonstrated awareness of suffering but could not help identify the perpetrators. Nevertheless, they emerge as wrenching and vivid moments in Jewish memories of the "Gypsy camp." Many Jewish witnesses described the night as the worst they experienced in Auschwitz, largely based on the sounds they heard.[70]

Seeing, hearing, and smelling the suffering of others were impressions that survivors often found difficult to forget. In Auschwitz, it was the memory of months or even years of serial murders, while at temporary killing sites—the "snake pits" that Sutzkever conjured in his poem—survivors recalled singular incidents. Yet, in all of these cases, these sensory experiences clearly moved those who recounted them.[71]

Witnessing the killing of members of another community left some victims attempting to make sense of their own survival. We find this in Romani reports about the murder of Jews in Transnistria, the administrative name of Romanian-occupied Ukraine.[72] In 2013, a Romani woman from a family deported from Moldavia to Transnistria told an interviewer of her encounter with a killing operation when she was a young teenager: "The Jews were also shut up in a stable, but they were burned, killed alive. And we were fortunate, because the Queen Maria had posters sent saying that the Roma from Moldavia were a happy and useful people."[73] This story as well as others that portrayed the miraculous rescue of Romanian Roma by a beneficent queen (who had in reality died before the regime deported Roma), allowed Romani witnesses to explain their own survival where so many others perished.[74]

Other testimonies primarily convey dread regarding the atrocities survivors witnessed against people they hardly knew. The account by the Jewish brothers Michael and Zvi Rajak of the mass murder of Roma in the town center of Glubok (today's Hlybokaye in Belarus) is typical in its vivid and horrifying detail. Their testimony in their community's memorial book told of how the Germans forced Romani children to sit naked on the cold ice, forcing their parents to watch them perish in agony before the Germans murdered everyone in a nearby forest.[75] Another Jewish survivor who grew up about a hundred miles south in Iwieniec (today's Ivyanets in Belarus) recalled that he had seen about 1,000 Roma who had been traveling with their animals and wagons as they were murdered by Einsatzgruppen outside of town.[76]

Exchanges

In contrast to these acts of witnessing from afar, personal transactions and regular physical encounters with the property of other victims gave Jews and Roma a better understanding of each other's situation. This process did not always lead to greater empathy, however. At times, such interactions became the basis for expressions of solidarity while, at others, they intensified animosity. Sometimes, both types of reactions coexisted.

Contact often started with exchanges of information. Whereas certain hard-earned intelligence about food, jobs, or the vulnerabilities of overseers was a scarce resource, other knowledge could be imparted more easily. Rumors about the truth behind official announcements, the progress of the war, and the fate of loved ones with whom people had lost touch were a central currency of life under persecution.[77] Jewish and Romani prisoners passed on such rumors in camps, both among themselves and to one another.[78]

Even information about the fate of other groups could offer valuable hints about one's own future in this context. Some of the first alarming accounts of mass murder to reach the ghettos concerned the fate of both Jews and Roma. The so-called Grojanowski report, written under a pseudonym by a man usually identified as Szlamek, is the best known of these: Szlamek had escaped the Chełmno (Kulmhof) extermination camp and gave an eyewitness account of gassings with exhaust fumes in vans to Emanuel Ringelblum's Oneg Shabbat group in the Warsaw Ghetto, where it became part of their hidden archive.[79] While he spoke at some length about the extermination of Jewish communities, his testimony largely dealt with the murder of Roma from the Łódź ghetto.[80] In gruesome detail, he reported how "Gypsies" arrived in truckload after truck-load only to be murdered in gas vans and buried in large pits dug by a small group of Jews doomed to meet their own deaths soon afterwards. News of the murder of Austrian Roma thus served to warn Jews in the Warsaw Ghetto of their own potential future as victims of the Nazi machinery of death.[81]

The experience of sharing such crucial information had the potential to create meaningful and lasting ties between Jewish and Romani prisoners. One German Sinto related how he had learned about the murder of all remaining Romanies in Birkenau's camp BIIe from two Jewish prisoners who serviced rail lines close to the liquidated camp before all three ended up in camp Dora. When he told his story to prosecutors two decades later, this Romani survivor knew of the postwar emigration to the United States of his one-time Jewish interlocutors and was able to identify one of them by name.[82] Another Jewish witness mentioned in a 1997 interview how a Romani woman named Rose, tasked with delivering materials between camps, memorized the names of Jewish women imprisoned in Kaiserwald (Riga) in order to tell them to men who had been deported to Tartu, before memorizing the names of the Jewish men in Tartu to report them back to the women held in Riga.[83] In this case, a Romani woman served as the crucial link between dispersed Jewish families.

Roma and Jews also regularly interacted with each other when necessity drove them to barter for food and other essential goods. These exchanges could both save and endanger lives, and witnesses sometimes recount them with less seriousness than they offer in accounts of atrocities. The artist Yehuda Bacon, who was deported to Auschwitz-Birkenau from Theresienstadt as a fourteen-year-old, described his interactions with young Romani prisoners through the fence that separated their two adjacent subcamps.[84] In a 2018 conversation with me, he spoke of the antisemitic and anti-Czech attitudes he witnessed among German Sinti when he traded with teenagers from the neighboring camp.[85] Yet, the perception of prejudice did not stop trade. He told of how starving Jewish children agreed to give Romani girls bread for a pot of mustard, only to realize that they had been handed sand with a thin layer of mustard on top. Bacon related his deep sense of betrayal at the time but noted that from the distance of several decades, he believed he had simply been "angry like a child." He then explained that to get back at them, the Jewish boys from Theresienstadt promised to give the Romani girls bread if they lifted their skirts. The Romani girls kept their end of the bargain but this time the Jewish boys didn't follow through. Bacon's story thus ends with a moment he described as a juvenile attempt at revenge. In other instances, the consequences of deals going poorly could be more violent.[86]

Roma and Jews also handled the possessions of expropriated or murdered individuals from the other group. European society was awash with the earthly possessions of its Jews and to a lesser extent with the possessions of expelled or murdered Roma.[87] While the Nazis made sure to retain everything with substantial monetary value, many objects transferred between Jews and Roma had only local worth. Yet, even when things with little peacetime value changed hands, these transactions could trigger strong emotions.

In her 1996 video testimony, Nina Michowski, a Jewish woman who survived in hiding after fleeing the Siedlce ghetto, recalled how possessions influenced her feelings toward Roma:

> The Gypsies were somehow free to leave the ghetto in this area. And they would come and they would beg. And sometimes I hated them for my stupid reason. Because you know the Gypsies were always dressed in those colorful outfits, which was rare actually. But they were differently dressed. And they would come and they would wear a men's coat, a woman's coat you know this. And I was jealous. I said, how come those Jewish people were murdered and the Gypsies [...] are there. And they are wearing, are wearing [...] the coats of those Jewish people. And they were still, they could come out of the ghetto and beg, you know. I said, how come my people had to die, were murdered, such a horrible thing and they are free. But unfortunately, few months later they were rounded up and they were also sent to crematoriums the Gypsies, you know, like the Jews. They were the second ones.[88]

Michowski's statement captures the sentiments that the asynchronous and related persecution measures against both groups could stir among their

victims. Siedlce was a major Jewish ghetto that saw an influx of German Romanies in 1941 as well as Roma from the region by May and June 1942.[89] Many
of the German Romanies interned there reported that they had seen the killing
of Jews in the ghetto.[90] In October 1942, the Nazis moved some Jews and
Roma to a different location, and subsequently relocated them to a new encampment on November 25.[91] According to the recollections of the head of
the Jewish Council, the Nazis forced Jews and Roma of the new ghetto onto
railway cars, deporting them to their deaths at Treblinka.[92] It was in this context that Michowski was able to see the Roma who had been spared deportations wearing clothes she identified as having belonged to Jews.[93] It was not
unusual for people to take things that the original owners could no longer use,
but it was unusual for a member of the targeted victim group to be able to
observe the process. In Chełmno, for example, no Roma were left to witness
how the Jews who were ordered to dig burial pits had put on the clothes of the
recently murdered Roma to warm themselves—or how the Germans forced
these Jewish gravediggers to lie atop the bodies of murdered Roma before
shooting them.[94] Survivors like Michowski, who understood both the final
outcome and the coincidental nature of such appropriations, later considered
their feelings of jealousy naive in the context of the calamity that eventually
engulfed both groups.

The recognition that prisoners faced "choiceless choices" pervades most
testimonies on the labor that prisoners were required to perform as part of the
Nazis' efforts to rob and kill their victims.[95] This was the case in Auschwitz-
Birkenau, where Romani prisoners built the infamous arrival ramp and were
subsequently tasked with unloading luggage that Jews had left in trains or on
the ramp, extracting food items, and bringing clothes to storage facilities.[96]
Property taken from Jews ultimately fueled much of the internal economy of
Auschwitz-Birkenau. This involved valuable goods, which could be sold on the
black market and collected at the part of Birkenau called Canada, but also more
mundane items, such as the sweets the SS physician Josef Mengele distributed to the children of the "Gypsy camp" in an effort to boost his popularity.[97]
No victim could survive and remain detached from these transactions in concentration camps, much like every prisoner was in some way involved in
contributing to another group's confinement and extermination. The Roma
who participated in the construction of the ramp created to facilitate the murder of Jews in 1944 themselves slept in a camp built largely by Jews in 1943.[98]

However unavoidable, many of the decisions survivors made and the ways
that they became implicated in the machinery of extermination and exploitation

left lasting scars and doubts. This is evident in the recollection of Walter Winter, a German Sinto who served in the German army and subsequently survived Birkenau's "Gypsy camp." In multiple interviews recorded on video, audio tape, and in writing, he tells of his encounter with Hungarian Jews detained at BIIe while he was there. According to his testimony, he convinced a new prisoner who had a young son to barter his valuable boots for some bread. Winter explained how he felt sorry about the transaction but claims that he knew that these Jews would soon be gassed anyhow.[99] His rationalization of the trade he made and his desire to address the moment in his various testimonies reveal Winter's ongoing struggle with this memory.

The Dead

At the height of persecution, Jews and Roma had to deal not only with living members of the other group and their belongings but also with each other's dead. This was the result of pragmatic decisions by the Germans or their allies who sought laborers to deal with the physical remains of those they had murdered. The ghetto of Jadów is typical in this regard.[100] According to the small Polish town's memorial book, the Germans sent Roma to the Jewish ghetto in 1942, where some moved into apartments and others stayed with their families in wagons.[101] The anonymous author who gave the account reported that the Nazis shot many in this first group of Romani deportees, before moving an even larger number of Roma to the gates of the ghetto, forcing them to dig graves, and proceeding to murder them. The last stage of the process involved ordering the Jews to fill the graves.[102] Detained, dispensable, and later earmarked for death, Jews and Roma were a natural source of free labor for the Nazis, as they had been in Labor Camp Bełżec, the extermination camp Chełmno, and other camps.

The Nazis also identified Jewish cemeteries as an obvious place to dispose of dead Romanies. In Łódź, Jewish laborers were forced to pick up the dead from the Romani camp every morning and bury them in the Jewish cemetery. (The German Ghetto Administration disdainfully gave the order under the single heading "Removal of Excrement and Corpses."[103]) The Jewish Council ordered the bodies brought there in a special wagon and assigned them special plots.[104]

Pragmatic considerations about the availability of labor similarly guided the decision-making of Nazis and their allies when they ordered Roma to handle the Jewish dead.[105] The best-known case of such orders comes to us from Romania, where authorities forced thousands of Jews from Iaşi onto freight trains in late June 1941. The vast majority perished in these overcrowded cars, dying of thirst, starvation, and heat. On July 1, one train arrived in the town of Târgu Frumos, where Romanian police shot many of the surviving Jews. Since the mayor did not have the resources to dispose of the remains of those who died on the train, he requisitioned local Roma and, later, local Jews to bury 650 bodies of Jews who had perished in the wagons.[106] The mayor and an observer who watched Roma sell food and water to Jews trapped in the wagons attributed the Romanies' involvement to their desire for the property of the dead.[107] In reality, all objects deemed of high value ended up in non-Romani hands, as was also true elsewhere. The recruitment of Roma for this work was partly a reflection of their dire economic situation, their marginal status in the community, and the perception of authorities and neighbors that handling corpses was a "dirty" activity.[108]

Even after the war, Roma occasionally dealt in one way or another with the physical vestiges of the Jewish genocide. In Kremnička, where Nazi-allied Hlinka Guards had committed the largest massacre on Slovak soil after the unsuccessful Slovak National Uprising, partisans, Jews, and Roma were among the 747 dead discovered in pits following the war.[109] When exhumations began in the summer of 1948, relatives of those who died in the region took the pilgrimage to the site, hoping to identify family members among the corpses, sometimes based on their clothes.[110] One Jewish survivor reports how the authorities tasked Roma with the gruesome physical labor of digging up the corpses. According to this witness, the Romani men laboring there comforted the Jewish survivor as she vainly looked at corpse after corpse hoping to find her parents' remains.[111]

Shared Spaces and Hierarchies

Jews' and Romanies' sense of the shared threats they faced created opportunities for mutual ties in other instances as well. These included moments of rescue and joint resistance that inspired two of the most elaborate poems of wartime Jewish-Romani relations: Sutzkever's "Petro, the Gypsy" and Papusza's "Tears of Blood." These two poems represent attempts by Jewish and Romani authors, respectively, to capture moments when persecution bound their two groups together. Sutzkever's poem is part of a larger epic cycle on the Vilna ghetto and tells the life of the "Gypsy" knife sharpener Petro, whose shop is in the designated Jewish living area of the city. As the Germans liquidate the ghetto, Petro smuggles a Jewish child through the sewers into the forests, where he hands the orphan to a Romani woman and says, "Save him! The child remained from thousands of mothers, with the love of thousands you shall love him."[112]

The Romani poet Bronisława Wajs, better known by her Romani name, Papusza, drew on similar motifs in her poem "Tears of Blood." [113] Arguably the most renowned Romani poet of the twentieth century, Papusza had grown up in a traditional Polska Roma community in Poland. Having survived the war by hiding in the woods along with her family, she wrote her works in Romani before having them published in the Polish translations of the writer Jerzy Ficowski.[114] While the majority of Papusza's poetry uses natural imagery to express her sense of loss in the face of destruction, "Tears of Blood" describes her wartime experiences in concrete terms, describing the solidarity she felt for persecuted Jews and the Jewish children who found their way into the forests.[115]

> I saw a beautiful young Jewish girl,
> shivering from cold,
> asking for food.
> You poor thing, my little one.
> I gave her bread, whatever I had, a shirt.
> We both forgot that not far away
> were the police.
> But they didn't come that night.[116]

Elsewhere in the poem, she implores a bright star to blind the Germans "so the Jewish and Gypsy child can live" and also seeks to protect two Jews who were the sole survivors of their families.[117] Together with the work of Sutzkever, Papusza's poetry memorializes moments of shared Romani-Jewish battles for survival and resistance in Nazi-occupied Europe.[118] These acts of joint resistance extended beyond partisan activity: in the ghettos in Radom and Tarnów, Roma participated in the smuggling networks and illicit supply chains that fed starving Jewish ghetto inmates.[119]

While these narratives of rescue and resistance focus on bonds created under duress, others emerged from long-standing relations, such as arrangements in which Roma had performed domestic work for Jews. Such individuals often shared a table with their Jewish employers and were especially close in cases when Romani women worked as nannies for Jewish families.[120] Thanks to the work of Milena Hübschmannová, a pioneer in the field of

Romani Studies, many such relations in rural eastern Slovakia are well-documented.[121] There, Romani interlocutors expressed the sense that these relations were better than those with non-Jewish Slovaks: they found that Jews tended to pay them in cash rather than in kind and were more likely to invite them into their houses than were Romanies' non-Jewish Slovak employers in the region. Yet, even in such cases, a hierarchy inevitably persisted in these relations. It was the Jewish merchant of textiles, wood, or foodstuffs or the head of a Jewish household who paid for Roma's services and thus also had the power to end the relationship.[122]

At times or in places where anti-Romani policies were not consistently applied, Roma sometimes found that they were able to aid the Jews who had once been their neighbors or employers.[123] Two Jewish sisters from Slovakia remembered, for example, how a Romani boy their Orthodox Jewish family had taken in from a nearby village before the war subsequently managed to supply them with food once they were transferred to the local ghetto.[124]

Other stories of rescuing former employers mirror the experiences that Sutzkever and Papusza rendered in poetic form. The best known is that of Hajrija Imeri-Mihaljić, a Romani woman who saved a Jewish child whom she cared for as a nanny. The child survived because Imeri-Mihaljić took her to a remote village in Kosovo and adopted her into her Muslim Romani family. Such actions often eluded formal records. Imeri-Mihaljić's case is one of the few exceptions: she became the only Romani person to be awarded the official title of Righteous Among the Nations for saving a Jewish life.[125]

Yet, different, much more contentious close relationships between Jews and Roma dominate most genres of recollection. When members of one group were in charge of another, this power dynamic indelibly shaped memories associated with the other group. Which group was on top and which was on the bottom largely depended on local circumstances. In some contexts, the Nazis ordered Jews to take charge of Romani victims. In Łódź, German authorities tasked the Jewish Council with setting up the infrastructure of the "Gypsy ghetto," for example.[126] This meant that a Jewish engineer received the order to arrange for new barriers that divided the Jewish and Romani sections of the city. The Jewish soup kitchen had to supply the new camp with food, and the Jewish Council had to organize the payment of electricity bills and the removal of human waste.[127] Those Jews who understood what was taking place in the Romani ghetto worked in the new camp or knew people who did.[128] Many of these responsibilities were fatal for those involved. When typhus broke out in the Romani ghetto, Jewish doctors and nurses were ordered to tend to sick Roma there, and many perished as a result.[129] Since all of the Roma in the Łódź "Gypsy ghetto" either died of typhus or were murdered, we cannot know how they felt about their relationship with the Jewish administrators arranging their food, Jewish police guarding the gate between the two camps, Jewish workers burying their dead, or the Jewish doctors attempting to treat them.[130] Elsewhere, however, Roma did leave testimonies about their strained interactions with Jews in positions of relative power. These included accounts of beatings they received from Jewish ghetto police or of their attempts to dodge Jewish ghetto police when smuggling food into the ghetto.[131]

The most lasting memory of unequal Jewish-Romani relations during the war was of the hierarchical use and abuse of power in the concentration camps.[132] While there were several places where Jewish victims reported interactions with Romani overseers, none left a mark as consequential as the brief moment when Jews from northern Transylvania were deported to Birkenau's "Gypsy camp" in 1944.[133] During a period of anywhere between two days and two weeks, according to different accounts, hundreds of Hungarian Jews from the region remained under the control of Romani prisoners. Crammed into tight barracks on one side of BIIe, they experienced the blows and mistreatment of their overseers as an introduction to camp life. These interactions between a handful of German Sinti and a group of Jewish deportees from Hungarian-controlled Transylvania clearly scarred the Jews who lived through that moment and subsequently played an oversized role in trials and literary accounts.[134] It is important to take such accounts seriously as individual experiences of suffering. Yet it is useful to remember that they tell us little of the hierarchies that existed between Roma and Jews across Hitler's Europe. Jews were more often in charge of managing Roma simply because they were available for the task, especially in the many spaces that were first established for the detainment of Jews and only later used to imprison Romanies.

The common suggestion that the Germans bestowed on Roma certain privileges over Jews tends to be based on a selective interpretation of individual cases. Yet the underlying narrative of conflict illustrates the violence possible between people who often shared few connections and were put under grueling conditions. We can see this in some of the most wrenching accounts of clashes, such as in the testimonies of the Dutch Jewish survivor Donald Krausz. In his interviews with the Shoah Foundation and Yad Vashem, as well as in written recollections, Krausz, a young teenager at the time of his deportation from the Netherlands, describes sharing barracks with German Romanies in the men's camp in Ravensbrück and Sachsenhausen.[135] In every version, his conflicts with "Gypsies" are the main theme, involving not just adults but also Romani boys who, he reports, beat Jewish boys. He attributes this in part to the antisemitic indoctrination that the German Sinti in his barrack had been exposed to as army conscripts before 1941 but also to their low status "from a refinement point of view."[136] Reading his account against the grain and alongside those of other Jewish and Romani survivors confined together suggests that much of the violence revolved around issues of status, shaped by individuals' expectations about social hierarchies, self-assertion, and honor.[137]

Such issues appear prominently in Elie Wiesel's *Night,* among the best-known memoirs of life in a Nazi camp. The original Yiddish version of Wiesel's famous book contended with the same linguistic and cultural baggage evident in other Yiddish writing from the era. He used the term *zigeiner* ("Gypsy") as a qualifier to describe something chaotic and disgraced: the leftover property of Jews strewn on ghetto streets appeared like a "Gypsy market" (*zigeiner-mark*); standing isolated on the street he is "like a Gypsy"; and the act of being forced to stand up and sit down to be counted is akin to being treated like a "Gypsy gang" (*zigeiner-bande*).[138] Wiesel's description of his interactions with Romanies in Auschwitz in both the Yiddish and revised French and English versions of *Night* disrupts his casual and caricatured portrayals of "Gypsies." It depicts his father's traumatic encounter with a Romani kapo as a pivotal moment after his deportation from Transylvania.[139] According to Wiesel, after his father politely inquired where he might find the restrooms, the "Gypsy" in charge stared at him and then beat him in response. Wiesel depicts his father's disgust at such "barbarians" and describes his own realization that he was now in a world where he could not defend his father.[140] Considering his portrayal of "Gypsy" ways in the Yiddish edition, Wiesel may well have perceived the affront as particularly egregious because it was inflicted on him and his fellow deportees by people they had traditionally considered to be below them.[141]

These conflicts were most explosive when the stakes were highest and where members of both groups were in close contact but had little chance to build familiarity. One German Jewish witness mentioned similar violence, reporting on an all-out collective attack by Jewish and non-Jewish female prisoners on Romani women in their labor unit. In her account, she relates the suspicions that festered between Romani women and others during their transport across Germany from Beendorf to Hamburg.[142] Speaking to a local oral history interviewer in New Jersey in 1993—and thus with some distance and opportunity to reflect—she claimed:

And the Gypsies were talking amongst each other and since we didn't understand it, we didn't pay attention. But with us was also a Hungarian girl who did understand them and who also spoke Polish. With us also was Roshi Klein who spoke Polish. And very quietly in Dutch and in German, she told us that the Gypsies had planned to murder as many as needed so they could sit comfortably, as soon as [it] got dark enough that they could do this. Because there was some light streaming into the cattle cars. Being forewarned we could help ourselves. We pulled. They had long hair. We pulled their hair, we punched. Nothing. Nobody got killed. We got hurt but we didn't get killed. We were the only cattle car where everyone got out alive.[143]

The implication that Romani women had killed Jewish prisoners in the other cattle cars allowed this particular witness to make sense of her experience. This unlikely claim is not corroborated by any other source and thus may not tell us much, if anything, about what actually happened in the other train cars that day. Yet it tells us a great deal about this particular survivor's attempts to legitimize the violence she recalled between people who were experiencing the tense and perilous last days of the Nazi regime together with people they could not understand and did not trust. Physically close, members of both groups often became competitors and, less commonly, allies; they became subsumed into the general category of "victims" of Nazi racial policies only in retrospect.

Separate Suffering, Shared Archives

Decisions by the Nazis and their allies at various administrative levels shaped interactions between Roma and Jews from the early era of racial legislation to the mass murder of both groups from 1941 to 1945. These decisions were decentralized. The Nazis forced their victims to oversee other victims, handle their property, and dispose of their corpses based on local exigencies and circumstances. Therefore, general statements about what the German state and its allies wanted explain little about the situation of both groups as related targets of their policies. No abstract ideological hierarchy or master plan emanating from Berlin determined that, in Łódź, Jewish police guarded the gate between the Jewish and the "Gypsy" ghetto, whereas Sinti kapos in Auschwitz-Birkenau were responsible for overseeing Transylvanian Jews. An integrated account of the particular and overlapping experiences of both victim groups requires us to move beyond the ideology and motives of the center of power to the logic of local implementation.

The vast majority of Roma and Jews did not have a shared experience of persecution under Nazism. They suffered next to but rarely with each other. Nor did proximity necessarily invite solidarity or familiarity. In fact, the more detached modes of knowing about the suffering of others—seeing, hearing, or smelling their fate—often led to unequivocal expressions of solidarity, while closer and more intense involvement with other victims tended to inspire more ambivalence. This situation created a paradox: the most sympathetic accounts are often those of people who observed members of the other group from a distance and whose empathy was thus formed on a foundation of limited personal knowledge.

The Jewish and the Romani Holocausts left a legacy of complicated relations that are refracted through distorting filters. We learn about them largely from the accounts of Jews who arrived at such interactions with preconceived ideas about Roma but little familiarity with them. These testimonies reach us principally through the collection efforts and archives built by Jews to memorialize their own destruction. Both the witness accounts themselves and the institutions that house them thus, by their very nature, skew toward the story of the Jewish Holocaust first and foremost and the Romani Holocaust only secondarily, incidentally, and partially. This unevenness is compounded by the fact that the broader public still knows relatively little, if anything, about the Romani genocide.

Studying Romani-Jewish relations in the shadow of the Holocaust also reminds us of what is unique about the history of these two groups. In some respects, the fight for recognition of the Romani genocide is a familiar one. Many other groups who have suffered genocide and mass violence have similarly struggled to ensure that their own experiences of atrocity be granted political recognition, media and curricular attention, and space in our monument landscape equal to what the Holocaust has received. Yet there is a fundamental difference in how the cases of the Jewish and Romani Holocausts relate to one another. The Jewish and Romani catastrophes are not merely comparable events. They occurred next to each other and were perpetrated by the same people, at the same time. This entangled persecution revealed a longstanding experiential gap between these groups, even as it created individual opportunities to bridge it.

What ties Jews and Roma together is ultimately not so much a shared history of injustice but a shared will to record and repair that injustice. The Jewish and Romani prisoners who handled each other's property and corpses during the war rarely knew anything about the lives they came into contact with in the process. Yet, they are forever associated with each other because their traces reach us through the same archival and knowledge infrastructure that survivors and liberators began building after the war.

2

Surviving Postwar Reconstruction

LISTS OF NAMES sealed the death sentences of Jews and Roma during the Nazi era, but after the war, lists—including those compiled by the Nazis and their allies—became tools to help them reconstruct their devastated lives.[1] Those who survived the genocide depended on others' compilations of names to prove their eligibility for benefits as victims of Nazism and—more immediately—to locate living relatives or learn more about the fate of those who had perished. While the International Tracing Service maintained the largest archives of names, Jewish communities and various other organizations created their own lists.[2] Representatives of victim groups relied on these lists to argue their cases and to convince other institutions and states to allocate resources to their charges. In Austria, the Action Committee of Those Persecuted for Their Descent, assembled many such lists based on a dizzying array of criteria, including: children of school age who had been in concentration camps; non-Jews who had been forced to wear the Jewish star and who now lived in the American zone of occupation; stateless Jews who had benefited from United States food distribution campaigns; and prisoners who spent between three and three and a half years in concentration camps.[3] The leadership of the reconstituted Jewish community had founded the Action Committee in February 1946 to fight for the rights of Jewish survivors at a time when the main association of Nazi victims and resistance fighters (the KZ-Verband) represented only victims of political persecution.[4] It is thus not particularly surprising that all such lists, which the Action Committee collected and then transmitted to the official Jewish community, dealt primarily with individuals who had been persecuted as Jews—all except for one, that is: the "List of Gypsies Registered with Us" (see Figure 2.1).[5] This unusual document, retained by Vienna's Jewish community, records the name, birthdate, and place of residence of thirty-three Romani men and women who were registered by

Wien, 17.7.46

Liste der bei uns registrierten Zigeuner

		22.Rasdorf 31
		22.Rasdorf 31
		Nieder Absdorf Hof
		" " Hof
Hussak Adolf	24. 1.1917	" " Hof
		" " Hof
		" " Hof
Hussak Hermine	28.8.1919	" " Hof
		" " Hof
Horwath Kathar.	11.8.1923	" " Hof
		" " "
Horwath Anna	19.9.1912	" " "
		" " "
		" " "
Horwath Magd.	2.1.1899	" " "
		" " "
		" " "
		Urschendorf bef Wr.Neustadt Kreis Neunkirchen
		Nieder Absdorf Hof
		" " "
		" " "
		Nieder Absdorf Hof
		" b " "

FIGURE 2.1. "List of Gypsies Registered with Us," Archive of the IKG Vienna, Bestand Wien, A/VIE/IKG/III/SOZ/1/4 (Loan Collection VWI). Names are made illegible to protect the privacy of individuals whose deaths could not be confirmed.

the Jewish-led Action Committee in 1946. Most belonged to the extended
Gussak and Horwath families.

Among the Roma included on the list were two individuals who had become a couple after their liberation from concentration camps: Adolf Gussak
(sometimes Hussak) and Hermine Horwath. Both were clearly scarred by
their experiences, with their health in tatters and their families decimated.
Gussak had lost his first wife and son; Horwath, her parents and four siblings
in the camps.[6] Nothing remained for either of them after they returned home.
Gussak was an orphan who had been raised by a priest and had never owned
property. Horwath's family had owned a tiny house (of about 200 square feet)
and vineyard in the Austrian province of Burgenland, but neighbors had taken
ownership of their home after the family's deportation. Such experiences were
typical. Researchers working for the Austrian Historians' Commission on the
seizure of property during the Nazi period and postwar restitution have identified multiple similar cases of real estate stolen from their Romani owners, none
of which were returned after the war.[7] Writing about the couple in 1958, one
interviewer suggested that "shared experiences, shared suffering brought them
together."[8] That suffering did not end with the conclusion of the war in 1945.

In the summer of 1946, the remaining members of Adolf and Hermine's extended families found themselves in Niederabsdorf, a hamlet in Lower Austria
close to the border with Czechoslovakia, where many Slovak Roma had worked
as agricultural laborers before the war.[9] By late June 1946, members of each
family left the town, then in the Soviet zone of occupation, for Vienna and
sought out an organization that could certify their status as victims of Nazism.[10]
The main association that could do so had been formed by the Jewish community:
the Action Committee. Here Jewish survivors and administrators—such as the
later general secretary of the Jewish community, Wilhelm Krell—certified their
status as victims of Nazism, which promised preferential treatment with the
authorities. The central office of the KZ-Verband, dominated by political persecutees, then checked these applications and frequently rejected them, because
they did not wish to be associated with victims who were stigmatized as asocial,
work-shy, or inclined toward criminality.[11] In this context, the Horwath and
Gussak families' registration with the Jewish-led Action Committee begins to
come into focus: there were no equivalent bodies formed by or for Sinti and
Roma in the city to work on their behalf, while non-Jewish associations did not
reliably serve Romani survivors.

After the war, Roma began to appear in documents created by Jews and
Jewish institutions not merely as clichéd figures but as individuals who shared

something fundamental with Jews. In a sense, this is hardly surprising, for each group's experience of liberation had a great deal in common. As members of both groups emerged from the daily threat of extinction—whether they had survived labor camps, remained in hiding, been spared deportation, or lived through the war outside areas under Axis control—Jews and Roma alike hunted for missing relatives and encountered hostile neighbors.[12] Frequently Romani and Jewish returnees alike found little sympathy among defeated or liberated populations who also considered themselves victims of the war and continued to regard both Jews and Roma with suspicion. Neither anti-Romani nor anti-Jewish sentiments disappeared with the collapse of the Nazi regime.

Yet, the situations of the two victim groups also had important differences. Just as Jews and Roma had experienced and responded to crises differently in the past, they did so again after the war. Whereas Romani survivors relied principally on kinship networks for relief, Jews turned to familial ties as well as international associations and state-recognized national bodies.[13] Jewish aid organizations that had existed for many decades—in particular the American Joint Distribution Committee (JDC), founded in 1914 to help Jews during World War One—offered essential support at a time of scarcity, when every calorie mattered.[14] Jewish organizations also effectively combined political lobbying with aid on the ground, providing Jews with the resources that Romani survivors such as Adolf Gussak and Hermine Horwath also hoped to access in the wake of the war. Efforts to establish a new order after the chaos of World War Two thus affected Jews and Roma differently. This asymmetry gave Roma incentives to seek out Jewish networks as they rebuilt their lives.

Different legal frameworks and approaches to national reconciliation also influenced the evolution of Jewish-Romani relations. In the immediate aftermath of the war some of the most intense conflicts over Jewish and Romani rights in Europe occurred in the US zones of occupation in Germany and Austria, which saw a substantial influx of displaced persons (DPs). In these areas, Jews sometimes found themselves in the position to influence the rights and resources that Romani survivors could access. No doubt, the Roma who registered with the Jewish-led Action Committee hoped that this would be the case for them. The rest of this chapter explores how Roma and Jews entered into a new phase of their relationship as members of each group struggled to reconstruct their lives. As they tried to satisfy their basic needs, they tended to encounter each other with prewar ideas still in place. Yet, their parallel efforts to seek justice began to unite them in new ways as fellow victims.

Migration and Reconstruction

For a number of reasons—including varying access to institutional and political resources—Jews and Roma tended to make different choices about where to settle after World War Two. Whereas the majority of Roma did not stray far from areas where they had lived prior to the war, most Jews who remained in Eastern and Central Europe or returned to the region after 1945 came to understand their continued presence there as temporary. This became apparent in the paths Jews traced through Europe after the war and in their vocal demands to be allowed entry into Palestine, under British control until 1948. In the immediate postwar years, nearly 200,000 Jews passed through the US zone of Austria, and an even larger number lived temporarily in the US zone of Germany, usually with the intention of continuing on to Palestine or other destinations overseas.[15] The majority were Polish Jews who had survived the war in the Soviet Union and had been repatriated to Poland but considered the postwar situation there untenable.[16] After Polish residents of the city of Kielce killed forty-two Jews in an anti-Jewish pogrom on July 4, 1946, many became convinced that there was no place in postwar Poland for Jews. Temporarily moving to places such as Bavaria and Hesse, eastern European Jewish survivors organized themselves quickly but also relied on an infrastructure created by large Jewish institutions such as the JDC and non-Jewish entities such as the International Refugee Organization (IRO).[17] Within a matter of years, these and other Jewish survivors participated in a mass migration that eventually shifted the centers of Jewish life away from Europe to the United States and Israel. Whereas approximately 58 percent of the world's Jews lived in Europe in 1939, the number dropped to 35 percent by 1945 and 26 percent by 1970—with the majority of those who remained in Europe now residing in the Soviet Union, France, or the United Kingdom.[18] As a result of these demographic shifts, few Jews lived in areas with large Romani populations after the late 1940s.

Roma, by contrast, remained in their countries of origin in East-Central and Southeastern Europe in much larger numbers. A small number fled states in the process of a communist takeover, such as Czechoslovakia and Yugoslavia, but the majority remained in their prewar countries, where they stood out after wartime and postwar ethnic cleansing made these countries much less diverse.[19] In such places, it was not merely the Jews who had all but disappeared; within their newly constituted borders, states like Poland and Czechoslovakia also lost their substantial Ukrainian and German minorities, respectively.[20] This newfound national homogeneity often rendered Roma the most visible remaining outsiders.[21]

Though it is true that they stayed in part because of limited access to networks that could help them cross borders and establish new lives abroad, many Romani survivors also found new opportunities in postwar Central and Eastern Europe. In Czechoslovakia, Roma moved from rural Slovakia into Czech industrial areas that had been purged of most of their German-speaking inhabitants, finding prospects for employment and, in some cases, improved living conditions, in the process.[22] Communist regimes also discovered Roma as part of a revolutionary remaking of social relations. Czechoslovak officials came to portray the "Gypsy" industrial laborer as the ideal Stalinist worker, representing the regime's ability to transform even those who had once occupied the very bottom of the social hierarchy.[23] Such policies of uplifting Roma according to state plans entailed the elimination of economic niches Roma had once occupied as well as the forced destruction of Romani settlements, while at the same time promising new paths of social mobility.[24]

In Western Europe, Romani experiences in the postwar era had more in common with patterns developed in the prewar era, particularly at the level of official state policy, and often with adverse consequences. In France, for example, prefects who had been in charge of camps for "nomads" established during the war—a category they often treated as equivalent to "Gypsy"—refrained from releasing all inmates at the war's end.[25] Until 1969, the French state even maintained the same registration system for so-called nomads that was previously used by the Third Republic (1871–1940) and the Vichy regime (1940–44) during the Second World War.[26] In this context, postwar French officials' attempts to settle, assimilate, and discipline "Gypsy" populations led to onerous restrictions as part of general "security" measures intended to aid normalization. Liberation in France—and elsewhere in Western Europe—thus took on a different hue for Romanies than it did for Jews, who no longer encountered bureaucracies with expertise in tracking them.[27]

In Germany, too, Romani populations continued to face the threat of police and administrative repression. After 1945, German police authorities and ministries of the interior sought to implement repressive measures they had previously deployed against Sinti and Roma in the German Empire (1871–1918) and the Weimar Republic (1918–33).[28] Postwar German authorities maintained separate registries and employed police officers assigned to track "Gypsies"—now identified using new terms such as *Landfahrer* ("traveler" or "vagrant"). Although the Western Allies did not have a comprehensive plan for the treatment of Romani survivors, US and British occupation authorities rejected punitive measures that singled out one racially defined group or allowed for incarceration without judicial review.[29] Their influence sometimes mitigated punitive conditions for Roma and Sinti in Germany, yet Allied interventions in this area remained limited.

The Bavarian workhouse Rebdorf clearly illustrates continuities in the treatment of people the state identified as—or grouped together with— "Gypsies" before, during, and after the war. The workhouse was active from its founding in 1857 through the Nazi years, and into the postwar period. Although the legal details that led to the incarceration of individuals deemed "lazy" changed over time, the principal process by which they arrived in Rebdorf did not: workhouse detainees were apprehended and relocated by the fiat of high-ranking local administrators and were never put on trial. Many after 1945 were imprisoned on the basis of prewar legal precedents. These included a 1924 federal law mandating forced labor for unemployed, able-bodied welfare recipients as well as a 1926 Bavarian law against "Gypsies, Vagrants, and the Work-Shy."[30] The Nazis had used both laws extensively and sometimes transferred inmates between Rebdorf and better-known concentration camps such as Dachau.[31]

Even after the province became part of the US zone, Bavarian authorities continued to detain individuals as "Gypsies," "work-shy," or "idlers" in Workhouse Rebdorf.[32] What changed was that the United Nations Relief and Rehabilitation Administration (UNRRA) and, later, the IRO began operating a camp for displaced Lithuanians in the monastery next door.[33] While authorities did not leave a record of the official relationship between these two camps, we do know that American officials who were also overseeing the DP camp soon became uncomfortable with the presence of the labor camp in their midst. During a series of inspections of Workhouse Rebdorf in 1947, US occupation authorities found eleven inmates interned according to the 1926 law against "Gypsies" and the "Work-Shy" and ninety others brought there under the cover of other decrees against idlers.[34] The people identified with a "Z." next to their name on the list of inmates had been sentenced to the longest periods of imprisonment—usually around two years, as opposed to the more common half-year to one-year convictions. Although the presence of a "Z." next to inmates' names did not necessarily indicate an ethnic Romani background, it presumably meant that such individuals had been detained using laws against "Gypsies" (Zigeuner).[35] That the majority of Rebdorf's inmates had been imprisoned without judicial review or appeal proved worrisome to local US officials, who demanded a repeal of the 1926 Bavarian law against Gypsies and the Work-Shy and the immediate release of all inmates.[36] Bavarian authorities responded to these orders reluctantly. Despite the clear instructions of the Bavarian chancellery in Munich, at least three prisoners remained in custody at Rebdorf on the orders of a Bavarian judge.[37] While the Bavarian authorities duly reported this decision to US military authorities, it seems no further action was taken to advocate on behalf of the remaining detainees.[38]

These practices were holdovers from earlier regimes, but they were also characteristic of Western European postwar reconstruction projects. Only a few months after US occupation authorities sought to intervene on behalf of those imprisoned at Rebdorf, the Bavarian parliament debated possible new measures to deal with so-called asocials and work-shy individuals. Several members of the Christian Socialist party, or CSU, proposed the following bill: "To ask the state government to initiate immediate negotiations with the military government to vacate camp sites (Dachau) as quickly as possible in order to build a work camp for asocial elements."[39] The bill's sponsor, conservative deputy Hans Hagn, a representative of the Christian worker unions, cited a police report from Munich that demanded action against a variety of people, ranging from dealers on the black market to vagrants, none of whom could be convicted because they claimed they were simply searching for lost relatives. In response, a Social Democratic representative suggested that building material for labor camps might be put to better use as housing for workers who had found employment but remained homeless. Nevertheless, he ended up supporting the measure and the Bavarian parliament unanimously approved the bill, which asked the Americans to reconstruct Dachau or another site as a facility for the internment and reeducation of work-shy individuals. The principal disagreement that surfaced once the bill was passed on to the government for implementation was not whether to support such a program but what the new camp should be called: with the experience of Nazi camps fresh in people's memories, the Bavarian Chancellery sought to find alternative names for the site, suggesting either "forced labor" (*Zwangsarbeit*) or "work education camp" (*Arbeitserziehungslager*). Eventually, the Ministry of Labor and Social Welfare settled on the older term workhouse.[40]

While none of these debates directly targeted Romanies, Bavarian lawmakers' attempts to reestablish legal mechanisms for the internment of vagrants and the work-shy illustrate how postwar policies affected people whom the authorities identified or treated as Gypsies.[41] It is certainly suggestive that the postwar Bavarian government sought to create a new workhouse for "work-shy" individuals on the grounds of one of the best known Nazi concentration camps, only months after Americans forced the closure of another workhouse for individuals detained under the kinds of laws used against "Gypsies" and the "work-shy." Indeed, given the state's history of interning Romanies under similar pretenses, this move signaled the renewed precariousness of Romani life in the region after the war. Reconstruction in the Cold War West meant many things: the creation of democratic states and the reestablishment of the rule of law—including the right to property—but also a renewed idealization of disciplined workers and, soon, worker-consumers.[42] Because state officials continued to associate Romani and "Gypsy" populations with vagrancy and a resistance to regular work, they remained at a disadvantage amid new efforts to shape the whole population into economically productive citizens.

Economic arguments, security concerns, and established preconceptions about the purported racial characteristics of "Gypsy" types also drove the management of postwar migration. While these stereotypes differed from those about Jews in some respects, both Jews and Roma faced discrimination in the administrative processes that gave preferential treatment to people deemed most useful for postwar reconstruction. The first schemes for mass resettlement under the aegis of the IRO—including "Operation Black Diamond" to Belgium, "Westward Ho!" to Great Britain, and the "Metropolitan Scheme," which directed migrants to France—were all aimed at tapping into DPs as a labor pool.[43] While the IRO established eligibility based on applicants' personal history, including the continuous threat of persecution, the selection commissions for immigrant countries were more preoccupied with finding good workers. Since national selection commissions made the final determination about resettlement, opportunities for new beginnings in the early Cold War West had more to do with perceptions of an individual's productivity and work ethic than with their experience of past injustices. These decisions were often influenced by racialized stereotypes about productivity.[44] The IRO, for its part, created lists of "resettlement handicaps" that included racialized, religious, and ethnic categories. Next to health, age, and occupational "handicaps," the IRO noted that "Asiatics" and "Moslems (non-Turkish speaking)" were unlikely to be accepted for immigration.[45] While Jewish aid organizations could offset some of the stigmas about unproductive Jews by promising support for immigrants in their new home countries, no comparable developments eased fears about Roma when it came to migration. Many administrators remained convinced that "Gypsies" would be unable to fit into a productive economic order and that it was therefore futile to support their emigration.[46]

Romani and Jewish prospects were even more unequal in terms of compensation, even though members of both groups faced serious disadvantages compared to political persecutees.[47] Restitution and compensation laws tended to focus on individuals who were citizens before a certain prewar cutoff date, or those who could establish a record of national merit—for example, activity in the resistance. Western European reconstruction was not only a hemispheric project under the US umbrella driven by Marshall Plan aid but also a national project aimed at restoring the authority of various postwar nation-states in the region.[48] The resulting compensation criteria regularly excluded Jews, many of whom were not citizens of the countries from which they had been deported. This was true, for example, for approximately 50 percent of the Jews in France and as many as 90 percent of the Jews deported from Belgium.[49]

However challenging the circumstances were for Jewish refugees in postwar Western Europe, they were more dire still for those registered as "Gypsies." Being categorized as a "Gypsy" not only undermined attempts to remedy past injustices but also made an individual the target of further injustice. Facing ongoing suspicion and discrimination, it made sense for Roma to draw a closer relationship to Jews who had survived the war—comparing their experiences to Jewish experiences, seeking the aid of Jewish organizations, or deciding that their best hope was to ask to be treated like Jewish victims. After all, despite the intense conflicts that regularly ensued between German police and Jewish DPs accused of black-market activities during this period, at least no political party had suggested the establishment of new camps designed to imprison Jews after the war.[50]

Categories of Victimhood

The list of "Gypsies registered with us" preserved by Vienna's Jewish community suggests that new, countervailing pressures nevertheless incentivized people to get registered as a "Gypsy" because it offered potential benefits that competed with older disincentives driven by patterns of police surveillance and the targeting of Roma as vagrants and work-shy. In these contexts, Romani survivors such as Gussak and Horwath decided to reveal that they had been persecuted as Gypsies and seek rights as such.

The histories of the international organizations that managed displacement and migration after the war offer some hints about how the term "Gypsy" slowly shifted from a criminological category to a legal one that established certain rights. For Roma and Sinti, as well as others who were identified or identified themselves as "Gypsies," however, such changes were not only slow but also at times seemingly arbitrary. Whereas prosecutors at the Nuremberg trial clearly named "Gypsies" as a group that experienced genocide, the international organizations chartered by the Allies and eventually controlled mostly by Americans, did not treat "Gypsies" as a legal category.[51]

This was the case with UNRRA, the first organization to work on behalf of postwar DPs between 1943 and 1947. UNRRA's main task was to offer legal and material support to individuals displaced during the war and facilitate their repatriation. The organization's mandate primarily entailed returning nationals to their home countries, even if it sometimes meant ignoring what the people in question wanted. Instructions distributed to UNRRA eligibility teams thus demanded that classifications follow only national designations, a development which came to influence later reviews and decisions about applicants. Categories that did not clearly map onto existing nation-states fell to the wayside, as an administrative order of March 11, 1946 made clear. "Such categories as 'Arabs,' 'Mongolians,' 'Gypsies,' 'Kalmycks,' 'South Americans' and 'White Ruthenians' are incorrect. The reporting of nationalities should be in reference to the country of which they are citizens or nationals. The only exception to this should be in the case of 'Jews,'" it explained.[52]

UNRRA's policies found their continuation in the categories employed by the IRO. The annex to the IRO's 1947 constitution, which defined eligibility for services, only allowed members of two groups to claim that they were unable to return to their former country of residence without having to substantiate the threats they faced: Jews and Spanish Republicans.[53] All other refugees had to demonstrate either reasonable fear of ongoing persecution or compelling political objections to repatriation across the descending Iron Curtain. What is more, to be considered victims of Nazi persecution, all others had to prove their precise history of internment, whereas Jews and Spanish Republicans merely had to show their identity as members of one of those two groups. Many Romani refugees—especially those fleeing from Czechoslovakia and Yugoslavia in the late 1940s—thus had to establish their continuing persecution (under communism) to receive any relief. It was in this context that Rudolf Braidić, the Romani refugee mentioned in this book's introduction, highlighted how he suffered like the Jews in his application. Yet, the process proved easier when officials on the ground began improvising to get around their explicit instructions. They judged Romani refugees to be worthy of being taken into Western Europe as refugees due to "compelling family reasons arising out of previous persecution," and thus reinterpreted IRO regulations to treat Roma as they treated Jews.[54] In so doing, they established "Gypsy" as a rights-bearing category, as a result of local administrative fiat and without cover from their own political leadership.[55]

Such a move required making Romani applicants visible through the application of "Gypsy" as an ethnic (as opposed to a social) category. US army personnel who created the first intake files of survivors with the help of other inmates and translators initiated this process. While filling out the requisite forms, they regularly crossed out the preprinted national designation—"German" on the German-language form or "Polish" on the Polish-language form—only to replace it with "Gypsy" (see Figure 2.2).[56]

Local IRO administrators then had to decide what to make of people registered using this category. The 330 and 243 applicants who registered as "Gypsies" in IRO files from Germany and Italy, respectively, give some sense of how the process worked.[57] Frequent mention of the Romani language among refugees' application forms implies that many self-declared as "Gypsies"; in other cases, interviewers suggested that the determination was ultimately theirs to make, regardless of how the applicants described themselves. (One Italian interviewer noted, "Applicant is really a Gipsy," and thus concluded, "This family, being gypsy, cannot be accepted by any selection mission."[58]) Despite the suspicions of certain interviewers, the IRO ultimately deemed the vast majority of these 573 "Gypsy" applicants eligible, at a considerably higher rate than the organization's average claimant. Indeed, the organization declared as eligible for support 87 percent of applicants in Germany and 90 percent of applicants in Italy who were registered as "Gypsies."[59] More striking still, Roma who came from Czechoslovakia had a 78 percent eligibility rate at a time when other migrants from these areas were often denied support because the organization deemed them to be economic refugees.[60]

For a period of approximately half a decade following the Second World War, the designation "Gypsy" thus functioned as a privileged rather than prejudicial category.[61] These developments had a precursor in the early Soviet Union. In the 1920s, Soviet programs of economic advancement for oppressed nationalities allowed for a brief renaissance of Romani cultural production—including a Romani state theater—and incentivized Roma to declare themselves as "Gypsies."[62] Whereas these Soviet policies had emanated from those in power, the reevaluation of the category "Gypsy" during the immediate postwar era did not. It was, rather, the result of the impromptu actions of officials in direct contact with survivors who decided to register people as "Gypsies" either against official instructions (as was the case with UNRRA), or without any clear guidelines in place for doing so (as was true for the IRO). These local decisions nonetheless gave Sinti and Roma access to the resources of some of the most influential international agencies of the immediate postwar years. Whether or not they made it explicit, administrators started to treat "Gypsies" the same way that Jews were already treated in these contexts.

To be sure, this transformation occurred largely in arenas where international rather than national imperatives predominated. At the level of national bureaucracies, expertise on Romanies remained squarely in the hands of law enforcement, welfare, and health officers, who continued to think about Roma along racialized lines. Such individuals generally viewed "Gypsies" as a challenge to public safety and social peace that had to be managed, often by removing them from a given jurisdiction. German authorities in many areas, for example, challenged the citizenship of Romani survivors, including men whom the state had drafted into the German army before 1941.[63]

International organizations, by contrast, had a different task. Due to their broad geographic scope, they were unable to define temporary relocation as success: they measured their accomplishments by the yardstick of permanent resettlement. Their different missions meant that their approach to Roma was more accommodating and thus, for a time, more beneficial than were most local and national administrative settings. Bringing Roma under their purview also removed Roma from situations in which they tended to be heavily surveilled and criminalized, giving them access instead to material aid and administrative and financial support for emigration. In this respect, their situation resembled that of Jewish survivors in the immediate postwar period.

This shift was also possible because some individuals working for the IRO recognized that Roma and Sinti had suffered their own systematic persecution during the war and factored this into their deliberations. Even when the details remained murky, interviewers could choose to use their knowledge of anti-Romani measures to make a case on behalf of Romani claimants. As one sympathetic IRO employee put it when describing the wartime decisions of an applicant who fled from a German-occupied area in today's Slovenia: "At arrival of German forces he had to escape from there and come to Italy because Germans were persecuting and shooting gypsys as well as jews."[64] The same interviewer implored the responsible officer to consider the persecution Romanies had suffered under Nazism: "PLEASE, consider his origin with respect

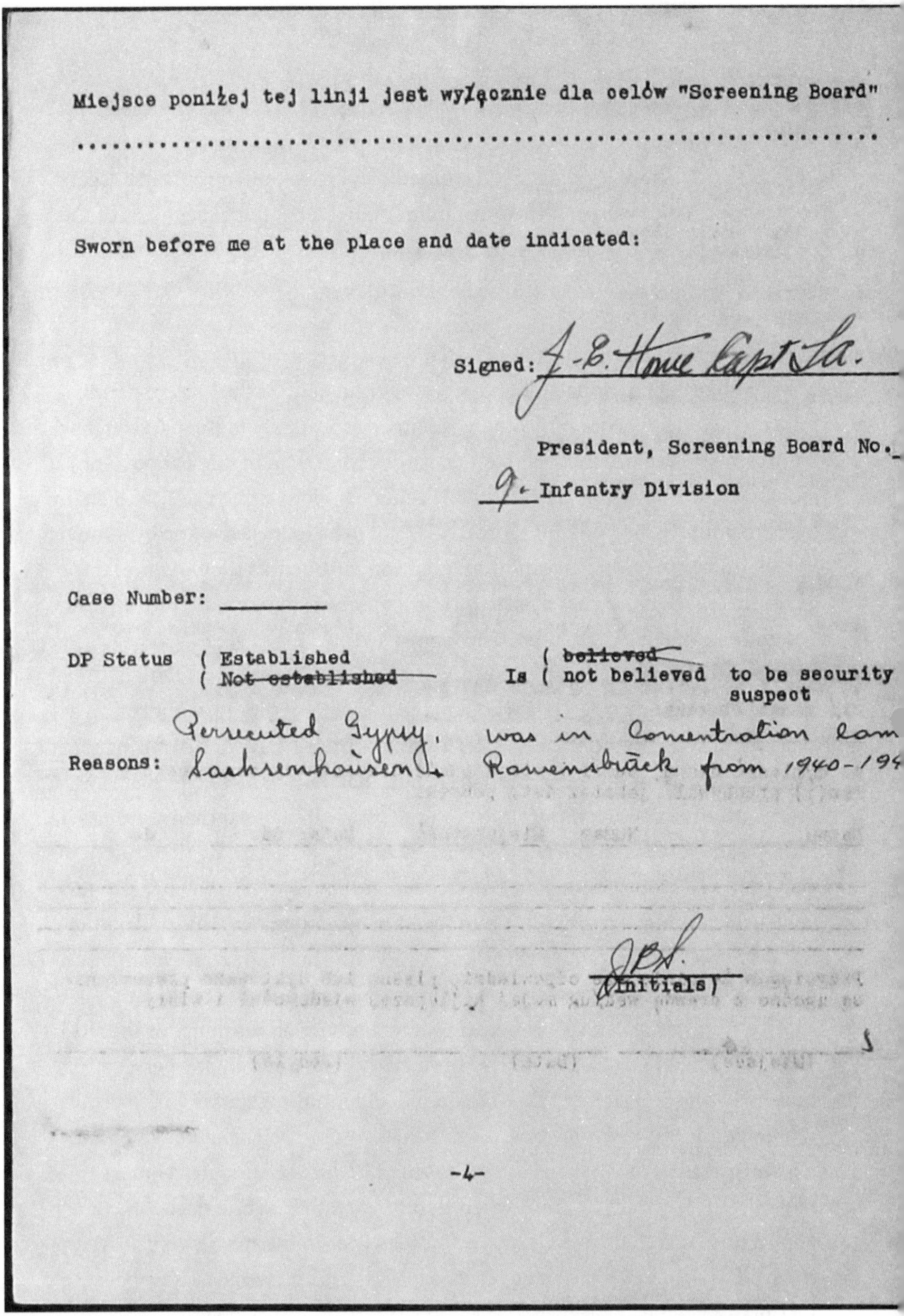

....

Sworn before me at the place and date indicated:

Signed: *J-E. Howe Capt Sa.*

President, Screening Board No.

9 Infantry Division

Case Number: _____

DP Status (Established
             (~~Not established~~   (~~believed~~
                                  Is (not believed to be security
                                                           suspect

Reasons: *Persecuted Gypsy. was in Concentration cam Sachsenhausen u. Ravensbrück from 1940-194*

(Initials)

-4-

FIGURE 2.2. Last and first page of the 1946 DP Questionnaire of Josef (Józef) Freiwald with the preprinted "Polish" crossed out and "Gypsy" inserted. The questionnaire also has Freiwald listed as stateless, which was later revised to "Russian" based on his birthplace. *Source*: 3.2.1/79094710/ITS Digital Archive, Arolsen Archives.

FREIWALD, Jozef.

EJWALD J.

USA Form No.
P/G-1
1 June 46)

HEADQUARTERS
THIRD UNITED STATES ARMY
-.-

C m 1
R-33

Polish 1057

Gypsy

P.St.5

KWESTIONARJUSZ DLA D.P.

er Obozu DP_____ Wiek _36_ Płeć _M._ Numer Karty porz.DP 2497920

lne Instrukcje: WSZYSTKIE PYTANIA MUSZĄ BYĆ ODPOWIEDZIANE. DRUKOWAĆ
ODPOWIEDZI.

eli odpowiedzi dane są niezupełne lub fałszywe, będzie Pan (i) karany
podstawie amerykańskiego wojskowego prawa karnego.

iejscach przeznaczonych dla obydwóch "Tak" i "Nie", posługujcie sie
-em dla oznaczenia Waszej odpowiedzi.

Nazwisko (polska pisownia): _Frajwal._ _Józef_
(Nazwisko)   Ekaterinoslaw   (Imię)   (Imię panienskie)

a. Kraj i miejsce urodzenia _Rosija._ b. Data urodzenia _17.12.1910_
(Data, miesiąc,
rok)

a. Wasza narodowość _Stateless_ b. Wasza Religia _R. Katolik_

c. W dniu 31 Sierpnia 1939r. jakie było Wasze (Legalne Obywatelstwo _stateless_
(Adres _Warszawa_

a. Dokładna pisownia Waszego nazwiska po niemiecku _Frajwal Josef_

b. Podać inne nazwiska Pan(i) ma lub miał:

Nazwisko	Gdzie używane	Data
	Nie miałem	

Podać nazwiska innych członków Waszej najbliższej rodziny obecnie w
Niemczech:

Nazwisko	Stosunek pokrewieństwa	Miejsce pobytu	DP (tak lub nie)
Frajwal Maria	żona		tak
4 synów			tak

a. Jaki jest Wasz szczególny zawód, przemysł lub profesja? _muzykant_
b. Wypełnić poniżej rodzaj pracy Pan(i) miał jakoteż miejsce pracy
(robotnik,biuralista,zarządca, majster itd) dla każdego z lat
wymienionych (rozpoczęwszy we Wrześniu 1939r. i kończąc w Maju 1945r)

-1-

to the objections."[65] Although it is difficult to discern precisely what the inter-viewer knew about the mass murder of Roma or Jews during the war, like many of the protagonists of this book, he decided that their experiences were similar enough to warrant juxtaposition in some form.

Each time Romani survivors gained new rights based on comparisons to Jews, they found new reasons to employ historical argumentation when mak-ing their claims. They were not alone in doing so. Ethnicized histories of vic-timhood and heroism became the principal idiom of self-assertion across the political spectrum following the war, to the point that life in DP camps pro-pelled the nationalization of different groups, such as Lithuanians, Poles, and Jews.[66] Collective histories also remained pivotal to rights talk after 1945, even as the debate shifted from minority rights to individual rights.[67] When the 1951 Refugee Convention defined refugees as those with a "wellfounded [sic] fear of being persecuted for reasons of race, religion, nationality," it compelled those who sought these rights to attach their biography to a familiar story of collective persecution.[68] Roma experienced the full effect of this turn to the politics of history following the close of World War Two.

The first practical step for many survivors was still to demonstrate their persecution on an individual level. As one Romani survivor, Oswald Hertz-berg, who struggled to locate relevant historical documents as evidence of his past suffering explained in a letter to the ITS in January 1950: "I am facing nothingness and could start a new life if I could show proof of my imprison-ment in a camp."[69] Although the man in question had been interned in three different concentration camps during the war (Auschwitz, Flossenbürg, and Dachau), his fate after the war's end hinged on his ability to substantiate his experiences officially through historical documentation.

Proof of imprisonment only mattered in the chaotic postwar years, how-ever, if it attached to a collective story of persecution. Individual biographies had to match administrative categories, whether they were decreed from above or improvised from below.[70] Hence, there was good reason why Roma found themselves on lists with Jews and lists created by Jews as soon as they volunteered their names for registration. Jews' experiences during the war were still better known, and documenting them tended to accrue certain legal rights, such as resettlement aid and financial compensation. Proving suffering in the same places as Jews, or in similar ways, was often Romanies' best bet at receiving recognition and compensation of their own after the war. Members of both groups became administrative kin, even as their experiences often re-mained apart.

Roma and Jews in DP Camps

While Jews and Roma had similar needs after the war, they rarely inhabited the same spaces, except for during a very brief period after the liberation of the camps. When they crossed paths subsequently, it was often due to their efforts to rebuild their lives. In most cases, Roma and Jews encountered each other as fellow sufferers or supplicants. The parallel travels of Jewish and Romani survivors to the mass graves at Kremnička, in Czechoslovakia, mentioned in the previous chapter, are a case in point. Here members of both groups sought to identify corpses of family members among the hundreds of dead discovered at the killing site, with Romani workers performing much of the labor of exhumation. Chance encounters between members of both groups likely happened as they both endeavored to reconstitute their lives in the shadow of genocide, including the act of testifying in front of war crimes commissions or registering with state offices dealing with housing, education, welfare, and citizenship matters.

Yet when they returned home after a day of waiting in line to receive food, official papers, and rights, Roma and Jews usually ended up in different places. The case of the large number of DPs streaming into the American and British occupation zones of Germany is instructive in this regard. Various prisoners liberated from camps stayed in facilities established on former campgrounds in the months after the war, living in dismal conditions. For Jewish prisoners, circumstances improved after a committee under Earl S. Harrison reported to President Harry Truman in August 1945 about the dire situation of Jewish survivors in US care. Responding to the concern that targeted aid for Jews might lead to tensions with other DPs, American and British authorities decided to house Jewish DPs in separate camps. These camps originally accommodated a small number of Jews who found themselves on German territory in the summer of 1945. They were only a miniscule part of the larger population of five to seven million displaced persons in Germany. Yet, while members of other population groups slowly found old or new homes, these camps eventually accommodated the over 100,000 Jews who fled Poland and other Eastern European countries after the summer of 1946. In these camps, Jewish life flourished for several years before the majority left for Palestine or overseas destinations. Many Jews on German territory lived in these Jewish spaces, with a substantial number moving into rental apartments with support from Jewish organizations.[71]

Romani survivors in countries under Soviet control moved into the western zones of occupation in much smaller numbers, and when they did, allied administrators assigned them to camps with non-Roma from the same region.[72] Roma refugees in Germany were subsequently torn between affiliation with individuals of the same nationality and affiliation as "Gypsies." Indeed, while many Roma who came to the US Zone of Germany from the east found their first homes in DP camps designed for citizens of a particular country, others resided in separate unregulated or semi-regulated settlements. A significant number selected the latter option over the former, such as the many Polish Roma who spent time in the Polish DP camp Hohenfels before joining other Roma on travelers' campsites, such as one in Venloerstraße in Cologne, which the Nazis had created as a forced settlement for "Gypsies" during the war. In the wake of the war, Romani survivors as well as some non-Romani people without housing had chosen to create a settlement of their own at the same site.[73]

Conditions for new Romani migrants to Germany were generally dismal. Their situation resembled that of Jewish refugees in the chaotic months immediately after liberation. The Freiwald family's struggles illustrate these challenges and remind us of what it meant to be without international protectors or local allies. As was true for so many refugees during this period, the details of Josef (Jozéf) and Maria Freiwald's fate before arriving in Germany cannot be ascertained with any certainty from extant documents. According to one version, Josef Freiwald was the child of Romani farmers from Bukovina who had given birth to him during their travels in Russia.[74] In 1930, at age 30, he left for Poland and returned to Czernowitz, where he claimed to have married his wife, with whom he eventually had eight children. Josef Freiwald then worked as a textile peddler in Poland or moved with his family across Europe, performing as a musician in Serbia, Latvia, and Sweden, according to different accounts.[75] After German authorities arrested him in Poland in 1939, he was deported to Buchenwald while his wife and children were sent to Ravensbrück, where two of their children perished. Immediately after the war, the family found itself in the western occupation zones of Germany and received UNRRA aid until the organization closed in 1947.[76] He was one of the liberated survivors whom US officials registered with UNRRA as "Gypsies," against the regulations (see figure 2.2 above). Josef initially sustained himself playing music for US troops in Bad Arolsen, where he was paid in cigarettes. The family later moved to Krondorf, where Josef traded in textiles in 1948. His income was clearly insufficient to feed his large family, and the extra allotment from the municipal welfare office in Krondorf did not fill the gap.[77]

By 1949, the family once again lived in a camp, this time in Schwandorf am Anger, inhabited mostly by Russian DPs, a nationality IRO officials decided he shared simply because he had been born on Russian territory. The legal counselor who prepared the family's documents for emigration described their dreadful situation in a report: "The Russians who live there have poor trailers. The family of Josef Freiwald does not have a trailer but a wooden shack without windows. The family Freiwald consists of 8 persons, including 6 children between the ages of 6 months and 11 years and these children suffer from Tuberculosis and Rachitis; they have no clothing and their wood shack is beyond description."[78] An officer from the social service branch was similarly dismayed and explained the grim living conditions of the family of eight on merely nine square meters (or 100 square feet).[79] The same official demanded that the family be granted assistance from the IRO as a hardship case. Around the same time, Brazilian authorities rejected the family's immigration bid because two of their children had been diagnosed with tuberculosis.[80] Josef agreed to train as a car mechanic and IRO officials reported that he made a good overall impression. None of that helped. Their poor living conditions made it even harder for the family to leave Germany. Limited resources and a dearth of voluntary organizations dedicated to their aid put them in a desperate position.

Jewish survivors in Germany were unlikely to witness the difficulties of the Freiwald family or any of the other Romani DPs in the country, for that matter. Jews lived largely either in separate camps or in urban areas, whereas the new Romani settlements—like the old ones they often reinhabited—were located remotely, toward the urban periphery. The rare sighting of identifiable groups of "Gypsies" was thus something noteworthy in Jewish camps. One trace of such a contact appears in a journal kept by members of a socialist collective— the kibbutz Ma'apilim—in the DP camp Feldafing in Bavaria, which housed only Jews.[81] Members of the group, consisting mostly of Polish Jewish survivors, maintained a shared notebook in 1946 and 1947 that contained their activities, ideas, satirical commentaries, and short mottos. One line in a list of miscellaneous notes written by a woman named Batya Goldman reads: "I use the opportunity and make friends with a group of Gypsies [*a zigeiner grupe*]."[82] This is all we learn about her new friendship, which appears to have been unusual enough to warrant special mention. (Indeed, there is no indication in the journal that she or any members of her collective deemed contact with any other nationality as noteworthy.)

Other interactions reflect the uneven infrastructure supporting Jewish and Romani attempts to rebuild shattered lives. Sustained contacts were most likely in places where Jews were the dominant group. Whereas only a few years earlier, proximity to Jews would have been a sign of impending doom, in the postwar period the possibility of remaining close to Jews could offer hope. This shift is reflected in the testimony of a Romani survivor who spent time in the largest camp for Jewish DPs after the war, Bergen-Belsen, which was set up in former army barracks close to the grounds of the defunct concentration camp by the same name.[83] Anita Schopper, a Romani survivor, told a Jewish interviewer in the 1990s that she and a friend found it comforting to go to the Yiddish theater in the camp after liberation.[84] Having learned Yiddish from her fellow prisoners during the war, she reported that they had even told the authorities that they were Jewish. Such interactions were clearly important for the people who experienced them: Schopper described these visits to the Yiddish theater as her first opportunity for escapism after the ravages of the war.

The experiences of Anita Schopper and Batya Goldmann proved the exception. Jewish inhabitants of DP camps were at least as likely to encounter Roma in the abstract as in person. Yiddish-speaking survivors continued to listen to songs about Gypsies or composed in "Gypsy-style," much as they had in the Warsaw Ghetto. Around the time that Goldman registered her attempts to befriend local Roma, other Jewish survivors in the Zeilsheim DP camp gathered to hear the famous Polish Jewish singer Lola Folman perform romanticized ditties about "Gypsies" for their entertainment.[85] A largely parallel and at times intersecting search for a new postwar life did not erase the old ways of seeing each other.

Managing Survivors:
A Jewish Administrator and his Romani Clients

Some of the most sustained contacts Roma had with Jews were not with Jewish DPs but with Jewish administrators. Romani relations with Philipp Auerbach, who eventually became one of the most influential gatekeepers of survivor rights in the US zone of Germany, illustrates the ambivalent relations between different survivors. Auerbach, who served as State Commissioner for Racial, Religious and Political Persecutees in Bavaria, is remembered today both for his meteoric rise and precipitous fall from grace.[86] He was the subject of a widely reported embezzlement trial that ended with his conviction in August 1952 and his subsequent suicide. In a sense Auerbach is postwar Germany's emblematic tragic hero—a man who rose to power due to his peculiar talents, which brought about his downfall and eventual death. His relations with Romani survivors add another layer to his complicated persona.

Although he grew up with relative financial security, Auerbach had to start from scratch several times over the course of his short life.[87] After graduating from a traditional Jewish religious school (or Talmud-Torah) in Hamburg without a high school degree, he joined his father's company, which traded in chemicals and minerals. During his apprenticeship, he learned chemistry in a trade school. His father owned a tungsten mine in Spain, and from 1929 to 1930 Auerbach managed his father's holdings there. Soon after his return from Spain, the family company went bankrupt, and Auerbach found himself forced into new business ventures. The Nazi rise to power in January 1933 accelerated this process. Befitting his upper middle-class Jewish background, Auerbach had been active in the liberal party (the DDP) and in the Weimar Republic's center-left militia, the Reichsbanner. He thus appeared on the Nazis' radar early and was arrested for ten days in February 1933. By 1934, Auerbach managed to flee to Belgium with his wife and newborn child. Unlike other exiles, Auerbach quickly got back on his feet. He opened a highly successful chemical business in Belgium, which employed as many as 2,000 employees at its peak, according to one biographer.[88] His company profited mainly from the export of chemicals to Republican forces during the Spanish Civil War.

Auerbach's luck ended once again with the outbreak of World War Two. The Germans had stripped him of his nationality and due to the interventions of the Antwerp Jewish community, which deemed him politically unreliable, the Belgians denied him citizenship. When German troops entered the country, Belgian authorities arrested him in Antwerp. From this moment until his liberation in Buchenwald in 1945, Auerbach passed from camp to camp; the Belgians initially deported him to France, where he was interned in multiple camps, including Vernet, St. Cyprien, and Gurs.[89] In August 1942, the French Vichy regime handed him over to the Germans under the charge of "high treason." The Germans first held him in the police prison on Berlin Alexanderplatz and then in Auschwitz, Groß-Rosen, and, finally, Buchenwald. With each internment, Auerbach managed to assume special roles: he introduced himself as a doctor of chemistry in French camps, acted as a translator while imprisoned in Berlin, and served as a chemist for the disinfection unit in Buchenwald.[90] After the war, one of his fellow inmates filed a complaint against Auerbach for joining kapos in abusing prisoners in Groß-Rosen, but other prisoners swore under oath that the accusations were untrue and both Belgian and Bavarian authorities dismissed the charges.[91] Regardless of whether there were merits to the case against him, no one could doubt that Auerbach was a resourceful man.

After the war, Auerbach worked for German authorities in the British zone of occupation, a position he received due to his personal relations with members of the British intelligence service. There he established the patterns that would eventually lead to his rise and fall in Bavaria. After working briefly for an office that dealt with welfare for victims of persecution, he headed another office tasked with identifying Nazi criminals in the North-Rhine province. In both positions, he was an eager advocate for the rights of Jewish victims and a zealous investigator of German officials. Research conducted by his team led to the resignation of Düsseldorf's major Wilhelm Füllenbach, among others.[92] Auerbach soon began a probe into the Nazi past of the province's governor (Oberpräsident) Franz Lehr. In December 1945, the British sacked Auerbach, arguing that he was damaging their popularity through his revelations about the continued presence of former Nazis in state positions. They also accused Auerbach—in this case, correctly—of claiming a doctorate in chemistry that he never actually received.[93]

It is a testament to the limited communication between the Allies and the chaos of postwar bureaucracies that Auerbach nonetheless managed to convince the Bavarian government and US occupation authorities to install him in a similar position in Munich less than a year later, in September 1946. His new employers hired him in part due to their knowledge of his influence among newly established Jewish communities in Germany. They also presumed that he had extensive international contacts. Because Auerbach's position was meant to be temporary—and thus never fully integrated into the structure of Bavaria's Ministry of Interior—he ended up with a great deal of leeway to pursue his own ideas. In his new role, Auerbach oversaw state aid for all persecutees, excluding those residing in DP camps—at least in theory. In reality, his office's files—such as the correspondence between his Munich headquarters and its branches throughout Bavaria—dealt mostly with the problems facing Jewish victims.

In many respects, Auerbach was an outsider in his job. Although Jewish DPs appear to have respected him, his political outlook was largely at odds with theirs. Whereas Auerbach supported the reconstruction of a Jewish community in postwar Germany (as did the small number of surviving German Jews), most Jews stranded in the country and around the world considered such an outcome neither likely nor desirable.[94] His views on the future of German Jewry also inflected his view of the past. In his unpublished dissertation of 1949, Auerbach claimed that resistance to the Nazi regime was impossible due to its totalitarian character, thus exculpating the German population from crimes committed in its name.[95] Such statements would not have sat well with the majority of Eastern European Jews, who tended to understand themselves as the "surviving remnant" of the Germans' assault on the Jewish people. At the same time, Auerbach had no desire to absolve those who had most actively supported the regime. He closely tied reparations to the prosecution of committed Nazis. Thus, he demanded from the US administration that members of the Nazi party should be forced to pay double their contributions to the party over the years as a fine, so that these funds could be used to support the regime's victims.[96]

Although Auerbach sometimes spoke like a German-Jewish patriot—a deeply unpopular position among Jews in the postwar period—his approach to administrative tasks also departed from the traditions associated with the German civil service. Auerbach improvised, cut corners, and was often outright careless in his dealings. In this respect, he was closely attuned to the needs and political demands of his charges, who often expressed impatience with bureaucratic rules established by their former tormenters. Auerbach's appointment also served German authorities, who wanted a Jewish administrator to deal with Jewish immigrants to minimize tensions and appease skeptical outside observers. As importantly, they sought someone with a knack for cutting through red tape. Indeed, the Bavarian government purposefully created a position that both legally adjudicated claims on behalf of the state and lobbied for its claimants at the same time. Auerbach became the embodiment of this paradox, which he resolved by leaning into his function as lobbyist.

There was a price to Auerbach's activities. He bartered favors, requested longer opening times for the nightclubs of acquaintances, demanded a fast car and a gun to protect himself, and gave every indication of being thoroughly convinced of his own importance.[97] In one case, he had an employee fired because she was unfriendly to him on the phone before she realized who he was.[98] Auerbach acted like an enlightened autocrat, breaking rules in the name of justice but also infusing his own narcissism into his advocacy efforts.

These characteristics not only made him an easy and frequent target of attacks but also affected Sinti and Roma who lived in his area of jurisdiction. And his record with these communities was decidedly mixed. On the one hand, Auerbach stands out as one of the few administrators on record defending Romani survivors against accusations of criminality. Indeed, in a short article that appeared in the newsletter of Bavaria's Committee of Political Persecutees, Auerbach introduced his arguments to his mostly non-Jewish readers with an unusual analogy: just as the Germans could not be collectively condemned for Nazism, Roma did not deserve to be collectively portrayed as criminals.[99] What is more, he felt strongly that Roma deserved the sympathy of the German public for what they had suffered during the war. For Auerbach this was also a personal matter. He recalled seeing multiple generations of Romani families suffer in bug-infested cells next to his own while he was incarcerated in the police prison on Berlin's Alexanderplatz. He also spoke of witnessing SS guards force young Romani women to have sex with them in Auschwitz while noting that the same guards often had no compunctions about killing Romani men, at times in the very same places where they had sexually assaulted Romani women.[100] As Auerbach explained it, the Germans—or rather "we Germans," since he regularly included himself in that collective—would only truly escape the curse of the Third Reich once all stereotyping of Roma was relegated to the past.

On the other hand, and despite his attempts to elicit sympathy on their behalf, Auerbach's position toward Roma was ambivalent at best, as his reactions to conflicts surrounding the Bayerisches Hilfswerk demonstrate. When the organization was founded in 1945 to help victims of Nazi racial laws, it excluded prisoners with a criminal background, which disproportionally affected Romani prisoners, given their history of being surveilled and targeted by the police, often for minor infractions of onerous special laws. (The other group most significantly affected by this decision consisted of former camp inmates whom the Nazi regime had deemed "asocial" or "habitual criminals.")[101] Widespread prejudices against those who had been persecuted as "Gypsies" led some to ask whether they should be excluded by definition.[102]

Such pressures were precisely those that compelled Romani victims sometimes to claim to be Jews. The Hilfswerk sent a list with members of one extended group of Sinti families to the criminal police and Auerbach, claiming that they had identified themselves as Jews or partial Jews. According to the Hilfswerk's registration officer, they were "concealing their Gypsy characteristics," and "baptizing their most recent children according to Jewish rites." (This comment is a telling reminder of how little the non-Jewish victims' organization understood Jewish religious practices.)[103]

Confronted with such suspicions, Auerbach opined that Roma and Sinti were clearly racial persecutees and should categorically be treated as such—a policy the Hilfswerk appears to have generally pursued.[104] Yet even in his pleas for cultural understanding, Auerbach inserted his own misgivings about the group. Although he claimed that "Gypsies" had only a proportional number of so-called "asocial elements" among them, he insisted on the need to rehabilitate or exclude certain "Gypsies" from the broader community. In his words, Germans should "approach them with love, because only thus will it be possible to turn the few remaining Gypsies into full members of our human society." In so doing, they would "have to distinguish in this task between those Gypsies who were persecuted for racial reasons and those who were demonstrably imprisoned for asocial behavior."[105]

For Auerbach, distinguishing between the worthy and the unworthy was a major task. He did this in part by running criminal background checks to determine applicants' eligibility for support. This procedure also allowed him to limit the number of Romanies under his care. Arguing that greater numbers of Sinti and Roma should be excluded from support due to their criminal records, he sent the German police a list of 300 "Gypsies" registered with the Bayerisches Hilfswerk for a background check.[106] This was not unusual: for some state authorities that dealt with compensation payments, criminal background checks were a standard procedure.[107] In Auerbach's case, it was noteworthy because he proved much more flexible when it came to Jewish victims. Indeed, he does not appear to have requested comparable systematic background checks for Jews in his jurisdiction and even defended several of his Jewish employees with known criminal records.[108]

His office also created additional hurdles for Romani applicants. According to the rules Auerbach helped establish, his office supported all Jews not living in DP camps in Bavaria, irrespective of the details of their persecution. Roma, by contrast, had to prove that they had been imprisoned.[109] In this regard, he followed the differential treatment established in the IRO's statutes regarding Jews, Roma, and others. When applying for relief in Auerbach's jurisdiction, Roma also faced much greater scrutiny regarding their past lives than Jews did. Auerbach understood the need to be flexible with Jews who crossed zonal boundaries in Germany, but clearly did not apply the same approach to Nazism's other racialized victims. Auerbach sought to ensure that the Roma and Sinti he dealt with had established proper residence in Bavaria. As he stated bluntly in his correspondence with US occupation authorities: "We must be careful in avoiding that those gipsies who run about consider Bavaria an asylum and come over because they are cared for there [Bavaria]."[110]

Restitution, a central concept of the reconstruction era, could also be turned against Roma. This is evident in Auerbach's dealings with Munich's small Romani community. In February 1947, Auerbach sent a letter to Louis Miniclier, chief of the US Military Government's Public Welfare Branch, to explain his position on the lodging of 400 Sinti and Roma in Bavaria's capital.

Although he admitted that members of this group had been victims of Nazism and were technically under his protection, he insisted that it was imperative that they not "become a nuisance and endanger public safety and order." He then described the difficulties caused by twenty-one "Gypsies" who were illegally occupying an apartment in town as well as the trouble caused by a Romani family that had taken to using a room in their apartment as a barn for their horses. On another occasion, Auerbach spoke of a different group of Romani men, suggesting that they were "terrorizing the whole area."[111]

The official recommendation Auerbach issued to the military government in response is remarkable for its simultaneous use of the language of compassion and its almost total disregard for Romani survivors' economic reality:

> For reasons of humanity and with regard to the fact that these people suffered in the concentration camps, I cannot incur the responsibility of turning them out of doors with the present severe cold. Starting from the standpoint that a repair of the wrong done by the Nazis must have an end when the individuals have reached their status quo ante, I believe it best to set them an adequate term of thirty days to remove back into their gypsy wagons and to earn their life and sustenance and to procure their lodging in the same manner as they did before the racial laws became effective in Germany.[112]

The key idea for Auerbach was his suggestion that the state's interventions should focus on returning people to their way of life before persecution and internment. Yet in this case, that restitution of the status quo ante did not require an investigation into the history of the individuals involved. Instead, Auerbach drew on a romanticized, collective image of Gypsy nomadism. The hundreds of Sinti and Roma who strove to make ends meet in the Bavarian capital during his tenure as state commissioner may well have lost their former houses, apartments, trailers, cars, and other possessions, but in Auerbach's eyes, their future lives required no capital beyond what he described as their "gypsy wagons."

This was not how Auerbach dealt with most of his Jewish claimants, for whom he regularly sought the material restitution of lost property on an individual basis. More importantly, he understood that only new forms of welfare could help his Jewish charges reconstitute their lives—an awareness he clearly lacked when it came to Sinti and Roma survivors who similarly depended on new types of support to reestablish themselves after the Nazis had murdered their kin, destroyed their livelihoods, and devastated their social networks. While Auerbach recognized Roma as victims of Nazism, he found it difficult to extricate himself from a logic of economic reconstruction that defined Gypsies as a threat to the stability of the economy and society. Auerbach was hardly alone in his ambivalence as a Jew toward Roma as fellow victims. He was merely unusual in the level of authority he exercised over large numbers of Romanies in the postwar era.

Auerbach's unequal approach to Jews and Romanies did not prevent him from gaining a favorable reputation among the region's Sinti and Roma, who noted his grandiose rhetoric and his undeniable willingness to go the extra mile for victims of racial persecution. According to a 1948 report from the Bavarian police, local Romanies described Auerbach as their protector in their interactions with the authorities.[113] The conflicts that eventually reached Auerbach started one August night of that year, when neighbors called the police and asked them to come to an apartment building in the Munich suburbs where several Romani men and women were hosting a loud party in the apartment of a Romani Auschwitz survivor. The police handed out citations to several of the partiers and shut down the event. When the police returned the next month to end another large party at two a.m. and issued citations to two participants, the same two individuals allegedly smashed their neighbor's windows in retaliation. The third time, the police arrived two weeks later to respond to calls of another celebration with a dozen inebriated people, and the conflict escalated further. The Romani partiers reportedly began insulting the officers as "SS pigs" and told them that Auerbach would make sure that they would lose their job.[114] It appears that such threats had a certain effect: the other inhabitants in the apartment building suggested in a written complaint that there was no point in pursuing their Romani neighbors' removal as long as Auerbach was going to defend them.[115]

Yet despite the hopes of these Romani individuals, Auerbach made sure that the German police knew that these "Gypsies" could not expect any special protection from him and gave the authorities permission to move against the offending parties. He also assured the police that he was going to threaten the accused with removal from his welfare rolls if it turned out that any of them were under his office's care.[116] It is clear from this case that Jews in positions of power had suddenly come to play a role in conflicts between Romani citizens and the state in ways that would have been unimaginable in previous centuries.

Projecting Power

When Romani survivors invoked Auerbach's name in their dealings with their neighbors and police, they articulated a theory of Jewish power that would have been familiar to the broader German public, many of whom came to consider postwar Jews to be privileged—with extra food rations or allocations of apartments, for example—or even, at times, above the law. This theory of Jewish power was flawed on many levels. It underestimated the ability of different authorities to stifle Jewish efforts at compensation and restitution and overestimated the sway Jewish lobbyists or officials had over the non-Jewish politicians who made the final decisions in such cases.[117] Most dominant postwar parties in European countries tended to privilege political victims at the expense of Jewish survivors in legislation on financial compensation, since doing so supported narratives of national resistance to Nazism. Moreover, after the initial push for retribution, they soon sidelined all victims—whether political or racial—in decision-making so as to facilitate reconstruction by integrating those who had been complicit with Nazism during the war.[118] The antifascist consensus of the immediate postwar period gave way to the anticommunist consensus of the Cold War.

Romani impressions that people like Auerbach could serve as omnipotent protectors were also erroneous from the start. Despite his bluster and ability to bend the rules for a short time, Bavarian politicians gave Auerbach space to act only as long as doing so proved beneficial to them. Most commentators agree that his arrest for embezzlement was a direct result of his detractors' sense that he outlasted his usefulness once most Jewish DPs had emigrated. In this sense, Auerbach's rise and fall is a study not in the reality of Jewish power but rather in its fragility. Auerbach was arguably harsh when Roma began to invoke his protection not only because of his prejudice against members of that community but also because their claims potentially endangered his position. He had more power than they did, to be sure, but even he was aware of the limits of that power. It is precisely this delicate dance between unequal partners who both sought to enter society from the margins that characterizes Jewish-Romani relations after 1945.

As was true for the period before 1945, Romani-Jewish "relations" during the postwar era were multifaceted. They consisted not only of personal interactions but more often of a relationship that emerged from a complex projection of power—including the power of new administrative categories—across social space. Roma who fought with the police in the Munich suburbs did not know Auerbach personally, nor were they likely aware of his checkered track record, but they understood that the new Jewish lobbyist in town might have the potential to change the circumstances of their own lives. This was also the situation of the Roma who registered with the Action Committee that members of the Jewish community had founded in Vienna: they found themselves in front of Jewish administrators because Jews had become the foremost group to receive support based on their status as racial victims of the Nazis, after intensive struggles to be included in compensation and aid schemes.

Yet, at this point—during the first years after the war ended—the intensity and depth of this relationship remained limited. Only in the 1960s would a new generation of Jewish lawyers and historians start to make a difference in Romani politics and communal life, as would a new set of non-Jewish allies on the left. The Gussak family—who registered with the Jewish-led Action Committee in 1946—soon found help from both directions. Hermann Langbein, a lapsed non-Jewish communist, former secretary of the International Auschwitz Committee, and one of the earliest figures to promote the narrative of the Jews' particular history of Nazi persecution among non-Jewish camp survivors, came to the aid of the impoverished Romani family in 1961.[119] By then, Adolf Gussak was partially disabled, and Hermine Horwath had died, likely due to the abuses she had suffered in Nazi camps. Langbein organized donations so that their indigent children would be able to receive Christmas presents.[120] A few years earlier, he had also arranged for Gussak to be interviewed for the oldest Jewish Holocaust archive in the world, the Wiener Library in London, where Gussak's account of his experiences under Nazism became one of the earliest Romani testimonies available to scholars.[121]

This would be the ultimate legacy of relations between Jews and Roma during the early postwar years. Although these groups continued to have little contact and different experiences in the postwar era, their collective interests slowly began to overlap, generating the material connections that bound them together: shared archives, almost all of which began with shared lists.

3

Blank Pages:
Early Documentation Efforts

IN THE LATE 1940S, no one was as dedicated a collector of information on genocides as Raphael Lemkin. The Polish Jewish lawyer coined the term genocide in 1944 and made it his life's mission to popularize it and codify it in international law. To do this, he needed not only a compelling concept but also case studies that could persuade politicians, legal specialists, and commentators around the world to support the Genocide Convention of December 1948. Lemkin had spent years of his life campaigning for such an agreement, and he spent years afterwards convincing states to ratify it. This meant promising many things to many different people. To a Greek representative, he suggested that the convention would punish the abduction of Greek children by communist guerrillas; to American Italian associations he conveyed that it might protect 200,000 Italians in Eritrea and 20,000 in Yugoslavia.[1] For general audiences, he often referred to a host of historical genocides to show the term's relevance, from the killing of Waldensians as Christian heretics in the Middle Ages to the German Empire's murder of the Herero in German South West Africa in the early 1900s.[2]

The murder of Europe's Roma had a special place in Lemkin's campaign for his concept of genocide. Around the same time that Avrom Sutzkever contemplated in his postwar poem whether anyone would remember the murder of the "Gypsies," Lemkin made sure the fate of Roma would find mention in courts of law. Owing to Lemkin's personal intervention, the Nuremberg trial's indictment included genocide, and Romani victims appeared as paradigmatic in the term's first use in an international trial context: "They [the accused] conducted deliberate and systematic genocide, viz., the extermination of racial and national groups, against the civilian populations of certain occupied territories in order to destroy particular races and classes of people and national, racial, or religious groups, particularly Jews, Poles, and Gypsies and others."[3] Lemkin continued to refer to this triad of victim groups over the next years, indirectly reminding readers of the Romani Holocaust as part of his public relations work for the concept of genocide. Lemkin could relate to the treatment of Jews and Poles from personal experience as a Polish Jew who had fled the country in September 1939, leaving behind many members of his extended family. He had studied decrees aimed at the destruction of Jewish life and Polish national culture in his 1944 volume *Axis Rule in Occupied Europe.*[4] But what did he know about the Romani Holocaust?

We can get a sense of Lemkin's challenges in this regard if we retrace his efforts to locate documents on the Romani genocide. As a lawyer, he first searched through seized German documents and trial depositions. These documents were the lifeblood of any legal work, and his letters demonstrate that he made good use of what little one could glean from the limited legal sources available to him, including killings at Auschwitz and Majdanek and some of the Nazi medical experiments discussed at the so-called Doctor's Trial of 1946–47.[5] When he exhausted these documents, he turned to acquaintances who might have been in a position to offer clues. We can see this in his correspondence to someone named Hélène, who appears only under her first name in his writings. She was one of many women who briefly served the financially bankrupt Lemkin as unremunerated assistants (and were often his lovers). An employee for Radio France, she seems to have supplied mostly anthropological articles on Romanies from popular magazines.[6] Lemkin also turned to Jewish archivists and testimony collectors, who constituted a new type of historical expert. Among those he contacted was Isaac Schneersohn, the director of the Center for Contemporary Jewish Documentation (CJDC) in Paris and cousin of Menachem Mendel Schneerson, the head of the Chabad-Lubavitch movement. One of the central nodes of Jewish postwar efforts to assemble information on the catastrophe that befell European Jewry, the CJDC suffered financial difficulties in the late 1940s. In one of his letters soliciting donations addressed to Lemkin, Schneersohn added: "We are using this occasion to send you 2 documents that will be of interest to you. They refer in particular to the genocide of the Gypsies."[7]

None of this seems to have satisfied Lemkin, who continued his search for material. Finally, he turned to the obvious experts on the subject: scholars who studied Roma. Their largest professional organization, the Gypsy Lore Society, had its seat in Liverpool, where one of the society's veterans, Dora Yates, had kept it alive throughout the war. Lemkin wrote to the society and reached Yates, who had just published an article on the Nazi murder of Roma for the Jewish magazine *Commentary*.[8] The two letters with material she sent to Lemkin in New York must have been disappointing. From the extant correspondence, it becomes clear that Yates could offer only a few published articles from the Gypsy Lore Society's journal.[9]

Lemkin's final work is a good indication of the difficulties anyone—even a determined, well-connected lawyer such as Lemkin—would have encountered in the quest to "memorialize the Gypsy extermination," following Sutzkever's lead. In the 1950s, Lemkin set out to write a book that could both introduce the concept of genocide and constitute a massive compendium of genocides throughout history. By his death in 1959, Lemkin had assembled an impressive amount of information on most of the genocides he hoped to analyze. His unpublished manuscript, which is housed in the collections of the New York Public Library, includes a chapter on "Gypsies." It consists of the title and an otherwise blank page.[10]

Some of the earliest collectors of experiential accounts struggled to fill that void. The rest of this chapter deals with three of them: Dora Yates, David Boder, and Estelle Goldstein. In their own ways, all three failed to adequately document Romani suffering. Their failures reveal the conceptual and practical challenges of postwar efforts to record the fate of Roma. But their engagement with the Romani genocide also speaks to a larger point Sutzkever had raised in his poem "Encamped Gypsies." It lends insights into how people learn—or fail to learn—about the suffering of others.

Dora Yates and the Failures of Traditional "Gypsy" Studies

Yates, Lemkin's correspondent, the long-serving secretary of the Gypsy Lore Society and editor of the society's journal, was the most prominent Jewish scholar of Romani culture to deal with the genocide.[11] The fifth of eight children, Dora Yates was born in 1879 to an established British-Jewish family. Her parents were Hannah and George Samuel Yates, a tobacco importer and warden of Liverpool's Old Hebrew Congregation. Through her father's sister, Clara, Dora was the first cousin of Herbert Samuel, a successful liberal politician who became Great Britain's first High Commissioner for Mandate Palestine.[12] This connection was not a coincidental relationship to a famous man, but rather an indication of her family's place within a small network of influential Jewish families, or the "Cousinhood," as one scholar has called it.[13] Even though her branch was less affluent than other parts of her extended family, and despite her later financial difficulties, Yates's sheltered upbringing could not have been more different from that of the people she eventually came to study.

In this regard, Yates was typical of those who turned to Romani studies in Western Europe before the war. In France and the United Kingdom, scholarship on "Gypsies" was often the preoccupation of well-off men, but even when this was not the case, interest in Roma usually signaled a desire to encounter a group whose upbringing and experiences were worlds apart from that of those entering the field to study them. Echoing others, Dora Yates explained her own encounter with British Romanichals in a local encampment in 1903 as the discovery of a different, mysterious culture that required initiation from a seasoned guide. She remembered feeling "almost the thrill of a novitiate who first beholds with his own eyes the object of his worship."[14] Studying a group that they defined as enigmatic and difficult to fathom—no matter how many hours they spent in conversation with its members—Yates and her colleagues also prided themselves on their own revolt against stale social norms.[15] Yates and other leading figures of the Gypsy Lore Society, including her mentor John Sampson, idealized Romanies' freedom and rebellious minds and portrayed themselves as equally free-spirited in their pursuit of these elusive subjects.

This dynamic must have appealed to Yates not just as a someone seeking to emancipate herself from her family but also as a woman who sought new opportunities. While her sister Lucy Keyser Yates became a journalist and advocate for women's labor rights, Dora broke the glass ceiling in her own way: in 1900, she became the first Jewish woman to receive a Master of Arts (in English) at a British university.[16] Most scholars rightly emphasize that the Gypsy Lore Society was a difficult place for women. Women were sidelined there just as they were in most academic disciplines, but, more specifically, male scholars saw this field of study as a place of masculine freedom, where they could live out their sexual fantasies—sometimes with those who worked for them and sometimes with those they purported to study.[17] Despite these challenges, Yates seems to have perceived her role as a Romani Rawnie—a female scholar of the Roma—as a mark of independence. Traveling around in her own horse-drawn trailer, never marrying, living much of her life with her sister, she established a life according to her own rules, far away from the social obligations she grew up with and the "card-parties" she detested.[18]

Yates' path was unusual in another important respect: neither Jewish men nor Jewish women contributed substantially to scholarship on Romanies before World War Two. This contrasts with the considerable European Jewish interest in the Middle East and the Muslim world in the nineteenth and early twentieth century. Antisemites had long depicted Jews as "Asiatic" and, at times, similar to Arabs. Many Jews reacted by playing up their ability to understand the Orient.[19] In contrast, while there were certainly some non-Jews who construed a shared origin of Jews and Roma or equated their patterns of transnational mobility, few Jews found it opportune to claim any proximity to Romani culture.[20] Even Yates made no such assertions. She reported that her dark complexion helped her blend in with Romani interlocutors during fieldwork and found herself sometimes racialized by Gypsy Lorists—her mentor, for example, described her as the "fair flower of Palestine" in a romantic poem he sent her—yet even Yates did not think that Jews had an innate appreciation of Romani culture.[21] On the contrary, she viewed the study of Roma as a sentimental craft that required learning and dedication.

Much like those obsessed with the Orient or new-age mysticism, Yates wrote about "Gypsies" as a form of cultural criticism that was difficult to pin down ideologically and that consciously ignored any attempts at Romani politics. For Yates, "Gypsies" were primordial natives, whose disappearance heralded a disenchanted, somber age.[22] The image of "the last Gypsy" invoked by Sutzkever resonated with the elegiac tone of Romani Studies as practiced by members of the Gypsy Lore Society and the celebration of freedom by Yiddish-speaking youth who gathered for "Gypsy evenings" at New York summer camps in the 1930s.[23] Yates and her fellow Lorists also worried constantly about the possibility that Romanies might lose their cultural purity, and they thus dismissed all Roma who did not meet their criteria of what it meant to be a "Gypsy."

Yates—like Sutzkever—changed her outlook in the face of unprecedented violence against Roma. Yates wrote weekly letters to the Chicago businessman Alfred E. Hamill between 1936 and 1946 that reveal the tension between her prewar interest in Romani folklore and her need to account for wartime atrocities. Hamill was an investment banker and a trustee and later president of the board of trust of the Newberry Library, a prestigious independent research library in downtown Chicago. He had originally contacted Yates in her official role as secretary of the Gypsy Lore Society. Within months, they became friendly, soon familiar, and then outright flirtatious with each other, without much prospect of a physical meeting. At the time of their correspondence both were middle-aged and living in dramatically different circumstances. Hamill was a wealthy philanthropist, married with children and grandchildren, while

Yates was a single woman in her 50s who shared a home with her unmarried older sister. While Hamill was busy traveling the Americas to discover new artifacts for his collections, Yates endured the war in England on the brink of financial ruin, her home rendered uninhabitable due to an indirect bomb hit during the Liverpool Blitz of May 2–8, 1941.[24] Yates looked up to Hamill and clearly had a romantic interest in him. Her weekly talks, as she called her missives, were love letters, reflecting a relationship that was likely one-sided and never consummated.[25]

Throughout their correspondence, Yates explained her interest in Romani culture as a matter of "romanticism," as she called it herself, and romanticism and politics did not go well together in her view. She delighted in Hamill's report that he found what she called "pre-Cortesian" Indians in Mexico who did not know anything of the ongoing world war in 1942.[26] Finding people utterly disconnected from the day's news indicated a much longed-for state of innocence. Her interest in Roma was similarly driven by thirst for the pure and untainted rather than a desire to overcome injustice. Yates could thus be arbitrary in both her affection and disdain for different groups. In a letter to Hamill, where she recounted a memory of kissing a chimney sweep as a little girl out of compassion for his dreadful "black man's countenance," she explained: "And perhaps that's why I grew up with an uncanny liking for the 'down-and-outs' of this life, and a passion for Gypsies. (Negroes, however, I am ashamed to confess, I still cannot abide!)"[27] The statement is revealing because it contrasts so clearly with the sentiments of activists who later turned to the Romani genocide: by the 1960s many would equate the struggle of the African American civil rights movement with that of the Roma.[28]

Yates' approach to Romani life was essentially disconnected from her political commitments, including her expressions of support for persecuted Jews. In her work for Jews escaping Nazism, she followed her father's example: George Samuel Yates had supported the cause of Jewish refugees in the 1880s, serving as a delegate to North America for the British Mansion House Committee, a fundraising and aid endeavor for Jews fleeing Russia established in 1882.[29] Over fifty years later, Yates organized her own relief effort in Liverpool for Jewish students and scholars from Germany.[30] The venture, which started in 1938, was modest considering the magnitude of the crisis. Yates and her associates found fellowships and housing for a small handful of students who were already in the UK, out of a total of over 50,000 Jewish refugees fleeing Germany to the British Isles at the time.[31] Even if her efforts were limited in scale, Yates was acutely aware of the dangers German and Austrian Jews faced under the Nazis and pledged to do her part. The reality of displacement also entered her family life. Her brother took in a young German-Jewish refugee whose father perished in one of the early concentration camps, and her nephew eventually married their houseguest.[32]

Yates never initiated or joined any equivalent efforts on behalf of Roma and Sinti, although she dedicated her long life to studying them. The only account of her political advocacy for "Gypsies" and Travellers in Britain before the war is likely apocryphal. Based on a personal conversation with Dora Yates, one scholar claimed that the young Yates successfully lobbied her cousin Herbert Samuel for an exemption in the 1908 Children's Act that allowed children not to attend school in the summer if their parents were traveling.[33] This frequently repeated claim merits skepticism, however. The amendments to the bill that offered exemptions came not from Samuel but from the liberal Lord Russel in the House of Lords.[34] As Parliamentary Under-Secretary of State for the Home Office, Samuel merely defended these changes to the original bill in the House of Commons on the logic that the bill might otherwise seem "too severe on the class of respectable gipsies [sic]." Yet Samuel made sure to signal to Parliament that he accepted his liberal colleague's suggestions "with very much reluctance."[35] Since Samuel expressed unenthusiastic support for an exception demanded by others, it is hard to see what Yates' role could have been in shaping the bill's final form.[36] She certainly understood herself as an advocate for Romani culture but, until the late 1930s, this did not translate into the kind of political activism she exhibited on behalf of fellow Jews.

The turning point in Yates' views about policies affecting Roma came with the war and emerged from her growing perception of Jews and Roma as fellow sufferers. It is impossible to reconstruct exactly what she knew about Nazi atrocities and when, but her correspondence indicates her limited understanding of what was transpiring during much of the war. Although forced sterilization policies against Roma appalled her, her correspondence with Hamill suggests that, until 1942, she remained mostly preoccupied with the annihilation of Jews.[37] In a letter she sent him shortly before Christmas of that year, she confided that "massacres of the Jews in Occupied Europe" were "such a terrible crime against humanity itself, that one stands aghast at the seeming indifference of the rest of mankind to this hideous mass cruelty. Thank God that in your country and mine we have managed to rescue a few refugees from this general holocaust."[38] By 1943, however, Yates started to speak of Jews and Roma together as those who "from time immemorial" have faced "the concentrated hate of the barbarians."[39] Although letters from most of her friends on the continent did not reach her anymore, some unidentified missives or bits of news had clearly convinced her to consider the victimhood of Romanies and Jews together. In spring 1943, she wrote to Hamill, "For it is Gypsies as well as Jews that the Nazis are trying to exterminate in this year of grace 1943!"[40] From this point onward Yates added a decidedly political dimension to her studies on Roma life and culture.

Jews were not just a point of reference—they were the main audience for her writing on the Nazi genocide against the Roma. Her most elaborate treatment of the subject appeared in the US-based Jewish magazine *Commentary* in 1949.[41] Largely drawing on accounts from Romani survivors and scholars affiliated with the society, she explained to Jewish American readers how Hitler had aimed to wipe out a second group alongside the Jews. Among her informants was Vanya Kochanowski, a Romani survivor who published an account on the fate of Latvian Roma in the journal Yates edited for the Gypsy Lore Society.[42] Citing victim testimonies she received in her capacity as the Gypsy Lore Society's secretary, Yates reported on the mass murder of Roma in Latvia, Serbia, Croatia, and Germany. Beyond offering her historical account of the Romani genocide, Yates pleaded with her readers to respect Romani survivors by sparing them from forced assimilation and sedentarization programs that restricted their free movement and choice of residence in the present.[43]

With some trepidation, Yates also opened the *Journal of the Gypsy Lore Society* to reports on the fate of Europe's Roma, turning it into the principal venue for publishing information on the Romani Holocaust in the postwar years.[44] There was nothing inevitable or obvious about this. As early as 1941, Hamill had suggested that she solicit a piece on "Gypsies in Wartime," but Yates could not find anyone to write such an article.[45] It might be true that some scholars had been worried about the safety of their Romani informants, as she intimated in her letter to Hamill, but whatever the case, her later choice to begin publishing in this area was also a departure from the apolitical romanticism the Society provided to its dues-paying members. The French diplomat and former political concentration camp prisoner Frédéric Max submitted the first article in the *Journal of the Gypsy Lore Society* that dealt with the murder of Romanies in Auschwitz and their status as prisoners in Buchenwald and two French internment sites.[46] Having learned to speak some Romani, he reported on the accounts Romani prisoners were willing to entrust with him as well as the reports of Jewish prisoners who had some knowledge about the "Gypsy camp" in Auschwitz.[47] Revealingly, Yates felt the piece would meet with approval because it was "written with sufficient restraint and illuminated by a keen enough observation of Gypsies in captivity as to make it wholly tolerable to our members."[48] Without anthropological commentary, Yates implied, Gypsy Lorists would have little interest in a report on the persecution of their subjects.

The journal's coverage of the Roma genocide remained riddled with contradictions. Both Yates and the society at large rarely attached the same status to Romani voices that they did to those of non-Romani researchers.[49] When Roma expressed political opinions, Yates and her colleagues suspected them of merely mimicking the positions taken by the non-Romanies in their environment. To Yates, the fact that a Romani author, Matéo Maximoff, submitted an article on "Germany and the Gypsies: From the Gypsy's Point of View" to her journal in January 1946 signaled a fundamental change. In a letter to Hamill, she described this disconcerting new situation: "It is a queer thing, is it not, Hugo? when the Gypsies themselves can plead their own cause in print."[50] On the whole, the *Journal of the Gypsy Lore Society* remained a venue for scholars and laypeople whose accounts of Romani suffering were tainted by a fundamental distance from their subject. Reports by the devout Catholic Geneviève L'Huillier on the fate of Romani inmates in the Poitiers camp for nomads, for example, emphasized the pedagogical challenges she had as a teacher for interned minors rather than the history and injustices of French internment policies.[51]

Yet, none of this changed the fact that there was no publication in the world that could surpass the *Journal of the Gypsy Lore Society* as a source of information on the Romani Holocaust during this period. This had to do, in part, with the range of articles the periodical published immediately after the war and the diversity of its authors, which included scholars and survivors. Depositions for postwar commissions and trials remained in the collections of governmental and intergovernmental agencies, whereas the society's journal was a relatively accessible publication where interested parties—such as Lemkin—who knew little or nothing about the subject could find accounts of the Romani genocide.[52]

Despite her openness as an editor, Yates and other members of the society did not adapt its mission to new realities. The society remained perennially in search of content that fed their readers' linguistic and folkloristic interests. Yet, it did not systematically collect stories of persecution, death, and survival, nor did its members concede that the unprecedented murder of Europe's Roma might require novel approaches. Yates herself published a collection entitled *A Book of Gypsy Folk-Tales* in 1948, with stories from all over Europe.[53] Even though she was well aware of the destruction of Romani life by this point, she made no mention of the fact that many of the people who would have told these stories were dead.[54] In a state of denial, Yates continued to collect stories that catered to readers' hopes for exotic tales instead of those that conveyed the suffering of her age.

David Boder's Interviews with Jewish Survivors

Most Jews who struggled with Sutzkever's call to "memorialize the Gypsy extermination" after 1945 made no claim to expertise on Romani life and barely understood the fate of Romanies under Nazism. More often than not, they encountered these other racialized victims incidentally when they engaged with the Jewish genocide. As a result, they were coincidental and unwitting contributors to knowledge about the Romani genocide whose efforts and accomplishments in this field often became fully apparent only decades after they died. The experiences of David Boder, a psychiatrist who traveled through war-torn Europe to record conversations with Jewish survivors, exemplifies this process. Setting out to preserve the experiences of one group, he inadvertently documented his own transformation as a person hearing and learning about the tragedy of another.

Like other Jews who returned to Europe with the Allies, Boder had a circuitous life path. Born in Lithuania in 1886, he had studied in St. Petersburg and Leipzig before eventually making his way to Mexico City during the Russian Civil War (1918–20). After five years in Mexico teaching at the National University, he moved to the United States, where he received additional training. After graduating with a master's degree from the University of Chicago and a PhD in psychology from Northwestern University, he secured a position in the psychology department at the Lewis Institute (called the Illinois Institute of Technology after 1940).[55]

In 1946, Boder departed for Europe with heavy tape-recording equipment to interview Jewish DPs. This was a bold move for various reasons. European states were still recovering from the war, and Boder did not have a permit to enter the US Occupation Zone of Germany, where most Jewish DPs could then be found. When he arrived in Paris, he stepped foot in a devastated and chaotic world with a brand-new recording device to do something no one had done before. Indeed, the novelty of his tools was so central to his endeavors that in grant applications he promoted his project as an experiment in the use of new technologies.[56] There were some obvious advantages to recording interviews, rather than collecting written depositions or working from interview notes. Boder could analyze nuances in his subjects' voices, for example, and determine their mood when they explained their experiences under Nazism. Such methods also had their technological limits, however. For sixty years, researchers exclusively accessed these recordings in transcription and in Boder's translation. Archivists only discovered and digitized copies of the original interviews in the 2000s, when new formats and distribution methods allowed the public to hear them for the first time.[57]

Boder understood that the major state institutions that might fund such a trip did not consider the documentation of Jewish history a priority. He thus emphasized universal, social science questions in his letters to state bodies. Indeed, when writing to the French embassy to request a visa, he completely omitted any reference to Jews.[58] Yet, there were also Jewish organizations, including B'nai B'rith and the American Jewish Congress, whose support he could realistically hope to receive.[59] Boder thus had financial incentives to focus on recording Jews' experiences in particular. Explaining these pragmatic considerations to the director of the Jewish Charities of Chicago, he wrote: "The gist of it is that I shall not hesitate to convert the investigation into what may be called a Jewish project, if under such circumstances either the Joint Distribution Committee or the American Jewish Congress should be willing to take this study under their wing."[60] As marginal as Jews remained within the broader landscape of reconstruction-era Europe, and as difficult as their position remained in relation to state actors there, Jewish organizations clearly exercised a countervailing pull and were influential enough to persuade Boder to change his pitch.

Boder was principally interested in recording memorable, detailed, and compelling accounts. Before beginning his recordings, he appears to have asked some survivors to convey things that were "interesting."[61] His interviews are essentially extended attempts by two parties to figure out what might qualify as such. Although he interviewed mostly Jews and asked about the fate of Jews, Boder—and thus, indirectly, also his interlocutors—developed a concern with Romani experiences as well. As a result of this commitment, fifteen out of 118 extant interviews include references to "Gypsies." For a project that set out to collect accounts of Jews' experiences the fact that nearly every eighth interview discussed Romanies is remarkable. In most cases, it was Boder who brought up Roma—at least once he understood that his interviewees might have something to say on the subject. Boder repeatedly interrupted his interviewees to pose clarifying questions, often touching on topics that did not emerge again in later testimony projects, such as detailed descriptions of violence, including revenge killings after the war.[62] The fate of Roma was one such topic: it emerged out of his own desire to put on tape lesser-known or surprising details that rarely made it into newspaper articles.

When Boder arrived in Paris to interview Jewish DPs, he knew little, if anything, about the persecution of Europe's Roma. Yet his encounters with Jewish survivors exposed him to confusing, contradictory stories about these other victims, which piqued his curiosity. Boder learned from an interviewee that there had been "Gypsies" in Nazi concentration camps on the very day he first started recording testimonies, at the Chateau Boucicaut, an institution for young Jewish survivors located in a small suburb of Paris. In this former retirement home for department store workers, Boder spoke to Mendel Herskovitz and learned about the young man's deportation from his home in the Polish city of Łódź to a factory where he performed forced labor and, eventually, to Buchenwald. The narrative climax of Hershkovitz's story was his liberation: Hershkovitz was particularly proud to have avoided deadly evacuations through a combination of cunning and luck.[63] The evacuations started with functionary prisoners herding other prisoners out of the building. Hershkovitz called these kapos Germans. When Boder asked, "Germans?" Hershkovitz clarified, "Gypsies," leading to a short back-and-forth in which Boder tried to confirm that he heard correctly. These German "Gypsies," the eighteen-year-old survivor explained, had "helped the SS."[64] Hershkovitz returned to the subject while discussing his liberation. He had been hungry and went to find a person from the same group of prisoners who had driven him out of a hiding place during the evacuation. This person, we learn again, was a "Gypsy" whom he forced to give up his ration of bread. Hershkovitz eventually let him go, rather than exacting revenge on the spot—a decision Hershkovitz regretted.

If Boder's first encounter with stories of Romani prisoners was disconcerting, he heard an even more confusing account from another young man at the same home on the very same day. Kalman Eisenberg reported that all "Gypsies" had been murdered just as he arrived in Buchenwald. In his account, they were not gassed but all burned alive. To Boder, this seemed unlikely. He wondered, how does one burn people alive? Eisenberg doubled down on his story: he had seen it himself, he insisted. The Germans dug pits, filled them with wood, poured gasoline on them, and then forced the Roma into the pit. To ignite the fire, they threw hand grenades.[65] Hershkovits and Eisenberg both sought to offer their interlocutor remarkable accounts, yet their accounts seemed contradictory. Were the Roma corrupt prisoners or the victims of the most heinous crime?

The next day, a young woman at the home offered yet another fundamentally different account. Fela Nichthauser told Boder about her encounters with other prisoner groups in the typhus block at Bergen-Belsen.[66] Nichthauser highlighted her good relations with German "Gypsies." This clearly sounded unusual to Boder, who started to wonder how many Romani prisoners had been in the block. Nichthauser clarified that there had not been many and immediately switched topics. Even if they did not dwell on the subject, Boder had now heard a third time about "Gypsies" during his first two days interviewing Jewish survivors in Europe. From then on, he dealt with Romanies' presence in the camps as an established fact. The next day, Boder introduced the topic in his recorded conversation with a young interviewee rather than waiting for the survivor to come forth with stories about Roma: "Tell me one thing I have heard already, people had told me. There was talk about Gypsies."[67]

Apparently inspired by these early encounters, he asked other survivors in France, Switzerland, and Germany about Roma under Nazism. He wanted to know from one Mennonite woman who was interned at a camp in Neustadt in western Prussia, for example, if she had seen Jews in the camp. She had not, so Boder inquired about "Gypsies" instead, whom she had also not seen.[68] In another case, Boder introduced his question in a peculiar manner: "I have some psychological questions. Have you heard anything about the Gypsy lagers?"[69] There is no indication on the recording or in his publications how this would have connected to the topic of psychology. Perhaps Boder sensed that Jewish survivors' answers about Roma had more to do with their own state of mind than Romani realities.

Boder's questions inspired some elaborate testimonies on the subject. The richest comes from Helene Tichauer, who was deported on one of the earliest trains from her hometown of Bratislava to Auschwitz, where she eventually performed secretarial duties for the camp's registry office. Due to her position, Tichauer had better connections within the camp than most other prisoners and thus a more precise understanding of the camp's inner workings. Indeed, her interview was so detailed that it became the subject of a book, in which five established historians analyzed her testimony from different perspectives.[70]

Tichauer's account provided Boder with additional information about rumors surrounding "Gypsies" and their presence in Auschwitz.[71] According to Tichauer, "reliable sources" had revealed to her in Auschwitz that the Germans had started interning "Gypsies" because they wanted to convince Hungary to deport its Jews.[72] Until 1944, Hungary did not deport its Jews, as she knew, and the "Gypsies" were meant to be exchanged for them, she claimed. The logic of her explanation becomes somewhat obscure at this point. Hungary, she noted, had many more "Gypsies" than Germany. Why that would make Hungary desire more of them is unclear. The theory—as implausible as it may sound—made sense to her because it fit into another set of events, closer to her heart: she viewed the creation of the "Gypsy camp" in 1943 as an indication of the impending doom of Hungarian Jewry, a premonition she claimed to have secretly conveyed to contacts in Hungary as a warning.

Despite her puzzling and contradictory theories about the reasons behind the persecution and deportation of Roma, Tichauer also supplied a good deal of information that conforms to established accounts of Birkenau. She spoke about the resistance of Romanies in Birkenau, the transfer of the young and healthy to other camps, and the eventual gassing of the remaining prisoners. Her sources were clearly diverse. Not only did she speak to other Jewish prisoners, but she also met Romani women in Ravensbrück who had come from Auschwitz. She addressed the accounts Boder had heard about Roma being burned alive in camps. The Germans had no reason to make their job any harder, she explained, and used the same process for all victims. "The gassing," she noted, "proceeded in a very courteous [höflich] manner."[73] It was purposefully designed to calm down the victims and was thus efficient for the murderers.

Despite her personal relations with Romani prisoners, Tichauer had an ambivalent view of Roma. She spoke of German, Czech, and Hungarian Roma she encountered in Auschwitz as "quite intelligent elements, also really very valuable people," who had been trained in various professions.[74] She clearly thought of this as a compliment, even if she used language that she likely heard from Nazis. Both her use of "value" and the reference to people as "elements" distanced her from the people she described, speaking like an administrator rather than a fellow inmate. She also contrasted the Romani prisoners she met with "nomadic Gypsies" (*Wanderzigeuner*), whom she perceived as without "value" and outside her circle of solidarity. Romanies in Auschwitz, by contrast, had a central place in her image of the camp. She explained how their quarters were located so that they witnessed the Jews marching toward the gas chambers and crematoria. Ironically, Roma whose fate Boder only knew vicariously through Jewish testimony were themselves the closest witnesses to the destruction of the Jews in Auschwitz.

Boder also encountered stories of Romani suffering in the testimony of Anna Kaletska, a Polish Jewish woman who lost her husband and son in the war. Kaletska survived the Grodno Ghetto and Auschwitz, and Roma appeared at a pivotal moment in her account. Reporting how she had nearly lost all hope while interned in Auschwitz-Birkenau, she told of regaining the resolve to live when she met a distant cousin who looked like her daughter. After describing her subsequent struggle to stay alive with the extra rations she procured by cleaning her block, Kaletska mentioned the extermination of the "Gypsy camp" in early August 1944. For Boder and Kaletska this event was relevant for different reasons. Boder interrupted her narrative and asked her about Romani prisoners, giving Kaletska a chance to speak briefly on the horror she felt when she witnessed their mass murder. She speculated that Romani inmates might not even have been gassed because the screams and commotion had been so loud when their camp was liquidated. It then becomes apparent why this moment was crucial for Kaletska: she had remarked aloud while back in Birkenau that these images from the "Gypsy camp" were worse than any hell Dante could have imagined—"Dante was a dog; they know it much better"—and this comment led to a vital friendship between Kaletska and a literary-minded Polish block leader who overheard her comment and protected her from then on.[75]

In the voice recording, it is clear that Kaletska experienced the destruction of the Romani camp as an emotional turning point. Yet, that is not the main reason she spoke about this episode from Birkenau to a stranger equipped with a recording device. Instead, this low point was part of a series of events, starting with the encounter with her cousin, that ended up leading to her survival. Boder's interjection, more than anything else, marked the Romani experience as something relevant. The magnetic tape thus recorded a shared moment of learning when a survivor and a sympathetic interviewer refined their understanding of the type of questions and observations they considered meaningful. In contrast to the agenda-driven process that marked the efforts of others to understand the Romani genocide, Boder and Kaletska experienced an unplanned interaction. In their fragile and often ineffectual attempt to understand each other's concerns, they flagged for future listeners that something momentous had happened in Auschwitz to imprisoned Roma.

Boder reflected on these episodes in an article that he revised for over a decade. He wrote "The Tale of Anna Kovitzka [sic]: A Logico-Systematic Analysis or an Essay in Experimental Reading" in December 1946, shortly after returning from Europe. He obsessed over polishing it for submission to such an extent that he ended up never publishing it. In all of its different versions, the article includes an analysis of Kaletska's statements on Roma alongside further comments on their fate. Boder claimed that "[m]ention of the Gypsies occurs frequently in the interview[s]" but failed to note that he himself had often brought them up, thus leaving out the crucial details both of his own shaping of the interviews and of his sustained interest in learning about the fate of Romanies during the war.[76] That process had serious limitations because he never spoke to Romani survivors, a fact he remarked upon later. In the essay, he described how he saw "Gypsies" traveling in carts in western Germany but reflects that he never managed to "get hold of a single Gypsy for an interview."[77]

Unable to speak to Romani survivors, Boder's interpretations instead replicated his own biases as well as those of his interlocutors. In his essay, he focused on the Nazis' alleged privileging of Roma over Jews and stories about Romani prisoners' brutality against Jews. He also presented as fact the rumor that the Germans had originally tried to convince Hungary to deport its Jews by promising the Hungarians that they would return Europe's "Gypsies" to Hungary, their alleged homeland. Interviewing only Jews about Roma created one-sided historical narratives, even as it left important clues that something significant had happened both to Roma and between Jews and Roma during the war.

The fate of Boder's interview with Kovitzka, which had impressed Boder sufficiently to compel him to write an article on the subject, illustrates how different layers of the interview slowly disappeared together with an acknowledgment of the process that had generated them. In its first published version of 1949 in *I Did Not Interview the Dead*, Boder included detailed transcriptions of both his questions and his subject's answers.[78] These were also retained in the careful translation created under Boder's auspices for a five-volume anthology of interviews he donated to a select number of research libraries.[79] The most popular edition of his work changed the text, however. Seeking to create a more coherent narrative out of the jumble of back-and-forths that originally characterized the collection, Donald Niewyk's compilation of Boder's interviews, published in 1998, omitted many of Boder's interruptions.[80] This edition still allows readers to grasp why Kaletska wanted to talk about the subject: it is apparent even in the abridged version that her reaction to the collective murder of Auschwitz's Sinti and Roma permitted her survival. Yet, something was missing. First, the shortened version deleted Kaletska's recollection that "Gypsies" had not been tattooed and her speculation that they might not have been gassed but put to death on the spot in more violent ways. This not only omitted crucial (albeit erroneous) information but also cut much of the emotion from her account. On the tapes, it is apparent that Kaletska's speculation about the method of killing was largely an expression of her shock at the dreadful sounds emanating from the camp. More importantly, the rhythm of the conversation also changed once it was abridged. While the tapes and Boder's transcript invited the listener or reader to dwell on the situation in the "Gypsy camp," later readers might easily miss this part. It was not the answer but the omitted question that had originally stopped the flow of the conversation and marked the extermination of Roma in Auschwitz-Birkenau as something relevant.

Scholars have debated the degree to which interviews like those collected by Boder were forgotten in the decades after the war.[81] Boder's work appeared in edited versions, and some social scientists even used it to form new theories about human behavior, but for decades after Boder conducted the interviews, no one mined them for historical information. The fate of his project shows that although there was never complete silence around the history of Nazi genocide, the topic proved marginal for most scholars and laypeople for many decades.

Even if they had paid attention to these sources, it is unclear what scholars might have gleaned about the Romani genocide from the contradictory information found in Boder's interviews. What would a historian in the 1950s do with the claim by the Auschwitz survivor George Kaldore, for example, that Romani prisoners in Birkenau donned Hasidic hats, which they had somehow acquired from rabbis?[82] Boder's interviews surely could have served as kernels that might have seeded a broader understanding of Romani experiences but read in isolation they were—and remain—inadequate as sources for Romani history. Most of all they represent a one-sided account of the complicated wartime relationship between two groups.

Many of the accounts Jews gave of Roma following the war described harsh competition in the camps. Such accounts of conflicts in turn deterred straightforward attempts to recover the Romani genocide. For example, Alexander Gertner, a Hungarian Jewish survivor, reported on his interaction with Romani prisoners in Auschwitz-Birkenau after Boder prompted him to talk about the subject.[83] Gertner shared the experiences of many other Transylvanian Jews, such as Elie Wiesel, who faced Romani kapos for a short period after their deportation to the infamous camp. As he spoke about different Romani inmates who had been put in charge of Jews, Gertner bemoaned how even the youngest Roma thought it was their right to hit Jews. As he put it ironically: "It was a good deed to beat us." (The original Yiddish is more colorful: "*Es var a mitzve tsu kloppen*.")[84] Such mediated stories had little use for later researchers who cared about Romani experiences and were irrelevant to those who cared only about Jewish experiences. It is no coincidence that Gertner's interview did not make it into Niewyk's popular edition of Boder's interviews. These kinds of interviews are difficult precisely for scholars like Niewyk, who made a point of acknowledging Romani history.[85]

Accounts such as Gertner's, which presented Roma as victimizers rather than victims, seemed to undermine the idea of parallel genocides that Niewyk was committed to promoting. Niewyk's solution in his commentary on another account lays bare this problem. He added a footnote denying that there had been Romani kapos, writing instead that Roma were only given a role in orchestras but not any other camp function.[86] This approach might have helped Niewyk support his larger vision—that of treating the Romani and Jewish genocides in tandem—but it does not conform to what is now broadly known about the position of Romanies in various camps during the war years. Roma served, on many occasions, as kapos. We need not shy away from this knowledge, uncomfortable as it is. In other instances, Jews ended up in positions of more power over Romanies, and the tables were turned. A proper reckoning with the entangled history of Romani-Jewish relations requires us to think about all of these examples, in all of their complexity.

Boder's interviews are challenging sources to use, yet they are indispensable for our understanding of Jewish-Romani relations and prisoner relations at large. They tell us a number of things. First, they illustrate the tenuous distance between prisoners—when sometimes even the most sympathetic Jewish commentators spoke about Roma like administrators. Yet they also remind us that the suffering of others across a fence had a deep emotional impact on Jews contemplating their own fate. Finally, they show how a scholar who became attuned to this fact might grow curious about the experiences of these other prisoners whom his Jewish interviewees mentioned so often, leading him to ask questions that few others asked at the time.

The Goldstein Commission

The curiosity about Romani experiences of genocide that Boder developed incidentally was also evident in a different, administrative effort to document Nazi atrocities against Jews in the immediate years after the war. Between 1951 and 1952, Jewish Holocaust survivors from all over Belgium received requests to come to the offices of the Ministry of Reconstruction in Brussels. There they were interviewed by several people, including Estelle Goldstein, a Social

Democratic journalist hired for the purpose of conducting a survey of Jews' wartime experiences.[87] The resulting questionnaires were unusual in Belgium, where authorities had sufficient information to understand crimes committed against the Jewish population on their territory but did not recognize Jews as a distinct category of victims in need of special protections within the context of the country's welfare policies.

Postwar Belgium's compensation and welfare laws were the result of negotiations in 1946 between the left-wing government and the Catholic opposition. The communist Minister of Reconstruction, Jean Terfve, the driving force behind the new laws, devised a consensus solution by which various political groups—from the Catholic right to the communists—received support and recognition for their suffering during the war, largely to the exclusion of Jewish victims. While Belgian-born Jewish deportees to the camps received substantial benefits, they received no official recognition, a status that was reserved for various categories of political resistance fighters and prisoners. Foreign-born Jews, on the other hand, could only receive financial support from the state if they could prove their participation in resistance activities.[88] And foreign-born Jews constituted the vast majority of Jewish survivors in Belgium.[89]

In the first years following the conclusion of World War Two, Belgian authorities had collected some information on the murder of Belgian Jews, but there was much left to do. A report published by the Belgian War Crimes Commission in 1947 gave a solid overview of antisemitic persecution by the Nazis, drawing in part on testimonies collected by two Jewish organizations, the Conseil des Associations Juives de Belgique and the Aide aux Israélites Victimes de la Guerre.[90] This report did not elaborate on the crucial distinction between Jews with and without Belgian citizenship. Nor did it translate into laws benefiting Jewish victims.[91]

Goldstein's bureaucratic odyssey exemplifies the challenges that Jewish claimants faced in this environment. Around the time that Goldstein was interviewing others and directing the effort to understand the fate of Jewish survivors in Belgium, she found that she too was expected to explain her wartime activities to Belgian officials. Hailing from a liberal, non-observant Jewish family in Antwerp, Goldstein appears to have become political early on. In her memoirs she describes how she became a leftist at age eight, after she met revolutionary socialists Karl Liebknecht and Rosa Luxemburg at a relative's home.[92] During the interwar period, she represented Belgian socialists at international women's meetings and edited a feminist journal. These activities left her highly exposed after the German invasion in 1940. Although she managed to obtain false papers and lived under the pseudonym Marie Boulard until the end of the war, she was nonetheless detained for four months—from November 28, 1942 to April 6, 1943—at St. Gilles prison under the suspicion that she belonged to a resistance network. Postwar Belgian authorities did not challenge the fact of her arrest or her remarkable account of remaining unrecognized as a Jew during her months-long imprisonment; nevertheless, they refused to give her the status of political prisoner.[93]

It was difficult for Goldstein to prove that she had been part of a resistance network because she was arrested on the first day of her clandestine activities. Her principal Jewish contact in the resistance turned out to be in the pay of the Gestapo and soon betrayed Goldstein and several others in Belgium and the Netherlands. Another fellow resistance fighter and close friend was eventually identified as Jewish and deported to Auschwitz, where she perished. By the war's end, the only living person who could attest to Goldstein's involvement in the resistance was the Gestapo double agent who was convicted after the war and discredited as a witness. As a result, a Belgian court ruled on November 14, 1950 that Goldstein could receive the financial and welfare benefits of political persecutees but would not be permitted to call herself a "political prisoner." An appeals court confirmed that decision on February 16, 1951.[94] Only solid documentation of persecution and resistance translated into full recognition and compensation in postwar Belgium. Goldstein must have understood this better than most as she set out to document the fate of Belgian Jewry for a ministry that had just denied many of her own claims.

The Belgian path toward compensation created unique pressures for documentation. To prove their eligibility for state support, the most prestigious class of claimants in the Belgian system—political prisoners—was subjected to what one historian has referred to as "the criterion of suffering."[95] A central question behind state payments and recognition was how courageously individuals had behaved after their arrest, not simply the reason for their arrest or how long they were imprisoned. As a result, Belgian ministries were more interested than authorities in other countries in understanding the level of suffering people endured at different locations during the war. The Belgian Ministry of Reconstruction sent emissaries across Europe to help make such determinations, creating some of the most comprehensive lists of camps available in the postwar period. Belgium also maintained active permanent missions in France and to the International Tracing Service in Bad Arolsen.[96] As it investigated the fate of particular individuals and groups during the war, the

Belgian Ministry of Reconstruction developed its own agenda, creating an ever more complex system for documenting the wartime persecution of Belgian residents anywhere in Europe.

This tendency toward maximal documentation can explain the unorthodox methods that Belgian administrators used when filling out the questionnaires of the Jewish survivors they interviewed. These interviewers tended not to conform to the blank fields reserved for answers to various biographical questions. Instead, they often left these fields blank while filling the margins of the forms with long narratives and explanations of survivors' experiences. When a pattern seemed unusual—such as when interviewers realized that not all Jews had been deported from Belgium in infamous cattle cars—they provided detailed descriptions to explain any discrepancy from the anticipated narrative.

The Belgian ministry's questionnaires include surprising information on the fate of people deported to the camps as "Gypsies." Although there was no explicit question printed on the questionnaire about Roma, thirteen percent of Jews interviewed (54 out of 403) volunteered information on people they called "tziganes" or "zigeuners." Most of these commentaries appeared in a field reserved for "additional remarks." In nine cases, the questionnaires indicated merely that the witness had no contact with "Gypsies." The only possible explanation for such unusual comments about the absence of relations is that ministry officials explicitly and regularly asked Jewish survivors whether they had contact with Roma during their imprisonment. The Belgian interviewers' curiosity about the fate of Roma during the war also becomes apparent in an administrative note that appears on the questionnaire of a Jewish deportee who explained that she saw "Gypsies" at the transit camp in Malines and could attest to their transportation to Auschwitz in separate train cars in the twenty-third convoy.[97] A note left behind by a Ministry of Reconstruction administrator (most likely Estelle Goldstein), added in large letters with a red pen, read: "Voir Remarque Tziganes" ("See comment on Gypsies").

Jewish interviewees usually provided brief and descriptive answers about their experiences with Roma during the war. The majority noted the camps where they had seen "Gypsies" (including Malines, Auschwitz, Ravensbrück, and several labor camps). They also spoke of their fellow prisoners' maltreatment and mass liquidation, often highlighting the fact that Romanies had remained separate from Jews. Of the eight survivors who offered explanations comparing the fate of Jews and Roma in the camps, only one said that Roma were treated better than Jews, while three reported that they were treated worse, and four explained that the two groups were treated in the same manner.

What was the agenda of the Belgian administrators who signed off on this project? In the absence of any official inquiry into Romani victims of the war, ministry officials may have been instructed to collect general information for future possible claims by Roma. Or perhaps they were just trying to fill in gaps in their knowledge of wartime persecution.[98] Whatever the answer, the ministry's officials worked with what they had—a large number of Jewish claimants who were readily available as informants.[99]

Goldstein's survey was revolutionary in the Belgian context. It not only identified but also singled out Jews as victims of racial persecution and prepared reports on their deportation from Belgium and France that could support Jewish claims for compensation and recognition.[100] Originally "forgotten victims" themselves, Belgian Jews were asked to speak about the experiences of another largely ignored victim group whose fate they only knew from distant observation. Even those Jews who suggested that Roma had been treated worse than Jews indirectly found their experiences recognized as the benchmark for the treatment of racial persecutees. The questionnaires that illustrate the silencing of Roma thus enabled the empowerment of Jews. This is the enduring paradox of the Goldstein commission's documentation work.

The First Romani Archives of the Holocaust

Just as the Belgian questionnaires produced knowledge about Roma while centering the position of Jewish victims, Romani Holocaust Studies would eventually emerge as a field dominated by historians trained to study the Jewish Holocaust, while Romani Studies largely remained the domain of linguists, musicologists, anthropologists, social workers, and folklorists. Yates' willingness to write on the persecution of Roma for *Commentary*, a Jewish publication, and her inability to bridge prewar Romani Studies and Romani Holocaust history within her discipline is typical. This bifurcation meant that those who could speak to large numbers of Roma and had the resources to record their statements for posterity gave little support to historians who began their work decades after the fact.

While prewar attempts to document Jewish popular culture became the starting point of postwar efforts to collect Jewish stories about the Holocaust, projects to gather Romani stories remained often an antiquarian and romantic pursuit among non-Romanies.[101] This, in turn, meant that Roma had essentially no say in how their folklore was collected, stored, or interpreted. Some Romani victims spoke about their experiences in public forums, such as in trials or the offices of concentration camp associations and refugee organizations, but these stories usually did not find their way into the collections of scholarly institutions dedicated to their culture, such as the Gypsy Lore Society.

There were certainly some records produced of Romani narratives in the postwar years, but they have serious limitations. States and new international bureaucracies created their own collections of stories, based on the accounts that survivors had to give to acquire some type of right—whether it was the right to receive support from the International Refugee Organization or compensation from the German government. These brief accounts often tell us more about the administrators who produced them than the people who filled them out as supplicants. Since people tell their life histories for a particular purpose in a given setting, this is a familiar problem to anyone reading, listening to, or watching biographical accounts. Yet, there is a good reason that most scholars working on the Jewish Holocaust typically use administrative accounts only to supplement others: they have much richer testimony at their disposal from survivors who left their impressions in a great variety of other, non-administrative settings. These accounts, encouraged by other survivors who were often involved in the collection of stories before the war, are missing in the Romani case.

The few exceptions to this rule suggest what might have been possible had more people cared. One of these rare attempts to record stories from Roma came from a small initiative in Munich, called Die Vergessenen (The Forgotten), founded in early 1946 by two non-Romani former prisoners of Dachau, the painter Karl Jochheim-Armin and the graphic designer Georg Tauber. The organization's driving force was Jochheim-Armin, a political prisoner who was recategorized as "asocial" in 1939, allegedly to rationalize his continued internment.[102] Building on his own experience of marginalization, Jochheim-Armin was interested in offering representation for two "forgotten" groups—"asocials" and "Gypsies"—both of which continued to be targeted by the state after the war.[103]

Soon renamed Interessengemeinschaft Deutscher Zigeuner (Association of German Gypsies), Jochheim-Armin's small organization represented German Sinti in their claims against municipal and state institutions, helped them locate living relatives, and identified the graves of dead relatives. A newsletter featured short narratives of several Sinti camp survivors.[104] Perhaps due to his sense of the shared plight of Roma and asocials both during and after the war, Jochheim-Armin adopted the "Gypsy" cause as his own in a public letter addressed to the international tribunal convened at Nuremberg where, he complained, "we Gypsies noted the disturbing fact that our blood sacrifice was not mentioned with a single word."[105] Such efforts had little effect, however, largely because a personal feud between Tauber and Jochheim-Armin dissolved the association in a matter of months. With their efforts to collect testimony cut short, the organization—echoing its name—has been almost completely forgotten today.[106] Even without such personal squabbles, the continued discrimination against both Roma and so-called asocials in the postwar era complicated any efforts at an alliance.

Other collections solidified around Romani demands for state recognition of particular policies or camps in the postwar struggle for compensation. Most writing on the matter took the form of petitions or short articles in the newsletters of survivor organizations. Austria was one of the first places where a number of victims came together for the common purpose of compensation. Beginning in November 1940 Austrian Roma from the province of Burgenland had been deported to the camp Lackenbach, where they were housed in unhygienic conditions and forced to work. Lackenbach continued to exist even as the Nazis deported many of its inmates to the Łódź ghetto—all of whom were then sent to their deaths in Chełmno—or to Auschwitz. Following precedent in Germany, local municipalities funded the camp and the Viennese criminal police administered it, making it an exception in the minds of postwar administrators who did not recognize it as a concentration camp. As a result, the Austrian state denied imprisoned Roma papers to certify them as victims of Nazi camps and limited their compensation payments.[107]

In 1952, several Roma from southern Burgenland started collaborating with the association of former concentration camp prisoners, the KZ-Verband, which was dominated by communists after 1948, to change this situation. The association, which had a mixed track record regarding the inclusion of Roma, proved inclusive in this case and joined the lobbying effort to have Lackenbach classified as a concentration camp. In their magazine, *Der neue Mahnruf*, the KZ-Verband called for witnesses to the camp to come forward and frequently addressed the plight of Austrian Roma.[108] Although the state withheld legal recognition of the camp as a concentration camp for compensation purposes, these struggles were not in vain.[109] They left traces of documentation that future scholars would eventually make use of, albeit only after many decades. Although the Documentation Center of Austrian Resistance kept the originals and catalogued them—and even though one of the archive's staff historians, Selma Steinmetz, used them in her own publications—the field as a whole only rediscovered them as sources in the 2010s.[110] More common was another story exemplified by the documentation that Boder and the Goldstein commission created: the appearance of Romani experiences in the margins of the growing archives of Jewish experiences.

4

Asymmetrical Justice: Roma and Jews in the Courtroom

WRITING IN 1946, the novelist Matéo Maximoff expressed Romani victims' demands for justice:

> We, the Gypsies, the freest people in the world, together with the people of all the United Nations, we demand that the Gypsy martyrs at Auschwitz be avenged, like those of France or Poland, not by the fury of barbarism but by the hand of Justice. [...] Shall we Gypsies, one asks, ever have an Allied Court of Justice which will demand the punishment of these monsters, the assassins of 500,000 Tziganes? Since the United Nations desire to do justice to all the peoples who fought for the freedom of the world, why do they not consider justice for us also, and therefore institute an enquiry into the source of these monstrous Nazi orders to assassinate the whole Gypsy race?[1]

Maximoff, only twenty-one-years old and about to publish the novel, *The Ursitory*, which would make him Europe's most celebrated Romani author, understood that justice required many things: evidence, round numbers that could be easily communicated, and a narrative that allowed victims to make claims for redress. Justice also came in many forms: the criminal prosecution of the perpetrators, restitution, compensation, states' public acknowledgment of past suffering, and, most importantly for Maximoff, an end to restrictions on the everyday movement of his people. Referring to Roma as the "freest people in the world," he couched the latter demand in imagery that likely resonated with the romantically inclined readership of the *Journal of the Gypsy Lore Society*, where his article appeared.[2] Yet, to break the cycle of anti-Romani persecutions, he knew he would also have to invoke his group's collective status as victims of a common enemy—a status ideally conferred upon them by a court with international standing and supported by the victorious powers who were remaking the borders of Europe.

Asking a question that was as much historical as existential, Maximoff demanded to know from an international trial: "What was the motive which induced these Nazis to carry out such wholesale massacres of our race?" For Maximoff, as for many survivors of persecution, this was not a political but a personal question at a time when survivors, professional commentators, and even casual observers of European events understood the magnitude and outlines but not the details of Nazi murder policies. Nine months after submitting his piece in January 1946, Maximoff learned that forty members of his ethnic subgroup who lived in Kraków had been murdered during the war by the Germans.[3] Trials like those organized by the Allies in Nuremberg and many other states across Europe promised to elucidate the past in the process of offering justice to survivors like Maximoff.

Maximoff explained why Roma deserved their own international tribunal in terms that appealed to the war's victors. He situated Romani deaths in a global struggle to defeat Nazism, rather than depicting Roma as mere victims of state violence. Citing Romani contributions to resistance activities in France and Belgium, he underscored that "we have fought side by side with you," the "people of all the United Nations," and thus positioned Roma as legitimate participants in the construction of a new legal and political order.[4] In his depiction, the "freest people in the world" had joined the French battle for freedom from Nazism.[5]

To explain his cause to the international readership of the *Journal of the Gypsy Lore Society*, Maximoff also drew comparisons to extermination policies against Jews. He explained the mass death of Romanies in Auschwitz in relational terms: "For, like the Jews, our race has been swept out of Europe by a nation of 'over-lords.'" He was also the first to popularize the idea of 500,000 Romani victims, at the very moment when the international tribunal in Nuremberg gave official support to the figure of six million Jewish victims of Nazism.[6] These references and others in documents created by Romani authors or submitted on their behalf reveal their assumptions about their readers' greater familiarity with the Jewish genocide than with their own.

Maximoff called for international justice just as Jewish organizations and individuals were fighting to have anti-Jewish policies acknowledged at Nuremberg. Over the next decades, as new forms of national and transnational justice emerged, Jewish and Romani demands to hold perpetrators accountable became only more entangled. On the one hand, as the victim of genocide replaced the political deportee and the resistance fighter as the iconic victim of the radical evil of Nazism, Roma and Sinti increasingly looked toward Jewish successes to define their own expectations of justice. On the other hand, the legal innovations, documentary work, and new narratives that Jews brought to the courtroom had unexpected consequences for the Romani quest for justice, as Jewish efforts simultaneously revealed and obscured aspects of Romani persecution.

The three trials at the core of this chapter demonstrate these unintended outcomes: the International Military Tribunal at Nuremberg in 1945–46, alluded to by Maximoff; the 1961 Eichmann trial; and the 1963–65 Frankfurt Auschwitz trial. Nuremberg encapsulated the brief promise of international justice; the Eichmann trial, the possibility of national justice in the name of the victims; and the Frankfurt trial, the possibility of national justice in the country of the perpetrators. Each differed in terms of the knowledge and documentation they produced, the consequences for the writing of Holocaust history, and for the survivors drawn into these trials as witnesses. All three show how Jewish and Romani interests could overlap or, just as often, be at cross-purposes—with profound consequences for the shape of our archives and the way we write the history of the Holocaust. Finally, a fourth type of legal reckoning innovated by Jewish claimants delivered some of the justice denied in criminal proceedings and unexpectedly advanced knowledge of the Romani genocide: international civil litigation.

Nuremberg and the Making of Unequal Documentation

In December 1945, around the time Maximoff was preparing his article, the lawyer Jacob Robinson reported to the World Jewish Congress (WJC) in New York about the international trial against twenty-four leading Nazis taking place in Nuremberg. Since 1940, the WJC had worked behind the scenes to raise awareness of the wartime mass killings of Jews, supplying evidence to decision-makers in Washington and London. Once discussions about postwar justice started in earnest in 1942, the organization pleaded that a tribunal give adequate attention to the plight of Jews.[7] The Lithuanian-born Robinson, who stood at the helm of these campaigns and in front of the WJC's team in New York that December, was a veteran of organized Jewish politics and a major interwar advocate of minority rights.[8] He had advised the Lithuanian government in its endeavors to protect Jews as a newly defined national minority and headed an alliance of minority parties—including German and Polish representatives—in the Lithuanian parliament from 1922 to 1926. He subsequently sought to use supranational institutions such as the Congress of European National Minorities and the League of Nations to advocate for Jewish collective rights. These efforts coalesced into the founding of the WJC as a sister organization of the American Jewish Congress in 1936.[9] After fleeing the Nazi advance and arriving in New York in 1940, he established the Institute of Jewish Affairs with the aim of supplying information for the WJC's diplomatic and political campaigns during and after the war.

Looking back at the first two months of the Nuremberg trial, Robinson noted many successes but also challenges. Among his greatest concerns was the legal framing of the crimes committed against Jews in this first and only attempt by all four Allies to sit in judgment together over the Nazi regime's senior leadership. In early discussions about a future indictment, US and British planners had considered accusing captured Nazi leaders only of committing war crimes. These crimes, codified in international treaties or defined by convention, had a secure place in international law. A tribunal on war crimes could draw on existing legal precedent and avoid the accusation that the Allies were meting out the arbitrary justice of the victors. Yet for those advocating for Jewish victims, a narrow definition of war crimes was unacceptable, since it would make impossible a comprehensive prosecution for the mass murder of Jews. In the traditional definition of war crimes, only actions against enemies during wartime could be considered. This would remove from the court's jurisdiction systematic atrocities that Nazi and Axis governments had committed against their own populations, as well as prewar actions, including Nazi measures against German Jews before 1939. This limitation would also be true of "crimes against peace," a category proposed by the Soviet Jewish lawyer Aron Trainin to allow aggressive wars to be a chargeable offense—which was applied for the first time in Nuremberg.[10] Lobbying from Jewish organizations led political leaders in Washington and London to agree, hesitantly, to widen the definition, but prosecutors decided to walk a middle path.[11] Only when the racial persecution of Jews before the outbreak of hostilities could be said to have contributed to a larger plan to commit war crimes or "crimes against peace" would they include these incidents in the indictment.[12]

The key term in the prosecution's attempt to expand the geographic and chronological scope of their case was "conspiracy." Conspiracy was a term drawn from US legal discourse, often used in antitrust and organized crime cases. The US prosecutor's team under Robert Jackson introduced it as an innovation in international law, despite resistance from French and Soviet prosecutors.[13] In Nuremberg, it was the first count of the indictment, which accused some of the defendants of "formulation or execution of a common plan or conspiracy to commit, or which involved the commission of, Crimes against Peace, War Crimes, and Crimes against Humanity." While all four counts of the indictment dealt in some form with crimes against Jews, the prosecution used the first count—the conspiracy charge—to answer Maximoff's question concerning the Nazis' motives. According to the indictment, the disenfranchisement, deportation, enslavement, starvation, murder, and mass extermination of Jews was part of a plan to consolidate control over conquered territories.[14]

The result was a combination of two competing narratives about the German state's crimes: one claimed that Nazi elites and Hitler in particular had plotted from the beginning to eliminate the Jewish people through mass murder. The other centered on the Nazis' conspiracy to commit war crimes, a claim that could in turn explain all other accusations.

This two-fold argument about a premeditated antisemitic plan to murder Europe's Jews and an all-encompassing design for world domination left a paradoxical legacy. The court discussed and preserved a large corpus of documentation and information on the Jewish genocide. "No other crime had been mentioned as often and as persistently, in such grisly detail and on a comparative geographical scale. Jews were by far the most often mentioned religious or ethnic group in court," the historian Kim Priemel noted.[15] And yet, while prosecutors sometimes emphasized that the killing of Jews was the Nazi regime's most egregious transgression of human norms, they were equally adamant that these crimes were part of a yet larger scheme for aggressive war.

The famous first salvo of the trial, Robert Jackson's opening speech as US Chief Prosecutor articulated this dual narrative. He introduced "Crimes Committed against the Jews" as a distinct part of the indictment: "The most savage and numerous crimes planned and committed by the Nazis were those against the Jews."[16] Within minutes he added: "It was a policy directed against other nations as well as against the Jews themselves. Anti-Semitism was promoted to divide and embitter the democratic peoples and to soften their resistance to the Nazi aggression."[17] The latter statement made it sound as if antisemitism was merely instrumental, a tool to undermine the resolve of other states amidst an ongoing effort to subjugate them.[18]

The judgment sent the same inconsistent message. The court acknowledged the persecution of Jews in great detail, beginning with the antisemitism of the early Nazi party and the notoriously vulgar newspaper *Der Stürmer* (whose editor, Julius Streicher, was on trial) and culminating with the killings by Einsatzgruppen and in extermination camps. They cited seized documents and crucial testimony by high-ranking officials in the machinery of death. Yet the judgment did not accept the theory of early anti-Jewish measures as part of war preparations: "The persecution of Jews during the same period is established beyond all doubt. To constitute crimes against humanity, the acts relied on before the outbreak of war must have been in execution of, or in connection with, any crime within the jurisdiction of the Tribunal. The Tribunal is of the opinion that, as revolting and horrible as many of these crimes were, it has not been satisfactorily proved that they were done in execution of, or in connection with, any such crime."[19] Even as it rejected its jurisdiction over part of the violence committed against Jews, the court not only accepted their mass murder as a fact but also the account of the Holocaust as the regime's defining crime. Nazi documents—starting with the Nazi party program of 1920—proved the crime's premeditation. The Romani Holocaust, which the court treated neither as a central ideological aim of the regime nor part of a conspiracy for war, remained marginal in this framework.

Speaking months before the court would hand down its judgment, Robinson was hopeful that the collective Jewish interest he sought to represent would be well served by this novel interpretation of conspiracy charges in international law. In his New York speech, he took full credit for devising this approach, telling his WJC colleagues: "The Four Power Agreement has indicated our theory of the extension in time and space of the orthodox definition of war crimes, which actually amounts to the recognition of the identity of the Jewish people, as the chosen victim of Nazi persecution."[20] Robinson knew that the reduction of all Nazi actions to a single plan for warfare was a forced argument, yet he wholeheartedly endorsed the underlying assumption that the systematic killing of Jews required a premeditated plan. He and the WJC leadership lacked access to the internal deliberations of Nazi state and party institutions but had arrived at such an understanding of Nazism during the war by reading antisemitic sources expressing the desire for destruction.[21] Today we would call their outlook intentionalist: the theory that Hitler and top Nazi leaders intended the mass murder of European Jews from an early stage. This contrasts with functionalist accounts that emphasize haphazard responses, experimentation, pressure from different levels in the administration, and the iterative nature of the path toward genocide. For Robinson and other Jewish observers, the intentionalist approach was the clearest way to articulate their claims that the victims of this crime were not individual Jews but the Jewish people as a collective.[22] Jewish DPs who voiced their opinions on the trial had similar legal priorities. They demanded a role in the process of justice and wanted the court to treat the crime against them as something distinct, and thus as central and premeditated.[23] Many Romani victims might have shared these sentiments even if the intentionalist template established at Nuremberg would have posed serious challenges for them, as we will see.

In his speech in New York, Robinson cited the various legal concepts that had helped him establish his distinctive approach. He was especially supportive of the category "crimes against humanity," which had been introduced into Nuremberg planning meetings by the Jewish legal thinker and Cambridge professor Hersch Lauterpacht.[24] Once it became an independent count of the indictment, the phrase covered persecution on "political, racial, religious grounds" in the execution of the conspiracy charge.[25] The second term was Raphael Lemkin's new coinage: genocide. The concept remained marginal at the International Military Tribunal but would come to dominate discussions in the following decades. In his speech, Robinson complained about this term's inclusion in the indictment, one of his many issues with the chaotic process of negotiating a shared indictment with multiple parties. Robinson was not philosophically opposed to Lemkin's innovation, as illustrated by his later support for the genocide convention.[26] Nor was there any principled resistance from the Institute of Jewish Affairs, or the body that oversaw its activities, the WJC, beyond early skepticism that states would be willing to codify and prosecute genocide.[27] Apart from the pragmatic and accurate assessment that Lauterpacht's notion had more traction, Robinson seemed personally appalled by the particular example given, at Lemkin's suggestion, of genocide:

> Suddenly the idea of 'Genocide' (Lemkin's term) came into being, and the term was inserted into the document but was not developed. As example of the application of the concept of 'Genocide,' 'Jews and Gypsies' were cited. When I saw that, I got mad, because it so reeked of the Nazi method of humiliation of Jews by putting them in a class with the gypsies. It is a doubtful source of satisfaction that the word, 'Poles' was inserted to make the phrase read: 'Jews, Poles and Gypsies.'[28]

Robinson was not only offended by the association of Jews with Roma, he also believed others would see things the same way. It may well be that Robinson changed his mind over the next decades, since he later made copious notes on scholarship about the Romani genocide.[29] At this point in time, however, his comments served as an expression of a commonly held bias that he believed might undermine his advocacy for the Jewish cause. Robinson spoke as a Jewish lobbyist, fighting for justice for one group. When he reported to a smaller circle of WJC leaders four days later, he once again emphasized the need for a "collectivistic approach to the Jewish case" and listed the names of Jews involved in Nuremberg who he believed would help him—from the French substitute judge Robert Falco to the many Jews dealing with the translation and analysis of documents behind the scenes.[30] Scholars telling the story of the Nuremberg trials' successes and failures in capturing and prosecuting genocide inherited this perspective of an uphill battle to establish the Jewish genocide.

Departing from the singular narrative about Jewish efforts to overcome antisemitism allows us to see the logic behind the substantive Romani absence from Nuremberg. Even though prosecutors used general terms such as "racial persecution" and "crimes against humanity" throughout the trial, Roma appeared mostly in enumerations of victim groups, much as they had in the definition of genocide. Karl Jochheim-Armin, speaking for the Association of German Gypsies that he had co-founded in 1946, was technically incorrect when he wrote an open letter to the Nuremberg court, complaining that "we Gypsies noted the disturbing fact that our blood sacrifice was not mentioned with a single word."[31] Yet, he was correct to note the absence of their fate in anything but cursory terms.

The evidentiary legacy of the Nuremberg trials reflects this as much as anything that occurred in the courtroom. To the chagrin of many bored observers, the International Military Tribunal and many of the subsequent trials were largely based on documentary evidence rather than testimony. The reliance on seized Nazi paperwork followed the dual assumptions that it would suffice for convictions and that it offered conclusive historical proof of crimes. Many who thought professionally about the relationship between law and the politics of history, such as Robinson, agreed. In his New York report to the WJC, Robinson noted with satisfaction that most of the trials' documents had been seized by the United States, which now controlled them and would "lend-lease" them to other prosecution teams.[32] Unlike other states, the US was also committed to publishing these sources. This emphasis on documents and the will to make them available immediately, albeit in limited print runs, would be a major result of the trial.

The documentary trail left by the series of Nuremberg trials became foundational for research on the Jewish Holocaust and, by extension, the Romani

Holocaust. The case for the former is much clearer. Publication of the forty-two volumes of trial records (Blue Series) and twelve volumes of evidence of the International Military Tribunal in Nuremberg (Red Series), as well as the fifteen volumes documenting the subsequent US-led trials (Green Series), such as those against Nazi doctors or the Einsatzgruppen killing squads, was one of the lasting legacies of postwar trials.[33] In an age when historians and courts viewed testimony from victim witnesses to be of limited use, these authorized publications of Nazi documents offered unassailable evidence to those who wanted to write the history of the Jewish genocide and, later, the Romani genocide. These volumes were not perfect, nor were they universally available.[34] Yet they were invaluable resources for researchers and remain so even today.

Authors of the earliest histories of the Holocaust, such as Léon Poliakov, Gerald Reitlinger, and Raul Hilberg, whose works leaned heavily on these materials, also profited from the way prosecutors presented the documents. The Red Series, prepared by American and British prosecutors, included bibliographic essays with lengthy expositions on the accusations and lists of materials that pertained to them. In a chapter entitled "The Persecution of the Jews," prosecutors outlined a chronology of anti-Jewish radicalizing measures that follows the information Robinson supplied to US prosecutors and their support staff. It takes readers from Hitler's statements to discrimination, violence, and extermination programs, and then supplies 130 references to published evidence cited in the essay. In his 1951 *Harvest of Hatred*, Poliakov not only drew heavily on the content of this volume but also emulated its form, arranging his argument around long passages of perpetrator documents. "Wherever possible, to forestall objections, we have quoted the executioners rather than the victims," he wrote.[35] Nuremberg records formed the core of this effort. There was no comparable essay on the persecution of Roma that could have helped scholars like Poliakov reconstruct Romani persecution.

Despite these challenges, the few documents that appeared in the earliest attempts to write the history of the Romani genocide emanated from these trials. Among them was a 1939 memorandum on a solution to the "Gypsy question," which the governor of Styria, Tobias Portschy, had submitted to the Nazi party chancellery. It outlined an entire anti-Romani worldview, and for Poliakov and others, Portschy's suggestions were the equivalent of Hitler's statements in intentionalist accounts of the Jewish Holocaust.[36] Scholars also frequently cited another document that would prove crucial for the compensation claims of German Sinti and Roma: the minutes of the January 30, 1940 conference that resulted in the principal decision to deport 30,000 "Gypsies" from Germany to the newly established Government General in occupied Poland.[37] This published material helped Romanies challenge restrictive German compensation practices and formed the nucleus of early Romani Holocaust accounts. It also allowed Poliakov to include a two-page summary of extermination policies aimed at Romanies in his groundbreaking survey of the Jewish Holocaust.[38]

However deficient Nuremberg investigations and conceptualizations might have been when it came to crimes against Jews, they were more egregious still when it came to Romani victims. Prosecutors focused on a small set of institutions within the Nazi state and party apparatus, such as the SS, Gestapo, and army command. As the historian Donald Bloxham noted in his sweeping critique, this approach distorted the breadth of the German population's guilt.[39] It turned the SS into the "alibi of a nation" and allowed many German administrators and members of other armed formations to remain under the radar of criminal investigations and denazification procedures.[40] In the case of the Romani Holocaust, the same limitations led to an even more dramatic outcome. Neither the Romanian and Croatian regimes, which enacted autonomous murderous policies against Roma, nor the criminal police and municipalities involved in the persecution of German Sinti and Roma played a role at the Nuremberg trials.

During the trials, previous knowledge of Nazi extermination policies—based in part on information supplied by Robinson and the WJC—allowed prosecutors, investigators, and interrogators to seize on opportunities to reveal the immensity of the crime against Jews but not against Roma. This was evident in the stunning testimony that Rudolf Höß, the former commander of Auschwitz, gave to investigators and subsequently the court. In affidavits and in his cross-examination, Höß openly spoke of mass killings at the camp, even exaggerating the numbers of victims. In his appearance in the courtroom at Nuremberg's Palace of Justice on April 15, 1946, Höß confirmed his earlier statement that two and a half million individuals were murdered and another half million died of starvation and disease under his watch. The enormity of the crime was impossible to miss, as was the main target of the killing operations he commanded: his statements focused mostly on the murder of Jews, including nearly 400,000 Hungarian Jews in the spring of 1944. His testimony became one of the building blocks that established Auschwitz as the central location for a different kind of crime, shifting public debates from the general rejection of authoritarian terror to an understanding of genocide. Yet while Höß volunteered information once in captivity, it took an able interrogator,

Assistant US Prosecutor Whitney Harris, to recognize the significance of what Höß had said behind closed doors and to prompt him to elaborate on the mass killing of Jews in the court room, thus changing perceptions about the centrality of the Jewish genocide for an understanding of Nazi crimes.[41]

The absence of references to Romanies in Höß's testimony is telling because the Auschwitz commander eventually became the main source for early accounts of Romani suffering in Auschwitz. After he was called to the stand in Nuremberg, the British extradited Höß to Poland, where he waited ten months in a Kraków prison before he was tried and sentenced in Warsaw and subsequently executed in Auschwitz. In prison, he wrote an autobiography that appeared in Polish translation in two editions that were known to some specialists.[42] Only the German edition in 1958 and the first English and French translations in 1959 attracted the attention of Holocaust scholars and nonspecialist readers in the West.[43] In his exculpatory text, Höß elaborated on the plan to murder Sinti and Roma under his control. His statements were often inaccurate, misdating deportations to Auschwitz and conversations between him and Himmler about the Romanies' fate. He also portrayed himself as a savior, allegedly trying to rebut Himmler's extermination decision with the argument that many Romani deportees were good Germans—indeed, sometimes fellow Nazi party members—and should be spared. The memoir also depicts Roma and Sinti as nonideological and eternal children whom he loved for their simplicity. Despite its tendentious and self-serving aspects, Höß's memoirs gripped many readers who were struck by his open admission of guilt. Many historians and activists quoted from the book, even if they challenged its details and tone.[44] Prosecutors relied heavily on Höß, including those who drew on his descriptions as they prepared an indictment chapter on the "Gypsy camp" for the later Frankfurt Auschwitz trial.[45] Nuremberg prosecutors were not aware of this information, however, because they did not ask for it. Had they approached interrogations and cross-examinations with the same sensitivity and material preparation they had given to the subject of the murder of Jews, more evidence on the Romani genocide would likely have appeared earlier.

A similar oversight characterizes another consequential perpetrator testimony on the killing of Jews. The International Military Tribunal witness testimony of Otto Ohlendorf, head of Einsatzgruppe D, shifted attention from the camps, which were central to early debates, to mass shootings. Called by the British on January 3, 1946, Ohlendorf surprised the public with his open admission that he oversaw mass killings, stating in the courtroom that units under his command had shot some 90,000 individuals. He explained how Jews were identified, assembled, and eventually murdered using various methods, and elaborated on his personal preference for executions at a distance over killings by firing a bullet in the neck or gas vans. In his first appearance in Nuremberg's Palace of Justice, Ohlendorf spoke at length about Jews but not about Romanies—once again, because no one asked him to.

This changed when he became one of the accused in a separate trial dealing with Einsatzgruppen killings, the ninth trial under US control in Nuremberg, and a key source for one of the most murderous episodes of the Romani genocide. While other Einsatzgruppen sporadically included in their shooting campaigns Roma they had encountered, Einsatzgruppe D was the first to engage in the wholesale murder of all Roma under the unit's control, starting with two mass shootings of settled Roma in the southern Ukrainian city of Nikolaev in September and October 1941.[46] Ohlendorf's testimony at the Einsatzgruppen trial confirmed the general policy behind these killings and established that "Gypsies" were to be shot like Jews in German occupied Soviet territories.[47]

Ohlendorf's statements at the trial left a complicated legacy. The emphasis on the Einsatzgruppen allowed historians to grasp the extent of the Romani genocide, drawing attention to the systematic murder campaigns against Roma in Poland and the Soviet Union. Yet this did not help claim-making by Romani survivors, who largely experienced concentration camps or had managed to avoid arrest during the war. Their demands for compensation and recognition depended on their ability to show that deportation and imprisonment were part of a premeditated plan of racial persecution and murder.

Scholars and activists often cite Ohlendorf's statements to establish the targeting of Roma as a comparable crime to the mass murder of the Jews, but his testimony is also remarkable for its inability to settle the question Maximoff had raised: why did the Nazis target individuals as "Gypsies?" Ohlendorf's cross-examination in the Einsatzgruppen trials by the US prosecutor James Heath, and the famously interventionist judge, Michael Angelo Musmanno, is instructive here:[48]

HEATH: On what basis did you kill gypsies, just because they were gypsies? Why were they a threat to the security of the Wehrmacht?

OHLENDORF: It is the same as for the Jews.

HEATH: Blood?

OHLENDORF: I think I can add up from my own knowledge of European history that the Jews actually during wars regularly carried on espionage service on both sides.

MUSMANNO: You were asked about gypsies.

HEATH: I was asking you about gypsies, as the Court points out, and not Jews. I would like to ask you now on what basis you determined that every gypsy found in Russia should be executed, because of the danger to the German Wehrmacht?

OHLENDORF: There was no difference between gypsies and Jews. At the time the same order existed for the Jews. I added the explanation that it is known from European history that the Jews actually during all wars carried out espionage service on both sides.

MUSMANNO: Well, now, what we are trying to do is to find out what you are going to say about the gypsies, but you still insist on going back to the Jews, and Mr. Heath is questioning about gypsies. Is it also in European history that gypsies always participated in political strategy and campaigns?

OHLENDORF: Espionage organizations during campaigns.

MUSMANNO: The gypsies did?

OHLENDORF: The gypsies in particular. I want to draw your recollection to extensive descriptions of the Thirty Year War by Ricarda Huch and Schiller—

HEATH: That is going back pretty far in order to justify the killing of gypsies in 1941, isn't it? [49]

Ohlendorf's tendency to return to the regime's motive for killing Jews rather than Roma and his far-fetched reference to the Thirty Years' War (made more absurd by the fact that neither Huch nor Schiller mention "Gypsies" in their books on the war) allowed for different interpretations. Perhaps he had revealed the regime's attempt to relate the two groups to each other, giving prosecutors an opening to investigate crimes against Roma using tools similar to those used to investigate crimes against Jews. Alternatively, perhaps he could not articulate a coherent reason why units under his command murdered Romani populations in southern Ukraine because there was none. Historians and Romani activists preferred the former interpretation, but the court decided that the latter was more likely. The judgment in the Einsatzgruppen case shows that even explicit testimony on the Romani genocide in a trial that revolved around one of the most murderous parts of the campaign against Europe's Roma did not always prompt the courts to settle on a clear narrative. Musmanno and his colleagues concluded:

The Einsatzgruppen were, in addition, instructed to shoot gypsies. No explanation was offered as to why these unoffending people, who through the centuries have contributed their share of music and song, were to be hunted down like wild game. Colorful in garb and habit, they have amused, diverted, and baffled society with their wanderings, and occasionally annoyed with their indolence, but no one has condemned them as a mortal menace to organized society. That is, no one but National Socialism which, through Hitler, Himmler, and Heydrich ordered their liquidation. Accordingly, these simple, innocuous people were taken in trucks, perhaps in their own wagons, to the antitank ditches and there slaughtered with the Jews and the Krimchaks.[50]

These lines read like a caricature of Maximoff's arguments. Where the Romani writer expressed the puzzlement of the victims about their fate, the court announced that the motives behind their killing proved a mystery; where Maximoff catered to his readers' romantic imaginary of "Gypsies" as joyful emissaries of freedom, the court reduced them to colorful musicians; where Maximoff combined an emphasis on Romani innocence with a heroic narrative of their contribution to the war, the court only saw "simple, innocuous people." It remained an open question why Roma were "slaughtered with the Jews."

In its crudest form, the intentionalist narrative is a morality tale that lends itself to educational initiatives at schools and museums. It not only invited inaccurate conclusions about the origins of genocide but also gave Germans and their Cold War allies an opportunity to blame the Jewish Holocaust on a select group of fanatical, conspiring leaders who manipulated the larger population. Whatever its deficiencies, the intentionalist interpretation did not hurt Jewish victims in their claim-making. On the contrary, it helped communicate the "why" of anti-Jewish violence and resonated with the experiences of most Jewish victims. For Romanies, by contrast, intentionalism made it difficult to prove what they understood to be self-evident: that they were targeted as "Gypsies" in the same way that others were targeted as Jews. For Roma, unlike for Jews, the courts left the "why" question unanswered.

In other ways, too, the international tribunal at Nuremberg had negative consequences for subsequent Romani experiences with the legal system. The Nuremberg trials established the Jewish Holocaust as a known and knowable fact, and this could be used against Roma. This proved true in the case against a police officer from Würzburg in 1953, in a period when trials against Nazi perpetrators came to a near halt in Germany. A lower-level court acquitted the criminal police officer who admitted his involvement in anti-Romani roundups and deportations because of various character statements in his favor. The court concluded that the accused could not have been a true Nazi because of his regular church attendance and conflicts with the regime over religion. Prosecutors decided there was no point to an appeal, since the officer had no reason to see measures against "Gypsies" as an ideological crime, noting that general knowledge of events did not allow for "parallels to be drawn to the deportation and destruction of Jews."[51] In the words of prosecutors in Würzburg: "The accused could not have possibly understood the measures against Gypsies as one of the many steps in a systematic campaign of destruction as one would in the case of long-term measures against Jewish fellow citizens, which emerged from the universally known program of the NSDAP."[52] Ten years later, when Romani survivors sought to revive investigations against the police officer, prosecutors reiterated this claim. They told Romani survivors that it could not be apparent to police officers that they would cause serious harm to Sinti and Roma like them—adding that Auschwitz's "Gypsy Family Camp" was not a place they would have considered an obvious place of extermination.[53] The successful dissemination of the Nuremberg trials' intentionalist narrative—the idea of a preconceived plan for the murder of Jews, traceable to the Nazi party program of 1920—allowed German authorities to argue that no similar plan existed for Roma.

Maximoff and Robinson had similar hopes in the winter of 1945–46 and yet the small successes of the Jewish quest for justice did not improve the situation of Romani victims. Arguably, the popularization of the Nuremberg definitions and narratives coincidentally made the Romani genocide that much harder to see. The often distanced and tense relations between Jews and Roma during the war, and the unwillingness of Jewish political activists like Robinson to bring attention to the Romani genocide, were one matter. More important were the unintentional consequences of Nuremberg. On the one hand, efforts by Robinson and his collaborators to document the Jewish Holocaust facilitated later work on the Romani Holocaust. At the same time, the intentionalist narrative established at Nuremberg highlighted the elusiveness of any comparable document trail that might explain the persecution and murder of Sinti and Roma. Since the Nuremberg proceedings and document collections showed the regime's singular intentions with regards to Jewish victims, courts assumed the Nazi state's unclear motivations regarding Romani victims. They treated the Romani genocide as an aberration precisely because they expected it to have left the same traces as had the Jewish Holocaust but without mobilizing the resources to recover them.

The Eichmann Trial and the Hope for Victims' Justice

After eight Israeli agents abducted Adolf Eichmann in Buenos Aires in the spring of 1960, Israel's prime minister, David Ben Gurion, decided to stage a trial that would serve both judicial and educational purposes. The Nuremberg trials were largely based on confiscated German documents, but the Eichmann trial anchored the proceedings in lengthy survivor reports.[54] The staging of these witnesses put a new focus on the Jewish Holocaust and reshaped expectations of victim-centered justice far beyond Israel.[55] In the process, it also shone a light on the Nazi genocide of Europe's Romanies.[56]

The prosecution made deliberate attempts to draw attention to the Romani Holocaust. For the first time in a trial against a major war criminal, the mass murder of Roma appeared as an independent charge.[57] Count eleven of the fifteen-count indictment read: "The Accused committed acts during the period of the Second World War which are to be defined as crimes against humanity in Germany and the occupied territories when, together with others, he caused the deportation from their places of residence of tens of thousands of Gypsies, their assembly in places of concentration, and their dispatch to extermination camps in the areas of the German occupation in the East, for the purpose of murdering them."[58] This was the most serious crime Eichmann could have been accused of in relation to Roma, based on §1 of the Israeli Nazis and Nazi Collaborators (Punishment) Law of 1950. A conviction on this count alone would have merited the death penalty.

The level of evidence necessary for a conviction for "crimes against humanity," which Israeli legislators had introduced after they saw its first use at Nuremberg, required limited research on the part of prosecutors. The officials who drafted the Israeli laws had not expected to find Nazi war criminals under their jurisdiction. They had originally tailored the 1950 law to permit the punishment of Jews who aided the Nazis.[59] Whereas "crimes against the Jewish people" assumed a systematic attempt to destroy Jewish communities in whole or in part (equivalent to the definition of genocide in the United Nations' treaty of 1948), that was not the case for "crimes against humanity." To demonstrate that Eichmann had committed "crimes against humanity" against Roma, prosecutors only had to show that the deadly deportations he organized took place "on national, racial, religious or political grounds."[60] Investigators nevertheless cast a wider net.

Avner Less, the German-born Israeli police captain who interrogated Eichmann for 275 hours over eight months in 1960 and 1961, worked to link

Eichmann to crimes against Roma. Following instructions to use persuasive rather than coercive interrogation methods, Less did not press Eichmann on the subject. Instead, he tied his questions to concrete documents in order to slowly draw out the confessions he sought from Eichmann. The first time the topic briefly came up, Eichmann seemingly admitted his guilt on what would later be count eleven of the indictment. But he quickly backtracked: after Less asked if section IV B 4 of the Reich's Security Main Office, which Eichmann headed, was responsible for deporting "Gypsies" to extermination camps, Eichmann answered with an affirmative "Jawohl," but immediately added the qualification that he did not know if that indeed included "all Gypsies." He only admitted to his involvement in the deportation of Roma to the Ghetto Łódź, which, incidentally, was the only crime against Romanies the prosecutor would be able to prove in court. Eichmann claimed not to remember if "Gypsies" were also gassed in Auschwitz.[61]

Less returned to the topic in another interrogation session a month and a half later. Once again, he hoped to ascertain Eichmann's precise authority. This time they discussed Eichmann's responsibility for deportations of Poles, "Gypsies," and Jews from the Warthegau, parts of Poland that Germany had annexed in 1940. In this context, Eichmann explained that "with the Gypsies we also only [dealt with] the transport-technical issues, because the Gypsies— I think—they only came under my jurisdiction much later. And once I got them, there were none left."[62] This remained Eichmann's defense in his pretrial statements. He insisted that in the countries he was in charge of there had been very few Roma. This was also his response to Less's question: "What was actually the reason that all those Gypsies were exterminated?"[63] Like Ohlendorf before him, Eichmann had no useful response. He merely insisted that research and administration of Gypsies had not been part of his office's agenda. This answer, unlike others he gave, was accurate, for Romani affairs had been the responsibility of the German Criminal Police, not Eichmann's office.[64]

Although these exchanges add little to our understanding of Eichmann and the Nazis, they help us understand what interrogators like Less knew about the Romani genocide. His grasp of the Romani Holocaust emerges in his brief exchange with Eichmann about the numbers of Roma targeted by Nazi policies. Eichmann claimed that in Germany there could have only been 5,000 or 6,000 "Gypsies." Less wanted Eichmann to speak about the larger Romani populations farther east, however, and asked if there had not been between 700,000 and a million "Gypsies" in places like Poland, Romania, Russia, and Hungary.[65] Eichmann again returned to his main argument: he did not know such things because he had not been responsible for dealing with Romanies. Less did not insist. It is clear from his suggestive questions, however, that he perceived the genocide of the Roma as a substantive issue that could tie Eichmann to serious crimes against another group, beyond the Jewish victims at the center of the investigation. In fact, Eichmann and Less agreed during the interrogations that the systematic mass murder of Roma had taken place. Eichmann merely denied his involvement in major parts of the crime.

Once the trial started, witness testimonies became the main vehicle for communicating Eichmann's involvement in Nazi crimes to a wider public. The key testimony on Romani experiences came from Aron Bejlin, a Jewish physician who worked in the Auschwitz "Gypsy camp" during the war.[66] He was part of a group of Jews in similar positions who, by way of their medical work, knew of the fate of Roma in camps. As early as October 1945, a Jewish doctor by the name of Charles Bendel had testified at the Belsen trial organized by British officials about his time working with Mengele in Auschwitz's "Gypsy camp," and told the court about the mass murder of 4,500 Romanies in the gas chambers in the summer of 1944.[67]

Bejlin's testimony was especially prominent and detailed, offering observers a glimpse into the realities in Auschwitz's "Gypsy camp."[68] Bejlin began his account in September 1943, when the Nazis ordered him and other doctors to set up medical facilities in a section of Auschwitz-Birkenau.[69] Explaining his observations in BIIe, Bejlin told the court—and thus also global audiences—about the deportation of Roma from various countries as well as the murder of Romani prisoners who remained in the "Gypsy camp" until August 1944. Bejlin recounted being ordered to turn off the lights in the orphanage after it was emptied, and how he was nearly confused for a "Gypsy" only to be told: "If you are a Jew you still have a few weeks left. March to your block!"[70]

Such stories evoked a sense of shared victimhood between Roma and Jews. This made possible a sympathetic interpretation of Romani persecution at a trial that aimed to educate the citizens of a self-declared Jewish state about a key moment in the history of the Jewish people. However, the majority of Bejlin's testimony did not fulfill that function. Instead, it drew stark divisions between Jewish and Romani victims. This was noticeable in Bejlin's racialized language. When Hausner asked him in general terms about the inmates of the new camp, Bejlin felt compelled to explain the inmates' appearance: "All of them Gypsies. Naturally, amongst these Gypsies there were also blond types with blue eyes. Either they were offspring of mixed marriages, where the wife did not want to part from her husband, or they were the second generation.

At any rate we had blond Gypsy men and women."[71] Since no one in the court had intimated anything about the way "Gypsies" looked, Bejlin was apparently having an argument with himself about preconceived ideas about the "non-Aryan" appearance of Roma.

In other parts of his testimony, Bejlin discussed Jews and Romanies in even more overtly racialized terms. As he detailed how Romani prisoners contracted specific illnesses, Bejlin repeatedly contrasted the camp for "Gypsies" with the one he suggested had been designated for "whites" (*machane levanim*).[72] Although Bejlin explicitly called Jews "whites," he did not refer to "Gypsies" as "blacks." Yet that was the implication. Other Jewish survivors were more explicit. Judith Sternberg, a Jewish Auschwitz survivor from Hungary, produced her account of life in the camps in the late 1950s. Her memoir explains how she was shocked upon seeing a group of particularly dark-skinned prisoners arrive in Auschwitz. She noted: "[S]ome of them looked like Negroes. Since there were no colored people in Europe, their appearance caused much speculation, and we thought for a while that the Germans had already conquered America. We were very glad when we learned they were dark-skinned gypsies from Hungary, not colored people from America."[73] Writing at the dawn of the US civil rights era, Sternberg used the blackness of African Americans as a hyperbolic image to explain how physically different—and thus alien—these deportees appeared to her.[74] Bejlin's depiction of Roma as non-white was not unique among Jewish survivors, and state attorney Hausner was hardly the only prosecutor to encounter such descriptions.[75]

Such language usually went unremarked in court, as did other politically inconvenient statements from witnesses. But not this time. To Hausner's credit he did not let this comment stand. Instead, he interrupted the witness to declare, annoyed (as audible on recordings): "There is an unpleasant taste to this [*ta'am lo na'im*]—let us rather talk of a camp for Gypsies and camps for others, with your permission."[76] The Eichmann trial's chief prosecutor showed remarkable sensitivity to the introduction of racialized terminology in the courtroom at a time when few others even bothered to comment on similar statements.

Even though Hausner was unwilling to allow his Jewish witnesses to place the Nazis' Jewish and Roma victims into racial hierarchies, he nonetheless directed discussions away from their shared suffering under Nazism. Having made the fateful decision to ask Bejlin about German Sinti and Roma who had been members of the German armed forces before being sent to Auschwitz, Hausner prompted Bejlin to speak at length about Romani antisemitism. This

departed from Hausner's strategy of avoiding any mention of victims' complicity.[77] In his response, Bejlin remarked that he heard German Romanies shout
"Heil Hitler" at their Jewish doctors in Auschwitz. He also alleged that he saw
young Romani boys and girls in the uniform of the Hitler Youth and its corresponding organization, the Bund deutscher Mädel, while he was interned
there.[78] Another of Bejlin's memories involved his experience with his first
Romani patient in the camp, who, he recalled, refused treatment from Bejlin
because he was Jewish. Unlike his other anecdotes, this one was more ambigu-
ous: the same woman eventually came to regret her actions, Bejlin explained,
once she realized that they all faced the same fate.[79] It is unclear whether he
meant to offer a cynical reading of this encounter or to leave open the possibility of Romani-Jewish solidarity after the Holocaust.

Such portrayals of Romani antisemitism were surprisingly common in the
decades following the war. In his 1953 book *The Final Solution*, which served as
the main source for the prosecution team's analysis of Eichmann's crimes,
Reitlinger made a similar claim.[80] Like Bejlin, Reitlinger concluded his brief
account of Sinti and Roma in Auschwitz by highlighting their antisemitism:
"It seems that, while in Birkenau, they often expressed their approval of the
measures meted out to the Jews."[81] A similar picture emerged from the accounts
of Auschwitz's commander Rudolf Höß, who described his attempts to save
Romani prisoners who had been faithful Nazi party members. Both Reitlinger's
and Höß's texts had recently appeared in German, the foreign language most
familiar to Israeli investigators, in 1956 and 1959, respectively. These biased
accounts were no doubt the basis for Hausner's questions. When he posed
them, he pushed Bejlin, whether knowingly or not, to repeat the claim that
many Sinti and Roma had been sympathetic to Nazi ideology.

Since Bejlin was the sole witness testifying to Romani victimhood, the
prosecution presented a distorted image of the past. The experiences of German Sinti were exceptional in the context of the larger Romani genocide, and
their persecution had its own logic and tragic turns. In the right forum, it might
well have been (and may still be) productive to ask how certain German Sinti
came to embrace a particular promise for integration into the German nation
or even accepted certain ideas espoused by the Nazis. A Jewish court—which
this court of the State of Israel claimed to be—sentencing the (non-Romani)
man responsible for sending hundreds of thousands of Jews to their death was
not such a forum.[82]

A counterfactual thought experiment can help us understand the fruitless-
ness of Hausner's questions in Jerusalem. Let us imagine that a postwar

Romani state had put Arthur Nebe on trial.[83] Nebe was in some respects Eichmann's equivalent for the Romani genocide. As head of the Reich Criminal
Police Office, he devised and implemented various anti-Romani policies. Like
Eichmann, Nebe also committed crimes against different victim groups:
among other things, he was head of the Einsatzgruppe B, which killed tens of
thousands of Jews, Roma, and suspected resistance fighters in the Soviet
Union. Nebe was killed in March 1945 by the German state as a traitor due to
his involvement in the attempt on Hitler's life of July 20, 1944. For the sake of
this thought experiment, however, let us imagine that he survived and that a
Romani state arranged for a massive public trial. What would we think if the
prosecutor did not call a single Jewish witness? What would we say if instead
the only mention of Jewish suffering came from a former Romani kapo who
was asked to explain how the *Sonderkommando* of Jews, who were forced to
burn the corpses of fellow Jews, functioned? And what if that Romani witness
was then asked to speak about Jewish doctors' disregard for Romani inmates?
Who would accept the idea that a Romani kapo in Auschwitz was the right
person to give a comprehensive perspective on the conditions of Jews in Birkenau, especially at the first public trial on the matter?

Such a counterfactual scenario, one that captured the perspective of other
victims, was not alien to the court. Indeed, the three presiding judges enter-
tained a similar thought experiment about a "Gypsy state" in their judgment.
They inserted it at a crucial juncture in the argument to explain the all-
important question of Israel's right to try Eichmann for crimes committed
before that state's creation.[84] International critics and Eichmann's lawyer, Robert Servatius, had argued that Israel did not have the authority to adjudicate
the case, challenging—among other things—the legitimacy of retroactive
laws. Countering such arguments, the judges offered this hypothetical
scenario:

> Let us take an extreme example and assume that the Gypsy survivors—an
> ethnic group or a nation who were also, like the Jewish People, victims of
> the 'crime of genocide'—would have gathered after the War and established
> a sovereign state in any part of the world. It seems to us that no principle of
> international law could have denied the new state the natural power to put
> on trial all those killers of their people who fell into their hands."[85]

The judges' thought experiment reflected the court's view of Roma as victims of a similar crime to the one Jews experienced during the war. This was
clearly not the result of the prosecution's efforts, which faltered. Although the

court convicted Eichmann for crimes against humanity for the deportation of "Gypsies," it noted that the prosecution did not prove that Eichmann knew of their fate.[86] Hannah Arendt seized upon this point in her famous report on the trial in *Eichmann in Jerusalem*. She contended that the mass murder of Roma was "common knowledge" and also that Eichmann had admitted his involvement in the Romani Holocaust in interrogations, and concluded, "He was guilty of their extermination in exactly the same way he was guilty of the extermination of the Jews."[87] Not only did Arendt overstate her claim that Eichmann had admitted his involvement, she also missed the novelty that an Israeli court had declared the murder of Roma a parallel crime. At the same time, although the court acknowledged the crimes committed against Europe's Roma and invoked Romani demands for justice to legitimize its jurisdiction over the case, it never commented on how the "Gypsy survivors" they referenced might have felt about the proceedings.

The absence of Romani witnesses and narratives during these proceedings alone was unremarkable: many groups were not properly represented in Jerusalem. The prosecution also failed to call Jewish survivors from Bulgaria or North Africa as witnesses, as various observers noted. Others complained that a single Greek Jew who spoke at the trial became the voice of all of Sephardi Jewry.[88] It was not the absence of Roma but rather their strange presence that makes the Eichmann trial significant. The Israeli court showed both substantive neglect in regard to the Roma (by failing to prove the case of systematic murder) and interest in an ideological reading of Jewish-Romani relations. Different members of the court in turn portrayed Roma as potentially hostile non-Jews, in the mode of other Europeans who had failed Jews in the diaspora (following Bejlin's logic) or, like the Jews, innocent victims awaiting their national redemption (according to the judges' reasoning).

In all these contradictory ways, the Eichmann trial addressed Romani life and death under Nazism as a coincidental part of its attempts to give a human face to the Jewish genocide. Hausner had not asked Bejlin to take the stand because of Bejlin's ability to support the eleventh count of the indictment. Instead, the prosecutor chose witnesses with an eye to covering different locations, the novelty of each story, and their eloquence, as the historian Hannah Yablonka has noted.[89] Bejlin was articulate and could add something to the prosecution's legal case because of his knowledge of the extermination process, including details about the use of Zyklon B for gassings. Bejlin's status as a well-known epidemiologist had gotten him deployed to the "Gypsy camp," after all. Like all the survivor witnesses they called, the judges were willing to let Bejlin speak at length as long as he did not stray too far from the court's concerns. The Eichmann trial included Jewish survivors' statements about Romani experiences incidentally and by chance. The court's main interest in this case was to offer a forum for Jewish victims to speak, not to understand what Roma experienced.

This left a mixed legacy. In some respects, the Eichmann trial's treatment of the Romani genocide mirrored the International Military Tribunal's treatment of the Jewish genocide. In both cases, the court considered the fact as proven but relegated it to a secondary role in the larger narrative of the trial and diminished its relevance in the final judgement. However, in contrast to Nuremberg, the Eichmann trial did not leave a documentary trail for researchers. Historians of Romani history have found no reason to mine the court records for useful information.

Yet what the trial lacked in substance it made up for in being a replicable model of justice. Romani survivors found many of the images emanating from Jerusalem to be convincing: the focus on a single defendant who was the main culprit of a singular crime tried by those who claimed to speak for the victims fascinated many survivors. Romani activists who wanted to imagine what true justice looks like referred to the Eichmann trial later. So did individual Roma and Sinti who demanded criminal prosecution of those who harmed them. As one Romani survivor in Würzburg argued in a letter accusing a Bavarian police officer of complicity in deportations: "What Eichmann was for the Jews in the Third Reich, Blüm was for the Gypsies who lived in Unterfranken and Würzburg."[90] Paradoxically, a trial that offered no new information on the Romani genocide and featured mostly disparaging testimony about Sinti and Roma made it easier for Romani survivors to explain the type of justice they wanted to achieve.

The Frankfurt Auschwitz Trial and the Paradoxes of Witnessing

Just before Ben Gurion ordered Eichmann's abduction, a new wave of investigations in Germany produced a treasure trove of information on the history of the Jewish Holocaust and, to a lesser degree, the Romani Holocaust. The sheer number of West German investigations into killings from different types of German units and authorities across Europe, the mass of witness testimony these inquiries produced, the prosecutors' careful documentation, and the effective indexing of information distinguish them as sources for the global study of genocide. Much of what we know about the Holocaust, and in particular, the history of the various state organs that executed and initiated murderous policies on the ground, comes from these efforts, directed after 1958 by a central coordinating body, the Central Office of the German Justice Ministries for the Investigation of National Socialist Crimes of Violence.[91]

These consequential investigations and trials would have made little sense to people like Maximoff. German lawmakers and legal practitioners, wary of retroactively applying statutes to crimes, had individuals stand trial for murder or accomplice murder based on the German penal code. Prosecutors had to prove that lethal consequences were the result of a particular individual's intentional heinous act performed "to satisfy their sexual desire, out of greed or other base motives, maliciously or treacherously."[92] This emphasis on the subjective motives of individuals outside the larger apparatus of murder had somewhat paradoxical effects.[93] Prosecutors had a greater chance to obtain convictions if the accused had acted independently rather than implemented the larger plan for genocide that prosecutors had established at Nuremberg. Not only did courts find few opportunities to reflect on the larger crime, but prosecutors also pounced on any scrap of evidence suggesting that there had been no higher orders. One investigation into the two leading figures of the Reichskommissariat Ostland who had given orders to shoot Jews and Roma, for example, began in 1967 after prosecutors discovered in a Lithuanian book that they could not match these local commanders' directives to instructions from Berlin.[94] If these officers had acted according to their own malicious intent, that would legitimize a murder trial according to the German penal code. Consequently, neither the Jewish nor the Romani Holocaust were the central subject of German trials, even though both Jewish and Romani victims could stand at the center of proceedings, as happened in the Frankfurt Auschwitz trial.

The Frankfurt investigation's starting point was a series of accusations by a former Auschwitz prisoner named Adolph Rögner, an exceedingly unlikely person to have launched a trial. Rögner was in Auschwitz because the Nazis considered him a habitual criminal, so he did not profit from the postwar camaraderie that political prisoners and Jewish prisoners experienced. Indeed, most political and Jewish victims during and after the Nazi period kept their distance from those detained in concentration camps as "criminals" and were happy to see them excluded from associations of former prisoners.[95] Rögner's postwar life did nothing to aid his integration into victim communities. At the time of his first encounter with prosecutors, he was serving jail time once again—in Hohenasperg prison, no less, which the Nazis had used since 1940 to house Sinti and Roma before their deportation to the east. He also spent most of the early 1960s in a psychiatric hospital.[96] Having deemed him unreliable, prosecutors did not call Rögner as a witness during the trial that he had set in motion.[97]

It was nonetheless Rögner's 1958 letter to German prosecutors and the International Auschwitz Committee in Vienna informing them of the crimes the SS-captain Wilhelm Boger had committed in Auschwitz that initiated the largest German postwar trial to deal with Nazi atrocities. Rögner's original deposition included the accusation that Boger had killed two Romani prisoners who refused to enter the small crematorium in Auschwitz's main camp together with fifty other Roma and Sinti.[98] Rögner's statements inspired prosecutors to seek out new witnesses, including Romani survivors, to learn more about the fate of these prisoners. Although prosecutors were never able to build a case based directly on Rögner's statements, their subsequent investigations led to new accusations that made their way into the indictment. Among these were accusations leveled at another SS-officer, Franz Hoffmann, for murdering Romani prisoners while he was head of the "Gypsy camp" and for killing an unnamed Romani prisoner with a bottle.[99] The court eventually deemed Hoffmann guilty of premediated and malicious murder in these incidents.[100]

The early emphasis in investigations on the murder of Sinti and Roma left traces in the indictment. The long historical section on the systematic killing of Jews and the function of Auschwitz, written with help from Hans Buchheim, Martin Broszat, and Helmut Krausnick of Munich's Institute for Contemporary History, offered more detail than any previous trial document on the Romani genocide.[101] Their expert opinions, published later in the two-volume *The Anatomy of the SS State*, is today remembered as a groundbreaking description of the concentration camp bureaucracy and the Holocaust.[102] Yet, given the scarcity of information available on the Romani genocide, their survey of the Romani fate in Auschwitz also set new standards.[103] Prosecutors declared in their indictment that Jews and Gypsies were the main groups the Nazis had classified as "inferior races" and that "the largest part of imprisoned Gypsies died in the camps by the end of the war, especially in Auschwitz-Birkenau." [104]

This attention to Romani victimhood in the indictment did not, however, translate into a larger role for Romani witnesses. We can see this in the prosecutors' chapter on the destruction of the "Gypsy camp."[105] Prosecutors relied mainly on the memoirs of Auschwitz's commander Rudolf Höß and, once again, the Jewish survivor Aron Bejlin's testimony to support their interpretation.[106] Romani witnesses did appear in the indictment, but only to prove crimes against individual prisoners and not in the historical sections that explained the broader context of Nazi genocidal policies.[107]

The largest group of witnesses to shape the narrative offered in court and by the press were former political prisoners. They had the best knowledge of the camp because they frequently held supervisory functions there, had the best chances of survival and the most robust networks after the war, and were the earliest group to lobby for a major trial against Auschwitz camp officials.[108] Some also had an intimate familiarity with the "Gypsy camp," such as the former prisoner head of BIIe, Hermann Diamanski.[109] Yet no one was as influential as Hermann Langbein, who served as the secretary of the International Auschwitz Committee until 1959. Although prosecutors considered him a gadfly for prompting them to take Rögner seriously, Langbein was also a longstanding advocate for Romani rights and compensation, as we have seen.[110] An important witness on conditions in the camp during trials, he also prepared others for their testimonies and convinced disillusioned survivors to speak in court.[111] Although he did not refer prosecutors to Romani witnesses directly, Langbein facilitated the testimonies of other political prisoners with knowledge of the "Gypsy camp," some of whom in turn named Romani survivors in their depositions.

Despite such efforts, Jews' accounts of Auschwitz-Birkenau disproportionately influenced public perceptions of the fate of Romani prisoners. This happened because of the profound distrust that prosecutors and much of the postwar West German public felt toward political prisoners. In particular, camp survivor organizations with large memberships in Eastern Europe were dominated by communists who conducted regular purges of their organizations. Langbein was among their victims: after he had dared to criticize the Soviet invasion of Hungary, the Eastern European representatives who dominated the International Auschwitz Committee ousted him as secretary in 1959.[112] Although German prosecutors felt compelled to rely on contacts with these survivor associations to identify witnesses in Poland and arrange for their exit visas, they were never comfortable doing so. By contrast, they had less conflicted interactions with Jewish organizations and Jewish survivors whom they did not associate with a political enemy. Indeed, even when they perceived the demands of Jewish associations as an imposition, Frankfurt prosecutors fostered close ties with organizations such as the World Jewish Congress and its Institute of Jewish Affairs.[113]

A second factor that accounts for the significant role of Jewish perspectives in depictions of the "Gypsy camp" was the appearance of a memoir by Lucie Adelsberger, another Jewish physician in BIIe, which swiftly became the most influential published narrative about Auschwitz's "Gypsy camp." Like Bejlin, Adelsberger worked in BIIe and knew Roma from the infirmary. Although her 1956 German-language account of her time in Auschwitz was not successful with general readers, prosecutors and survivors circulated it among themselves as a particularly revealing testimony.[114] Langbein, for example, received the volume as a present in 1958 from Eva Reichmann, the head of the Wiener Library's research division, and in turn recommended it to the numerous survivors and journalists who contacted him with questions about Romanies in Auschwitz.[115] The Frankfurt court also sought to learn more about Adelsberger's experiences with Roma in Auschwitz and arranged to have her interviewed through the German General Consul in New York, where she lived after the war.[116] It was not her deposition but her written testimony that mattered, however. Even though her name did not appear prominently in the proceedings, Adelsberger's narrative influenced prosecutors and witnesses because it was a book that could be shared, rather than a deposition available only to prosecutors, defense lawyers, and accused.[117]

The eventual experience of witnessing in court and the role their testimony played for the framing of Nazi crimes was similar in many respects for Jews and Roma. Since German courts could only prosecute Nazi perpetrators under regular murder statutes, the court relied on precise testimonies about individual, extraordinary killings rather than the regular machinery of death in operation at Auschwitz.[118] Testimonies thus served a different role than they had in Jerusalem: in the Eichmann trial, Israeli prosecutors called witnesses to give a human face to the Jewish Holocaust, whereas in Frankfurt, prosecutors and lawyers needed these personal details to get a conviction.

Survivors of Auschwitz who testified—regardless of the reasons for their persecution—were often disheartened by their experience in the courtroom. Defenders and judges regularly argued that it was not only contradictions in an account's details that might make a testimony unreliable but also any expression of emotions. Exposed to such onerous expectations and the regular pressures of a criminal trial, witnesses in Frankfurt spoke about their own experiences only to have defenders and judges drag them into callous cross-examinations that cast doubt on many of their statements. Witnesses also had to accept that the court's interest in the sadism of individual SS men overshadowed a broader reckoning with Nazism's genocidal legacy. Jewish and Romani survivors' experiences were similar in all these regards.

Yet Romani witnesses also struggled with different and additional challenges. Most importantly, fewer Romanies were present during the proceedings. Only four spoke in the trial, while two others had their depositions read because they could not appear in person. This was in contrast to the eighty-eight Jewish witnesses called by the court.[119] This imbalance was compounded after each of the six Romani depositions failed for different reasons, to the point that none made much of an impression on the court or the public. One Romani witness, Bruno Stein, had trouble explaining how he knew the name of an accused he believed to have seen selecting Jewish prisoners at the ramp. In his case, the court set unrealistic standards when it presumed that prisoners could remember who had first pointed out the name of an SS officer to them two decades earlier.[120] Another Romani witness, Paul Morgenstern, spent much of his testimony in silence, waiting for the court to decide whether it would allow questions from an attorney for a joint plaintiff about sterilizations in Ravensbrück.[121] After multiple misunderstandings and discussions about the permissibility of surprise evidence regarding crimes committed in other camps, Morgenstern was able to speak briefly on the subject in question. Morgenstern's testimony thus became the occasion to clarify a fundamental procedural decision that might have been resolved much earlier, rather than on the sixty-sixth day of the trial. His testimony on the Nazis' forced sterilizations of Romani prisoners entered the public record, but only at the price of a harrowing day in court.

The most vexing issue for Romani witnesses, however, concerned pretrial investigations. Witnesses often had to correct statements recorded by the special investigative unit of the criminal police responsible for collecting initial depositions. In the cases of two Romani survivors, Waldemar Schröder and Max Friedrich, the protocols proved utterly inadequate. Both witnesses, who were related by marriage and lived at the same address, were interrogated together in the same room at a police station four years earlier. The investigating police officer apparently chatted informally with both men together and then created separate depositions for each of them to sign.[122] Each deposition ended up as a confused mix of the two testimonies. The officer even accidentally attributed several identical sentences to both witnesses. During the cross examination of the two witnesses the court struggled to figure out who said what.

The resulting exchanges in court were embarrassing to state authorities and humiliating to survivors. In the end, neither witness could testify on the issue that had brought them to the witness stand. Both clarified in court that they did not personally see the accused SS-officer Franz Hofmann forcing prisoners to perform so-called "Sport," a euphemism for a form of lethal collective torture.[123] These difficulties aggravated one of the two witnesses, Max

Friedrich, who became increasingly upset as lawyers and judges asked him to address what turned out to be his relative's observations instead of inquiring about his own experiences. Court audio recordings register his growing agitation. Distressing to the witness, the testimony was also useless from a legal standpoint. The sloppy pretrial investigation had turned Friedrich into a witness whose testimony seemed full of contradictions.

It is not difficult to imagine how frustrating these experiences must have been. Romani survivors regularly faced suspicions that they were unreliable witnesses and also remained the target of heavy, coercive policing in West Germany after the war. While Jewish witnesses also experienced unfriendly cross-examinations, most lived outside of the court's jurisdiction and did not endure ongoing persecution by the state. Romani witnesses were compelled by law to speak about their past—like all other witnesses within the court's jurisdiction—only to see that the police who still systematically surveilled them wrote up reports that rendered their testimony useless.[124]

The fact that Roma testified at the Frankfurt Auschwitz trial has largely been forgotten.[125] They apparently did not make much of an impression at the time either. News reports rarely mentioned the "Gypsy camp" in Auschwitz and, when they did, they focused on the testimonies of more prominent non-Romani witnesses, such as Hermann Langbein and Hermann Diamanski.[126]

By a twist of fate, however, Friedrich's appearance in court ended up having a lasting effect on our knowledge of the Frankfurt Auschwitz trial. His testimony became the subject of debates in a trial nearly three decades later. In 1988, during the proceedings against Ernst August König, a block leader in the Auschwitz "Gypsy camp," the defense asked the court to admit Friedrich's recorded testimony as evidence.[127] König's lawyer, Georg Bürger, hoped to demonstrate that Friedrich was contradicting himself in his testimonies over the years.[128] The state attorney who tried to get a conviction for König, by contrast, argued that the incompetence of his predecessors made these testimonies useless and that any contradictions were thus irrelevant.[129] This controversy over the reliability of Friedrich's testimony inadvertently led to one of the greatest breakthroughs in research on postwar Holocaust trials. In the mid-1980s, audio recordings from the Frankfurt Auschwitz trial remained hidden away in a storage room in the prosecutor's office. The court's request put in motion a series of inquiries about the tapes, which the president of the district court in Frankfurt am Main eventually transferred to the central state archives of Hesse in April 1989. Friedrich's largely inconclusive testimony—which never touches on König—is the reason scholars today have unfettered access to audio recordings of 430 hours of Frankfurt trial proceedings, including the statements from no less than 318 witnesses.[130] The searing and immaterial testimony of a German Sinto now allows historians and anyone in the wider public to listen to the proceedings of Germany's largest Holocaust trial.

Knowledge Production:
From Criminal Courts to Civil Litigation

The Nuremberg trial, the Eichmann trial, and the Frankfurt Auschwitz trial each represented moments of promise and disappointment for Jews and Roma. For the victims of Nazi racial persecution, the International Military Tribunal raised hopes that the victorious powers would be able to deliver justice in a form that acknowledged the specific policies aimed at them. Compared to Romani victims who found their case ignored, Jewish victims could hear crimes against them discussed at length—even if they were subsumed under other crimes. More importantly, US prosecutors published trial material in a format that laid the groundwork for future research on the Jewish Holocaust and supplied some of the basic building blocks for scholarship on the Romani Holocaust. Yet, the unequal documentation of the two genocides and the tendency to explain mass murder as a premeditated plan expressed in the Nazis' ideological statements since the early 1920s prejudiced the handling of survivor claims. Maximoff demanded clarity about the persecution of Romanies during the war from an international tribunal. Yet, the only such trial on Nazi crimes that ever took place merely highlighted the unsettled origins, intention, and chronology of the Romani genocide in comparison to the Jewish one.

The Eichmann trial promised a new form of national justice, organized by those who claimed to speak for the victims. It created the paradigm for a victim-centered Holocaust and genocide trial that few other courts could deliver. While it technically should have dealt with crimes against humanity committed against Roma, it did so in a highly circumscribed and limited way. The courtroom proceedings had little to offer to Romani survivors. Although prosecutors successfully used documentary evidence to show that Eichmann organized the deportation of Austrian Roma and Sinti, they made no effort to prove the Nazis' genocidal plans. Witness testimony, which was more central for the reconstruction of historical context than in any previous trial, merely underlined the tensions between Jews and Roma that Nazi camp administrators had purposefully used, and exacerbated, to manage their prisoners.

Romani activists were nevertheless inspired by the political logic of Jewish efforts at redress.[131] In 1961, when Ionel Rotaru, a Romani activist who styled himself king of the "Gypsies," announced his plans to travel from France to the trial in Jerusalem, he expressed his fascination with the idea of such proceedings.[132] The early period of international Romani activism, which culminated in the first World Romani Congress in London in 1971, began around the time of the Eichmann trial. When Romani activists organized across borders to demand compensation and sought dignified ways of articulating their past suffering, they had in mind the kind of justice imagined in the Jerusalem court's hypothetical formulation. The Eichmann trial was of interest to Romani activists because they embraced it as a model for a genocide trial dominated by narratives of victims, not because of anything individuals said in the courtroom.

The Frankfurt trial represented attempts by Nazi Germany's successor state to use regular criminal proceedings to try individuals who had gone beyond the call of duty to implement the regime's genocidal policies. It was neither an attempt at an all-encompassing reckoning with the war's darkest moments (as Nuremberg was), nor an attempt to imagine a new victim-centered justice (like the Eichmann trial). Although Jewish narratives of suffering were omnipresent at the trial, the "centrality of the Jewish dimension of the mass murder at Auschwitz did not emerge with any great clarity," in the words of historian Devin Pendas.[133] Something similar could be said for the Romani dimension, only here personal narratives were even more effectively silenced by the court's treatment of witnesses.

With its focus on a single camp that was a central location for the internment and murder of Jews and Roma, the Frankfurt trial reinforced the impression that crimes against Roma were similar in some respects to those committed against Jews, yet juxtapositions of the two also highlighted their differences. We can see this in the framing of the testimony of a Romani witness who did not appear in court. Elisabeth Guttenberger gave a deposition under oath that had to be read at the trial because she was unable to attend for health reasons. Her account of her time as a Romani prisoner who worked as a registry clerk nevertheless reached a wider audience than the recollections of other Romani witnesses, thanks to Langbein. He included a version of her trial account in a collection of testimonies that he published as a companion volume to the trial in 1967.[134] Guttenberger also had the opportunity to speak in a feature that Langbein arranged for German radio in 1962.[135] His introductory statement to the radio segment underlines what he thought people knew about Auschwitz from the Eichmann and Frankfurt trials: "Most victims in Auschwitz were Jews [...] Yet, they were not the only ones whom Hitler destroyed for 'racial reasons.'"[136] This juxtaposition, which gave Langbein an opening to introduce a lesser-known victim group, quickly devolved into an unfavorable comparison. After Guttenberger's account of her arrest and deportation, the moderator continued: "The Gypsies were treated preferentially in Auschwitz." Although his point of comparison in this problematic statement remained implicit, it is clear that Langbein sought to measure Romanies' suffering against that of Jewish victims, whose story had been told at greater length at both trials.[137]

While states did not organize other international or Eichmann-style national tribunals for Nazi crimes, trials under German law (and the national laws of other European states) remained a distinct possibility. It was the only justice in a criminal court that Romani victims and their families could realistically achieve. After decades of filing complaints against individual police officers and SS guards, the Romani rights movement finally succeeded in bringing one Auschwitz guard to justice in the late 1980s—Ernst August König, whose trial led to the recovery of the Frankfurt trial tapes.[138] The trial was a success in the sense that the accused was convicted with heavy involvement from the largest German Romani organization, the Central Council for German Sinti and Roma, which supported witnesses. Yet, much like all the trials that took place after the first Frankfurt Auschwitz trial, the König trial garnered much less attention. The progress toward the recognition of the Romani genocide that observers saw in the trial was an expression of perceptions that had already begun to shift. The larger conceptualization of the crime, in the court and in the press, was symptomatic of a slowly changing understanding of the Romani genocide, which the German government officially acknowledged in 1982.

The most transformative legal innovation occurred in a field that Maximoff never could have imagined. Rather than criminal trials, civil litigation gave Jewish and Romani survivors access to new types of justice and compensation shortly after the König trial. Starting with three class action lawsuits filed in New York federal courts against Swiss banks in 1997, lawyers used the idiosyncrasies of the US legal system to bring various European corporations to justice.[139] The collective structure of these suits shaped the information gathered as well as which categories of individuals would qualify as victims. Given their broad scope, these suits allowed law offices to hire experts—such as historians—to collect evidence beyond the abilities of individuals.[140] Incentivized to represent the largest number of people possible, the lawyers who worked on the suits against the Swiss banks and, later, German industry included Romani victims in settlements with special funds set aside for them as part of a larger category of "victims or targets of Nazi persecution."[141]

Roma also found representation in the 1999 fairness hearing where the court confirmed the settlement. "We are very happy to know that this time, nobody forgot about us," stated Roman Kwiatkowski of the Association of Polish Roma.[142] Settlements additionally covered the opening of archives and convinced twenty-four European governments to install commissions to investigate the history of their country under Nazism, including national complicity in Nazi crimes.[143] Some of these, such as the Austrian Historians' Commission and the Wiesel Commission on the Holocaust in Romania, also published authoritative reports on the persecution, expropriation, exploitation, and mass murder of Roma.[144]

This final stage proved to be a brief window of opportunity in the search for legal redress. US courts opened the possibility of such litigation through its Alien Tort Statute with landmark decisions in 1980 and 1995, and subsequently closed it when the Supreme Court restricted the right to sue foreign private companies in 2013.[145] This does not preclude the use of alternative mechanisms, such as litigation in European courts, or other legal threats to those who profited from the property or labor of Nazism's racialized victim groups.[146] Especially regarding looted art, litigation has not ended. The most effective tool to seek a remedy for Nazi crimes is nevertheless weakened. In this sense, it resembles the even briefer moment, reflected in Maximoff's essay, when international criminal justice seemed possible for victims of Nazi genocides.

The outcome of that final—fourth—mode of justice also reminds us of an insight that emerged from the three major criminals discussed above: even where states create new possibilities to address historical injustices, the focus on one victim group does not always translate easily into advantages for others. The implementation of the settlements that allotted funds to specific categories of Romani victims often required documentation that Roma were less likely to have than other claimants. As a result, the celebration of their inclusion in settlements soon gave way to resentment over the inability to access promised funds. As in the past, administrative demands for documentation disadvantaged Roma, much as it would other populations who had historical reasons to avoid heavy policing and bureaucratic surveillance.[147] Those who fail to account for the relations between different types of victims and the fundamental differences in their condition can inadvertently create new injustice in their own quest for justice.

5

Jewish Institutions and the Rise of Romani Holocaust Scholarship

WHEN EARLY ROMANI RIGHTS organizations began their work, evidence of Nazi crimes committed against them would have been invaluable, yet reliable information was in short supply. In 1960, the year before the Eichmann trial, the Central Committee of Gypsies discovered this after they sought help from the principal academic institution in Germany that dealt with the history of Nazism. Having written to the Institute for Contemporary History in Munich to ask for numbers of victims, members of the committee found that the institute had very little to offer. Siegfried Fauck, who answered from Munich, struggled to identify reputable literature on the subject.[1] Aside from the opinion his colleague Hans Buchheim had written on a single episode in the longer history of the Romani Holocaust, Fauck relied mainly on numbers he found in Dora Yates's short 1949 article for *Commentary* and Joseph Tenenbaum's 1956 survey history *Race and Reich*.[2] Fauck may have missed some works, such as Léon Poliakov's *Harvest of Hate*, but most scholarly publications—including Poliakov's—only included a short section on Roma in any case.[3] There was little anyone could find with a subject heading search, even in well-stocked research libraries.

State offices were similarly eager for information. Authorities in charge of compensation for victims of Nazism regularly exchanged paperwork on the subject with authorities in other states dealing with related matters. One file in particular made the rounds in 1959. The compensation authority for the West German state of Schleswig-Holstein sent a dossier to fourteen other official institutions, including the finance administrations of other West German states and the foreign ministry, on the fate of the Sinti and Roma deported from Germany to occupied Poland in May 1940.[4] The office had interviewed multiple victim witnesses and collected testimonies, Romani petitions to Nazi authorities, and even some personal letters exchanged between German Sinti during the war to demonstrate that the state had no obligation to pay the deportees as individuals who had suffered racial persecution. The pièce de résistance was the 1950 testimony of a German Sinto who allegedly stated under oath that he had reported about his experiences in Poland to avert illegitimate claims for compensation by other Romani victims. For historians, such explanations of witnesses' motives immediately raise a red flag, since they suspiciously—and conveniently—attribute administrators' biased ideas about Romani dishonesty to a Romani victim. Yet, administrators who closely scrutinized every piece of evidence from applicants tended to treat such complicated material as validation for their position that the state should reject applications for compensation from Sinti and Roma deported in 1940.

Such a prejudiced approach to Romani claims is typical of the fraught relationship between Romanies and the state in the years following the war. Still, the immense effort that German civil servants invested in supporting their case is surprising. Collecting a multitude of sources from different locations, bureaucrats essentially performed the work of historians. The responsible compensation officer in Schleswig-Holstein with the fitting last name Zornig ("angry" in German) showed extraordinary initiative in his attempts to disseminate his dossier across the country so as to ensure that no West German state would pay compensation in similar cases.[5] The file eventually made its way to the International Tracing Service and, from there, to Belgium, where the administration for war compensation filed it away as one of their only documents on Romani victims.[6] In an information desert, clearly marked files with a biased selection of testimonies could assume exaggerated importance for administrators searching for guidance.[7] Other documents lay dormant in poorly indexed files at state archives, but Zornig's dossier formed a significant part of how the German bureaucracy "remembered" what it did to its Romani citizens.

Over the next fifteen years, German Sinti and Roma as well as international Romani activists would seek allies in their quest to overturn European states' control of information. To do so, they relied on people who had acquired substantial non-state expertise on the subject: Jewish survivor historians and archivists who had found positions at various institutions dedicated to reckoning with the Nazi past. The labor of these individuals together with the work of Romani activists eventually led to the publication of the first comprehensive book on the Romani Holocaust in 1972, Donald Kenrick and Gratton Puxon's *The Destiny of Europe's Gypsies.*

The Jewish lawyers, scholars, and public figures at the center of this chapter initiated a slow shift in public and scholarly perceptions of the Romani Holocaust at a moment when knowledge of the Jewish Holocaust was still limited. Even as various states actively undermined the efforts of Romani activists to gain recognition of their victimhood, these Jewish individuals worked to bring to light the stories of the Holocaust's Romani victims. Yet, despite all that they were up against, they did not labor alone. Their work was supported by a number of close-knit networks that in turn relied on various Jewish and Jewish-led institutions. It was this broader constellation that allowed a small group of professionals and public intellectuals to transform our narratives about the Nazi genocide, making their history not only one of individual initiatives, but also of the infrastructure and resources people need to rewrite history successfully.

Kurt May and the United Restitution Organization

Across Europe, Romani survivors' demands for recognition took different forms, each inflected by the political climate in a particular country, national narratives of complicity and heroism, and bureaucratic legacies. Certificates conferring some protected status for racial and political persecution under Nazism or resistance activity were largely national issues, although international organizations such as the International Tracing Service often supplied crucial documentation. Restitution, compensation payments, and pensions depended both on national legislation and agreements between different countries and West Germany, as the internationally recognized successor state to Nazi Germany. Such agreements sometimes forced victims of Nazism who lived outside of Germany to apply for compensation to their postwar states, which would fund awards from German reparations payments.

In theory, victims or their kin had to apply as individuals to receive compensation for stolen property, lost income, or unlawful imprisonment. They had to fill out forms; find physicians who would attest to health issues; solicit affidavits from fellow persecutees; collect documentation on property, incarceration, and personal status; and submit their file at an office responsible for compensation or restitution payments.[8] Many did not wish to spend weeks or months compiling documents about a painful past for payments that observers might perceive as absolution for the perpetrators.[9] Even those who were well-versed in dealing with state agencies and willing to subject themselves to such a procedure often found it difficult to prepare the necessary paperwork without legal aid. Confusing categories, deadlines, and procedures over-whelmed individual victims acting on their own.

Adding to survivors' frustrations, a claim's success often depended on cir-cumstances that had little to do with an individual's experience during Nazism. Driven by Cold War politics, West Germany refused to make payments across the Iron Curtain, for example.[10] Such policies affected Romani victims more than Jews. Since most Romani survivors—and most individuals forced into German slave labor programs—lived in Eastern Bloc countries, they were in-eligible for payments according to West Germany's Cold War-inspired poli-cies. The majority of potential Jewish claimants, by contrast, lived in the United States, Israel, Great Britain, or France. As a result of these and similar limitations, individuals who had been interned in the same camp or ghetto might receive very different forms of compensation, or no compensation at all. One's place of residency before, during, and after the war, the type of in-carceration, and the exact wording and origin of orders leading to persecution affected the particular payments people could claim.

That last criterion—the wording and origin of orders—derailed many Ro-mani applications for compensation in the 1950s. German compensation law required proof that the Nazis had acted according to a particular set of motives—political or racial in nature—to qualify for payments for unjust in-carceration, loss of economic opportunities, and lost income. Courts generally accepted that Roma experienced racial persecution after February 1943 when the Nazis started rounding up European Romanies and deporting them to Auschwitz-Birkenau. Administrators and courts disagreed on the nature of policies initiated by municipalities or articulated as anticrime measures before that date, however. Courts regularly challenged claims that earlier instances of deportations or imprisonment could be deemed racial persecution, including the forced removal of German Sinti and Roma to occupied Poland in May 1940, an act which brought many of its victims to Labor Camp Bełżec.

In landmark decisions on January 7, 1956, the Federal Court of Justice, West Germany's highest court of appeal for criminal and private law, overturned lower courts that regarded these earlier deportations as racially motivated. Ruling on two independent cases concerning a Romani man from Trier and a Romani woman from Koblenz, both of whom had been deported via Cologne in May 1940, the court issued nearly identical decisions. Although the Federal Court of Justice recognized that these deportations were unlawful, the justices insisted that they had resulted from military and policing considerations, not racializa-tion. They thus did not fulfill the requirements of paragraph 1 of German compensation law, which defined victims of Nazi persecution as political enemies of the regime or individuals persecuted "for reasons of race, faith, or worldview."[11] To review the eligibility of a large class of Romani claimants, the court not only reconstructed the regime's inner motivations but also ended up legitimizing the state's actions as rational, albeit excessive. The court viewed as a fact that "Gypsies" were "asocial" and that authorities could thus reasonably "approach the solution to the Gypsy Question from the essence of their race." According to the court's judgement, racial stereotyping based on policing efforts did not amount to persecution based on race; only if the original motive lay purely in theories of "racial biological insights" could claimants get compensation.[12]

A selective interpretation of anti-Jewish measures might have led to similar conclusions, yet the court was not eager to pursue its argument in that direction. Instead, it played the two victim groups against each other, describing the deportation, ghettoization, and murder of Jews as the paradigm for racial persecution as covered by paragraph 1 of German compensation law. The court noted that these early deportations spared some "Gypsies" and asked the public to consider that "the old and fragile and people with property had not been excluded in the deportation of Jews." These exclusions, the court determined, must mean that racial considerations were not operative in the Romani case. It was a contrived argument—any racist policy could first affect certain subgroups of a racially defined group. The contrast drawn to measures targeting Jews was also historically inaccurate. At various points, the Nazis selected Jews according to criteria such as their ability to work, which did not change the fact that all Jews, eventually, were marked for death.[13]

To some degree, this misinterpretation was the result of the very success of people like Robinson and the prosecutors' case at Nuremberg. The International Military Tribunal's endorsement of an intentionalist approach implied that "racial persecution" left an abundant record of political statements about intentions. Although West German compensation law did not spell out this assumption, the demand that others be measured against the yardstick of the experiences of Jews, the only other group in the category of racial persecutee, was met with an expectation that claimants could present comparable evidence for a master plan, and also that they could demonstrate each measure's relationship to that plan.

It took someone with Lemkin's sense of solidarity and Robinson's institutional connections to overturn these decisions. The Jewish lawyer Kurt May embodied both qualities. Although he had no known personal history of interactions with Roma, like Lemkin, he experienced their postwar treatment

FIGURE 5.1. Kurt May during World War One. Reproduced with permission from Tom Gross.

as an affront. Like Robinson, he formed part of the large number of legal experts who shaped Jewish postwar politics and our understanding of Nazism's historical record. A decorated veteran of World War One, May had worked as a lawyer at an appeals court in Jena until 1933, when, as a Jew, he was debarred and forced into emigration.[14] He fled to Palestine and opened Jerusalem's largest fashion store together with his brother.[15] In 1948, he returned to Germany to join the United Restitution Organization (URO) and became director of its Frankfurt Central Office in 1955.[16]

May's work would have been much less effective without that organizational base. The URO began as a cash-strapped legal aid organization that sought to help Jewish survivors make claims in German courts. Offering their support to applicants outside of Germany, they allowed Jews who had suffered under Nazism to demand restitution of property and compensation by simplifying the process for them, and without turning to non-Jewish German lawyers in the process. By the mid-1950s, the URO had built up a formidable presence—with May as its driving force and the key figure in its ground operations in Germany. In 1958, the organization had 1,026 full-time and 106 part-time employees, including 223 registered lawyers, and was managing 220,000 pending cases.[17] One historian has described the URO as the "brain-trust" that made possible other organizations' lobbying efforts.[18] Various individuals shared May's commitment to changing the discriminatory treatment of Sinti and Roma, but none could muster the professional apparatus he had at his disposal.

These efforts relied on legal and historical information, and the ability to bring together both realms of knowledge. The URO's extended foray into historical research began because of an obstacle in German law for Jewish claimants persecuted by regimes allied with Nazi Germany. West German compensation law determined that persecutes who were otherwise deemed eligible could receive payments for unlawful imprisonment by a foreign state as long as the Nazi government had initiated their arrest.[19] This put an incredible burden on courts to make a factual determination as to whether the German state was directly culpable for imprisonment in places such as Romania, Hungary, or Vichy-controlled Algeria. To establish their eligibility, Jews and other victims from these regions had to demonstrate not only that they had been deported at a particular time but also that the German state was involved. Before the issue was settled in the 1960s, whether they filed their claims with a court that was willing to accept German influence or not came down to luck. If they were unlucky, they would need to offer historical documentation that individuals rarely could supply. Most survivors did not have access to an academic library, let alone archival sources dealing with German and Axis governments' communications about their handling of Jews.

This was where institutions with resources to pay lawyers and historians came into the picture. The URO made a concerted effort to supply German courts with the necessary documents.[20] It could do what individuals could not: send teams to German, British, and US archives to search for historical evidence.[21] These efforts culminated in four volumes of German documents that demonstrated that the German state instigated the imprisonment of Jews across Europe and North Africa.[22] The URO's research helped bring about more consistent jurisprudence and prepared a legislative response that would settle the matter. In 1965, the German parliament amended the law and offered clear guidance on historical cases to be included. It determined that

FIGURE 5.2. Kurt May, director of the United Restitution Organization. Reproduced with permission from Tom Gross.

the German state considered all imprisonment due to racial criteria in Bulgaria, Romania, and Hungary after April 6, 1941 to have occurred at the instigation of German authorities. A combination of legal and historical work smoothed the way for compensation payments for a large number of European Jews.

None of this directly affected Roma, and yet the URO's approach to Jewish claims would fundamentally alter their chances of receiving compensation. The same network of people who created new source editions on the persecution of Jews and laid the foundation for new court rulings on Nazi-allied regimes soon turned to the most vexing challenge for German Romanies. The crucial figure at the center of these efforts was May, who used the URO's resources as well as his personal connections to change the German judiciary's practices.[23]

In his efforts to secure compensation for Romanies, May first turned to a historian at the Munich Institute for Contemporary History, Hans Buchheim. Founded as an independent research center in 1950 to investigate the history of Nazism, the institute produced an enormous number of expert opinions. In 1957, the institute advertised that it drafted approximately 150 responses to court requests for information each year.[24] Whereas the institute's scholars dedicated their academic research to the demise of the Weimar Republic, the causes of Germany's descent into Nazism, and German resistance, in their court opinions they frequently discussed the persecution of Jews.[25] Buchheim, an expert on the SS and its role in the state, was among the most prolific authors of these commissioned texts.[26] Hence, when he approached Buchheim, May was turning to a specialist who was already working at the juncture of academic publishing and the law.

It would be a stretch to describe the institute or Buchheim as part of a Jewish network. On the contrary, the exclusively non-Jewish members of the institute were united by their shared commitment to ignore their personal experiences in the Nazi era, whether as soldiers (Buchheim) or as members of the Nazi party (as was the case with longtime directors Helmut Krausnick and Martin Broszat).[27] Some members of the institute, including Buchheim, were also close to the German Secret Service and its leader, Reinhard Gehlen.[28] Gehlen had directed the Wehrmacht's intelligence service in the east during the war and surrounded himself with others who had illustrious careers under Nazism.[29] In short, the institute was a living monument to the paradoxes of German attempts to rebuild a democratic society from the ruins of a racist dictatorship with mass appeal. The institute's scholarly work revealed these same contradictions. Members of the institute emphasized scholarly objectivity to assert a distance from their own history and dismissed as unscientific the publications of Jewish historians such as Léon Poliakov and Gerald Reitlinger. They rejected the notion that Jews, and Jewish survivors in particular, could write a neutral history of the regime given their emotional investment in the topic.[30]

May nevertheless had a working relationship with members of the institute, including Buchheim. Organizations like the URO needed historians at state-funded institutions and the authority that society bestowed on them to make historical pronouncements. Buchheim and his colleagues in turn appreciated the connections abroad that people like May offered.[31] May and Buchheim remained formal with each other throughout their interactions but also found common ground in the endeavor to rectify the unfair treatment of Sinti and Roma by German postwar courts. As May put it in a letter to Buchheim: "It relieves my conscience to know that these Gypsies, who were hunted down by the Nazis, will finally get their right."[32]

Buchheim wrote an essay in response that challenged the Federal Court of Justice's 1956 decisions. Whereas Buchheim's expert opinions were usually responses to requests from the court, he wrote this essay at his own initiative. Aware of the legal stakes and judicial conventions, he argued in meticulous detail why the deportations of Romanies in May 1940 from western Germany to occupied Poland were racially motivated.[33] As a scholar of state bureaucracies, he clarified the distinction between the motivations of politicians and the language of their decrees. The mere fact that the regime did not identify a measure as racial did not preclude a motive grounded in racial science and a racialized understanding of national belonging. Even if early decrees led to the detention of Romanies as alleged "asocials," he argued, this term was deeply problematic considering the Nazis' tendency to lump individuals who did not fit into their vision of an ideal racialized community into that category.

Buchheim's essay allowed lower courts to ignore the Federal Court of Justice's decision, citing new factual evidence. May made sure of this, sending the piece to interested parties, and turning to someone whose opinion carried considerable weight among legal practitioners: he enlisted the help of Franz Calvelli-Adorno.[34] The first cousin of the philosopher Theodor Adorno, Calvelli-Adorno grew up Catholic in a well-off family in Frankfurt am Main. In 1929, he became a judge at the district court in Dortmund but was forced into retirement without benefits after only four years, due to his mother's Jewish background (she was the sister of Theodor Adorno's father). The ministry removed him from his position in July 1933 and denied his application to work as a lawyer.[35] While his children managed to escape to Great Britain on a Kindertransport, he and his wife could not secure emigration documents. He worked as a violinist and did some paralegal work for lawyers in Frankfurt before going into hiding to avoid conscription into forced labor as part of Organisation Todt. After the war, he rejoined the judiciary and rose to the position of presiding judge in Frankfurt's Higher Regional Court in 1951. In this function, Calvelli-Adorno was involved in judgments on Romani compensation and did his part to revise the judiciary's interpretation of historical facts.[36]

In his attempt to administer justice to all claimants of compensation for Nazi crimes, Calvelli-Adorno relied on May's work. He indirectly acknowledged his debts to the organization in a 1965 essay that praised the URO and May for shouldering the responsibility of carrying out unbiased historical research and factual investigations that state authorities were legally obliged to pursue but failed to initiate.[37]

Building on Buchheim's work and—even more decisively—on a collection of documents handed to him by the URO, Calvelli-Adorno published an essay that argued for a revision of the Federal Court of Justice's ruling to deny Roma automatic compensation for persecution experienced before 1943.[38] Even when the higher court had determined that "Gypsies" did not face racial persecution before January 1943, Romani plaintiffs could still try to establish such persecution on an individual basis. As a result, a whole series of courts in Oldenburg, Cologne, Hamburg, and Frankfurt had deemed such persecution a fact, even after the Federal Court of Justice's 1956 ruling. Calvelli-Adorno sought to prove that the materials collected in these lower courts added up to an outright refutation of the Federal Court of Justice's factual claims. Following

Buchheim's opinion, Calvelli-Adorno saw 1938 as a turning point in the racial targeting of Sinti and Roma but insisted that the severity of their persecution could only be explained by the emotional force of fanatical racism. Even when the Nazis had deemed someone to be "asocial," they applied such a term and murdered them with detectable enthusiasm only because the state promoted a racist vision of itself and its enemies. Calvelli-Adorno insisted that in all of these respects Roma were treated like Jews long before 1943. Ghettos where Jews and Romanies suffered next to each other were one example.[39]

In 1962, the Federal Court of Justice accepted compensation for damages from earlier persecutions in individual cases, and in a 1963 decision it followed Calvelli-Adorno when it recognized deportations of Sinti and Roma to Poland in 1940 as partly racially motivated.[40] This assessment allowed administrators to grant Romani claims for measures targeting them before 1943 even if they could not prove that racial motives were the decisive factor. Some appeals courts subsequently emphasized the similarity with the situation for Jews. In a 1964 decision in Schleswig-Holstein, the court underlined the parallels: "Gypsies were discriminated against and put in a similar position as were Jews who wore the Jewish star, when they had to have special Gypsy identity cards or sometimes wore an armband with the letter Z."[41] What is more, the very experience of seeing the murder of Jews in ghettos such as Siedlce must have weighed on them and reinforced their own experience of persecution, according to the judgment.

In a 1965 decision that further resolved the issue, the Federal Court of Justice sided with a Romani claimant who had been stripped of his itinerant trade license in 1938. While maintaining that courts had to evaluate the reasons for persecution, it argued that it was the state's obligation to prove that a Romani claimant was not subject to racial persecution.[42] This came close to a general recognition of their status as racial persecutees, equivalent to the practice in Jewish cases. Legislators recognized this shift when they permitted the resubmission of claims by those persecuted as "Gypsies" between December 8, 1938 and March 1, 1943 in its 1965 revision of compensation laws.[43] Unlike those persecuted as homosexuals or "asocials," Roma now had landmark decisions on their side, which administrators across West Germany generally honored.[44]

The people who made this change possible came from a variety of backgrounds and had diverse personal histories, yet their ability to act effectively depended on relations between Jewish lawyers and Jewish institutions. Although Calvelli-Adorno's influence was among the most visible, the labor that undergirded his contributions often went unacknowledged. This includes the work of Walter Schwarz, the lawyer who created the magazine that published Calvelli-Adorno's essay and printed all new judgements on restitution and compensation with commentary. Like Kurt May, Schwarz had managed to escape to Palestine during the war, where he eventually became a lawyer in Haifa. He returned to Munich as an Israeli citizen and a representative of the Jewish Agency for Israel in 1950 but soon established himself permanently in Germany again. He studied law in Heidelberg and built up a highly successful practice in West Berlin that focused on restitution law. Yet, his influence was even greater as a commentator and editor. His journal *Rechtsprechung zum Wiedergutmachungsrecht* (Jurisprudence Regarding Restitution Law) became the central forum for expert debates on the subject when university-based legal scholarship ignored the topic.[45] Without Schwarz, there would have been no commentary on these judgments and no change in jurisprudence on Sinti and Roma.

The other organization was May's URO, which worked closely with Schwarz. While Schwarz created the forum for a critical review of compensation practices, the URO brought together historians, lawyers, and victim advocates to help claimants individually and collectively. To do this, it built on the precedent set by Jewish associations founded in nineteenth-century Western and Central Europe to lobby for oppressed coreligionists abroad.[46] Such organizations had long drawn on historical knowledge to make their arguments. From the campaigns for the rights of Jews in the newly established state of Romania in the 1870s to the work of the Committee of Jewish Delegations at the Versailles Peace Conference, Jewish institutions sought to bundle different forms of legal, demographic, and historical knowledge to promote their agenda. Robinson's preparation for the Nuremberg trials on behalf of the World Jewish Congress had drawn precisely on this strength, as did the work of US class action lawyers who cooperated with Jewish organizations in the 1990s.

May's advocacy for Roma likewise relied on a larger network of postwar Jewish institutions that permitted his organization and many documentation centers to persist through difficult times. Two US institutions carried the burden of immediate aid to survivors after liberation: the American Jewish Congress and the Joint Distribution Committee, which both relied largely on donations from US Jews. Within a few years, the Conference on Jewish Material Claims Against Germany, known as the Claims Conference, became the most important backer of historical and legal work.[47] Twenty-two international Jewish organizations—including the American Jewish Congress, the Joint Distribution Committee, and organizations from Western Europe and Latin

America—founded the Conference in New York in 1952 to represent Jewish victims outside Israel in compensation negotiations with the Federal Republic of Germany. In the Luxembourg Agreement of the same year, West Germany agreed to pay three billion German Marks to Israel and 450 million Marks to the Claims Conference. These payments allowed the Claims Conference to support the URO when it lacked funds.[48] It also saved multiple Jewish documentation centers that aided the URO's historical work. After the initial burst of activity around historical commissions, most collections ended up in a few archives that were struggling to stay financially afloat by the early 1950s. The Center for Contemporary Jewish Documentation in Paris would have likely not survived with their collections intact without the support of the Claims Conference.[49] The Claims Conference also bankrolled Yad Vashem in its first decade, covering half of the Israeli state institution's expenses.[50]

The campaign to change compensation practices depended on such material connections, which were largely invisible to claimants. The campaign was also possible because the German state paid reparations to Jewish organizations based on a treaty that explicitly excluded non-Jewish victims (since neither Israel nor the Claims Conference could speak for them). May's initiative was even more directly tied to Jewish survivors in that they supplied the organization's funding after the mid-1950s. Historical collecting, trips to foreign archives, and legal work were possible because the URO worked with success fees of between 4 percent and 9 percent of the awards given to the Jewish claimants they represented.[51] These fees in turn created an apparatus that allowed for political campaigning that was unavailable to Romanies and other victims of Nazism, such as homosexuals or those deemed asocial. Good intentions mattered, but the tools of change were well-resourced networks that could assemble new information.

The Limits of Romani Self-Organization

While May broke new ground in aiding Romani compensation from German courts, Romani groups were also increasingly turning to arguments about historical justice. In West Germany, this orientation was unavoidable. Aware that West Germany was eager to distance itself from Nazism, Romani activists tried to change the state's understanding of their group by addressing its history of persecution. The statutes of one of the earliest Romani associations are instructive in this regard. In 1960, Sinti from the Frankfurt area founded a Central Committee of Gypsies to advocate for equality between non-Romani and Romani Germans and to promote the traditions of "Gypsydom."[52] The latter included: "The care of the memory of the Gypsies murdered by Nazism and the protection of their honor."[53] The organization also demanded fair rules for compensation. The most urgent task, in their view, was the legal recognition of Romanies living in German territory as German citizens whom the Nazis had persecuted.[54] These victims had the clearest path to compensation, and they were the Central Committee's most obvious constituents.

Yet the Central Committee, much like other Romani organizations, faced challenges that Jewish organizations did not. Jewish organizations had two advantages. The first came from years of formal organizing, whether in state-recognized communities, transnational political parties, or transnational philanthropic and lobbying organizations. Second, states had an interest in allowing Jewish organizations to speak for Jews, and none more than West Germany. When the newly established West German state under Konrad Adenauer engaged in negotiations for compensation in 1952, it decided to recognize two bodies as speaking for murdered and persecuted Jews: the state of Israel and the Claims Conference.[55] The Claims Conference would not have existed if Germany hadn't wanted to find a body that could represent Jews.

Before the 1970s, in contrast, Romani organizations could not rely on the goodwill of states as they attempted to self-organize. They also faced challenges because they had not previously formed international associations. Indeed, postwar Romani organizations—much like their interwar predecessors—did not form strong national organizations either, in part because they struggled to overcome their identification with individual Romani subgroups. Many Romani associations found that they had to respond to challenges to their legitimacy from some of the very people they claimed to represent in ways that Jewish organizations rarely did.

The attempts of Rudolf Karway, a Polish Rom, to found a civil rights organization in Germany in 1969 clearly illustrate these pressures. His International Gypsy Rights' Commission demanded a quicker path to citizenship for foreign Roma, the end of social and legal discrimination, and educational initiatives.[56] Yet, after he succeeded initially in garnering some political support, his organization dwindled due to criticism from within the Romani community. German Sinti fiercely resisted Karway's claim to represent all Roma and Sinti in Germany. One Sinto wrote to an administrator in his state, Baden-Württemberg, that he only wanted to be treated like a German citizen and did not want a foreigner speaking for him. He claimed that "Polish Gypsies" had abused him in concentration camps, and threatened that "murder and manslaughter" would ensue if the government recognized Karway.[57] Other Sinti organized to express similar sentiments.[58] Some cited their own service in the German army as proof of their patriotism and their rejection of foreign representation.[59] The first chairperson of the Central Committee of German Gypsies, Wilhelm Weiss, wrote to German President Gustav Heinemann that German "Gypsies" were deeply upset to have a foreigner from Eastern Europe demand compensation on their behalf.[60] When German Sinti coalesced in the late 1960s to seek political representation they did so by articulating a national response in opposition to an international organizing effort.

State officials prone to dismiss Romani political demands welcomed this confusion. When the Bavarian Ministry of the Interior assessed the need to coordinate with the Central Committee of German Gypsies, these state officials immediately pounced on the (erroneous) claim that one of the organization's officials was a Rom rather than a Sinto. They also turned to the criminal records of some of the organization's representatives, using the documentation created by the state's targeted policing to dismiss their claims.[61] This rejection was not universal, and in some quarters—including the office of the German president—the new organization and its messaging were well received. At the same time, this abstract goodwill had obvious limits. While German authorities understood that they had to negotiate with Jewish organizations—whether out of a sense of historical responsibility or pragmatism—they felt no obligation to deal directly with Romani organizations. Where Roma had reasonable collective demands, officials expected them to be made by social workers. As a result, Romani claimants sometimes came together for short periods—as in the case of *Die Vergessenen* in Bavaria, or to demand recognition of the camp Lackenbach in early 1950s Austria—but did not build institutions that resembled the URO in their ability to sustain a full-fledged legal and information infrastructure.

The French case illustrates in even starker terms how authorities effectively silenced Romani organizations and thus also inadvertently undermined Romani claims against Germany. In France, Romani activists faced aggressive methods of suppression in the 1960s. Across Europe, there was little international pressure to rethink the state's approach to populations described as "Gypsies," or, in France, as "nomads." The limited arguments that reached the German public about the state's historical responsibility to Romani victims did not exist in French debates. As a result, prewar registration and surveillance practices persisted into the postwar period in France with few changes. These continuities were clear in the central institution of Francophone

Romani Studies scholarship, the Association for Gypsy Studies (Association des études tsiganes), established as a joint venture between different ministries to monitor and reform so-called "nomads." Six years after its founding in 1949, the association published a journal, *Études tsiganes*, which remains the most important publication on Romani Studies research in French today.[62] Some of those involved with the journal and the association came from religious organizations, while others were scholars employed at universities, but most of them participated directly or indirectly in the French state's persistent approach of managing "nomads" as a problematic population. The same effort led to the creation of a new "National Committee on Information," generally referred to as C.N.I.N.,[63] which included local organizations of "nomads" and "Gypsies" under its umbrella but ultimately served as a tool of the French state.

Romani activists organizing for collective action had to contend with the combined force of the state and its experts. Around the time that Karway made his failed attempt to represent Sinti and Roma in Germany, Ionel Rotaru pursued similar aims in France with his Communauté Mondiale Gitane (World Gypsy Community). Like Karway, Rotaru was something of an outsider. Born 1918 in Bessarabia, he served as a conscript in the Romanian Army during World War Two and fled west in 1946. He escaped first to Italy and then to Egypt, where he applied for protection from the International Refugee Organization.[64] Allowed to settle in France, he sought to establish credentials to speak for a highly heterogeneous community. He declared himself Supreme Leader of the Gypsy People and henceforth appeared under the name Vaida Voëvod III. He thus drew on a tradition among Romani men of presenting themselves as "Gypsy kings," often to mediate between communities and states, regardless of their actual authority among diverse Romani populations.[65] In his choice of titles Rotaru followed in the footsteps of another Romani citizen of interwar Romania, G. A. Lăzurică, who had also adopted the title of Voivode of Roma in 1933. Lăzurică had exercised monarchic power to make a stalwart defense of the Orthodox church and to express sympathy with authoritarian politics.[66] Rotaru, by contrast, sought to associate himself with a new language of victimhood. In addition to this performance of natural communal authority, Rotaru also claimed legitimacy for himself and his organization through the history of Romani persecution. From the very beginning, the organization asked for "war reparations" to be paid to "Gypsies" by West Germany, seeking a recognition parallel to that achieved in 1952 by the Claims Conference and Israel. A periodical associated with the organization later called on French Roma to submit applications for

FIGURE 5.3. Ionel Rotaru (Vaida Voëvod III) explaining his demand for a Romani state in Somalia in the mid-1960s. Reproduced with permission from Ilsen About.

compensation to the West German state, albeit without much institutional support or hope for success.[67]

Rotaru's politics clearly annoyed French officials who placed him under police surveillance.[68] He broke with the French republican belief that the state only had to deal with social groups—such as individuals defined by unusual forms of mobility—rather than ethnic groups. Rotaru and his deputy, Vanko Rouda, were claiming precisely to speak as representatives of a national or ethnic community, asserting international legal standing, and even flirting with the idea of a Romani homeland in Somalia, Djibouti, or on an island in the Pacific (see figure 5.3).[69] Rotaru also approached members of parliament, prompting the leader of the center-right Gaulist faction to request background information from the experts at C.N.I.N. before he responded.[70]

Soon, leading figures associated with *Études tsiganes* and C.N.I.N. met to discuss the perceived provocation. Nicole Lafay, who was responsible for "no-mads" in the Ministry of Health, Louis Peyssard, inspector general for public health and population management and director of the C.N.I.N., and Pierre Join-Lambert, a member of France's Council of State who edited *Études tsiga-nes*, met with several stakeholders on October 28, 1964.[71] Among those present were missionaries in charge of "nomads," yet it was Lafay who seemed most shocked that Rotaru had declined to reveal to her whether he was Catholic or Pentecostal.[72] She suggested that this refusal was indicative of dangerous ten-dencies among these new activists, who seemed to depart from the familiar path of surveilled self-organization. She and the others thus contemplated radical action. One proposal was to deport the unwanted troublemakers to another country and to prohibit state bodies from any contact with the Com-munauté Mondiale Gitane. Peyssard, the highest-ranking administrator in the room, eventually concluded that his colleagues had gone too far and decided merely to prohibit Rotaru's activities.[73]

To suppress these unwanted voices in its midst, French authorities de-ployed a law against associations of foreigners decreed just before World War Two. The law of April 12, 1939 prohibited organizations controlled from abroad, led by anyone who was not a French citizen, or whose members were more than one-quarter non-French, unless they received special permission.[74] On the same day in 1939, the French government also decreed that all male refu-gees between the ages of 20 and 45 would have to serve in the French army. Both decree-laws (as they were officially called) were part of a flurry of mea-sures passed with special executive powers. Parliament had bestowed these powers on the government to address war preparations and the continuous flow of refugees into France.[75] A 1939 government report legitimized these new regulations as necessary to suppressing Nazi propaganda by organ-izations that sought to hide their connections to Germany.[76] The decree-law remained in force even after parliamentary rule was reestablished after the war and only abrogated in 1981. Hence an anti-Nazi law passed by executive fiat at the height of anti-refugee sentiment and anxieties of fifth columnists became a tool for government authorities to stop Romani activists from organizing. Per a decree of February 26, 1965, the state prohibited the Communauté Mon-diale Gitane.[77]

While this did not stop the emergence of a Romani rights movement in France, it would take years for Romani institutions to build up a level of expertise that could remotely match that of the URO.[78] From the 1950s to the 1970s, German and French Romani organizations faced hostile officials and tended to attract a limited number of followers. More importantly, they did not have access to the resources necessary to produce new historical knowledge. With its extensive staff of lawyers, connections to young and established historians, and international partners, the case of the URO demonstrates the immense resources needed to produce dependable information about the past. The impediments Romani organizations encountered and the efforts needed for effective lobbying help us to understand why Jewish organizations mattered to Romanies, who otherwise had few points of contact with Jews. The consequences of these disadvantages were clear to Romani activists if not necessarily to the Jewish scholars and representatives working in the field. Jewish institutions themselves were still working on the margins of mainstream historical debates and often struggled financially, making it hard for most Jewish intellectuals and community leaders to grasp the value their infrastructure might have for another group.

Jews and Early Research on the Romani Holocaust

The Jewish scholars and public figures who would start to change that worked in a plethora of institutions. Some of these institutions were originally established to document national struggles against Nazism or resistance activity, such as the Netherlands Institute for War Documentation (established 1945) or the Documentation Center of Austrian Resistance (established 1963). Both research centers emphasized political oppression and heroism and slowly turned their attention to the fate of the Nazi regime's racialized victims.[79] Other institutions had a clearer Jewish mandate, such as the Wiener Library in London, Yad Vashem in Jerusalem, and the Center for Contemporary Jewish Documentation in Paris. In different ways, each gave committed researchers and archivists opportunities to establish what would grow, within a few decades, into an infrastructure of Holocaust research centers, each with its own perspective and emphasis.

The earliest catalogued material on the Romani genocide emerged from this heterogeneous group of documentation centers. These institutions made available Nazi administrative files, in the original or in duplicates from state archives. Jewish Holocaust archives were also among the first to depart from a focus on heroism and to collect accounts from people whom historians understood mainly as victims.[80] Initially these archives housed some of the collections assembled by historical commissions in the immediate postwar period. After a short hiatus, they launched new testimony projects in the late 1950s and, with more resources and attention, in the 1960s, following the Eichmann and Frankfurt Auschwitz trials. Some of these efforts also included Romani survivors.

The Wiener Library was one of several institutions engaged in such work. Founded in Amsterdam in 1933 as the Jewish Central Information Office by exiled German-Jewish émigré Alfred Wiener, the organization was the first documentation center dedicated to the Nazi persecution of Jews. It moved to London in 1939 with its founder and slowly transformed into a Holocaust research center, archive, and library. Its testimony collections started in 1938, when the archive—still under its old name—assembled more than 350 eyewitness testimonies on the November Pogrom (Kristallnacht).[81] The Wiener Library's testimony collections grew in the 1950s under the direction of Eva Reichmann, who—together with Rachel Auerbach at Yad Vashem—pioneered the systematic collection of victim testimonies at a time when most historians dismissed them as unreliable and of limited use.[82] Reichmann worked from 1924 to 1938 for the Central Association of German Citizens of Jewish Faith, a large centrist Jewish organization founded to combat antisemitism. She fled to England with a doctorate in economics and received a second PhD at the London School of Economics, with a dissertation on "The Social Sources of National-Socialist Antisemitism."[83]

In 1957, the year that Buchheim published his study on the 1940 deportations, Reichmann hired a Viennese woman by the name of Emmi Moravitz to conduct interviews for her archive. Moravitz began working with few instructions, transforming her interviews into third-person accounts of survivors' experiences.[84] After receiving the first batch, Reichmann encouraged Moravitz to seek out Romani survivors—telling her that "we particularly hope for Gypsy-reports." Reichmann promised 250 Austrian schillings, or approximately $150 in today's value, per testimony.[85] Funds for the project came from the Claims Conference, which funneled money to the British archive by paying for Yad Vashem to purchase transcribed testimonies.[86] This allowed the library to employ a staff of four to five people to process and cross-reference the testimonies.[87]

Moravitz likely found Romani survivors to interview through her acquaintance Hermann Langbein, who had recommended her to Reichmann. Among the people she interviewed were Hermine Horwath and Adolf Gussak, the two Romani survivors who had ended up on the "List of Gypsies Registered

FIGURE 5.4. Eva Reichmann in the Wiener Library. *Source*: The Wiener Library Collections.

with Us" created by the Jewish-led Action Committee in 1946.[88] To the extent that we know anything about Horwath and Gussak today, it is because of all the people in this chain: Langbein, who knew them personally, and collected money to support Gussak when he was widowed; Moravitz, who spoke to them; and Reichmann, who worked for a Jewish institution that made their testimonies available for researchers.[89]

While Reichmann was mainly an organizer of knowledge, other Jewish professionals of the period set out to write the history of the Romani Holocaust. They usually identified as survivors and former resistance fighters who made it their life's task to keep alive the memory of murdered Jews. None embodied this approach more than Miriam Novitch, who collected material for a Jewish Holocaust archive and wrote the earliest historical survey of the Romani genocide. Born in 1908, Novitch grew up in Wilno (Vilnius) and moved to Paris after graduating from a Hebrew high school. A self-identified communist, she sought out the company of left-wing artists, and ended up marrying one of them: the painter Moshe Castel, who had arrived in the city from Jerusalem. The marriage did not last long. Castel returned to Palestine and Novitch—who called herself Marie at the time—stayed in France with their child. After France's capitulation to Germany, Novitch joined the communist underground until the Gestapo arrested her in 1942. Imprisoned as a foreign national in the Vittel camp, she met the love of her life, Yiddish poet Itzhak Katzenelson. She credited Katzenelson with converting her to Zionism and often presented her later work as a tribute to the author, who perished in Auschwitz. Yet, she remained committed to communist causes, as her postwar role as a functionary for a France-Soviet Union friendship organization demonstrates.[90] In the immediate aftermath of the war, she also ventured into documentation work, collecting testimonies on Nazi crimes for the Federation of Jewish Societies of France, an aid organization for foreign Jews established in 1923 that later engaged in underground resistance activities against the Nazis.[91] In 1953, Novitch moved to Israel and joined kibbutz Lohamei HaGeta'ot, known as the Ghetto Fighters' Kibbutz in English, a community consisting largely of Holocaust survivors.

Even among them she stood out as unusually scarred by her experiences under Nazism. Novitch assumed the position of head of collections for the kibbutz's museum dedicated to the Nazi murder of Europe's Jews and their resistance. Rather than simply work there, she lived there, sleeping in a small room inside the museum building. The historian Tom Segev wrote pointedly that she "practically transformed herself into an 'exhibit' at the Holocaust museum" she helped to oversee.[92] Novitch was singularly dedicated to building the museum's collections, while—according to her own account—neglecting her two children, who grew alienated from her in adulthood. Even visually, she marked her distance from society, wearing black and donning formal hats, in stark distinction to the more casual dress adopted by most kibbutz members.[93] Novitch was an avid fundraiser for the Ghetto Fighters' House Museum and its archive and one of the few women who contributed to the early historiography of the Holocaust with works on the extermination camp Sobibor and on resistance through the production of art. A pioneer of Holocaust scholarship but also someone who did not fit in, today she remains largely forgotten.[94]

Unlike Gerald Reitlinger, who abandoned the idea of writing on the Romani genocide in 1959 after realizing that there was no one-stop archive that might have served his purpose, Novitch was willing and able to create the very archive that would become the basis of her research. During various trips to

FIGURE 5.5. Miriam Novitch, archivist and
chief curator at Ghetto Fighters' House in Israel.
Source: The Ghetto Fighters' House Museum,
Israel, Photo Archive.

Europe, she collected primary sources that she deposited in her Israeli archive
and used for her own publications.[95] It was in this way that numerous testimonies and Nazi documents about the murder of Roma in Yugoslavia found their
way onto the shelves of the Ghetto Fighters' House.[96] Novitch's long travels
often combined lectures and archival visits, such as a trip from September 1963
to December 1964 that included a presentation on the Romani Holocaust
along with a visit to the Brno municipal archives, where she discovered multiple sources on Roma.[97]

The materials Novitch collected remained largely hidden from sight, but
her historical writing had a visible public impact. She was the first to undertake
a global history of the Romani genocide, where others treated it as a side note
of the Jewish Holocaust or only mentioned developments in particular
camps.[98] The model of the Jewish Holocaust was central for her extended
essay, "The Genocide of Gypsies under the Nazi Regime."[99] Adapting a quote

from Katzenelson's famous "Song of the Murdered Jewish People", which she had helped hide in Vittel, she noted that Jews and "Gypsies" were the only ones killed not for their attempts to defend their nation but rather for the mere fact of existing.[100] Her narrative from pre-1933 discrimination to liberation continuously drew out these similarities: many of her work's topic sentences began with "the Jews and the Gypsies." The phrase "like the Jews" appears on nearly every page.

Glancing at the footnotes of Novitch's essay, it is also apparent that historical writing on the Romani genocide emerged from Jewish Holocaust archives and collaborations between Jewish scholars. In some instances, she cited a "Gypsy file" created by archivists that scholars could use at the Wiener Library in London or the Ministry of Reconstruction in Brussels—the latter having been originally compiled with the help of Estelle Goldstein as part of her work on the Jewish Holocaust for the ministry. Even the few texts Novitch assembled from non-Jewish archives, such as the Auschwitz Museum or the Belgian Ministry of Reconstruction, became available to her as a result of her work on behalf of a Jewish Holocaust institution. She also cited books on the murder of the Jews from authors such as Raul Hilberg and Léon Poliakov, as well as wartime memoirs and testimonies from Jews. Except for some references to Romani voices—including the poets Matéo Maximoff and Papusza—Novitch's footnotes show that she built the edifice of this first history of the Romani genocide mostly on the foundation of work done by Jewish scholars on the topic of the Jewish Holocaust.

Jewish networks also played an outsized role in the publication process of Novitch's account of the Romani genocide. Her history first appeared as a published lecture from a conference on persecution and resistance that she attended during one of her trips to Czechoslovakia. At this point, her manuscript was nothing but a mimeographed set of papers that she circulated among interested parties. Novitch subsequently published a longer version with an Italian journal at the Sapienza University of Rome that pioneered interdisciplinary research on deportation.[101] All of these venues provided only limited audiences. Novitch finally reached a slightly wider audience through her friends in France. In 1968, the French Association of Jewish Medical Students published the essay in their newsletter and subsequently reissued it as a small booklet.[102] This last edition ended up at various research libraries, anchoring the slim collection of works on the subject of the Romani genocide.

While Novitch produced one of the foundational texts in the field, her scholarly contribution could not match the public visibility of Simon Wiesenthal's attempt to publicize the wartime fate of Roma. Famous as a "Nazi hunter," Wiesenthal rose to prominence with the trial of Adolf Eichmann, whom he claimed to have helped apprehend in Argentina. Although an internationally acclaimed figure, Wiesenthal was also an outsider in many respects. Like others who would later rise to prominence, Wiesenthal started with meager resources after the war. Since 1947, he had operated the Jewish Historical Documentation Center in Linz, which collected information to aid in the prosecution of Nazi criminals. Other documentation centers from the time, such as the Center for Contemporary Jewish Documentation in Paris, were equally strapped for funding.[103] While the French center survived, Wiesenthal's did not. He was forced to shut down his operation in 1954, although he managed to revive his endeavors in Vienna in 1961 under the name Jewish Documentation Center. Wiesenthal's daily struggles involved many compromises—such as a conflict-laden job with the Jewish Community of Vienna—that allowed him to continue his activities.[104]

More significant than these compromises, Wiesenthal was an outsider both within the Jewish community and among those seeking to understand the Romani Holocaust. He was a supporter of the conservative party in Austria and the right-wing Heruth movement in Israel (the predecessor to today's Likud party). This set him apart from the majority of Jews in his environment. In the 1960s and early 1970s, most Western European Jews supported center-left parties, while labor Zionists dominated Israeli politics and Vienna's Jewish community alike. Novitch, while a marginalized figure within her kibbutz, fit with the mainstream of Israeli and Jewish diaspora politics in her day. Wiesenthal's politics made him an unusual advocate for an expansive understanding of victimhood under Nazism.[105] An unconventional thinker, he combined right-wing Jewish nationalism with a demand to recognize the historical injustice and violence committed against multiple groups—including not only Roma but also Jehovah's Witnesses, homosexual victims of Nazism, and Native Americans.[106]

Wiesenthal's first steps in that direction followed a pattern of public relations work that he perfected over the years. In 1965, leveraging his celebrity status, he decided to send to German authorities several documents he discovered that linked Eichmann and his deputies to the deportation of Roma.[107] The documents offered some leads for a new investigation against an SS-officer by the name of Walter Braune, though Wiesenthal surely knew from experience that the authorities would need more than these limited documents to proceed.[108] Indeed, the prosecutors he addressed were not his main audience.

Wiesenthal was more concerned with attracting the attention of various media outlets. Having transmitted the documents as part of an open letter, together with a press release, he used the opportunity to put the Romani genocide on the agenda of major international newspapers.[109]

Two years later, Wiesenthal included a chapter on "The Extermination of the Gypsies" in his bestselling autobiography, *The Murderers Among Us*.[110] As one might expect from a memoir, it focuses on Wiesenthal's discovery of documents, starting with his chance discovery in 1954 of a telegram to Adolf Eichmann on the topic of deporting "Gypsies." Other coincidental findings and the holdings of "various Jewish archives all over the world" revealed additional clues, he noted, but "many details remain unknown."[111] Wiesenthal was not one to fill in these gaps himself. Instead, he used his position to facilitate the exchange of information between other institutions and to highlight the fate of a group continuously spurned.

More than anyone involved in the historical documentation process, Wiesenthal boosted the voices of Romani leaders in Germany, whose civil rights movement increasingly gained public attention in the late 1970s. Despite his own right-wing politics, Wiesenthal supported the campaigns of the Society for Threatened Peoples, an NGO associated with the student left that focused on supporting indigenous groups in the decolonized world. The association worked together with several Romani organizers, including the prominent activist Romani Rose. Wiesenthal attended some of Rose's press conferences, wrote letters on behalf of his organization, the Central Council of German Sinti and Roma, and became one of the German Romani movement's most reliable allies. In 1981, Wiesenthal wrote to Queen Beatrix of the Netherlands on behalf of Roma who were being threatened with expulsion.[112] He used his reputation as an advocate for a thorough legal reckoning with crimes committed against Jews—by then accepted as a tragedy with universal lessons—to support the campaigns of Roma who were still fighting for their basic rights.

One of Wiesenthal's close collaborators, Ben Sijes, soon began pursuing research on the Romani genocide as well. Born into a Jewish family in Amsterdam, Sijes identified politically as a council communist and worked for decades as a historian for the Netherlands Institute for War Documentation in his city of birth. In 1965, as Wiesenthal contacted prosecutors about the involvement of Eichmann's men in the deportation of Roma, Sijes started to investigate the history of anti-Romani policies in the Netherlands. In many respects, the collection he amassed to write his book proved as innovative as the book itself. The study took much longer to complete than he had hoped and appeared only in 1979.[113] Unlike Novitch, Sijes did not just draw on established collections and earlier testimonies. He also went directly to Dutch Romani survivors and interviewed them, mostly between 1970 and 1975, although many seemed reluctant to speak to him. Originally, he made these testimonies available only to a team of five master's students who ended up drafting most of his work.[114] Today, these interviews constitute their own collection at the Netherlands Institute for War Documentation. It is a peculiar set of papers, consisting largely of transcripts cut up to match analytical rubrics Sijes created. Yet, these are some of the earliest written traces that reflect the voices of Dutch Romanies.

Many institutions that can be broadly conceived of as Jewish Holocaust archives—even if they were originally founded to celebrate political resistance or national heroism—contain similar collections. One such archive, for example, is the Documentation Center of Austrian Resistance in Vienna, where the holdings on Roma come from another Jewish employee and former resistance fighter, Selma Steinmetz.[115] The files Steinmetz used to publish her 1966 volume, *Austrian Gypsies in the Nazi State*, among the earliest book-length histories of Roma persecution in a single country, made the Documentation Center one of the few places with properly labeled Romani testimonies and correspondence on Romani history in a publicly accessible collection.[116]

Why did Reichmann, Novitch, Wiesenthal, Sijes, and Steinmetz turn to the Romani Holocaust when few others even expressed interest in the topic? Some of them addressed this question directly, citing a chance meeting or occurrence that drew their attention to the fate of a group they hardly knew. Ben Sijes reported, for example, that an encounter with a Romani woman in 1961 piqued his interest. That year, he had organized the first big event with Simon Wiesenthal in the Netherlands—with heavy security because neo-Nazis had sent threats against the prominent visitor from Austria. At the end of the event, according to Sijes's account, a small woman approached and implored them to help her find her siblings. Showing Sijes and Wiesenthal a picture of children standing in a row with nuns after the war, she explained that this was the only image she had of them. According to Sijes, she told them that they had been separated because they were "Gypsies" and that her young brothers and sisters—like some Jewish children hidden in Catholic institutions during the war—could not be located. Her parents and nine other siblings had all been murdered. In his autobiography Sijes claimed that he and Wiesenthal bonded over this new mission, which also began their close friendship. They allegedly wrote to their wide network of acquaintances for help and began every phone conversation with: "So did you hear anything about the children?"[117]

Others had similar stories. In a 1985 interview, Miriam Novitch told a reporter who asked her about the beginnings of her interest in "Gypsies":

> For us, the Jews, the interest did not have to start. Injustice and suffering, that is our business. Always, in all of history. After the war, I saw a woman with the letter Z on her arm, and she was ashamed, she tried to hide it, because people always asked her if it was a phone number. I asked her, what is this, and she said that she is a Zigeuner, a Gypsy woman, and she told me briefly what happened to her. I decided that I have to figure out what happened to the Gypsies. Wherever I went, I immediately asked—maybe you saw Gypsies in the camp—maybe you know what happened to them?[118]

Like Sijes, Novitch recalled a first encounter that sparked her sustained interest in a silenced history of injustice. Like many others—including Kurt May—she also articulated her concern as a natural extension of her own identity. Each recounted a learning process that is audible in David Boder's 1946 interviews, in which listeners can hear him alter his questions to witnesses with every new mention of Romani prisoners and victims.

There are many more such stories of sincere commitments emerging from unexpected interactions during or after the war, yet these stories are also full of contradictions. Sijes tied his dedication to Romanies to his friendship with Wiesenthal, yet their correspondence reveals that this remained a marginal concern for them throughout the 1960s. The Romani woman at the event existed, but letters show that they both immediately lost her contact information.[119] Novitch may well have met one Romani survivor of Auschwitz after the war, but she also claimed in other writings that she published on the genocide of Roma because she saw that prosecutors in the Eichmann trial included the accusation that he deported "Gypsies" to their death in the indictment.[120]

These discrepancies do not negate the possibility that real encounters shaped the scholarly trajectory of these survivor-historians. But they do suggest that these individuals believed a narrative of discovery would help explain and validate their concern with a marginal topic. Having turned to the Romani Holocaust in their fifties and sixties, these Jewish historians were not part of the new circles who became increasingly interested in studying marginalized subjects. Indeed, their work remained largely disconnected from that of a new generation of politically active students and intellectuals who looked to outsiders—rather than just the working class—as focal points of their political activism. In various fields in the 1960s and 1970s, scholars conceived grand theories based on marginalized individuals. One of the most consequential was Michel Foucault's historical analysis of insanity in *Madness and Civilization*, which appeared in 1961. Many more turned to colonial subjects, women, and Jews, sometimes seeking to connect these disparate groups.[121] In this context, the image of the Jew became a staple of "theory"—a category of writing often associated with politicized forms of continental European philosophy. "Gypsies" might have made an excellent case study for grand theories, but none of the prominent thinkers on the topic of marginality paid much attention to them. Human rights campaigns sometimes supported Romani organizations or sought to represent them, but academics remained largely uninterested in their fate or history.[122]

When Sijes, Novitch, and Steinmetz began researching Romani history and talking to Roma, their essays appealed less to those who sought out new revolutionary subjects and more to those who cared about the history of genocide. Although all three identified as communists at some point in their lives, they wrote mostly for a readership of Nazi victims and their families, not for those identified with a particular party or with the political and cultural revolution of 1968.[123] Their stories of the discovery of "Gypsies" as Holocaust victims thus made the topic more legible or compelling to their particular audiences. Theirs was a world largely sustained by semi-official institutions that represented Jewish and non-Jewish groups defined by their interwar and wartime experiences. Novitch and Wiesenthal remained prominent supporters and honored guests at conferences of the international Romani rights movement. Survivor historians and survivor activists—rather than a new generation of Jewish 68ers—became the faces of Jewish-Romani solidarity well into the 1980s.

Networks, Relations, and Knowledge Production

The efforts of Jewish historical professionals in the 1960s culminated in the publication of the first comprehensive account of the Romani genocide: the 1972 volume *The Destiny of Europe's Gypsies*.[124] Co-written by a Jewish communist linguist, Donald Kenrick, and a "Gypsy" and Travellers' rights activists, Grattan Puxon, the project was made possible through the support of Jewish institutions—in particular the Wiener Library—as well as Jewish supporters such as the historian Norman Cohn. While neither Kenrick nor Puxon were of Romani or Traveller origin, the latter's deep involvement in Romani and

Traveller self-organization since the mid-1960s connected their work to social activism and encouraged community buy-in among various politically active Roma.[125] The volume marked the beginning of serious scholarship on the subject but was also a milestone in the collaboration between Jewish and Romani historical practitioners.

No doubt, much of the work that allowed them to succeed came from non-Jews and reached Puxon and Kenrick across the Iron Curtain. Jerzy Ficowski, mentioned above as the translator of the Romani poet Papusza, wrote essential works on Polish Roma, including detailed descriptions of their fate under Nazism; in East Germany, Rainer Gilsenbach collected Romani testimonies and made crucial contributions to the history of German Sinti.[126]

Yet, Kenrick and Puxon's achievement would have been impossible without Jewish survivors and the institutions they built to document and account for Nazi crimes. These individuals and organizations studied the expropriation, abuse, and murder of the Jews well before the "Holocaust" was a familiar term and when most state institutions established to illuminate the history of the Nazi era—such as the Institute for Contemporary History—treated the Jewish Holocaust as a niche issue within the larger history of Nazism and antifascist resistance. Romani civil rights activists could build upon the labor that Jews invested both outside and within state institutions. We need only read the acknowledgements for the "interim report" Puxon and Kenrick produced in July 1968 to recognize this.[127] Of the five archives they thanked for supporting their work, one was Romani: the private collection of the Communauté Internationale Tzigane, which had suggested that Puxon create such a compendium. Three others were Jewish institutions: the Center for Jewish Contemporary Documentation in Paris, Yad Vashem in Jerusalem, and the YIVO (Yiddish Scientific Institute) archives in New York.[128] Their footnotes also reveal their reliance on early Jewish historians of Nazi crimes, and no one more than Novitch.[129] Had the Central Committee of Gypsies written to the Institute for Contemporary History fifteen years later, rather than in 1960, they would have received a more substantial answer, thanks to work done largely by Jewish historians or by others writing with the support of Jewish institutions. In some respects, these Jewish networks helped Romani survivors and activists overcome the self-justifying narratives that dominated the state apparatus, displacing Zornig's file as the main authoritative information available to state agents.

Most of this historical labor emerged from interactions that do not deserve to be called dialogues. Even if these Jewish scholars and activists interacted with Roma, they did so as professionals talking with research subjects. In this sense, their work is as much a testament to the distance between them as to the unequal resources that members of both groups had at their disposal as they tried to grasp their persecution under Nazism. Yet, unlike in 1946, when Avrom Sutzkever wrote of the forgotten murder of Roma, and David Boder first learned to ask about their fate, this was not a matter of singular individuals anymore. It is unclear who read or heard Sutzkever and Boder, but there is little doubt that Wiesenthal, May, Steinmetz, Sijes, and Novitch formed part of a small coterie of individuals who could rely on other individuals and institutions to delve into the history of people they hardly knew. Their small networks created the basis for the more egalitarian alliances that would emerge between Jewish and Romani activists in later decades.

6

The Path to Shared Romani-Jewish Remembrance after 1978

EVERY YEAR ON AUGUST 2, Romani delegations travel to the Polish city of Oświęcim to commemorate the Nazi murder of all remaining prisoners in the subcamp for "Gypsies" in Auschwitz-Birkenau. Such gatherings at the memorial site started in the 1970s, originally attracting only small groups of Romani survivors and their immediate families. By 2014, the event had grown into a large multi-generational occasion to honor the dead and reflect on this defining moment in Romani history. The most visible group that year was composed of the teenagers and students who had arranged a large conference with experts and activists in neighboring Kraków in the days leading up to the event.[1] Organized by the Romani youth movement ternYpe, the events brought a thousand young Roma from across Europe to Poland that year.

This was a day dedicated to commemorating the Romani—not the Jewish—past at Auschwitz, yet it was hard to miss the subtle and not-so-subtle Jewish references. In contrast to the March of the Living, the best-known Jewish memorial trip, the young people emerging from their tour buses held up the flag of the Romani movement rather than that of Israel. Otherwise, the choreography seemed identical (see Figure 6.1). The procession of participants entering the Birkenau compound through the famous main gate could easily have been confused for a Jewish youth pilgrimage. Whether this was on some participants' minds or simply the result of the site's layout is difficult to say.

More direct and intentional were the references to Jews and Israel by leaders of the two organizations that brought the majority of survivors and older activists to the 2014 commemoration: Roman Kwiatkowski of the Association of Polish Roma and Romani Rose of the Central Council of German Sinti and Roma. In his address that day, Kwiatkowski cited the previous year's speech

FIGURE 6.1. Romani youth at a commemorative event in Auschwitz-Birkenau on August 2, 2014. Reproduced with permission of Márton Neményi.

by the Israeli ambassador, who referred to Jews and Roma as brothers and sisters.[2] (In 2014, the ambassador could not attend because the event fell on the Jewish Shabbat.) Commenting on the Gaza conflict raging that summer, Rose condemned certain criticisms of Israel as antisemitic and expressed solidarity with Israel as well as with Jews in Germany. Few lines in the speeches delivered that day received as much applause from the assembled Romani activists and survivors as Rose's statements defending the Israeli position on the 2014 Gaza war.[3]

For Rose and Kwiatkowski, solidarity with and support from Jews was an accomplishment. For decades, Romani leaders and their allies had fought for their group's equal recognition as victims of Nazism. The presence of Jewish as well as non-Jewish dignitaries at this gathering signaled their success in that endeavor.

Younger Romani participants, however, took a different approach, instead expressing their distaste for the type of politics such displays represented. After standing in the blazing sun for over an hour, they decided to leave the main gathering and hold a separate event at the site of one of the destroyed crematoria. There, the ternYpe leadership apologized for "political speeches" and staged a ceremony that contrasted starkly with that of the dignitaries. First, Andi Gergely, president of the World Union of Jewish Students, read a prayer in English.[4] Next, a Pentecostal preacher offered a blessing in Spanish. Finally, the organizers handed the microphone to a delegate from the Union of Jewish Students of France, Nethanel Cohen Solal, who intoned the Mourner's Kaddish, the Jewish prayer of the dead. After entering the compound in the style of the March of the Living and hearing Zionist speeches, hundreds of young Roma stood around Crematorium Five listening to a Jewish student reciting the traditional Hebrew words of mourning for Europe's murdered Roma and Sinti. Nearly seventy years after Sutzkever wondered how Jews could put the murder of their fellow sufferers into words and song, it seemed a new generation of Jewish and Romani activists had arrived at their own answer to that question. It was not the "melodious heroism" of Pushkin or the poetry of a non-Romani observer that brought together the two groups, as Sutzkever had once suggested, but a dialogue enacted in the language of traditional piety.

It might be tempting to see the scripted diplomacy of the older generation's event as more calculating than the spontaneous staging of shared prayers by younger participants. Yet, both parts of the August 2 ceremonies were simultaneously an expression of deeply felt sentiments of historical connection and an exercise in politics. Every participant standing on the grounds of the former Auschwitz-Birkenau camp on August 2 understood that for the rest of the year, this was a space of Jewish and Polish memory—with both Jewish and Polish representatives competing for interpretive control.[5] They also knew that in recent decades, Romani representatives and survivors had fought to be invited to Jewish Holocaust events. Whether they were young or old, whether this was their first trip abroad with friends or one of the last opportunities to see others who had suffered in the camp alongside them, they all understood that since the 1970s, the wider public regarded them as Nazism's "other" or "non-Jewish" victims.

A similar mix of psychological and political motives propelled Jews who had arranged such commemorations for their dead since the war. In most circumstances it proved impossible to disentangle the multiple concerns that informed public events. The larger world of archives, films, college courses, high school exhibits, textbooks, heritage trips, and local initiatives to hear survivors speak at school and community events emerged out of private desires that also made political sense.

This dualism of sentiment and politics is not an easy one. The role politics plays—or should play—when individuals invoke the Holocaust has always been contentious. Given the importance of institutions, memorial spaces, and funding organizations that have focused on the Jewish Holocaust since the 1970s, Romani activists seeking recognition for their group's genocide continue to work through these issues, as do their Jewish counterparts.[6] Much as in 2014, over the past decades, Romani participants regularly navigated their own internal divisions even as they found themselves in the middle of debates about the politics of memory involving Jews and other groups. At the same time, Jews deeply involved in the politics of their own group found themselves drawn to Romani civil rights work and Holocaust commemorations for reasons that were personal and political, in ways that would have been unimaginable in the decades immediately following the war.

An American Museum of the Holocaust(s)

The most remarkable shift in public debates on Nazi crimes took place in the second half of the 1970s, especially in Germany and the United States. Plaques for murdered Jews began appearing in German towns large and small, while in the United States, school districts and colleges started to include the Holocaust in their curricula.[7] In Germany, and, later, across Europe, this was the result of a few processes: Non-Jews were coming to terms with the Nazi past, were increasingly curious to know what their relatives did during the war, and developed a new sensibility to the haunting voids left by the murdered Jews who once formed part of their societies. In the United States, by contrast, this renewed interest was driven largely by Jews of different ages and persuasions, rather than non-Jews. As the historian Peter Novick has noted, for some American Jews, the threats to Israel in the 1967 and 1973 wars raised memories of World War Two, when US Jewry witnessed the destruction of European Jewry.[8] At the same time, children of survivors started to address histories that had previously been deemed private, drawing on the popular notion that addressing a traumatic past might have therapeutic effects. Accounts of past suffering also gained new meaning with the proliferation of identity as a political category and amidst a growing emphasis on the political importance of seemingly private concerns.[9]

These developments culminated with the airing of the NBC miniseries *Holocaust* in the United States in 1978 and Western Europe in 1979. The series reached an enormous audience across the Cold War West and transformed public perceptions of Nazism. Subsequently, the murder of the Jews came to represent Nazi Germany's defining crime, summed up with a single term in different countries, across multiple languages. *Holocaust* also entered the German language through the miniseries, and the debate sparked by the docudrama reinforced the transnational character of the new Holocaust memorial culture.[10] Among many Western European and US Jews, a consensus solidified that the Jewish Holocaust could be generalized as a warning to others, but that the event itself was distinct from the killing of other noncombatants during the war.

The murder of Roma assumed a strange liminal position in mainstream descriptions of the Jewish Holocaust as a kindred and related event that was nevertheless subordinate to the larger story of Jewish persecution. The NBC miniseries illustrates this logic. The main narrative concerned a Jewish and a Catholic German family and their respective paths into victimhood and complicity. Viewers learn of Romani victims only indirectly. In the first episode of the series, the Nazis arrest Karl Weiss, one of the protagonists, and send him to the Buchenwald concentration camp after Kristallnacht. At the camp, an older Jewish prisoner in the textile workshop explains the various signs Karl must sew onto prisoner uniforms. Each symbol and color stands for a different group: political prisoners, "asocials," homosexuals. Arriving at a brown triangle, the inmate tells Karl, "Brown is for Gypsies." Surprised, Karl asks, "Gypsies?" His interlocutor replies, "Sure, Buchenwald is full of them. They give the guards fits. The SS buried two gypsies alive yesterday. When they dug them out, their tongues stuck out like sausages."[11]

While such comments might have raised the issue of "other victims" for some—inspiring scholars to add "Gypsies" to educational material prepared to accompany the film, for example—the grotesque image voiced by the characters hardly humanized the Romani experience of genocide.[12] Instead it portrayed Romani prisoners as spectral figures who were discussed in strange and shocking terms but never appeared in the film. The miniseries, like so many depictions of the Holocaust that had come before it, offered a thoroughly Jewish perspective on the victimhood of Roma.

The Romani civil rights movement's discussion of historical injustice took place against this backdrop. With depictions of Jews as the paradigmatic victims of Nazism, other victims found themselves in the categories of "forgotten victims" or "non-Jewish victims." For those who came to be known under these terms, debates about the correct way for states and societies to remember the past had high political and emotional stakes. These controversies are part of the history that Romani activists openly or indirectly address at many commemorative events. Some of the most bruising experiences emerged from the earliest efforts to give an official, authoritative form to the new Holocaust consciousness popularized by the NBC series: the United States Holocaust Memorial Museum (USHMM).

The museum embodies the dual character of the new memory culture as an expression of heartfelt idealism and hardnosed politics. The latter was hard to miss. In 1978, President Jimmy Carter decided to form an exploratory committee—under Elie Wiesel's leadership—for a Holocaust memorial because of his administration's involvement in Middle East affairs. Many political commentators understood Carter's decision as a play for Jewish votes, noting that he had established the commission in response to criticism over the sale of fighter jets to Saudi Arabia and to allay fears that this signaled a loosening of traditional US ties with Israel. International politics would remain a continuous consideration in the institution's approach to how it represented and archived the past.

Those offering their vision of what an American museum of the Holocaust might be couched their ideas in terms that would appeal to a broad political base in the United States. Some European commentators associated the "Americanization" of the Holocaust with the banalization of the past for the sake of commercial exploitation and mass media consumption, but others in the United States understood the catchword Americanization in positive terms. Charged with exhibition planning at the museum from 1987 on, the Holocaust scholar and educator Michael Berenbaum argued that the term encapsulated the mission to explain the Holocaust to a diverse US audience in the name of a state that represented an increasingly multicultural society.[13] Berenbaum articulated his view in a much quoted essay on the uniqueness and universality of the Holocaust: "The task of the US Holocaust Memorial Council involved the Americanization of the Holocaust; the story had to be told in such a way that it would resonate not only with the survivor in New York and his children in Houston or San Francisco, but with a black leader from Atlanta, a Midwestern farmer, or a northeastern industrialist."[14] His aim was to Americanize without "dejudaizing"—another popular term with those involved in the debates of the 1980s and 1990s—by making the Jewish Holocaust into a lesson for all Americans.

Paradoxically Berenbaum's idea of universalization led to an emphasis on the uniqueness of the Jewish experience. To contemporaries, the limitations of Berenbaum's position were less obvious than that of Elie Wiesel, who insisted that the Holocaust was an unspeakable event that resists representation. Indeed, until today, Jewish policymakers and intellectuals sometimes perceive

Berenbaum's approach as the more inclusive of the two options.[15] But the consequences of Berenbaum's approach for Jews' relations with other groups is apparent in his comments on the Romani genocide. In the same essay, he introduces their fate in the following terms: "Gypsies shared much but not all of the horrors assigned to Jews. Romani were killed in some countries but not in others." For Berenbaum, the history of Roma, like the history of many other groups, had to be related to the larger Jewish story of genocide, so that Jewish history could become more intelligible to diverse audiences. Jews were imparting a lesson to fellow Americans, but in Berenbaum's vision they themselves had little to learn from the history of other victims.

This approach perfectly encapsulates the concessions that key players in the United States Holocaust Memorial Council (USHMC), the USHMM's steering and planning body, believed they could make in the 1980s and 1990s. Berenbaum reflected on these concessions in *A Mosaic of Victims: Non-Jews Persecuted and Murdered by the Nazis*, a volume based on a conference of the same name, held under the auspices of the USHMC at the US State Department in February 1987. The title reveals the apologetic thrust of both the event and the publication. Facing constant critiques from multiple constituencies— including Polish-American and Ukrainian-American associations—the USHMC addressed competing demands in one sweep.[16] The event combined an assortment of "non-Jewish" victims and framed the discussion in ways that were sensitive to the priorities of Jewish survivors and communally active US Jews, whose identification with the museum was crucial for its legitimacy and future success.[17]

Romani representatives did not challenge the centrality of crimes against Jews for the museum, but they did demand a seat at the table. And for the first time, there *was* a metaphorical table where decisions on the official representation of Nazi genocides would be made. Roma had organized nationally and internationally around compensation and recognition before. But there had never been a single institution entrusted with the task of representing a consensus account of the Holocaust to the nation and—due to its location—the world. According to the unchallenged understanding of everyone involved, Yad Vashem in Jerusalem was a site of Jewish memory, serving a state that claimed to be the answer to a history of Jewish persecution. Representatives of the Israeli institution could plausibly argue that their legal and moral mandate limited them to the representation of the Jewish Holocaust. Concentration camp memorials offered a clearer precedent. German Sinti were among the earliest non-state groups that successfully demanded spaces commemorating their dead in these camps, starting with a small memorial in Auschwitz-Birkenau's former "Gypsy camp," dedicated by Vincenz Rose and Oscar Bamberger in 1974.[18] Over the decades, many major camps received some monument or plaque that could become the focal point of ceremonies. Yet, these camps were largely sites of parallel memorialization, where survivors of particular groups could congregate around separate monuments, and sometimes received separate exhibit spaces.[19] At the USHMC, by contrast, Romanies hoped to be part of a council that would decide on a single canonical account.

In 1984, Barry Fischer, a Jewish constitutional lawyer who represented Romani clients in civil rights cases, arranged for a meeting in Los Angeles between Jewish museum representatives and Romani leaders.[20] The meeting put Romani concerns on the radars of Jewish decision-makers but did not change the USHMC's plans. A second, more confrontational strategy was modeled on successful demonstrations by the German Romani rights movement, which had organized a hunger strike at the former camp Dachau in 1980.[21] To press their issues, Romani activists, including the US-based Romani leaders John Tene and James Marks, demonstrated in front of the US Department of Labor building where the USHMC convened a meeting on July 20, 1984.[22] The protestors wore homemade versions of the striped uniforms associated with Nazi concentration camps to underscore their demand to be seen as fellow victims of Nazism and to have a representative on the USHMC. Despite these stark images, barely anyone noticed the protest.[23]

Purposeful and spontaneous actions that interrupted the USHMC's messaging proved more effective. Romani activists started appearing at the Days of Remembrance, the USHMC's main annual event commemorating the Holocaust in the Rotunda of the United States Capitol. In 1985, a Romani survivor began lighting his own candle, breaking the ceremony's planned choreography, and Romani survivors protested in front of the building when they did not find a place inside.[24] Around the same time, multiple Romani leaders and veterans of the Romani rights movement, such as Gratton Puxon, started a letter campaign for inclusion in the council. Slowly, the council realized it had to react. An internal memorandum on the "status of the P.R. siege by Gypsy groups," showed that the council's leadership was starting to be concerned about damage to the museum's public image.[25] In 1986, the USHMC's Director of Communications warned that "damage could be done to the Council if the worst happens and the Gypsies demonstrate" at the next Days of Remembrance Ceremony, scheduled for May 6 of that year.[26] She asked the head of

FIGURE 6.2. Roma protesting in front of a meeting of the United States Holocaust Memorial Council in Washington, DC, July 20, 1984. Reproduced with permission of Grattan Puxon Archive, Bishopsgate Institute.

the committee organizing these events, Sigmund Strochlitz, whether they wanted to do something or "accept the calculated risk of a demonstration."[27] Strochlitz, an Auschwitz survivor who remembered the night of August 2, 1944, when the Nazis killed all remaining Romani prisoners, decided to include them.

As a result, museum executives met with a range of people they understood as "Gypsy representatives" on May 5, 1986.[28] Romani activists demanded shared commemorative events and five positions on the supervisory council. Instead, they received what the museum had already conceded: there would be a separate ceremony for Roma in September 1986, and the event would be publicly announced at the Days of Remembrance. The fragility of that agreement is reflected in a last-minute memo to the USHMC's vice-chair before the ceremony at the Capitol Rotunda: "[W]e negotiated the text of this paragraph with members of the Gypsy nation yesterday. If no other speaker reads it, please do so. Very important. Our credibility is at stake."[29]

Other minor adjustments followed. At the special Day of Remembrance for Romani victims, Elie Wiesel promised "on my behalf and on behalf of my friends, that we shall do whatever we can from now on to listen better," and both Wiesel and Strochlitz referred to their memories of the mass killings of

Romani prisoners on August 2 in Auschwitz to explain their affinity with Romani survivors.[30] In 1987, the museum initiated an "Ethnic Outreach Program" on the "Fate of the Gypsies during the Holocaust." The planners explained that they were responding to "previous Council neglect of the Gypsy community" and proposed new commemorative ceremonies and a photo resource packet.[31] At the level of governance, some small changes occurred as well. Following public pressure, the White House appointed a Romani representative as one of the sixty voting members of the USHMC, starting with Romani professor of music, William Duna, from 1987–97.[32] The professor of linguistics Ian Hancock replaced Duna in 1997 for a five-year term, and, after a hiatus of over a decade, Barack Obama appointed the Romani sociologist and activist Ethel Brooks to the museum's supervisory body in 2016.[33] The superficial nature of such measures understandably irritated Romani activists, such as Hancock, who had worked for years to build relations with Jewish scholars and administrators.[34]

These limited concessions are indicative of the economic context for memory work that took hold in the United States, where institutions came to rely heavily on fundraising among religious and ethnic communities. Many of the early institutions that dealt with the Holocaust, such as the Wiener Library in the UK, the Ghetto Fighters' House in Israel, and the Center for Contemporary Jewish Documentation in France relied on a mix of payments from restitution funds (via the Claims Conference) and small-donation fundraising; others, such as the Netherlands Institute for War Documentation and the Institute for Contemporary History in Munich, were independent institutions backed by the state. States also governed and funded memorial sites on the grounds of former camps, often operating small educational departments and archives. As a public institution that relied heavily on private fundraising, the USHMM followed in the footsteps of these institutions. Yet with its mix of state funding and professional fundraising, the USHMM also embodied the deep roots of the US government's reliance on civil society groups for public services. Income tax exemptions established in 1917 that allowed certain individuals to deduct contributions from charitable, religious, or educational associations set the US on a unique path in this regard.[35] These tax rules, revised over the years, formed the regulatory backdrop to a shift in public attitudes toward giving that also transformed Jewish communal life and commemorative institutions.

US fundraising for Jewish organizations was not just quantitatively different from corresponding efforts to finance memorial and communal work in Europe, it was also qualitatively different. It was much more central to Jewish life,

Jewish nonprofit organization management, and the political environment. Museum planners conceived not only the narrative of the museum but also its economic structure in the middle of a revolution in philanthropic financing. By the 1950s, institutions that previously prided themselves on spending all the funds they raised began building endowments, which grew exponentially in the 1970s and 1980s.[36] In this environment, the original law establishing the museum, which Congress unanimously passed in 1980, promised only a limited budget for the institution, with the understanding that all building funds would have to be raised from donors.[37] Even though the USHMM could rely on a sizable federal appropriation to fund its basic operations and staff, beyond these essential functions, private donations and endowments supported programming. There was a strong assumption that the council would raise these funds from Jews who cared about Jewish history and politics.

This means that even when scholar-administrators like Berenbaum reflected on the responsibility to address diverse audiences, material and political realities amplified the voices of those who claimed to represent the Jewish mainstream. Given the museum's political origins, moral mission, and funding, it was easy to have debates among Jews about the role of other groups, rather than with those groups, even at a state institution with a largely non-Jewish staff. Council members and their critics could draw on larger debates about the role of Jewish suffering for Jewish identity because many of them thought that all of the important decision-makers would care about the Holocaust in precisely those terms. There was certainly a sense that Jews had to explain their vision to non-Jews: indeed, the council even hired pollsters to gauge how they might best explain why a Holocaust museum belonged on the National Mall in Washington DC.[38] Yet, this move merely underscored that this was a debate among Jews about how to communicate their priorities to a wider public.

None of this boded well for dialogue. Romani victims had no place in conceptual debates because there were few incentives to consider their viewpoints. Romani representatives did not speak for an influential constituency in the United States and had little access to decision-makers; nor could they promise much in terms of fundraising. Ian Hancock complained vigorously to his allies and the White House when Linas Kojelis, Reagan's liaison for relations to "ethnic groups" and defense policy, explained in 1986 that Romanies were not powerful enough as fundraisers to merit a seat on the council.[39] What Romani leaders understood as cynicism from politicians and Jewish representatives was the consequence of the tendency to outsource US government functions to public-private partnerships.

For their part, Jewish administrators left little evidence of having reflected critically on the financial realities and infrastructure that facilitated their work. In another incident, the council's director of communication tried to tell John Megel, who represented a Romani association called the Romani Council, that he could receive training in fundraising from other directors of Holocaust organizations.[40] The USHMC apparently intended this as a generous offer to compensate for the bad news they had given Megel: they were unwilling to pay for a traveling exhibit on the Romani genocide that he had planned. They did not pause to consider that Jewish fundraising relied on populations that saw significant economic success after World War Two and on communal institutions that benefited from decades of professional development.[41] Romani communities lacked similar potential and the apparatus to realize it. The US tax code's donation exemptions created an infrastructure that shaped Holocaust memory politics in ways that did not necessarily translate to other groups or countries.

Polemical claims about a "Holocaust industry" that reduces memorialization efforts to Jewish greed or self-interest obscure rather than expose these underlying dynamics. Endowments and annual fundraising have reshaped politics and knowledge production. They dominate private and public university life, for example. But at least this has sparked a robust debate on the conflict between an economic model of governance and another that emphasizes the public good of higher education. In contrast, the role of fundraising and endowments in the representation of historical injustice has not yet been a subject of serious debate. As a result, museum administrators and scholars have found it difficult to address disparities that endowments did not create but have nonetheless often reinforced.

Other structural decisions that had little to do with Romani claims also contributed to their marginalization in the museum's permanent exhibition, even as the administration was well aware of the museum's deficient coverage of non-Jewish victims of Nazism. Members of the museum's content committee understood the museum's public mission as one of radical accessibility. From the earliest iterations of the program in position papers, the committee's ambition was "to inform the visitors' moral imagination" rather than explore historical details.[42] Nothing should look like "a textbook on walls," according to the responsible committee, which wanted streamlined storylines.[43] In the conflict between exhaustive coverage—and thus inclusivity, as regards victims—and accessibility, the latter won out. Exhibition developers thus treated Romani history as an unnecessary complication unless it fit seamlessly within a timeline of anti-Jewish measures or could be represented by compelling artifacts. When intriguing display objects—such as a "Gypsy wagon" that the USHMM bought from a Czech film studio in 1990—were available, Romani experiences found space at the museum.[44] Yet, museum designers marked them as separate and somewhat marginal parts of the exhibit.

A Revolution at the USHMM: Archives and Research

When it came to high-profile commemorations and the popular permanent exhibit—the realms that mattered most to Romani and Jewish commentators—the USHMM's actions were a disappointment. Yet these failed opportunities obscure the museum's primary success: the USHMM developed into a major center for the collection of historical material and research on the Jewish *and* the Romani Holocaust, although the institution rarely highlights this work.

From its inception, it was clear that the museum would need auxiliary services that went beyond the infrastructure required to put objects into an exhibition space. The 1979 report by the President's Commission proposed that the museum house "a library, an archive of Holocaust materials, computer linkage to existing centers of Holocaust documentation, and a reference staff." [45] This language suggested some understanding that the museum would need professional expertise, learning materials, and access to digital technologies to fulfill its educational mission. Yet the report hardly expressed an ambition for the USHMM to become one of the world's premier research hubs on the Holocaust and the most important repository of archival sources on the subject.

Discussions about research and archival activities came surprisingly late in the institution's development. The first dedicated meetings on the topic took place when the Academic Committee began its work in 1989, nine years after Congress established the USHMC.[46] By the time staff members sat down with a few prominent scholars to hammer out what an academic committee could contribute, the council had resolved all crucial issues regarding the exhibit. This liberated the committee from dealing with contentious issues that garnered public attention. Whereas the permanent exhibit was not going to change for a long time, the committee took charge of the activities that required ongoing decisions: academic programming as well as the development of the archive and library. The key players in this early phase, Rabbi Alfred Gottschalk, the historian Raul Hilberg, and Michael Berenbaum, would remain the most vocal members of the committee in its first decade. German-born Gottschalk, a leader in Reform Judaism and the long-serving president of Hebrew Union College, chaired the committee.

Committee members understood that forming archives and facilitating research were activities that belonged together, and that decisions about the former would have to come first. The museum had started collecting artifacts for its exhibit and, in the process, built an apparatus for identifying, acquiring, and storing historical materials. With the slow opening of different communist countries during Perestroika and the revolutions of 1989, opportunities for the collection of material multiplied. When the Academic Committee began contemplating the creation of a new archive, negotiations to copy documents from Soviet and Romanian institutions were already underway, and a deal with the Soviets had already been signed.[47] Thus, even before the committee began considering the shape that the museum's research center would take, they had to tend to the urgent matter of defining the scope of archival acquisitions.

While heated public debates transpired over the representation of victim groups in the exhibition, archival acquisitions were a matter of expert deliberations that took place behind closed doors. Many decisions remained in the purview of professional staff who determined the budgetary and technological limitations of acquisitions before they presented options to committee appointees. Whether staff or committee members, everyone involved emphasized that relevance to the Jewish Holocaust was the vital criterion for acquisitions. Their task thus consisted largely of working through the catalog records of existing state collections and determining which holdings pertained to Jewish persecution and which belonged in the capacious category of everything else. This preoccupied staff and committee members to such an extent that other victim groups hardly came up. When they did, it was often to clarify that they did not belong in the museum's burgeoning archive. Early meetings determined that copies from the Extraordinary State Commission in the postwar Soviet Union should only include "records relating to Jewish losses," for example, without any reference to other targeted groups.[48]

The scholars on the committee were certainly aware of the broader conflicts over questions of victimhood that were taking place in the public square. In fact, they engaged in their own debates over uniqueness and universality—not surprisingly, perhaps, since many committee members, such as Berenbaum and the historian Yehuda Bauer, had already staked out clear positions in these debates. Most members feared that scholars might veer too far from Jewish issues. Several of them, including Gottschalk, successfully pushed to include language in the founding documents of the research institute to ensure that "we do not become universalistic."[49] They also openly discussed how to prevent future committee members from revisiting the institute's focus on Jews.

Out of the public eye, these professionals seemed to feel they could finally do their work without getting bogged down by interests they perceived as political. Without dissenters in the room, they agreed that the museum should collect in areas that matched their understanding of the Jewish Holocaust, even though some of the participants expressed the will to advocate for Romani rights and insisted on the relevance of their history in other contexts.[50]

Scholars who were able to make sense of these new archival holdings and provide feedback on their needs soon came to Washington. In 1991, the Academic Committee deliberated in earnest about a future research institute. After they considered and rejected the idea that the museum could train scholars as a university would, a consensus emerged that some sort of academic programming with conferences and fellows should exist.[51] A series of names were used for the resulting unit, starting with United States Holocaust Research Institute (1993), Research Institute (1996), and, eventually, the Center for Advanced Holocaust Studies (1997). In 2014, after a $10 million endowment from the Mandel Foundation, it became the Jack, Joseph and Morton Mandel Center for Advanced Holocaust Studies.[52] At its inception, the institute had sufficient funds only for a single invited scholar.[53] Soon, the museum secured resources to bring junior scholars to Washington as well, all based on money gathered from donors rather than government appropriations.[54] Over the years, this fellowship program would grow to become the largest of its kind in the world.

There is no record of major deliberations on the inclusion of Roma in this context, yet many small decisions contributed to making the USHMM into a hub for Romani Holocaust research, despite the insistence of many of its founding members that the museum concentrate on Jewish themes. The historian Sybil Milton likely got things started when she served on Berenbaum's staff and then as the museum's first Senior Historian from 1992 to 1995. In all her functions, Milton encouraged the study of Romani history by making sure that material on Roma ended up in the archive and found capable readers.[55] She also made clear to others that she disagreed with her superior, Berenbaum, and insisted on the need to emphasize the similarities between the persecution of Jews and Roma.[56]

The combination of ambitious collection building and a growing research program soon developed its own dynamics. The acquisition team purchased and copied material wherever they could but also needed to consider possible users, while academic reviewers selected visiting scholars based on their ability to use archival resources. This created a feedback loop. The more the institution collects on a particular theme, the more likely it is to fund scholars working with those materials; the more scholars come to the museum with an interest in a particular topic, the more likely the institution is to invest in making material on the topic available by purchasing collections and prioritizing the creation of finding aids and digitization. Reference librarians and archivists will also tend to be quicker to refer scholars to material that has been previously used.

The overlap between archival acquisitions and fellowship programming was most evident when it came to Romania. Radu Ioanid, a historian who worked on the persecution of Jews and Roma in Romania, headed the museum's section in charge of acquiring international archival material between 2000 and 2020. Under his tenure, the museum's acquisition team added material on Roma when the opportunity arose, even creating its own collection of Romanian records dealing with Roma derived from multiple archives.[57] At the same time, numerous scholars came to the museum to work on Romanian Roma. Between 1995 and 2020, half of the fourteen fellows working on Roma at the Center for Advanced Holocaust Studies focused on Romania. The steady stream of scholars using these materials in turn legitimized their acquisition, encouraging further collection building on the Romani Holocaust.[58]

None of this changes the fact that the USHMM and its subsidiary institutions, such as the Center for Advanced Holocaust Studies, were designed to lead education and research on the Jewish Holocaust. However, it does show how such institutions could become centers for the study of the Romani genocide through the invisible labor of individuals on the ground, changes in their scholarly focus, and the tendency to expand their mandate into adjacent areas of expertise. Proportionally, the collections made available, fellowships granted, and conferences organized on Romani matters remained small relative to the museum's original mission, but there was still no other institution that could rival the USHMM in its capacity to aid in the creation of authorized knowledge on the Romani genocide.

Private philanthropy as well as the geopolitical clout of the United States made all of this possible. The museum began acquiring its holdings after the end of the Cold War when the United States was able to build broad coalitions to meet its foreign policy goals. The importance of the United States for aspiring NATO applicants in East Central Europe aided the efforts of NGOs and institutions based on state-civil society cooperation to get privileged access to the region. As the United States began projecting its power—often with a stated concern for minorities in postcommunist Europe—the material traces of genocide became part of a transfer of knowledge and objects from former communist countries in Eastern Europe to the United States and Western Europe.[59]

We can glean how these transfers worked by examining a short controversy over documents from the famous secret archives created by the Oneg Shabbat group in the Warsaw Ghetto. The original records of the group belonged to the Jewish Historical Institute in Warsaw, which lent certain documents to the USHMM in the late 1980s.[60] Organizers anticipated that these documents, together with a milk can that Ringelblum used to bury his archive, would be prize objects at the museum's opening in 1993, which coincided with the fiftieth anniversary of the Warsaw Ghetto Uprising. The USHMM encountered some unexpected resistance, however, when the director of the Polish State archives in 1992 refused to renew the Jewish Historical Institute's loan of Ringelblum archive documents. Worried about the embarrassing loss of important items for display in the new museum, USHMM administrators and backers intervened with Polish officials. The USHMM's key argument concerned public opinion. President Lech Wałęsa of Poland had personally promised these documents to the museum during a visit to Washington, DC, and a council member, Miles Lerman, the USHMM's chairman from 1993 to 2003, made Polish officials aware that negative publicity would ensue from the retraction of that offer.[61] This argument likely convinced Polish authorities to agree to a new contract to lend different Ringelblum archive documents on a permanently renewable basis to the USHMM.[62]

Financial considerations were also at play, however, even if all parties emphasized moral arguments. Money rarely came up in official correspondence. Yet, in negotiations with the unresponsive head of the Polish state archives, the USHMM prepared to remind their interlocutors of the USHMM's investments in Poland. Among other things they had contributed a $50,000 phone system for the Auschwitz Memorial and a reproduction studio for the Majdanek Museum. Cooperation with the USHMM was indeed important and necessary for such institutions. The Jewish Historical Institute received a paper conservation laboratory worth an estimated $20,000, and the USHMM's director authorized the purchase of microfilm equipment for up to $12,000.[63]

There was nothing cynical about these expenditures. They emerged out of power relations between a state institution in the United States that had considerable donor backing and underfunded institutions in postcommunist

Central and Eastern Europe. Post–Cold War geopolitics and the often-unspoken financial realities guiding nonprofit institutions' ability to acquire material globally made possible the USHMM's rise to becoming a central hub of Jewish and, eventually, also Romani Holocaust Studies.

Recording Traces of Genocide in the United States and Europe

In polycentric Europe, there are no similarly consolidated archives of the Jewish Holocaust. Instead, historical document repositories, much like memory debates, tend to be national in character and focus on material produced within the state's borders. The European Union and other supranational organizations created common arenas for competition over monetary support but did not alter the local and diffuse nature of archival work across the continent. In the European Union, archives are one of the few areas where states can largely establish and enforce their own rules. Despite attempts to create a unified database of national collections, historians of Nazi persecution have to seek out material in traditional administrative archives, such as national archives, that preserve records on Nazi crimes as part of the paperwork produced by a particular bureaucracy. While it is not surprising that these institutions retain distinct collections, the dearth of research centers that provide fellowship programs and centralize information by duplicating materials from state archives increases the cost of historical scholarship. Consequently, visits to the USHMM are often familiar steps in the careers of European Holocaust historians, even if most of the USHMM's holdings originated in Europe. Those who want to seriously study the Romani Holocaust frequently face a choice of either working alone in decentralized state archives or joining a community of scholars at a highly accessible archive in the United States—but one tailored for historians working on the Jewish, not Romani, Holocaust.

The disparities in access to information are even starker when it comes to oral history, a crucial source for victim-centered research in general and Romani history in particular. Many interview initiatives in the United States, as in Europe, began locally. But only in the US did endowment funding and private initiatives permit the consolidation of collections in a few centralized spaces where the recorded voices of survivors are easily available.

The Fortunoff archive in New Haven, Connecticut, is an excellent example of these developments. Founded around the same time that a new generation of oral history projects also started in Germany, the Fortunoff archive grew out of a project by the New Haven Jewish Federation to record interviews for a film in 1979.[64] From these modest beginnings, a group under the leadership of the psychologist Dori Laub and several others developed the Holocaust Survivors Project. They managed to grow the project thanks to a grant from the Charles H. Revson Foundation, which allowed them to move the project to Yale University in 1982. Eventually, an endowment from Alan A. Fortunoff sustained the institution—subsequently known as the Fortunoff Archive— after 1987.[65] Had the institution relied only on local volunteers or project-based funding for academic work, which was common in Europe, it would likely have remained a disparate collection with limited access or been absorbed into larger archives, as was the case with many other local initiatives in the United States.[66]

US institutions also had the ambition to collect globally, unlike European institutions, which tended to focus more narrowly on recovering voices from their national past. This was true for the big archives such as the Shoah Foundation and the USHMM, but also for smaller institutions such as the Fortunoff Archive. US initiatives had focused largely on interviews with survivors in North America in the 1980s, but with the fall of communism, the Fortunoff Archive, like others, began collecting abroad, just as the USHMM embarked on its bold quest for archival acquisitions. That expansion began with a series of interviews from Serbia in 1989. The better funded Shoah Foundation and the USHMM would soon overtake the Fortunoff Archive's efforts, but even as one of the smallest and oldest of the major US Holocaust testimony archives, the Fortunoff Archive covered as many areas of Nazi persecution and communities of survivors as it could, collecting a total of over 4,400 interviews.

In this spirit, the Fortunoff Archive commissioned the first widely available audiovisual testimonies of Romani survivors. These were not the property of a single research project but instead part of a dedicated testimony archive. In 1991 the Canadian ethnographer Gabrielle Tyrnauer, supported by the US archive and a Canadian oral history project, conducted interviews with twenty-four Romani Holocaust survivors in Germany.[67] Tyrnauer, who fled Nazi-occupied Austria as a young child, often referenced her own Jewishness in her interviews with her Romani interlocutors. Her collection remained on analog media in New Haven for the next two decades, before her estate donated versions to the USHMM that were then digitized and made available online without restrictions. Long underutilized, her collection is among the most accessible set of Romani oral histories.[68]

In the 1990s and 2000s, US archives consolidated Jewish testimony collections in a few locations, which had far-reaching consequences for Romani testimony collecting. The largest of these archives, the Shoah Foundation, established by Steven Spielberg in 1994, aimed to become the central global repository of Holocaust testimonies. Its Visual History Archive, now hosted by the University of Southern California, consists of over 50,000 Holocaust testimonies, which follow a standardized method, and represents one of the largest audiovisual collections globally.[69] Like other archives, the Shoah Foundation eventually made efficient use of its expertise and added to its collections testimonies dealing with genocidal violence in South Sudan, Guatemala, Cambodia, and other locations. Even before the archive's leadership began documenting atrocities in other parts of the world, they made efforts to include Romani interviews. Suspecting that they might encounter difficulties recruiting survivors, they turned to individuals who could help: Romani Rose and Roman Kwiatkowski, who both spoke at and organized the official August 2 commemoration of the Romani Holocaust that opened this chapter. Although the Shoah Foundation was largely unsuccessful in its formal cooperation with Romani organizations, it nonetheless managed to assemble 406 interviews with Roma, making it the largest repository of its kind in the world.

Local initiatives in Europe have sought to build their own testimony collections, but US institutions have retained the advantage of having started earlier. They also benefit from long-term funding from endowment sources, as well as annual state appropriations in the case of the USHMM. By the time small Romani institutions began interviewing survivors in the 2000s, US endowment-driven archives that specialized in Jewish memory had created collections that dwarfed theirs, in both size and accessibility. European grassroots projects to interview survivors have in turn created a radically decentralized situation, where recordings often remain the property of individual scholars. In other cases, such as that of the Central Council for German Sinti and Roma, museums and associations have kept recordings in local collections without publicly available catalogs and with highly restricted access.

The consequences for Jewish and Romani history are profound. While Romani survivors and their descendants mostly lived, and still live, in Central and Eastern Europe, institutions in these regions have proven unable to compete with the USHMM, the Shoah Foundation, and the Fortunoff archive—or with Yad Vashem in Israel, for that matter. As a result, the most effective collections of Romani historical material are situated far from where the majority of the victims' descendants live.[70] Most Jewish Holocaust survivors and their descendants, by contrast, reside in countries where the most accessible collections have been assembled. The same economic and geopolitical realities that facilitated the growth of Jewish Holocaust Studies thus exacerbated the fragmentation of Romani sources and made it harder for scholars—but also advocates of Romani rights—to find relevant material.

The Romani Genocide, Israel, and Antiracist Memory

While US institutions transformed Holocaust documentation, most debates on the Nazi past and initiatives to commemorate Romani history took place in diffuse settings across Europe, where the political stakes were higher than in the US. In Europe, when activists demanded recognition of past injustice, they had on their minds the continuous injustice of the present: in many European countries, survivors and their family members lived among the perpetrators and in communities that had supported these perpetrators. They also remained targets of institutions that had aided in the identification, removal, expropriation, and murder of Roma. While postwar political conventions militated against open antisemitism, anti-Romani racism, or antiziganism, was ignored and unnamed. Unlike Jews, Roma continued to face systematic discrimination in housing, the labor market, and urban policy.

The first large international commemoration of the Romani genocide conveyed these realities unambiguously: in October 1979, advocates for Romani rights and human rights brought together survivors, activists, and politicians for an event in Bergen-Belsen, calling it "Gassed in Auschwitz, Persecuted until Today." The title, which was also given to a volume published the same year, encapsulated the sense that too little had changed for Sinti and Roma since the Nazi era. This was also the tenor of the foreword written by Romani Rose, the rising star of Germany's Romani civil rights movement. Rose emphasized that Sinti and Roma still suffered systemic marginalization and excessive policing.[71] Unlike most ceremonies dealing with Nazi crimes that emphasize "never again," many Romani commemorations demanded "not anymore."[72]

Jewish survivors played a notable role in this struggle. Their presence at the 1979 gathering underscored the relevance of Romani demands at a time when the German public was starting to confront the Jewish Holocaust in new ways. The ceremony in Bergen-Belsen took place nine months after the airing of NBC's *Holocaust* in West Germany and during parliamentary debates in Bonn on the extension of the statute of limitation for Nazi crimes.[73] In this context, Romani activists were glad to welcome official Jewish dignitaries such as

Heinz Galinski, the head of Berlin's Jewish community, who cited the two groups' shared experience as stigmatized minorities and acknowledged that Sinti and Roma, unlike Jews at the time, had to fight for the recognition of their fate under the Nazis.[74]

Most Jewish commentators acknowledged that their support for Romani struggles for equality came simultaneously from a place of shared otherness and of difference between the groups. This was evident in a speech delivered by the most prominent Jewish participant in attendance at Bergen-Belsen, Simone Veil. Much of the event's choreography and subsequent coverage focused on Veil, the newly minted president of the European Parliament and longtime minister of health in France (1974–79). At Bergen-Belsen, Veil spoke as a survivor of Nazi concentration camps to fellow survivors. Bringing her listeners back to the day of her liberation from the camp, where she had also lost her mother, she remarked that Jews and "Gypsies" both emerged from the ordeal that day, April 17, 1945, as "shadows without gender or age." Veil felt an obligation to be present at the commemoration, she explained, since both groups had "suffered together," and "together mourned our dead who were burned in the crematoria." She also told her listeners "that the ashes of all our parents are unified and that this monument here contains the last remains, some bone fragments, some ash, of all our parents."[75] Powerful and vivid, the image spoke of a shared death but not shared lives.[76]

Veil addressed this gap, in life, between Jews and Roma. Expressing sentiments common in other testimonies from Auschwitz—where she was imprisoned before her transfer to Bergen-Belsen—she emphasized the separate suffering of Jews and Roma. Segregated according to Nazi categories of persecution in the camps, everyone felt "their own misery," she noted. She candidly explained that Jews in Auschwitz-Birkenau sometimes envied their fellow Romani prisoners for remaining with their families. Like other Jewish survivors, she emphasized how these sentiments later turned into profound regret—and a sense of solidarity—once it became clear that the SS had murdered the remaining Romani prisoners. For Veil, this ambivalence lay in the past, superseded by the bonds created between two groups who had shared a fate.[77]

A prominent Jewish intellectual, Ernst Tugendhat, expressed feelings of shared experience and divergence differently. A well-known philosopher who wrote the foreword to a volume published in 1979 under the same title— *Gassed in Auschwitz, Persecuted until Today*—Tugendhat put the onus on Jews more decisively.[78] Unlike Veil, who endured Nazi camps, Tugendhat spent his early youth in exile, first in Switzerland and then Venezuela. The scion of a wealthy family of Czech industrialists, Tugendhat studied at Stanford and drew on utterly different experiences than Veil. Still, he opened his piece with similar observations. "Their fate makes Gypsies and Jews siblings," he noted. However, Tugendhat made clear that he referred only to a small slice of their history. For assimilated Jews, as he called people such as himself in his fore-word, life in postwar Germany was comfortable, despite the difficulties of the prewar and wartime periods. For Roma, by contrast, the nightmare had not ended. Indeed, he quickly switched from "we Jews" to "we Germans," empha-sizing that many Jews shared non-Jewish Germans' prejudices against Sinti and Roma.[79] Tugendhat thus implicitly questioned whether Jews were indeed natural partners in the Romani struggle for civil rights.

He did so at a moment when opportunities for different alliances with non-Jewish groups arose. By the late 1970s, many new organizations fought for human rights and could serve as useful allies.[80] These organizations included the Society for Threatened Peoples (Gesellschaft für bedrohte Völker), which had published Gassed in Auschwitz, Persecuted until Today and organized the event at Bergen-Belsen. This human rights organization dedicated months of intensive fundraising to pay for the 1979 event, subsidizing it with a payment of 46,000 Deutsche Marks (the equivalent of over $60,000 four decades later).[81] During the same year, the society also supported the Association of German Sinti under Vincenz Rose and the Romani Union in drafting and promoting a memorandum that included ten demands for the German gov-ernment in 1979.[82] In 1981, it helped organize and finance the Third Roma World Congress in Göttingen.[83] Such efforts were instrumental to the recogni-tion of the Romani minority, which made a great step forward when Chancel-lor Helmut Schmidt acknowledged the Nazi genocide against Sinti and Roma in 1982.[84]

The new human rights organizations that emerged in the 1960s and 1970s sometimes invoked Nazi crimes but did so in particular ways. The predecessor to the Society for Threatened Peoples, Biafra-Hilfe, was one of the organ-izations that used the memory of the Jewish genocide in its campaigns to ben-efit victims of violence outside of Europe. The founder of the Society, Tilman Zülch had co-founded Biafra-Hilfe to raise awareness of the deaths, largely by starvation, that Nigerian military forces had caused in the secessionist republic of Biafra in the context of the Nigerian Civil War of 1967–70.[85] This turn to conflicts abroad was part of the New Left's shift toward the decolonized Third World as the main target of its mobilization efforts in the 1960s.[86] At least early on, it was easy for activists to equate these struggles with those of Jews. Proponents of the Republic of Biafra saw Biafrans as the "Jews of Africa."[87] These descriptions convinced a number of German, British, and French commentators, who reinforced them with visual imagery that suggested similarities between murdered Biafrans and the corpses of Bergen-Belsen.[88] Biafra-Hilfe, following this logic, created posters with the slogan "A as in Auschwitz—B as in Biafra."[89]

Yet, while Auschwitz or Belgen-Belsen could serve as a powerful referent in these debates, leftist activists soon grew suspicious of contemporary Jewish and Israeli politics. On the one hand, certain postwar authors linked the history of colonial, white supremacist, and Nazi violence to offer lessons on European political pathologies.[90] In such cases, Jews could be seen as an inspiration for antiracist and anticolonial struggles, as the literary scholar and cultural critic Michael Rothberg has shown.[91] On the other hand, in the realm of international politics, left-wing and anticolonial activists perceived Israel as part of the colonial, not the anticolonial, world.[92] Its coordinated attack on Egypt with Great Britain and France during the 1956 Suez crisis only reinforced its status as an ally of the old colonizers.[93] While there was no single approach to Israel among leftist and progressive intellectuals and organizers, anticolonial movements and postcolonial states remained at odds with Israel in a variety of realms, ranging from the United Nations to many university seminar rooms, where those who prioritized the global struggle for social and racial justice challenged Zionist positions.

Jews were hardly "threatened" or "endangered peoples"—the titular victims to be protected by Zülch's organization. This adjective, more common today in debates on biodiversity and threatened species, made sense to activists when they campaigned to save indigenous populations in the Americas, Africa, or Asia during the late twentieth century. It was never meant to describe Western European Jews such as Tugendhat or Veil. Thus, while some activists called Biafrans the "Jews of Africa" to invoke parallels to Nazi genocide, few believed that Jews were the colonized of Europe. This was different for Roma, whom Romani and non-Romani activists alike understood as subject to an ongoing global racist regime of oppression. Members of various left-wing movements sometimes considered Roma as Europe's Third World, and the idea of being "threatened" also conformed to clichés that had long circulated among scholars intent on saving Romani culture, or "the last Gypsies."

Unlike others targeted under Nazism, such as political opponents, those deemed hereditarily ill or disabled, homosexuals, so-called asocials, and

Jehovah's witnesses, Roma and Sinti could adopt the language of anticolonial ethnic self-determination. From their inception, the international associations they founded focused on equity, access to all facets of citizenship, and group rights that mirrored those of minority rights activism, civil rights movements, and the Third World nationalisms of the day.[94] The notion that Roma were a non-territorial nation or a national minority also gained traction in Central and Eastern Europe after 1989.[95] Certainly, there were Romani constituencies in Western Europe that preferred to be understood as a minority culture within their larger respective nations—most leading German Sinti representatives, for example, asked for their group to be understood first as Germans— yet even they had to contend with other Romani groups within Germany that pursued different policies as well as an international Romani movement that demanded recognition in ethno-national terms.

The emphasis on Romani ethnic unity, reinforced by the narrative that Roma shared a history of migration from India in the Middle Ages, had drawbacks as well as clear advantages at different points. Assertions of a revolutionary ethnic identity made it difficult for Roma from countries in Cold War Eastern and Southeastern Europe (excluding Yugoslavia) to participate in efforts at international self-organization throughout the 1970s and 1980s, since Moscow-aligned communist governments were leery of such national claims among their citizens. At the same time, it made Romani civil rights a cause that could appeal to diverse actors who were eager to support postcolonial self-assertion. Thanks largely to the mediation of the senior Indian diplomat and linguist W. R. Rishi, the Indian state gave financial support for international Romani conferences early on, helped negotiate the attendance of Czechoslovak Roma there, and—together with Yugoslavia, a fellow nonaligned state—sponsored a 1977 resolution in a United Nations subcommission to recognize Romani people as having "historic, cultural and linguistic ties of Indian origin."[96] The flag adopted by the first World Romani Congress in 1971 reflects the ascendancy of these ideas: the designers put the dominant element of the Indian flag, the 24-spoke wheel (or Ashoka Chakra), on the "Flag of the Romani people."[97]

While such Romani nationalism could be understood to resemble Zionism, with its demands of a return to ancestral, biblical lands, most potential allies who supported anticolonial nationalism had soured on Zionism by the 1970s. Writing at this time when the Romani civil rights movements gained momentum, the sociologist Thomas Acton noted in his analysis of the International Romani Union (referencing the anticolonial thought of Frantz Fanon): "Fanonism and Zionism are not, of course, really compatible systems of thought."[98] Indeed, they were not—neither on paper nor in practice. Holocaust memory slowly became a preoccupation for the political center in much of the Cold War West, while groups further left in Western Europe, North America, and Israel identified with the Black Panthers and anticolonial movements.[99] The Israeli-Arab wars that had motivated many US and European Jews to support Zionism and highlight Jewish victimhood under Nazism also gave rise to an international movement to support Palestinian rights of self-determination.[100]

Israel's 1982 invasion of Lebanon and the First Intifada, which began in 1987, broadened the cleavage between left-wing parties and Zionism across much of the Cold War West.[101] In France, it coincided with a rise in the activism of descendants of Maghrebi migrants (who reclaimed the pejorative term *Beur* for themselves) as well as the surprise successes of the right-wing Front National, starting with municipal elections in 1983. These developments led to the creation in 1984 of a broad antiracist coalition in France, the organization SOS Racisme. The organization brought together self-declared Beur activists with the Union of Jewish Students (UEJF).[102] Although the focus on warding off the successes of the populist right under Jean-Marie Le Pen held the alliance together, the emotional force of the Israel-Arab conflict eventually made cooperation difficult. Indeed, even in its most successful years, the organization invested substantial energy to distance itself from Middle East politics. This is discernible in SOS Racisme's slogan: "We cannot solve the Israel-Palestinian problem on the banks of the Seine."[103] While promoting the idea that multicultural France was under attack from the right, SOS Racisme also had to manage tensions and accusations among its members. Beur activists suggested that the Jewish organizations in its midst supported a racist regime, and Jewish participants accused Beur activists of promoting antisemitic ideas. By 1991, amid debates on the Gulf War and the permissibility of head coverings for Muslim girls in public schools, the UEJF and SOS Racisme found themselves at loggerheads and ceased cooperation.

Similar fault lines developed in other European countries. In Britain, where an active anticolonial movement merged with intense anti-Zionism, tensions were sometimes even more pronounced. In Germany, by contrast, many in the mainstream Left and beyond believed that the country's historical culpability required a more restrained critique of Israel.[104] Yet in each context, members of Jewish student unions and others affiliated with organized Jewry knew that they might face questions about their loyalties and progressive credentials in light of events in Israel.

This affected individual Jews in different ways, depending on their political positions, which ran the gamut from support for the right-wing parties that came to power in Israel in 1977 to a rejection of Zionism. For most European Jewish organizations like official community bodies, Jewish youth movements, and student organizations, which felt an obligation to represent a perceived consensus position, the spectrum was much narrower. Those most likely to represent the Jewish community at commemorative events or to donate money for organized Jewish activities, tended to be more troubled by the rise of anti-Zionism. Indeed, fundraising efforts often emphasized ongoing threats to Jewish life as a means of mobilizing constituents.

In Cold War Eastern Europe, these debates unfolded differently. Most communist states promoted the rejection of Zionism from the top down. In some cases, this found expression in anti-Jewish campaigns, such as the one in Poland in 1967–68.[105] Official attacks against Zionism gave incentive to opponents of European communist regimes to express their sympathies with Israel—but also made it unattractive for Roma from Eastern European countries to associate themselves openly with Jewish politics.[106] Beginning in 1989, these countries experienced multiple, polarizing memory revolutions. Right after the fall of communism, recognition of the Holocaust became the unofficial benchmark for readiness to join the European Union. Yet, breaking with convention in Western European countries, which emphasized the singularity of Nazi crimes, official state institutions and populist parties in former Soviet Bloc countries also proclaimed the double victimhood of the nation under fascism and communism.[107] Paradoxically this self-portrayal as historical victims created openings to continue the pattern established under communism of downplaying the breadth of popular participation in the murder of Jews and Roma. In Eastern Europe, official museums and commemorative institutions have often depicted the Holocaust as a German crime with most members of their own nation as victims. At the same time, a segment of society acknowledges some level of national complicity in antisemitic violence—a position that often goes together with an interest in all things Jewish.[108]

In much of the former Cold War West, there were clear continuities between the youth activism of the 1960s, mobilization for the Third World, and critiques of Israel. But former Eastern bloc countries had a different relationship to the decolonizing world. Although the idea of a common front against western imperialism played a role in Soviet state policy and local youth activism in some Eastern European countries, NGOs as well as center and center-left parties that formed after 1989 generally did not associate themselves with these anticolonial traditions.[109] There was no Eastern European equivalent to Beur activism in France, nor did organizations on the left have to negotiate the legacies of anticolonial campaigning with alliances that included mainstream Jewish organizations. Instead, support for or rejection of Zionism transected the political spectrum in sometimes unexpected ways. Delegates from Jewish institutions might expect conflicts over representations of local participation in Nazi killings in Warsaw and Budapest but fewer critical questions about Israeli occupation policies than they might receive in London or Paris.

Romani Holocaust commemorations stand out in this memorial landscape bifurcated by individuals' conflicting ideas about national guilt and the relationship between different emancipatory struggles. As victims who faced continuous persecution from their neighbors and postwar states, Romani activists do not whitewash the history of local complicity with Nazism. Yet, they tend to avoid critiques of Israel. The latter point is remarkable, considering that many Romani activists have found inspiration in theorists who seek to overcome structural inequalities on a global scale. The canon of useful texts dealing with race and power is admittedly vast, much of it not necessarily concerned with the Middle East. It is certainly possible to read the classics of critical race theory, which focus on the social, legal, and economic underpinnings of white supremacy, and to think mainly of examples from the United States.[110] Yet, discussions of the exploitation of the Global South and the history of settler colonialism offer ample opportunities to seek common cause with critics of Israeli occupation policies. These are not alliances that most Romani activists highlight, however.

The major transnational Romani youth organization ternYpe is typical in this respect. Officially established by a diverse group of young Romani leaders in 2010, its most prominent project has been the annual event held on August 2, when its members from different European countries convene in Auschwitz.[111] Many young people who enter the world of activism on a heritage trip and others who are veteran organizers unite there under the banner of the Romani slogan "Dikh he na bister" ("Look and don't forget").[112] Such mobilization around memory issues highlights continuities with previous generations of Roma and Sinti fighting for equality and respect. Despite occasional tensions, the struggle for Romani civil rights and commemorations of the Romani Holocaust remain intergenerational endeavors. Accustomed to balancing the desire for a united front in the battle against discrimination and acknowledgment of each Romani group's distinctive culture and history, Romani movements have also proven adept at coalition building across political divides. Although ternYpe's attempt to empower Romani youth was radical in a number of respects, it accommodated coalitions with a range of Jewish activists—from those who are outspoken in their critiques of Israel to badge-wearing supporters of Israel. This is a remarkable feat in an era when most antiracist alliances between mainstream Jewish organizations and champions of human rights have become difficult. Romani activists found ways to combine Fanonism and Zionism in the 1970s and continue to do so into the 2020s.

The New Generation

Even as they discover shared interests in polarized societies, European Roma and Jews continue to work against a backdrop of past conflicts. The debates that leave the greatest mark, or scars, on Jewish-Romani relations tend to be ambitious projects—such as the USHMM—that claim to represent a national vision of the past. In Europe, for example, an especially acrimonious conflict developed over the push for a monument to the Holocaust in Berlin. In 1988, the journalist Lea Rosh and the historian Eberhard Jäckel called for a central German memorial. Many official supporters of the idea, including the project's initiators, were not Jewish. Indeed, the original petition noted that it was "a matter for the descendants of the perpetrators."[113] This approach departed from the US model: whereas Carter's commission recommended a museum as a living memorial that could fit into the US multicultural canon, German planners wanted a traditional monument that could stand as a reminder of German guilt. Soon questions arose about the space the monument would give to the experiences of Sinti and Roma and Germany's debt to them.

In response to the initiator's plans, Romani Rose demanded that Sinti and Roma should be included in the project to make it "a memorial for all victims." In 1991, the Central Council of German Sinti and Roma submitted a proposal for a monument that was separate but integrated into the Jewish one. In the conflict that ensued leaders of the Jewish community rejected the proposal. This group included Heinz Galinski, head of the Central Council of Jews in Germany, who had addressed Jews and Sinti and Roma as fellow victims in Bergen-Belsen in 1979. Fears that the gravity of the Holocaust as the defining event in German history could be diminished by conflating the experiences of different victim groups fueled these heated debates about the monument. The ultimate symbol of Germany's commitment to acknowledging its responsibility became a debate about whether adding the Romani genocide was an act of relativizing, and thereby trivializing, the Holocaust.

The result was a separate monument to the Romani Holocaust. Designed by a Jewish, Israeli artist, Dani Karavan, and administered by the foundation established to manage the Jewish site, the separate monument was clearly a compromise imposed on Romani representatives. Since its opening in 2012, the Romani Holocaust monument has nevertheless gained a prominent place in Berlin's memorial landscape.[114] Yet, much like the USHMM's permanent exhibition, it is inevitably also a monument to these hurtful debates.

Controversy over the historical place of both genocides continues today. Some conflicts have erupted over commemorative events, such as the decision of the Institute of the Terezín Initiative in the Czech Republic not to read Jewish and Romani names together at a ceremony in 2021.[115] In other cases, controversy has taken the form of academic disputes. The political scientist Guenther Lewy, for example, challenged the systematic and genocidal nature of Romani killings, both in articles and in the only book-length survey of the Romani Holocaust to appear with a major English-language press in the past decades. Scholars have overwhelmingly rejected his assertions, which also drew heavy critique from activists.[116]

Much like debates on the comparability of the Jewish Holocaust to other genocides and colonial violence, editorials and social media have often highlighted the most polemical voices, leaving the impression that divisions are the norm. Sporadic and intense moments of discord can obscure the fact that, over the past two decades, Romani and Jewish organizations have regularly collaborated and expressed shared understandings of the past. By the time Romani organizations convened the events in Birkenau in August 2014, leaders of important organizations representing Europe's Jewish youth—the World Union of Jewish Students, the European Union of Jewish Students, and the Union of Jewish Students of France—had presidents who pursued sustained involvement with Romani commemorations of the Holocaust and the ongoing struggle for Romani civil rights. Andi Gergely, Jane Braden-Golay, and Sacha Reingewirtz, the leaders of each of these institutions, respectively, made it their mission to use their organizations' leverage in campaigns with Romani partners. Commemorations and speeches at shared events were only the public face of relations they had already been cultivating as individuals and members of institutions for some time. Each spent many hours learning from their Romani peers, engaging in a dialogue about shared aims with other young lobbyists and working to build long-term alliances based on common interests and outlooks.

In France, after a hiatus of nearly a decade, SOS Racisme and the UEJF joined forces again in the early 2000s. As self-declared defenders of the republic, both organizations argued against their enemies on the right as well as religious fundamentalists.[117] Members of the two organizations belonged to a centrist progressive camp that did not seek to overcome the foundational values of the French state but rather to redeem their promise. In light of increasing violence against Jews and electoral successes by the extreme right across Europe, support for Israel did not divide the groups this time. Patrick Klugman, president of the UEJF in 2001–2003, and one of the contributors to *Zionism Explained to our Friends* (2003), later became vice-president of SOS Racisme.[118] The two organizations continued their cooperation into the period of Nicolas Sarkozy's presidency (2007–2012).

When Sarkozy announced the mass deportation of Romanian and Bulgarian Roma in the summer of 2010, the new leadership of the UEJF joined forces with SOS Racisme and FNASAT (Fédération nationale d'associations de Tsiganes), an umbrella organization representing a variety of Romani and Traveller groups.[119] In an ironic, theatrical protest, Arielle Schwab of the UEJF and Dominique Sopo of SOS Racisme deposited live chickens in front of the French Ministry of the Interior on July 29, 2010.[120] Playing with the stereotype of "Gypsy" chicken thieves, they pleaded for an end to deportations and anti-Romani violence in exchange for the animals the activists brought to the event. At stake, according to the UEJF, was "the principle of republican equality."[121]

This was the beginning of regular relations between the UEJF and FNASAT as well as other groups representing French Roma. The following year, FNASAT and the UEJF organized a joint trip for an intergenerational, international group of Roma and Jews to memorial sites in Poland. The group brought along a Jewish filmmaker, Anna Pitoun, who had worked on Romani themes before, to document the joint visit to Warsaw, Auschwitz, and Treblinka.[122] The trip included some tense moments. Pitoun directed her viewers' attention to several conflicts, including one where Romani painter Gabi Jiménez challenged Jewish students to think about the resources each group had at its disposal when telling their stories. This time, however, these tensions had an arena and were articulated by people committed to a shared journey, both physically and politically.

The rise of the Right and the politicization of anti-Romani policies after 1989 have driven much of this cooperation.[123] Ironically, just around the time Yehuda Bauer began to publish articles claiming that the Nazi persecution of Roma operated according to a different logic than Nazi measures against Jews, anti-Roma sentiment across Europe began to increasingly resemble threats European Jews knew all too well. Mirroring the history of antisemitism since the 1870s, antiziganism became a central tool for right-wing mobilization—sporadically in Western Europe and more consistently in Central and Eastern European countries that joined the European Union in the 2000s. Meanwhile, those opposed to the rise of populist and extreme right-wing parties turned the defense of Romani civil and human rights into central planks of their political agenda. Solidarity with Roma now signaled a defense of an embattled center, a political culture of human decency, and a hard-won liberal order that most speakers at Holocaust commemorations had championed for decades.

Similar processes took place across Europe, starting in countries where new right-wing parties first succeeded. In Austria, the rise of Jörg Haider's xenophobic Freedom Party and a racist terror attack in 1995 that killed four Roma in the town of Oberwart created new solidarities between Jews and Roma, who had previously found little ground for dialogue. Five decades after Adolf Gussak, Hermine Horwath, and their extended family registered as "Gypsies" with the Jewish-led Action Committee as a mere bureaucratic act, the Jewish community represented Austrian Romani interests in settlement negotiations for slave labor compensation.[124] In neighboring Hungary, a great number of Jewish and Romani activists collaborated in the shadow of the rise of violent antisemitic and anti-Romani politics and the anti-liberal policies of Victor Orbán's government. At cultural centers, theater productions, and youth events—and among student groups and lobbyists—new partnerships have emerged between members of both groups—to such an extent that it is difficult to trace them all.

Young activists who forged the closest bonds between associations that represented both groups began to increasingly resemble each other. In Europe, the growth of supranational agencies and the proliferation of NGOs that deal with a plethora of social, economic, political, cultural, and ecological issues have given rise to a new class of young activists trained on the job in nonprofit management, grant writing, and advocacy.[125] Individuals who met at lobbying events, meet-and-greets at the European Parliament, or thematic symposia sponsored by international foundations have conceived many of the projects that have brought together Romani and Jewish youth in recent years.

The geopolitics of memory did not create these initiatives, but they inspired a search for allies that brought Roma and Jews together in new ways. My 2011 conversation with Sacha Reingewirtz, the vice-president and later president of the UEJF, highlighted the challenges of memory competition.[126] As a progressive young lawyer, he was most concerned with the accusation that media coverage given to the Holocaust was displacing the history of colonialism.[127] Discussing activities that predated his tenure, Reingewirtz explained his Jewish student group's attempt to seize the initiative against this critique: "We thought that the best answer to that would be to show an interest in the memories of others rather than trying to compete with them. And so the union organized the first student trip to Rwanda in 2006." Rwandan students subsequently joined commemorations of the Holocaust in Kigali, while Jewish students joined others for ceremonies in honor of Rwanda's murdered Tutsis.[128]

The same logic facilitated institutional and personal engagement with the Romani genocide. In the past, some Jewish community leaders had believed that their insistence on the Holocaust's uniqueness would guarantee its relevance in public debates, but Reingewirtz and other Jewish student leaders arrived at a different conclusion. They saw the value in memory collaborations but also learned quickly that some alliances worked better than others. Even if strategic considerations catalyzed these relations, the results were profound. For example, Reingewirtz was willing to spell out the political logic of these alliances, but he was also a sincere partner to Romani activists and involved himself in Romani rights far beyond what would be required from a tactical perspective.

The Holocaust remained the linchpin of these efforts to think about Jewish and Romani history together. Even when Romani and Jewish representatives understood that their counterparts had many other concerns, commemorations were the key to their relationship. Between 1945 and the early 1980s, Jewish scholars encountered Romani history (though not necessarily Romani representatives) mainly through the subject of their treatment by the Nazis. In the 1980s and 1990s, new narratives of shared persecution led to erratic and often ambivalent encounters between individual Romani leaders and Jews involved in memory politics, including the conflicts around the USHMM's events in the Capitol Rotunda and the Holocaust monument in Berlin. European Jews and Roma inherited these fragile alliances in the 2000s. For many, a shared narrative of Nazi persecution was something not only to be commemorated at events but also something that could demonstrate inter-minority solidarity and affirm their embattled European identity. Common projects also reflect the shared dependence of Romani and Jewish activists on the goodwill of administrators in national and European Union funding agencies.

If such Jewish-Romani alliances were to fracture today, it would likely not happen because of the issues that generated controversy in the 1990s. Today, the most sensitive topic is not the uniqueness of the Jewish Holocaust but the politics of Israel—something many Romani activists avoid and that many Jewish activists wish they could avoid. This challenge is not so much a function of the personal opinions of the individuals involved, since many progressive Jews and Roma disagree with Israel's occupation policies and its disenfranchisement and subjugation of Palestinians. Nonetheless, they realize that any event can be derailed when someone brings up issues such as boycott and divestment from Israel. Joint commemorations of the Holocaust that emphasize suffering—whether unique or shared, particular to their context or generalizable in their lessons—now provide participants with a relatively safe political space by comparison.

Most Romani activists are sensitive to the history of conflicts between advocates for Romani rights and Jewish representatives in debates about the uniqueness of the Jewish Holocaust. Yet, in conversations with me, the same activists also described their work with Jewish organizations and individuals as the result of natural and even unremarkable alliances. Unlike their predecessors thirty years ago, Romani activists today have every reason to expect their Jewish counterparts to know something about their struggles and believe in their shared interests. Roma and Jews regularly form alliances that would have made little sense before the Nazi era and had little traction in the decades immediately after the war.

Admittedly, many of these relations are transitory and dependent on the goodwill of individual actors, yet they have proven to be surprisingly resilient. Unlike community-based institutions that become permanent through their professionalization and fundraising, these endeavors exist largely thanks to project-based funding from the European Union, member states, or private foundations, and then disappear again, only to give way to new collaborations. One such undertaking was the Europe of Diasporas network that assembled Jewish, Romani, Assyrian, and Armenian representatives in a single body in 2016.[129] Driven largely by students, this series of three conferences with members of four European minorities ended its activities in 2018 when its funding dried up. Yet, in the process, young Jews and Roma forged ties that continued after the original endeavor had ended, including some between the European Union of Jewish Students and Phiren Amenca, an organization that coordinates volunteers who work in Romani contexts. In August 2020, the two organizations published a joint open letter calling on European Union institutions to address the long-standing discrimination and scapegoating of Roma that was only aggravated by the COVID crisis. The letter ends with the statement: "Jewish Rights are Roma Rights and Roma Rights are Jewish Rights!"[130]

Significantly, expressions of solidarity—formerly restricted to moments in front of monuments on particular days—often happen on social media, where they remain archived on individuals' and institutions' timelines. In this context, the reciprocity of these declarations also becomes visible. To mention just one such example: On October 9, 2020, ternYpe joined the Jewish Student Union of Germany in commemorating a terror attack on the Jewish synagogue in the German city of Halle a year earlier.[131] Shortly afterward, the Jewish student organization lit virtual Hannukah candles each night in honor of a political cause, dedicating the sixth candle to Rom*nja and Sinti*zze (the gender-neutral form of Roma and Sinti).[132]

None of this undoes the history of the uneven resources that members of these two groups have before them. Good intentions and a will to learn do not change access to expertise or economic and political capital. Growing numbers of Jews have agreed to say that Roma suffered "like us," whereas Roma often continue to seek to make their suffering visible by claiming that they suffered like Jews. One is an act of solidarity with those who are not similarly recognized, the other a demand for justice. This makes full reciprocity unlikely, or at least costly. It is easier to imagine a Jewish student saying kaddish for the Romani dead at a ceremony in Auschwitz, than a Romani artist singing "Aušvicate hi kher baro" at an event commemorating the Jews murdered at Auschwitz. Yet, at least there is now an opportunity to tackle these inequalities as individuals join forces at events and in projects.[133] This is fundamentally different from the situation three decades ago.

Conclusion

Stages of a Relationship

THE PLAY *Roma Armee* (Roma Army), which opened at Berlin's Maxim Gorki Theater in 2018, reveals the challenges and opportunities of Romani-Jewish relations in twenty-first century Europe. Unlike traditional plays where actors work with preexisting materials and scripts, and are in this sense fungible, *Roma Armee* is about the biographies of the specific actors onstage. The mostly Romani actors speak about their experiences as people stigmatized for being Romani, Travellers, gay, queer, or poor; they dwell on violence and shame, on divorces and body image. Transformed in the able hands of the Jewish, Israeli director, Yael Ronen, into a fast-paced reflection on Romani and other identities, it communicates the profound investment in Romani politics by those onstage. Indeed, two of the actors, the Romani sisters Sandra and Simonida Selimović, developed the original idea, a theatrical realization of militant Roma self-assertion under the banner of a Roma Armee Fraktion (Roma Army Faction).

What is the role of Jews and other non-Roma in a piece about Romani marginalization and resistance? In one scene, the two non-Romani actors, members of the Gorki Theater's ensemble, discuss that question. One is Mehmet Ateşçi who talks about his Turkish roots and his life as a gay man. He acknowledges that his background differs from those of his Romani colleagues, but the experiences he addresses speak to the play's central, overlapping themes of gender, sexuality, economic status, and ethnic background. The biography of the other actor, Orit Nahmias, is not as easily integrated into the core themes of the play. As one might expect from such a show, Nahmias addresses her delicate position directly. Turning to the audience, she explores the challenges of comparing her upbringing as a heterosexual woman in a middle-class Israeli family with that of the others sharing the stage, whose backgrounds diverge in so many ways from her own.

The task is thorny because Nahmias and the others do not slot neatly into categories. Nahmias is a Jew, an Israeli, a woman who describes her struggles with her body image, and a foreigner in Germany. Does that make her one of the outcasts who forms an imaginary army? Or is she "white," the privileged majority named by the activist actors onstage and offstage? Although she is deemed non-white enough to be in the play, viewers are left to wonder whether her comfortable upbringing and her status as a "desired" foreigner reveal her as the oppressor the imaginary Roma army should combat. The play provokes the question but also reveals the impossibility of an answer. In a climactic scene, members of this Roma brigade start killing those who are too white, including the invisible director, leaving only Sandra Selimović onstage, who shoots herself. The quest for legitimacy as a pure victim and thus a pure revolutionary turns out to be a suicide mission, albeit one the play never fully abandons.

Even as no one can claim the title of ultimate victim, any challenge to Jewish victimhood on a Berlin stage comes with its own peculiar baggage. On the one hand, Jewish victimhood has a special status in postwar Germany as well as the European Union as a whole. On the other hand, grassroots mobilization often takes place elsewhere, such as during transnational protests for Black Lives Matter, where most (white) Jews face hard questions about their privileged position in society. Nahmias's role reflects this duality and its effects on Romani-Jewish relations. At least since the late 1970s, the dominant question was whether Jews would concede that Roma suffered "like them," historically. The USHMM and the Berlin Holocaust memorial are monuments to these debates. Nahmias indirectly addresses this history when she notes onstage that it is difficult to share victimhood. Yet this might well be one of her least convincing lines. For most of the play, she wrestles with her status as a member of a group identified with historical victimhood who stands alongside others who can report in more intimate and personal terms on their past and current humiliations. In the context of *Roma Armee*, the question has been inverted: not whether Roma suffered like Jews but whether Jews suffer like Roma. Romani Europeans—much like others deemed non-white in societies that continue to privilege whiteness—can point to continuous racism that shapes their everyday lives. The question Jews are forced to reckon with in many political contexts is whether and how this applies to them.

Running parallel to the everyday politics in which Jews struggle to find a place, some scholars and intellectuals still debate whether we should compare the Jewish Holocaust to other atrocities. The history of Jewish-Romani relations suggests that the question itself is misleading. It implies that we might make a decision not to relate one atrocity to another. And yet comparisons were a reality from the moment Jews and Roma saw each other in camps and ghettos. Comparisons were part of Nazi victims' existential desire to understand their own position, not an artifact of historical analysis. After the war, other biographical, legal, and professional considerations influenced these comparisons. There was no time when victims, survivors, prosecutors, judges, and historians did not compare the wartime experiences of Romanies and Jews, usually in ways that had immediate financial, legal, and political ramifications.

Yet many of the ethical challenges of comparison remained hidden. The visible part involved monuments and exhibits, the realm where direct conflicts between members of both groups tended to arise. These areas of representation are also at the center of most scholarly discussions. Scholars and public intellectuals frequently comment on Holocaust comparisons in films, monuments, and political statements. Such debates often gloss over the work of documentation and knowledge production that give depth and substance to popular representations. The arrangement of collections, historical analysis, and legal interpretation are undergirded by a largely unseen infrastructure that relies on long-term funding and professionalization. Some of the most crucial infrastructures—open, accessible, cataloged archives—often remain the purview of specialists. As we saw in the case of the USHMM, journalists and activists frequently identify Holocaust institutions with their exhibits rather than their archival collections, fellowship programs, and opportunities for academic debate.

Profound inequalities in the infrastructure of knowledge are difficult to change. Large, centralized research institutions with ambitions to collect globally, such as the USHMM or the Shoah Foundation, require substantial state and philanthropic funding and need to establish their legitimacy in an already crowded field of memory institutions. It seems safe to predict that there will be no Romani USHMM or Shoah Foundation.[1] The challenge is thus to imagine what it would mean to translate the dialogue that is already underway with a new generation of activists into the rigid structures of institutions with state-mandated missions, restricted endowments, and the understandable inclination of managers to avoiding anything that might offend the political sensibilities of their backers. How should the salaried guardians of the past deal with the histories of the marginalized, nested obscurely within the archives of other marginalized groups? It is not enough to address familial traumas, offer spaces to express collective histories, or promote artistic representations. Usable knowledge about past injustice requires resources.

While these resources remain unequal, the history of Romani-Jewish relations is also an unlikely success story. Groups that had little in common, moved in different ways through the world, and left different traces as they did so, eventually suffered next to each other without much understanding of each other's fate. Yet something emerged from this parallel suffering that left parallel records. Although the disparity between each group's ability to conserve history and to make political claims was never fully resolved, it did transform to the point that a new generation is now finding ways to heed Sutzkever's call for commemoration in creative ways. Jews and Roma, who once mostly saw each other as abstract reflections and familiar strangers, increasingly find opportunities to engage with their differences. As in *Roma Armee* they often work through their relationship in front of non-Romani, non-Jewish audiences who regularly overidentify with one or the other position, and who often applaud at awkward moments.

ACKNOWLEDGMENTS

THIS BOOK REVOLVES around the conditions that make knowledge production possible. Writing it sharpened my sense of indebtedness to the people and institutions that have allowed me to finish it. Many colleagues and friends have helped this work along with advice at different stages. It is a privilege to be able to acknowledge many of them here: Ilsen About, Thomas Acton, Henriette Aséo, Elizabeth Anthony, Gerhard Baumgartner, William Bila, Crispin Brooks, Ethel Brooks, Kateřina Čapková, Martin Dean, Celia Donert, David Feldman, Karola Fings, Petra Gelbart, Jay Geller, José Gotovitch, Daniela Gress, Wolf Gruner, Kent Hallman, Ian Hancock, Andrea Härle, Krista Hegburg, Mozes Heinschink, Anna Holian, Radu Ioanid, Karen Jungbluth, Sławomir Kapralski, Michelle Kelso, Samuel Mago, Gilad Margalit, Yair Mintzker, Stephen Naron, Katherine Lebow, Sebastian Lotto-Kusche, Franziska Reinhuber, Frank Reuter, Eve Rosenhaft, Helena Sadílková, Johnathan Sarna, Carol Silverman, Noah Shenker, Helmut Walser Smith, Dan Stone, Aleksandra Szczepan, Joanna Talewicz-Kwiatkowska, Benjamin Thorne, Huub van Baar, Barbara Warnock, Vita Zalar, and Ari Zev. Justin Cammy, Marc Caplan, Jordan Finkin, and Allison Schachter graciously consulted with me about my Yiddish literary translations. I am particularly indebted to those amazingly generous people who were willing to read draft chapters, including Emily Greble, Tom Gross, Lisa Leff, Allison Schachter, and Daniel Sharfstein, as well as the many colleagues who have given me feedback in workshops over the years. The two readers who anonymously reviewed my entire manuscript for the press offered crucial insights and support and deserve special mention even if I cannot cite them by name.

I could not have written this book without the help of those survivors, activists, and involved professionals who lent me their time and entrusted me with accounts of their experiences and with their wisdom. It is an honor to have the opportunity to mention all those who gave me permission to reveal their names here: Yehuda Bacon, Karin Berger, Jane Braden-Golay, Rita Cohn,

Werner Cohn, Barry Fischer, Emmerich Gärtner-Horvath, Petra Gelbart, Andrea Gergely, Henry Greenbaum, Ian Hancock, Andrea Härle, Mozes Heintschink, Saniye Jasaroski, Dani Karavan, Bill Kerrigan, Samuel Mago, Vera B. Moreen, Isaac Nehama, Paulette Nehama, Anna Pitoun, Sacha Reingewirtz, Rudolf Sarközy, and Clas Steinmann. I am also deeply grateful to Anton Tenser for starting to teach me Romani at the most inopportune of moments—the year we both became fathers for the first time.

For their help with locating archival material, I thank Patrice Bensimon, Jeffrey Carter, Ron Coleman, Stef Dickers, Peter Gohle, Megan Lewis, Werner Renz, and Vincent E. Slatt. My research assistants Eliza Gilbert, Audrey Hommes, Karolina Koprowska, Kamil Kudra, Ivana Lazaroska, Ewa Rutkowska, Jessica Winchester, and Bryant White helped me make sense of these archival materials, often in languages that I do not speak. *History & Memory* and *The Journal of Contemporary History* granted permission to include material that previously appeared in these journals. For their help improving the structure and prose of this manuscript, I would like to thank Daniela Blei and Pamela Haag, two wonderful editors with whom I had the privilege of working as I prepared my manuscript for submission. At Princeton University Press, I had the great fortune to work with Priya Nelson, whose astute interventions and careful hand helped me clarify and hone my arguments. My thanks also go to Barbara Shi and the rest of the team at the press for all of their work in helping to bring this project to completion.

This is also a book about the financial and material foundations of knowledge production, and it is a pleasure to be able to thank those institutions that funded this project over the years: the American Philosophical Society, the Jack, Joseph and Morton Mandel Center for Advanced Holocaust Studies at the United States Holocaust Memorial Museum, the Oxford Centre for Hebrew and Jewish Studies, the Vienna Wiesenthal Institute for Holocaust Studies, and the American Council of Learned Societies. Vanderbilt University, my academic home for the past years, has also offered crucial support with its infrastructure, research support, leave policies, and grants, including a Research Scholar Grant and a Chancellor Faculty Fellowship, endowed by John Eliot Hassenfeld. The questions my students asked in my course on the Holocaust at Vanderbilt offered the original impetus to start this book and helped me appreciate the challenges of discussing the Jewish and the Romani Holocaust together. The collegiality and support of my colleagues at Vanderbilt has also been invaluable, as is attested by the inclusion of many of their names above.

Pursuing this project has also helped me discover new communities and intellectual homes. Nowhere has this been clearer than in the case of the Prague Forum for Romani Histories. I am deeply indebted to the members of the Forum for letting me into their circle, and, in particular, to Kateřina Čapková, whose generosity and ambitious vision for the field of Romani history has remained a constant source of inspiration.

My enduring gratitude goes to my family. By convention they come last in acknowledgments, yet in many respects they came, and come, first. Writing this book has made me more keenly aware of the tangible and intangible things that my grandparents and parents passed on to me and my siblings. My children, who are younger than this project, teach me every day how thrilling and frightening it is to encounter new subjects. To my wife, Julia, I owe more than I can convey here. Her sense of empathy and responsibility, sensitivity to language, and keen eye for imprecise arguments has made this a better book even as it has made me more aware of my own limitations.

ABBREVIATIONS

AJA	American Jewish Archives
AT-OeStA	Österreichisches Staatsarchiv
AN	Archives Nationales
BArch	Bundesarchiv, Germany
BayHSt	Bayerisches Hauptstaatsarchiv
BGH	Bundesgerichtshof, Germany
CJDC	Centre de documentation juive contemporaine
DÖW	Dokumentationsarchiv des österreichischen Widerstandes
FBI	Fritz Bauer Institut
FBI SuR	Fritz Bauer Institut, Vernehmungen Sinti und Roma
GFH	Ghetto Fighters' House Archive
GLS	Gypsy Lore Society
JGLS	*Journal of the Gypsy Lore Society*
HHStAW	Hessisches Hauptstaatsarchiv Wiesbaden
IMT	International Military Tribunal
IfZ	Institut für Zeitgeschichte, Munich
IRO	International Refugee Organization
ITS	International Tracing Service
LA-NRW	Landesarchiv Nordrhein-Westfalen
NIOD	NIOD Institute for War, Holocaust and Genocide Studies
OLG	Oberlandesgericht
StK Auerbach	Staatskommissar für rassisch, religiös und politisch Verfolgte (Auerbach)

StAM	Staatsarchiv München
USHMM	United States Holocaust Memorial Museum
USHMM IA	United States Holocaust Memorial Museum, Institutional Archive
VWI	Vienna Wiesenthal Institute for Holocaust Studies
VHA	Visual History Archive, USC Shoah Foundation

NOTES

Introduction: Jews and Roma in the Shadow of Genocide

1. Avraham [Avrom] Sutzkever, "Taboren zigeiner," in *Lider fun yam ha-moves: Fun Vilner geṭo, vald un vander* (Tel Aviv: Farlag Bergen-Belzen, 1968), 273. Cited and published in translation with permission from Rina Sutzkever. All translations are mine unless otherwise noted.

2. Vanya Kochanowski, "Some Notes on the Gypsies of Latvia," *Journal of the Gypsy Lore Society (JGLS)* 25, 3rd series (1946): 34–39 and Vanya Kochanowski, "Some Notes on the Gypsies of Latvia: By One of the Survivors," *JGLS* 25, 3rd series (1946): 112–16. On "Aušvicate hi kher báro" see Dušan Holý and Ctibor Nečas, *Žalující píseň: O osudu Romů v nacistických koncentračních táborech* (Strážnice, Czech Republic: Ústav lidové kultury, 1993), chapter 5; Michael Beckerman, "The World According to the Roma," in *The Cambridge History of World Music*, ed. Philip Bohlman (Cambridge: Cambridge University Press, 2013), 696. The song appeared in print shortly after Sutzkever published his poem. See Jerzy Ficowski, "The Polish Gypsies of To-Day," trans. Józef Rotblat, *JGLS* 27, no. 3–4 (July–October 1950): 92–102.

3. PCIRO Petition for Review, June 17, 1948, 3.2.1.2/80327719/ITS Digital Collection, Arolsen Archives, USHMM; similarly: questionnaire of November 17, 1949, 3.2.1.2/80390272/ITS Digital Collection, Arolsen Archives, USHMM.

4. The most elaborate attempt to draw such parallels to the point of equating Jewish and Romani exclusion comes from Wolfgang Wippermann. See Wolfgang Wippermann, *"Auserwählte Opfer?": Shoah und Porrajmos im Vergleich: Eine Kontroverse* (Berlin: Frank & Timme, 2005); Wolfgang Wippermann, *Wie die Zigeuner: Antisemitismus und Antiziganismus im Vergleich*, Antifa Edition (Berlin: Elefanten Press, 1997). For a perceptive analysis of the differences in the treatment of Jews and "Gypsies" in art and literature, see Hans Richard Brittnacher, *Leben auf der Grenze: Klischee und Faszination des Zigeunerbildes in Literatur und Kunst* (Göttingen: Wallstein, 2012), 72–92. Iulia-Karin Patrut, *Phantasma Nation: "Zigeuner" und Juden als Grenzfiguren des "Deutschen" (1770–1920)* (Würzburg, Germany: Königshausen & Neumann, 2014) offers a particularly careful analysis of these confluences. For works drawing these parallels, see Wilhelm Solms, "On the Demonising of Jews and Gypsies in Fairy Tales," in *Sinti and Roma: Gypsies in German-Speaking Society and Literature*, ed. Susan Tebbutt (New York: Berghahn Books, 1998), 90–106; Andrea Geier, "'Deutsche Kunst?' Zur Wissensproduktion über 'Zigeuner' und Juden in Kunstdiskursen des 19. Jahrhunderts," in *"Zigeuner" und Nation: Repräsentation—Inklusion—Exklusion*, ed. Herbert Uerlings and Iulia-Karin Patrut (Frankfurt am Main: Peter Lang, 2008), 151–68.

5. The Soviet historian Yuri Slezkine has gone so far as to describe this dichotomy as an epic conflict between those rooted in the soil and "service nomads" like Jews and Roma. See Yuri Slezkine, *The Jewish Century* (Princeton, NJ: Princeton University Press, 2004).

6. Jews were also a clearer model for nationalists. See Wolfgang Altgeld, *Katholizismus, Protestantismus, Judentum: Über religiös begründete Gegensätze und nationalreligiöse Ideen in der Geschichte des deutschen Nationalismus* (Mainz, Germany: Matthias-Grünewald-Verlag, 1992).

7. On Jews, see in particular Sander L. Gilman, *The Jew's Body* (New York: Routledge, 1991); on Roma, see Peter Widmann, "The Campaign Against the Restless: Criminal Biology and the Stigmatization of the Gypsies, 1890–1960," in *The Roma: A Minority in Europe: Historical, Political and Social Perspectives*, ed. Roni Stauber and Raphael Vago (Budapest: Central European University Press, 2007), 19–30. Both Jews and Roma appeared as physically distinct in polemics against them long before the rise of biological racism. See, for example, Dana Y. Rabin, "Seeing Jews and Gypsies in 1753," *Cultural and Social History* 7, no. 1 (March 2010): 35–58. Such portrayals were similar enough to convince a handful of misguided ethnographic commentators to speculate about the shared origin of both groups. Johann Christoph Wagenseil produced the best-known theory on the Jewish origin of the "Gypsies" in 1697. On such comparisons, see Ulrich Kronauer, "Vom gemeinsamen Vorurteil gegenüber 'Juden, Zigeunern und derlei Gesindel' im 18. Jahrhundert," in *"Zigeuner" und Nation: Repräsentation—Inklusion—Exklusion*, ed. Herbert Uerlings and Iulia-Karin Patrut (Frankfurt am Main: Peter Lang, 2008), 137–50; Klaus Michael Bogdal, *Europa erfindet die Zigeuner: Eine Geschichte von Faszination und Verachtung* (Berlin: Suhrkamp, 2011), 147, 150–51. The theme of shared origins appears regularly into the present from ethnographic reports to religious internet postings. See, for example, Walter Starkie, *In Sara's Tents* (London: John Murray, 1953), 287; "The Jewish-Romani Connection: Are Gypsies Descendants of Tribe of Simeon?" *Ynetnews*, May 5, 2018, https://ynetnews.com/articles/0,7340,L-5248902,00.html.

8. Paul A. Hanebrink, *A Specter Haunting Europe: The Myth of Judeo-Bolshevism* (Cambridge, MA: Belknap Press of Harvard University Press, 2018).

9. See, for example, Richard Landes, "The Jews as Contested Ground in Postmodern Conspiracy Theory," *Jewish Political Studies Review* 19, no. 3/4 (2007): 9–34; Stephen Eric Bronner, *A Rumor about the Jews: Reflections on Antisemitism and the Protocols of the Learned Elders of Zion* (New York: St. Martin's Press, 2000).

10. This pattern holds for much of Europe but of course not every single location. For a sophisticated assessment of the different geographies in the Russian Pale of Settlement, which was the major center of Jewish life in Europe and its main area of out-migration, see Robert E. Mitchell, *Human Geographies Within the Pale of Settlement: Order and Disorder During the Eighteenth and Nineteenth Centuries* (Cham, Switzerland: Springer International, 2019). The isolation of Roma to less desirable areas continues to this day. See Giovanni Picker, *Racial Cities: Governance and the Segregation of Romani People in Urban Europe* (London: Routledge, 2017).

11. Jews were not always the most literate group in many East European contexts, but they nonetheless treated their generally high literacy rates as a useful way of distinguishing themselves from many of their non-Jewish neighbors. Shaul Stampfer, *Families, Rabbis and Education: Essays on Traditional Jewish Society in Eastern Europe* (London: Littman Library of Jewish Civilization, 2010), 190–210. There are no reliable historical statistics on Roma for much of Europe. However, the 572 individuals who registered with the International Refugee Organization as

"Gypsies" in Germany and Italy between 1947 and 1952 offer some hints about literacy rates among Romanies and the divergence among Romani groups. Not all files make a determination possible and illiteracy for the purposes of my count includes only people who were incapable of signing their name or who stated that they could not read and write. Of the 44 people who appear in files as German "Gypsies" (individuals who would likely self-identity as Sinti) the vast majority, 39 men and women (89%), were literate. Among the 42 people who identify as Czech "Gypsies" only 7, or 17%, appear to have been literate. The numbers are similar for Romanies from the Yugoslav-Italian borderlands (largely Sinti) who registered in Italy. Here 13 out of 66 individuals, or 20%, were literate. On these files, see Ari Joskowicz, "Romani Refugees and the Postwar Order," *Journal of Contemporary History* 51, no. 4 (October 2016): 760–87.

12. Steven E. Aschheim, *Brothers and Strangers: The East European Jew in German and German Jewish Consciousness, 1800–1923* (Madison: University of Wisconsin Press, 1982).

13. For an overview of modern Jewish politics, see Ezra Mendelsohn, *On Modern Jewish Politics* (New York: Oxford University Press, 1993). The best depiction of the situation of Eastern European Jews, pejoratively called *Ostjuden*, remains Joseph Roth, *Juden auf Wanderschaft* (Berlin: Die Schmiede, 1927). On the role Jewish solidarity networks play for Jewish migrants in comparison to Muslim migrants, see Ethan Katz, *The Burdens of Brotherhood: Jews and Muslims from North Africa to France* (Cambridge, MA: Harvard University Press, 2015); Maud Mandel, *Muslims and Jews in France: History of a Conflict* (Princeton, NJ: Princeton University Press, 2014).

14. For the spatial logic of exclusion, I am drawing here from Didier Fassin, *Humanitarian Reason: A Moral History of the Present Times* (Berkeley: University of California Press, 2012), 26.

15. Edgar Behr to Amt für Wiedergutmachung, August 23, 1952, Staatsarchiv Hamburg, 351-11-11393. I thank Anna Holian for sending me this document and explaining its background.

16. See, for example, testimony of Hadassah R., November 12, 1984, Fortunoff Visual History Archive, HVT-530.

17. See, for example, testimony of Marta Ernst, July 1991, USHMM, RG-50.719.0013. The Fortunoff copies of these testimonies are cut differently and sometimes omit parts that appear irrelevant to the recollections people have of the Holocaust.

18. For a description of this situation as living in a state of exception within the liberal order, see Jennifer Illuzzi, *Gypsies in Germany and Italy, 1861–1914* (Basingstoke, UK: Palgrave Macmillan, 2014).

19. See Tara Zahra, "'Condemned to Rootlessness and Unable to Budge': Roma, Migration Panics, and Internment in the Habsburg Empire," *American Historical Review* 122, no. 3 (June 2017): 702–26.

20. For an especially sophisticated analysis of the everyday perceptions of Romani alterity and the challenges this poses for historians, see the work of Eve Rosenhaft. Eve Rosenhaft, "Blacks and Gypsies in Nazi Germany: The Limits of the 'Racial State,'" *History Workshop Journal* 72, no. 1 (2011): 161–70; Eve Rosenhaft, "At Large in the 'Gray Zone': Narrating the Romani Holocaust," in *Unsettling History: Archiving and Narrating in Historiography*, ed. Sebastian Jobs and Alf Lüdke (Frankfurt am Main: Campus Verlag, 2010), 149–68.

21. Ulrich Friedrich Opfermann, "The Registration of Gypsies in National Socialism: Responsibility in a German Region," *Romani Studies* 11, no. 1 (2001): 25–52. On the arbitrary decisions as to whom to include in orders targeting "nomadic Gypsies," see Vladimir Solonari, "Ethnic

Cleansing or 'Crime Prevention'? Deportation of Romanian Roma," in *The Nazi Genocide of the Roma: Reassessment and Commemoration*, ed. Anton Weiss-Wendt (New York: Berghahn, 2013), 96–119; Martin Holler, *Der nationalsozialistische Völkermord an den Roma in der besetzten Sowjetunion (1941–1944)* (Heidelberg: Dokumentations- und Kulturzentrum Deutscher Sinti und Roma, 2009).

22. See Zahra, "Condemned to Rootlessness." On Jews, Muslims, and others targeted in interwar France, see Clifford D. Rosenberg, *Policing Paris: The Origins of Modern Immigration Control between the Wars* (Ithaca, NY: Cornell University Press, 2006); Margarete Grandner, "Staatsbürger und Ausländer: Zum Umgang Österreichs mit den jüdischen Flüchtlingen nach 1918," in *Asylland wider Willen: Flüchtlinge in Österreich im europäischen Kontext seit 1914*, ed. Gernot Heiss and Oliver Rathkolb (Vienna: J & V Edition, 1995), 60–85.

23. Ronald Schechter, *Obstinate Hebrews: Representations of Jews in France, 1715–1815*, Studies on the History of Society and Culture 49 (Berkeley: University of California Press, 2003), 154.

24. These included books, booklets, and pamphlets. Michael Meyer et al., eds., *German-Jewish History in Modern Times*, vol. 2, *Emancipation and Acculturation* (New York: Columbia University Press, 1996–1998), 31. On the role of pamphlets in debates on Jews, albeit later in the century, see Uffa Jensen, *Gebildete Doppelgänger: Bürgerliche Juden und Protestanten im 19. Jahrhundert*, Kritische Studien zur Geschichtswissenschaft 167 (Göttingen: Vandenhoeck & Ruprecht, 2005), 147–95.

25. See Shulamit Volkov, "Antisemitism as Cultural Code: Reflections on the History and the Historiography of Antisemitism in Imperial Germany," *Leo Baeck Institute Yearbook* 23 (1978): 25–46. Carl E. Schorske, *Fin-de-siècle Vienna: Politics and Culture* (New York: Vintage, 1981), 116–80.

26. The trial took place before the passing of the German Restitution Law (Bundesentschädigungsgesetz) in 1953 and thus follows the nearly identical stipulations of Hessian state law. "Gesetz zur Wiedergutmachung nationalsozialistischen Unrechts (Entschädigungsgesetz)" [August 10, 1949], *Gesetz- und Verordnungsblatt für das Land Hessen*, August 18, 1949, no. 26–27.

27. All quotes from "Beschluss der 2. Wiedergutmachungskammer beim Landgericht Wiesbaden vom 27. März 1952: Abschiebung von Zigeunern nach den Ostgebieten," March 27, 1952, 2 b (2) Wi K E 541–549, IfZ, MA-21.

28. Yehuda Bauer, "Whose Holocaust?," *Midstream* 26, no. 9 (November 1980); Yehuda Bauer, "Gypsies," *Encyclopedia of the Holocaust*, vol. 2 (New York: Macmillan, 1990), 634–38: Sybil Milton, "Gypsies and the Holocaust," *The History Teacher* 24, no. 4 (August 1991): 375–87; Yehuda Bauer and Sybil Milton, "Correspondence: 'Gypsies and the Holocaust,'" *The History Teacher* 25, no. 4 (August 1992): 513–21; Yehuda Bauer, "Comparison of Genocides," in *Studies in Comparative Genocide*, ed. Levon Chorbajian and George Shirinian (New York: St. Martin's Press, 1999), 31–43. Henry Friedlander, a historian of Germany and Milton's husband was also instrumental in revising scholarly approaches to Roma as part of his scholarship on Nazi euthanasia policies. See Henry Friedlander, "Step by Step: The Expansion of Murder, 1939–1941," *German Studies Review* 17, no. 3 (1994): 495–507; Henry Friedlander, *The Origins of Nazi Genocide: From Euthanasia to the Final Solution* (Chapel Hill: University of North Carolina Press, 1995).

29. Romani Rose, "'Für beide galt damals der gleiche Befehl': Eine Entgegnung auf Yehuda Bauers Thesen zum Genozid an den europäischen Juden, Sinti und Roma," *Blätter für deutsche*

und internationale Politik 43 (1998), 467–72. Yehuda Bauer, "'Es galt nicht der gleiche Befehl für beide': Eine Entgegnung auf Romani Roses Thesen zum Genozid an den europäischen Juden, Sinti und Roma," *Blätter für deutsche und internationale Politik* 43 (1998), 1380–86.

30. For a survey, see Anton Weiss-Wendt, "Introduction," in *The Nazi Genocide of the Roma: Reassessment and Commemoration*, ed. Anton Weiss-Wendt (New York: Berghahn, 2013), 1–26. Karola Fings, "Opferkonkurrenzen: Debatten um den Völkermord an den Sinti und Roma und neue Forschungsperspektiven," *S:I.M.O.N. Shoah: Intervention. Methods. Documentation* 2, no. 1 (2015): 79–101 offers a sophisticated response to the debates of the 1990s. Some articles only aim to show that Roma were not targeted in the same way. See, for example, Guenter Lewy, "Gypsies and Jews Under the Nazis," *Holocaust and Genocide Studies* 13, no. 3 (December 1999): 383–404. In other cases, this is part of a larger systematic argument about Jews and other groups. See, for example, John Connelly, "Gypsies, Homosexuals, and Slavs," in *The Oxford Handbook of Holocaust Studies*, ed. Peter Hayes and John K. Roth (Oxford: Oxford University Press, 2010), 274–92.

31. Weiss-Wendt, "Introduction," 24.

32. Christian Gerlach, *Extremely Violent Societies: Mass Violence in the Twentieth-Century World* (Cambridge: Cambridge University Press, 2010), 6.

33. On the implications of new surveillance economies on historical scholarship, see Ari Joskowicz, "The Age of the Witness and the Age of Surveillance: Romani Holocaust Testimony and the Perils of Digital Scholarship," *American Historical Review* 125, no. 4 (October 2020): 1205–31.

34. See, for example, Michael Werner and Bénédicte Zimmermann, "Vergleich, Transfer, Verflechtung: Der Ansatz der *histoire croisée* und die Herausforderung des Transnationalen," *Geschichte und Gesellschaft* 28 (2002): 607–36.

35. See Huub van Baar, *The European Roma: Minority Representation, Memory and the Limits of Transnational Governmentality* (Amsterdam: F&N, 2011), 307; Nadine Blumer, "From Victim Hierarchies to Memorial Networks: Berlin's Holocaust Memorial to Sinti and Roma Victims of National Socialism" (PhD diss., University of Toronto, 2011), 71.

36. See Gilad Margalit, *Germany and Its Gypsies: A Post-Auschwitz Ordeal* (Madison: University of Wisconsin Press, 2002). For a discussion of similarities in the role history plays for nationalism among the two groups, see Roni Stauber and Raphael Vago, "The Politics of Memory: Jews and Roma Commemorate Their Persecution," in *The Roma: A Minority in Europe: Historical, Political and Social Perspectives*, ed. Roni Stauber and Raphael Vago (Budapest: Central European University Press, 2007), 117–33, https://books.openedition.org/ceup/1418.

37. Saul Friedländer, *Reflections of Nazism: An Essay on Kitsch and Death* (New York: Harper & Row, 1984).

38. For scholars who have continued in this argumentative vein, see, for example, Omer Bartov, *Mirrors of Destruction: War, Genocide, and Modern Identity* (Oxford: Oxford University Press, 2000). For other exceptions that bridge this divide, see Mary Fulbrook, *Reckonings: Legacies of Nazi Persecution and the Quest for Justice* (New York: Oxford University Press, 2018); Eliyana R. Adler and Katerina Capková, eds., *Jewish and Romani Families in the Holocaust and Its Aftermath* (New Brunswick, NJ: Rutgers University Press, 2021).

39. See John Mendelsohn, "Trial by Document: The Use of Seized Records in the United States Proceedings at Nuernberg" (PhD diss., University of Michigan, 1974); cf. Donald

Bloxham, *Genocide on Trial: The War Crimes Trials and the Formation of Holocaust History and Memory* (Oxford: Oxford University Press, 2001); and the discussion in chapter 4. In the long run the large-scale efforts of survivors to collect testimony in the immediate aftermath of the war also changed the face of Holocaust historiography, yet this was a late development. On these collections, see Laura Jockusch, *Collect and Record! Jewish Holocaust Documentation in Early Postwar Europe* (New York: Oxford University Press, 2012).

40. This includes classics of the field, such as Christopher R. Browning, *Ordinary Men: Reserve Police Battalion 101 and the Final Solution in Poland* (New York: HarperCollins, 1992).

41. Michel Rolph Trouillot, *Silencing the Past: Power and the Production of History* (Boston: Beacon Press, 1995).

42. Michel Duchein, "The History of European Archives and the Development of the Archival Profession in Europe," *The American Archivist* 55, no. 1 (1992): 14–25.

43. Although they focused on communal material not collected by the state, Jewish archives often adopted principles and practices from state-based archiving. See Jason Lustig, *A Time to Gather: Archives and the Control of Jewish Culture*, The Oxford Series on History and Archives (New York: Oxford University Press, 2022).

44. Lisa Moses Leff, *The Archive Thief: The Man Who Salvaged French Jewish History in the Wake of the Holocaust*, The Oxford Series on History and Archives (New York: Oxford University Press, 2015); Lustig, *A Time to Gather*. See also Peter Fritzsche, "The Archive," *History & Memory* 17, no. 1–2 (August 2005): 39. For the most part, these archives followed an adapted principle of provenance (or *respect des fonds*). They copied selectively but usually kept collections of one producing agency together, rather than reclassify them according to themes. On the history and theoretical challenges of this approach to collecting, see Michel Duchein, "Theoretical Principles and Practical Problems of *Respect des fonds* in Archival Science," *Archivaria* 160 (January 1983): 64–82.

45. See Clifford D. Rosenberg, *Policing Paris: The Origins of Modern Immigration Control between the Wars* (Ithaca, NY: Cornell University Press, 2006); Ann Laura Stoler, *Along the Archival Grain: Epistemic Anxieties and Colonial Common Sense* (Princeton, NJ: Princeton University Press, 2009); Kathryn Burns, *Into the Archive: Writing and Power in Colonial Peru* (Durham, NC: Duke University Press, 2010); Kirsten Weld, *Paper Cadavers: The Archives of Dictatorship in Guatemala* (Durham, NC: Duke University Press, 2014); Katherine Verdery, *Secrets and Truths: Ethnography in the Archive of Romania's Secret Police* (Budapest: Central European University Press, 2014); Marisa J. Fuentes, *Dispossessed Lives: Enslaved Women, Violence, and the Archive* (Philadelphia: University of Pennsylvania Press, 2016).

46. The institution's complicated name reflects the jurisdictional challenges in a highly federalized state that it was meant to address: Central Office of the State Justice Administrations for the Investigation of National Socialist Crimes. See Annette Weinke, *Eine Gesellschaft ermittelt gegen sich selbst: Die Geschichte der Zentralen Stelle Ludwigsburg 1958–2008*, 2nd ed. (Darmstadt, Germany: WBG, 2012).

47. Vermerk, LKA/NW 23, Düsseldorf, April 25, 1986, Gerichte Rep. 118, no. 2493, 1593, LA-NRW; Vermerk, LKA/NW 23, Düsseldorf, June 9, 1986, Gerichte Rep. 118, no. 2493, 1635, LA-NRW.

48. Vermerk, LKA/NW 23, Düsseldorf, June 9, 1986, Gerichte Rep. 118, no. 2493, 1635, LA-NRW. Apparently, investigators had not noticed that the information the International Tracing

Service had sent them regarding individual Romani prisoners was based on these registry books.

49. State Museum of Auschwitz-Birkenau, *Memorial Book: The Gypsies at Auschwitz-Birkenau* (Munich: K. G. Saur, 1993).

50. Reisekostenrechnung, OStA Röseler, Cologne, December 19, 1985, Gerichte Rep. 118, no. 2491, 1131, LA-NRW.

51. See, for example, the controversial polemics by Norman Finkelstein in his *The Holocaust Industry: Reflections on the Exploitation of Jewish Suffering* (London: Verso, 2003) or Tova Reich's novel *My Holocaust* (New York: HarperCollins, 2007).

52. See Leo Lucassen, *Zigeuner: Die Geschichte eines polizeilichen Ordnungsbegriffes in Deutschland, 1700–1945* (Weimar, Germany: Böhlau, 1996).

53. On Yenish, or *Jenische* in German, see Thomas Huonker and Regula Ludi, *Roma, Sinti und Jenische: Schweizerische Zigeunerpolitik zur Zeit des Nationalsozialismus: Beitrag zur Forschung* (Zürich, Switzerland: Chronos, 2001). I use the British spelling for "Traveller" when I refer to a particular group of people in the UK and Ireland who identify under that name.

54. See Thomas Acton, "Modernity, Culture and 'Gypsies': Is there a Meta-Scientific Method for Understanding the Representation of 'Gypsies'? And do the Dutch Really Exist?," in *The Role of the Romanies: Images and Counter-Images of "Gypsies"/Romanies in European Cultures*, ed. Nicholas Saul and Susan Tebbutt (Liverpool: Liverpool University Press, 2004), 98–116.

55. Some historians have made great strides in this regard. See Ulrich Friedrich Opfermann, *"Seye kein Ziegeuner, sondern kayserlicher Cornet": Sinti im 17. und 18. Jahrhundert: Eine Untersuchung anhand archivalischer Quellen* (Berlin: Metropol, 2007).

56. One exception is the interwar Soviet Union. Yet, this too turned into a lethal risk when the Nazis used the registration as "Gypsy" under nationality in identity cards to identify and murder Roma in Soviet areas newly under their control.

57. See Michael Stewart, *The Time of the Gypsies* (Boulder, CO: Westview Press, 1997); Sławomir Kapralski, "The Aftermath of the Roma Genocide from Implicit Memories to Commemoration," in *The Nazi Genocide of the Roma: Reassessment and Commemoration*, ed. Anton Weiss-Wendt (New York: Berghahn, 2013), 229–51.

58. For an overview, see Yaron Matras, *The Romani Gypsies* (Cambridge, MA: Belknap Press of Harvard University Press, 2015). Like other marginalized groups, Roma have developed their sense of self and group coherence in resistance to powerful actors who have sought to control and surveil them. Illuzzi, *Gypsies in Germany and Italy*, 6; James C. Scott, *The Art of Not Being Governed: An Anarchist History of Upland Southeast Asia*, Yale Agrarian Studies Series (New Haven, CT: Yale University Press, 2009). For a critique of the homogenization that can come from generalizing about resistance, see Huub van Baar, "Enacting Memory and the Hard Labor of Identity Formation: Rethinking the Romani Movement and Its Historiography," in *The Identity Dilemma*, ed. Aidan McGarry and James M. Jasper (Philadelphia, PA: Temple University Press, 2015), 150–69, especially 154–55. For a new approach to resistance based on diverse sources, see Lise Foisneau, *Les Nomades face à la guerre (1939–1946)*, in collaboration with Valentin Merlin (Paris: Klincksieck, 2022).

59. On the First Serbian Gypsy Association for Mutual Support in Sickness and Death in Belgrade, see Elena Marushiakova and Vesselin Popov, eds., *Roma Voices in History: A Sourcebook* (Leiden, Netherlands: Ferdinand Schöningh, 2021), 180–90, and on the Hungarian Gypsy

Musician's National Association and the Hungarian Gypsy Musician's National Federation, see Marushiakova and Popov, *Roma Voices in History*, 467–549. Various mutual aid societies of Roma also emerged from Romani guilds (*esnafs*) in the Ottoman Empire. See Elena Marushiakova and Vesselin Popov, "Gypsy Guilds (Esnafs) on the Balkans," in *Roma: Past, Present, Future*, ed. Hristo Kyuchukov, Elena Marushiakova, and Vesslin Popov (Munich: Lincom, 2016), 76–89.

60. On the Soviet Union, see Brigid O'Keeffe, *New Soviet Gypsies: Nationality, Performance, and Selfhood in the Early Soviet Union* (Toronto: University of Toronto Press, 2013).

61. This is one of the results of the large collaborative research project "RomaInterbellum: Roma Civic Emancipation between the Two World Wars." See Marushiakova and Popov, *Roma Voices* and Sofiya Zahova, Raluca Bianca Roman, and Aleksandar Marinov, eds., *Roma Writings: Romani Literature and Press in Central, South-Eastern and Eastern Europe from the 19th Century until World War II* (Paderborn, Germany: Brill Schöningh, 2021).

62. György Majtényi, "The Memory and Histography of Porrajmos: Making a Transnational National Site of Memory," *S:I.M.O.N. Shoah: Intervention. Methods. Documentation* 8, no. 1 (2021): 86–103.

63. Readers will often see Roma in constructions such as Roma migration, instead of Romani migration. The descriptivist in me must concede that such usage—called a noun adjunct—seems acceptable to many native speakers. The prescriptivist in me would like to point out to writers and copyeditors that saying Roma Studies instead of Romani Studies is grammatically like saying Jews Studies. Unlike English speakers, German speakers are stuck with the noun adjunct. The old adjective *zigeunerisch* from the pejorative term *Zigeuner* is today understood to be racist, while German does not allow for the construction of an adjective from the terms Sinti and Roma.

64. Sinti representatives have frequently insisted on marking their distinction from Roma. As a result, "Sinti and Roma" is the universally accepted appellation in Germany. In Austria, where German debates have influenced common usage but where Sinti are a minority among the larger population of Roma, the accepted term has been reversed to "Roma and Sinti." On the role of Romani representatives and communities in naming practices, see Elena Marushiakova and Vesselin Popov, "Roma Labelling: Policy and Academia," *Slovenský Národopis* 66, no. 4 (2018): 385–418.

65. The term can also be spelled differently, including Pharrajimos or Porajmos. For an early use, see Ian Hancock, "The Porrajmos (Romani Holocaust)," *Nationalities Papers* 19, no. 3 (1991): 373–94.

66. Hancock acknowledges these possible meanings but has defended the term: Ian Hancock, "On the Interpretation of a Word: *Porrajmos* as Holocaust," *The Holocaust in History and Memory* 3 (2011): 19–24. For a critique, see János Bársony and Ágnes Daróczi, *Pharrajimos: The Fate of the Roma During the Holocaust* (New York: International Debate Education Association, 2007), x. As the title suggests, the authors nevertheless use the term. For another sustained critique, see Renata Berkyová, "Concept of the Porajmos as a Reflection of the Marginalization of Roma in Historiography," *Romea*, June 6, 2018, www.romea.cz/en/news/world/renata-berkyova -concept-of-the-porajmos-as-a-reflection-of-the-marginalization-of-roma-in-historiography.

67. The best-known early critique comes from the historian Walter Laqueur who called the term "singularly inappropriate." Yet he also conceded that the term was useful and continued

using it himself. Walter Laqueur, *The Terrible Secret: An Investigation into the Suppression of Information about Hitler's "Final Solution"* (London: Weidenfeld and Nicolson, 1980), 7.

68. Donald Niewyk and Francis Nicosia, *The Columbia Guide to the Holocaust* (New York: Columbia University Press, 2003), 45. Jon Petrie, "The Secular Word Holocaust: Scholarly Myths, History, and 20th Century Meanings," *Journal of Genocide Research* 2, no. 1 (March 2000): 31–63.

69. The term Holocaust also remains more common in publications than the other terms, as the authoritative international bibliography on the subject demonstrates: About and Abakunova, "The Genocide and Persecution of Roma and Sinti." See also Donald Kenrick, "Holocaust," in *Historical Dictionary of the Gypsies (Romanies)* (Lanham, MD: Scarecrow Press, 1998), 109–13. For a critique of the term Romani Holocaust, precisely due to the close relation and equivalence it implies to the Jewish Holocaust, see Konstanty Gebert, "Shoah and Porrajmos: Closely Connected, Yet Best Kept Separate," in *Beyond the Roma Holocaust: From Resistance to Mobilization*, ed. Thomas M. Buchsbaum and Slawomir Kapralski (Kraków: Universitas, 2017), 185–98.

Chapter One: Roma and Jews in Nazi Europe

1. On Sinti and Roma in Auschwitz-Birkenau, see Michael Zimmermann, *Rassenutopie und Genozid: Die nationalsozialistische "Lösung der Zigeunerfrage"* (Hamburg: Christians, 1996), 326–44; Guenter Lewy, *The Nazi Persecution of the Gypsies* (Oxford: Oxford University Press, 2000), 152–66; Slawomir Kapralski, *Roma in Auschwitz*, Voices of Memory 7 (Oświęcim, Poland: Auschwitz-Birkenau State Museum, 2011); Waclaw Dlugoborski, ed., *Sinti und Roma im KL Auschwitz-Birkenau, 1943–44: Vor dem Hintergrund ihrer Verfolgung unter der Naziherrschaft* (Oświęcim, Poland: Staatliches Museum Auschwitz-Birkenau, 1998).

2. Deposition of Konrad Reinhard, November 8, 1966, Vernehmungsprotokolle Sinti und Roma, Fritz Bauer Institute (FBI), 26–31.

3. Deborah Dwork and R. J. van Pelt, *Auschwitz* (New York: Norton, 1996), 338–43.

4. Michael Burleigh and Wolfgang Wippermann, *The Racial State: Germany, 1933–1945* (Cambridge: Cambridge University Press, 1991) offers the standard account with this focus. For recent revisions, see Devin O. Pendas, Mark Roseman, and Richard F. Wetzell, eds., *Beyond the Racial State: Rethinking Nazi Germany* (Cambridge: Cambridge University Press, 2017).

5. Zimmermann, *Rassenutopie und Genozid*, 167–75. On Nisko and unrealized ideas of deporting Viennese Roma to the "Jewish reservation," see Jonny Moser, *Nisko: Die ersten Judendeportationen* (Vienna: Edition Steinbauer, 2012), 55–56; Doron Rabinovici, *Instanzen der Ohnmacht: Wien 1938–1945: Der Weg zum Judenrat* (Frankfurt am Main: Jüdischer Verlag, 2000), 197–209.

6. Patrick Desbois, *The Holocaust by Bullets: A Priest's Journey to Uncover the Truth behind the Murder of 1.5 Million Jews* (New York: Palgrave Macmillan, 2008) popularized the term "Holocaust by bullets." Desbois' organization, Yahad-in Unum, has also been instrumental in identifying sites where Roma have been shot. On killings by the Einsatzgruppen, see Martin Holler, *Der nationalsozialistische Völkermord an den Roma in der besetzten Sowjetunion (1941–1944): Gutachten für das Dokumentations- und Kulturzentrum Deutscher Sinti und Roma* (Heidelberg: Dokumentations- und Kulturzentrum Deutscher Sinti und Roma, 2009).

7. On Croatia, see Alexander Martin Korb, *Im Schatten des Weltkriegs: Massengewalt der Ustaša gegen Serben, Juden und Roma in Kroatien 1941–1945*, Studien zur Gewaltgeschichte des 20. Jahrhunderts (Hamburg: Hamburger Edition, 2013). On Romania see Radu Ioanid, *The Holocaust in Romania: The Destruction of Jews and Gypsies under the Antonescu Regime, 1940–1944* (Chicago, IL: Ivan R. Dee, 2000); Jean Ancel, *The History of the Holocaust in Romania* (Lincoln and Jerusalem: University of Nebraska Press and Yad Vashem, 2011); Vladimir Solonari, "Ethnic Cleansing or 'Crime Prevention'? Deportation of Romanian Roma," in *The Nazi Genocide of the Roma: Reassessment and Commemoration*, ed. Anton Weiss-Wendt (New York: Berghahn, 2013), 96–119.

8. On the difficulty of estimating population numbers of German Sinti and Roma, given the conflicting social and racial definitions of demographers at the time, see Zimmermann, *Rassenutopie und Genozid*, 72–73. On the Jewish population, see the German state's estimate in the census for religiously-defined Jews (*Glaubensjuden*): *Volkszählung: Die Bevölkerung des Deutschen Reichs nach den Ergebnissen der Volkszählung 1933*, vol. 5, *Die Glaubensjuden im Deutschen Reich* (Berlin: Verlag für Sozialpolitik, Wirtschaft und Statistik, 1936), 7.

9. See, for example, Walter Stanoski Winter, *Winter Time: Memoirs of a German Sinto Who Survived Auschwitz* (Hatfield, UK: University of Hertfordshire Press, 2004), 27; testimony of Ludwig Georg, March 3, 1967, FBI Sinti und Roma (SuR), 227–28. German Romanies sometimes also referred to the greater resources at the disposal of Jews who sought to leave the country, see testimony of Ewald Hanstein, December 16, 1997, VHA 40368, USC Shoah Foundation, tape 3. Other Romani survivors highlighted their disappointment at having their careers in the Nazi regime's armed forces aborted, explaining that the regime's nationalism had attracted them. See, for example, Winter, *Winter Time*; testimony of Adolf Hermann S., June 10, 1987, Bl. 513–16, BArch 162/7348–7351.

10. Publication by the exiled Social Democrats, such as the *Deutschland-Berichte der Sozialdemokratischen Partei Deutschlands (Sopade)*, do not elaborate on such measures either. There are only some incidental asides on anti-"Gypsy" policies, such as this report (published in Paris) on Jews and "Gypsies" in labor brigades: "Die Lage jüdischer Schwerarbeiter: Wie sie ausgehungert werden sollen," *Neuer Vorwärts* 6, no. 286 (December 1938): 8, https://fes.imageware.de/fes/web/index.html?open=NV06048&page=7.

11. The regime had toned down its antisemitic propaganda, in the meantime, temporarily removing some signs prohibiting Jews from entering public spaces with an eye to appeasing the international community for the duration of the games. Saul Friedländer, *Nazi Germany and the Jews: The Years of Persecution, 1933–1939* (New York: HarperPerennial, 1998), 180–81.

12. Other camps were in Magdeburg, Braunschweig, Fulda, Hamm, Hanover, Herne, Kassel, Kiel, Oldenburg, Osnabrück, Ravensburg, Recklinghausen, Remscheid, Solingen, Flensburg, and Wiesbaden. For the full list with references to works on each camp, see Karola Fings, "Nationalsozialistische Zwangslager für Sinti und Roma," in *Der Ort des Terrors: Geschichte der nationalsozialistischen Konzentrationslager*, ed. Wolfgang Benz, Barbara Distel, and Angelika Königseder, vol. 9 (Munich: C. H. Beck, 2009), 195, 215–16. On Berlin, see Patricia Pientka, *Das Zwangslager für Sinti und Roma in Berlin-Marzahn: Alltag, Verfolgung und Deportation* (Berlin: Metropol-Verlag, 2013); on Düsseldorf, see Karola Fings and Frank Sparing, *Z. Zt. Zigeunerlager: Die Verfolgung der Düsseldorfer Sinti und Roma im Nationalsozialismus* (Cologne: Volksblatt Verlag, 1992); on Flensburg, see Sebastian Lotto-Kusche, "'. . . Daß für sie die gewöhnlichen

Rechtsbegriffe nicht gelten': Das NS-Zwangslager für 'Zigeuner' in Flensburg und dessen Wahr-nehmung in der Stadtbevölkerung," *Demokratische Geschichte: Jahrbuch für Schleswig-Holstein* 28 (2018): 225–38.

13. Fings, "Nationalsozialistische Zwangslager," 197; Pientka, *Zwangslager*, 122–33.

14. Simon Dubnov, *Velt-geshikhte fun Yidishn folk fun di eltste tsaytn biz tsu der hayntiker tsayt* (Vilnius: Yidisher visnshaftlekher institut, Historishe sektsye, 1938), 388. Dubnow's work ap-peared right after these policies were put in place. His notion clearly drew on a sense of the seemingly timeless disenfranchisement of Roma, not any specific policies.

15. Even where Romanies and Jews clearly faced similar policies, such as their exclusion from various welfare services, there are few hints that members of either group attributed this to a shared dynamic. On such policies concerning both groups, see Wolf Gruner, *Öffentliche Wohl-fahrt und Judenverfolgung: Wechselwirkungen lokaler und zentraler Politik im NS-Staat (1933–1942)* (Munich: Oldenbourg, 2002), 307–9.

16. See, for example, Mark L. Smith, *The Yiddish Historians and the Struggle for a Jewish His-tory of the Holocaust* (Detroit, MI: Wayne State University Press, 2019), on the early influence of survivor historians. Roma and Sinti were also not of interest to non-Jewish historians. In this period, they generally dismissed their Jewish colleagues and focused on sources produced by the most notorious Nazi agencies, rather than local municipalities or nonpolitical branches of the criminal police. Nicolas Berg, *The Holocaust and the West German Historians: Historical In-terpretation and Autobiographical Memory* (Madison: The University of Wisconsin Press, 2015).

17. Fritz Goldschmidt, "My Life in Germany before and after January 30, 1933," London, 1957, Wiener Library, 1656/2/5/756, 42.

18. Ibid., 43.

19. Increasing persecution and direct contact often merely reinforced such sentiments. The memoirs of Arnold Mostowicz, a physician in the Łódź ghetto, expressed this succinctly: "The news that reached the ghetto about the conditions in which the Gypsies lived (news that did not even describe the horrible truth) improved the morale of the Jews enclosed in the ghetto because it meant it was not they who were at the bottom. [. . .] The executioner allowed the victims to observe each other, but it must be remembered that there was never any feeling of sympathy or common fate between the Jews and the Gypsies." Arnold Mostowicz, *With a Yellow Star and a Red Cross: A Doctor in the Lódz Ghetto* (London: Vallentine Mitchell, 2005), 24.

20. "Juden, Zigeuner und Neger," *Die neue Welt* 9, no. 519 (December 6, 1935): 2; "Reichsmin-ister Dr. Frick über das Reichsbürgergesetz," *Jüdische allgemeine Zeitung* 15 (December 4, 1935); "Authentische Äußerungen zu den Nürnberger Gesetzen," *C.V.-Zeitung* 14 (December 5, 1935); "Der Sinn der Rassegesetzgebung," *C.V.-Zeitung* 14 (January 31, 1935).

21. Among the exceptions: see "Zigeiner un aiden-bezonder," *Heint*, March 12, 1939, 2, on the orders of the mayor of Cologne to teach "Gypsy" children in separate classes.

22. *Bulletin of the Jewish Telegraph Agency*, July 27, 1937, 3, www.jta.org/1937/07/27/archive /rumanian-gypsies-join-forces-with-anti-semites-seek-music-monopoly. On the Jewish Tele-graphic Agency see Jonathan Sarna, "The American Jewish Press," in *The Oxford Handbook of American Public Opinion and the Media*, ed. Robert Y. Shapiro and Lawrence R. Jacobs, The Oxford Handbooks of American Politics (Oxford: Oxford University Press, 2011), 544.

23. In reality, *Țara Noastră* was the organ of the General Association of Roma in Romania, which had aligned itself with the National Christian Party and its newspaper. On the paper's

antisemitism, see Sofiya Zahova, Raluca Bianca Roman, and Aleksandar Marinov, eds., *Roma Writings: Romani Literature and Press in Central, South-Eastern and Eastern Europe from the 19th Century until World War II* (Paderborn, Germany: Brill Schöningh, 2021), 102–3 and 116; on the underlying politics, see Viorel Achim, "The Roma Organizations and their Relations with the Romanian Politics in the 1930s," in *Nouvelles Études d'Histoire*, ed. Dan Berindei, vol. 12, *Publiées à l'occasion du XXIe Congrès International des Sciences Historiques, Amsterdam, 2010* (Bucharest: Editura Academiei Române, 2010), 93–94. For examples of articles from *Țara Noastră* with translation and a commentary by Raluca Bianca Roman, see Elena Marushiakova and Vesselin Popov, eds., *Roma Voices in History: A Sourcebook* (Leiden, Netherlands: Ferdinand Schöningh, 2021), 437–47. Hungarian Romani musicians also adopted a nationalist rhetoric as part of their push for protectionist policies, aimed in part at competing musicians. See Tamás Hajnáczky, "Trianon and Revisionist Gypsy Musicians," *Central European Political Science Review* 21, no. 81 (Fall 2020): 129–41.

24. *Bulletin of the Jewish Telegraph Agency*, July 27, 1937, 3.

25. "Zigeuner Rumäniens judenfeindlich," *Jüdische Rundschau* 42, no 60 (July 1937):11, based on JTA report; "Bukarest," *Der jüdische Herold: Unabhängiges orthodoxes Organ* [Bratislava, Slovakia] 13, no. 29 (August 1937): 4; "Die Zigeuner Rumäniens im judenfeindlichen Lager," *Die Wahrheit* [Vienna] (August 1937): 3; "Die Zigeuner Rumäniens gegen die Juden," *Der Israelit* 78, no. 33 (August 1937): 9.

26. On the arrests of Roma and statistics on their numbers in different prewar camps, see Zimmermann, *Rassenutopie*, 115–24.

27. See Nikolaus Wachsmann, *KL: A History of the Nazi Concentration Camps* (London: Little, Brown, 2015).

28. Labor Camp Bełżec did not make it into the vast list of camps produced by the Red Cross and the International Tracing Service after the war. International Tracing Service, *Catalogue of Camps and Prisons in Germany and German-Occupied Territories, Sept. 1st, 1939–May 8th, 1945* (Arolsen, Germany: International Tracing Service, 1949); Martin Weinmann and Anne Kaiser, eds., *Das nationalsozialistische Lagersystem =(CCP)* (Frankfurt am Main: Zweitausendeins, 1990). Interviewers and individuals tagging interviews also frequently confused the camp of 1940 with the later extermination camp of the same name. Whereas the Shoah Foundation has a separate entry for the labor camp, calling it Belzec I, many other institutions, including Yad Vashem and the Fortunoff Archive, do not. The memorial site in Bełżec does commemorate the labor camp and has started also to highlight the detention and murder of Sinti and Roma. See "80th Anniversary of Extermination of Roma and Sinti in the Labour Camp in Bełżec—Bełżec," Muzeum i Miejsce Pamięci w Bełżcu, accessed November 6, 2020, www.belzec.eu/en/news /80th_anniversary_of_extermination/1363.

29. On Globocnik, see Berndt Rieger, *Creator of Nazi Death Camps: The Life of Odilo Globocnik* (London: Vallentine Mitchell, 2007). The camp developed out of an earlier experiment in Lublin, the camp at 7 Lipowa Street. See Witold Wojciech Mędykowski, "Forced Labor in the Labor Camps," in *Macht Arbeit Frei?: German Economic Policy and Forced Labor of Jews in the General Government, 1939–1943* (Brighton, MA: Academic Studies Press, 2018), 138–39.

30. Jewish prisoners were guarded by people who were—in the broadest sense—their former neighbors: self-identified ethnic Germans from the Lublin region who were recruited to the Selbstschutz, a paramilitary unit under control of the SS that was responsible for numerous

atrocities. Peter R. Black, "Rehearsal for 'Reinhard'?: Odilo Globocnik and the Lublin Selbst-schutz," *Central European History* 25, no. 2 (1992): 204–26.

31. Zimmermann, *Rassenutopie*, 167–75.

32. A small number of Jews might have been in the camp already, according to the testimony of German Sinti regarding their arrival in the camp. See BArch B162/3231, 103, 115, 165.

33. See Robert Kuwalek, *Das Vernichtungslager Belzec*, trans. Steffen Hänschen, 2nd ed. (Berlin: Metropol, 2014), 251. On Polish Roma later, see Jerzy Ficowski, *Cyganie na polskich drogach* (Kraków: Wydawn. Literackie, 1965), 98.

34. See deposition of Mr. R., BArch B162/3231, 171.

35. The camp commander, Hermann Dolp, went missing in 1944 and was thus presumed dead. This was the main reason that the investigation did not lead to a trial. Zentrale Stelle der Landesjustizverwaltungen to Oberstaatsanwalt bei dem Landgericht Kiel, October 3, 1966, BArch B162/3231.

36. As in investigations regarding killings in Auschwitz, Romani survivors from Germany sometimes recalled that there might have been someone with the last name Kwiek among them, referencing a name that was common among Polish Roma and associated with the family that made most headlines. This was useless to prosecutors and—since they knew neither their first names nor nicknames—indicated distance between the groups. See deposition of Isenhard L., September 4, 1967, BArch B162/3231, for mentions of Kwiek. For others who could not remember names, see in the file Barch B162/3231: deposition of Heinrich S., November 9, 1967; deposition of Johann L., January 4, 1967; deposition of Helmut T., September 24, 1967; deposition of Fredi L., September 29, 1967; deposition of Waberlie W., July 10, 1967; deposition of Robert B., June 8, 1967; deposition of Bertha R., June 27, 1967; deposition of Liesbeth E., June 28, 1967; deposition of Elisabeth G., June 29, 1967; deposition of Andreas L., June 8, 1967.

37. Early camps had often specialized in particular types of prisoners. In 1937–38, the Nazis started to segregate Jewish populations in particular camps (Dachau) and separate groups of Jews in some blocks. See Wachsmann, *KL*, 125–28, 175.

38. See deposition of Heinrich Steinbach, November 9, 1967, BArch B162/3231, 85–89; deposition of Fredi Laubinger, August 29, 1967, BArch B162/3231, 108–12; deposition of Waberlie Weiß, July 10, 1967, BArch B162/3231, 113–20; deposition of Robert Brühl, Kiel, June 8, 1967, BArch B162/3231, 142–48. On Romani *Vorarbeiter*, see deposition of Johann Laubinger, January 4, 1967, BArch B162/3231, 97–99.

39. For other reflections on relational prisoner identities in the camps, see Paris Papamichos Chronakis, "'We lived as Greeks, and we died as Greeks': Salonican Jews in Auschwitz and the Meanings of Nationhood," in *The Holocaust in Greece*, ed. Giorgos Antoniou and A. Dirk Moses (Cambridge: Cambridge University Press, 2018), 157–80.

40. Testimony of Abraham Bulwa, May 4, 1998, VHA 49112.

41. Deposition of Selma Weiß, August 30, 1967, BArch B162/3231, 107. The refusal to testify can also help us grasp the trauma this caused. See, for example, the statements of Anna S., who reported in 1967 that she lost her 7 children in the camp and was thus mentally incapable of serving as a witness. Vermerk, LKPA Kiel—SK/NS, Lübeck, November 8, 1967, BArch B162/3231, 83–84. For memories of a Polish Rom who was in Bełżec as a child, see testimony of Jan Buriański, August 11, 2013, Association of Roma in Poland Archive, Oświęcim.

42. This was true, for example, in cases when families were forced to bathe naked next to each other, breaking communal taboos. See deposition of Mr. L., BArch B162/3231, 103. On the way gendered experiences of violence affected families, see Michelle Kelso, "Romani Women and the Holocaust: Testimonies of Sexual Violence in Romanian-Controlled Transnistria," in *Women and Genocide: Gendered Experiences of Violence, Survival, and Resistance*, ed. JoAnn DiGeorgio-Lutz and Donna Gosbee (Toronto: Women's Press, 2016), 37–72; Volha Bartash, "The Romani Family before and during the Holocaust: How Much Do We Know? An Ethnographic-Historical Study in the Belarusian-Lithuanian Border Region," in *Jewish and Romani Families in the Holocaust and Its Aftermath*, ed. Eliyana R. Adler and Kateřina Čapková (New Brunswick, NJ: Rutgers University Press, 2021), 17–41.

43. Deposition of Helmut Rose, [Berlin], December 14, 1966, BArch B162/28141, 105–12.

44. BArch B162/3231, "Einzeltötungen von Sinti und Roma in dem vom Selbstschutz im Jahre 1940 eingerichteten Arbeitslager Belzec / Distrikt Lublin," under the auspices of the prosecutor's office in Kiel. Since 2012, a monument has marked the place of the mass burial of the— mostly young—Romanies who died in Labor Camp Bełżec. See "80th Anniversary of Extermination of Roma and Sinti."

45. For a related analysis of similar traumatic experiences, see the analysis of the stories German Sinti told of poisoned bread in Bergen-Belsen. Heike Krokowski, *Die Last der Vergangenheit: Auswirkungen nationalsozialistischer Verfolgung auf deutsche Sinti* (Frankfurt am Main: Campus Verlag, 2001), 115–27. Rose's three-year-old son survived the camp. See CM1 of Helmut Rose and family, 3.2.1/79680653/ITS Digital Collection, Arolsen Archives, USHMM.

46. Etty Hillesum, *Etty: The Letters and Diaries of Etty Hillesum, 1941–1943*, ed. Klaas A. D. Smelik, trans. Arnold J. Pomerans (Grand Rapids, MI: William B. Eerdmans, 2002), 578. Here and in the following instances, I changed "Gypsy" to uppercase from the published translation, since Dutch does not distinguish between the lowercase proper noun and the uppercase personal noun.

47. Etty Hillesum to Christine van Nooten, Westerbork, July 1, 1943, in *Etty*, 612–15. Van Nooten was the secret lover of Hillesum's father.

48. For other similar uses before Roma arrived in the camp, see, for example, Jacob Boas, *Boulevard des Misères: The Story of Transit Camp Westerbork* (Hamden, CT: Archon, 1985), 67; Philip Mechanicus, "Journal: Camp de Westerbork 28 mai 1943–28 février 1944," trans. Laetitia Decourt, Hinde Kaddour, and Gaby Velthuys, *Po&sie* 142, no. 4 (2012): 86.

49. B. A. Sijes, *Vervolging van zigeuners in Nederland 1940–1945*, Monografieën—Rijksinstituut voor Oorlogsdocumentatie 13 (The Hague, Netherlands: Nijhoff, 1979), 119.

50. On the plethora of accounts we have in which Jews speak about the situation of Romanies in Malines, see the description of the postwar investigations by Estelle Goldstein's commission in chapter 3. See also Laurence Schram, "De Malines à Auschwitz: Déportation des Juifs et des Tsiganes du Nord de la France," *Tsafon* [Lille, France], no. 79 (2020): 75–96. In some camps in France, interactions were longer and more sustained, especially in Rivesaltes.

51. "News fun Up-State New York un Toronto," *Forward*, May 7, 1939, 7; "News fun Up-State New York un Toronto," *Forward*, April 23, 1939, 8; "News fun Up-State New York un Toronto," *Forward*, April 9, 1939, 8.

52. David Seltzer, *Besaraber lider* (New York: Farlag Soroki, 1937). For children's literature, see Kalmen Lis, "Tsigeiner," in *Kind un rind* (Warsaw: Shvalbn, 1936), 18, which includes images

of "Gypsies" dancing with a bear; Eliezer Shindler, *In shtile farnakhtn: Mayselekh fun Mizreh un Mayrev* (Vilnius: Grinike beymelekh, 1937), 16–17.

53. *Grodnoer Lebn*, June 30, 1939, 1. Throughout 1939, Radio Budapest also broadcast "Gypsy music" over short wave. See the schedule of the radio broadcasts in the 1939 editions of the *Folksblat* from Kaunas.

54. Some novels also included the lore—popular across various European populations—that "Gypsies" abduct children. See Isaac Metzker, *Toli un Tobi* (New York: Matones, 1936), 36–39. Josef Zelkowicz (or Yosef Zelḳoyiṭsh), a journalist, author, and diarist in the Łódź ghetto who died in Auschwitz, reflected on these stereotypes in times when old stories to scare children were overshadowed by realities that were more horrible than any fantasy. In a portrait of deportations in his private diary, he tells of the 6-year-old Rysiek Fajn who suspects the worst because his mother is giving him better food. He imagines the child wondering what might happen and has him think back to his parent's threats that the "Gypsies" will take him if he misbehaves. Yet, these tales are misleading: "[B]ut now . . . now everyone likes him so much. What's more, the Gypsies who used to be in the ghetto are all gone . . . So who would nab him? And why?" Josef Zelkowicz, *In Those Terrible Days: Writings from the Lodz Ghetto* (Jerusalem: Yad Vashem, 2002), 336. Raised in European contexts in which blood libel stories about Jews kidnapping Christian children to use their blood were common, Roma sometimes also held such beliefs. See, for example, testimony of Antonina Bogdanowicz, March 31, 1998, VHA 44556, seg. 34–35.

55. Meir Wiener, *Kolev Ashkenazi: Dertseylung* (Moscow: Emes, 1934), 94. On Wiener, see Mikhail Krutikov, "Wiener, Meir," *YIVO Encyclopedia of Jews in Eastern Europe*, November 4, 2010, https://yivoencyclopedia.org/article.aspx/Wiener_Meir. For similar uses, see Israel Ch. Biletzky, *Umru lider* (Tel Aviv: n.p., 1935), 87. For other references to blackness: M. Beregovski, *Yidishe folks-lider* (Kyiv: Melukhe-farlag far di natsyonale minderhaytn in U.S.S.R, 1938); David Pliskin, "Zigeiner in stetl," in *Vunderland lider un mayselekh* (Paris: Aroysgegebn durkh di tsugob-shuln bay der gez. Fraynt fun arbeter-kind, 1938), 48–50.

56. Shneur Vaserman, *Shvebelekh: Kinder-lider un poemes* (Buenos Aires: Mekhaber ba der mithilf fun kultur-hoyz Mendele, 1938), 50. Readers will also recall Sutzkever's reference to Romani "bearded men" and "daughters like black earth" in the poem that opens the Introduction to this book.

57. Eliezer Shindler, *In shtile farnakhtn: Mayselekh fun Mizreh un Mayrev* (Vilnius: Grinike beymelekh, 1937), 16. Shindler calls Romani "zigeiner-loshn." A second story deals with a "Gypsy" stealing corn from a mill. Shindler, *In shtile farnakhtn*, 17–18.

58. Elias Schulman, *Yung Vilne 1929–1939* (New York: Getseltn, 1946), 12–13.

59. A more literal translation would be that the "Gypsies want to fraternize [*verbridert*]." Shimshon Kahan, "Litvishe zigeiner," *Di Zukunft* [The Future] [New York] 37, no. 8 (August 1932): 474. A proponent of a Jewish settlement area in Soviet Birobidzhan, Kahan may have been alluding to the work of Romani activists who embraced the Bolshevik's policies on nationalities in the 1920s. See Brigid O'Keeffe, *New Soviet Gypsies: Nationality, Performance, and Selfhood in the Early Soviet Union* (Toronto: University of Toronto Press, 2013). For Yiddish-language reports about Romani collective farms (*Sovkhoses*), see David Pinski, *Rayzebukh* (Warsaw: David Pinski bikher, 1938), 194–95. In his writing, Kahan joined a small group of other non-Romani artists and writers who lived with and sought to become cultural ambassadors for

Romanies during the first part of the twentieth century. See also Jan Yoors, *The Gypsies* (New York: Simon and Schuster, 1967); Jan Yoors, *Crossing* (New York: Simon and Schuster, 1971).

60. One person Shimshon Kahan clearly influenced was Sutzkever, whose series of texts on Roma can also be understood as his attempt to build a poetic monument to his murdered friend, Kahan. Other Jewish intellectuals, such as Emanuel Ringelblum, organizer of the Oyneg Shabbes archive in the Warsaw Ghetto, remained more ambivalent in their depictions of Roma. His diary entries from the ghetto describe conflicts between Jews and Roma as well as claims that Roma stole from Jews, although he also seems to have admired their will to resist. Joseph Kermish, "Emmanuel Ringelblum's Notes, Hitherto Unpublished," *Yad Vashem Studies* 7 (1968): 177–78.

61. USHMM, RG-15.079M, 392, RING. I/1108/2 (1427). See Anna G. Piotrowska, *Gypsy Music in European Culture: From the Late Eighteenth to the Early Twentieth Century* (Boston: Northeastern University Press, 2013), 86–99.

62. Isaschar Fater, *Yidishe muzik in Poyln tsvishn beyde velt-milhomes* (Tel Aviv: Velt-Federatsye fun Poylishe Yidn, 1970), 356.

63. The song was first published after the war. Szmerke Kaczerginski, ed., *Lider fun di getos un lagern* (New York: Tsiḳo, 1948), 41. On the song, see "Tsigaynerlid: Gypsy Song," in *Yes, We Sang!: Songs of the Ghettos and Concentration Camps*, by Shoshana Kalisch with Barbara Meister (New York: Harper & Row, 1985), 87–91.

64. German courts obsessively dissected all the possible ways individuals might see the events, since they had to establish a witness's visual identification of perpetrators. My question is different, however. Even when prisoners did not see enough to identify individuals due to obstructions or distance and as a result of the regular curfew (*Blocksperre*) when trains arrived, they could still often make out enough to become witnesses of another group's destruction. See, for example, deposition of Arono Franz, FBI SuR, 121–25; deposition of Elfriede and Siegfried Blum, February 8, 1967, FBI SuR, 140–41; deposition of Reinhold Seeger, February 10, 1967, FBI SuR, 143–47; deposition of Helmut Anton, February 23, 1967, FBI SuR, 197–98; deposition of Robert Wappler, March 3, 1967, FBI SuR, 208–12. On the role the clear identification of perpetrators plays in different testimonial genres, see Hannah Pollin-Galay, *Ecologies of Witnessing: Language, Place, and Holocaust Testimony* (New Haven, CT: Yale University Press, 2018), 107–55.

65. On the history of these deportees, see Julian Baranowski, *The Gypsy Camp in Lodz, 1941–1942* (Łodz, Poland: Archiwum Państwowe w Łodzi & Bilbo, 2003).

66. She subsequently claimed to have also seen Germans throwing babies out of third and fourth story windows. Testimony of Manya Altman, October 24, 1995, VHA 7907, seg. 25.

67. Testimony of Ya'akov Drori, January 15, 1998, VHA 40753, seg. 112. Similar testimonies about screams in Łódź: testimony of Lucie Bailer, June 12, 1995, VHA 3334, seg 54; testimony of David Brin, July 13, 1997, VHA 34126, seg. 45–46; testimony of Bronislaw Zajbert, March 20, 1996, VHA 12644, seg. 46. Others noted that one could hear Romanies' music in Łódź: testimony of Ze'ev Barats, May 12, 1998, VHA 44169, seg. 54; testimony of Irena Libman, reprinted in translation in Shmuel Krakowski, *Chełmno: A Small Village in Europe: The First Nazi Mass Extermination Camp* (Jerusalem: Yad Vashem, 2009), 54. Other Jewish witnesses broke from the dominant theme of continued cries of anguish coming over the fence to depict the Roma as a happy, eternally singing people. See testimony of Yaakov Drakhman, January 20, 1998, VHA 40370, seg. 45.

68. Indeed, as one memoirist noted, individuals in the ghetto were not even sure whether the inhabitants of the "Gypsy camp" were indeed "Gypsies" or instead Hungarian Jews or perhaps Yugoslav partisans with their families. Oskar Rosenfeld, *In the Beginning Was the Ghetto: Notebooks from Lodz* (Evanston, IL: Northwestern University Press, 2002), 42.

69. For the most recent estimate on the number of individuals killed (4,200–4,300), see Helena Kubica and Piotr Setkiewicz, "The Last Stage of the Functioning of the Zigeunerlager in the Birkenau Camp (May–August 1944)," *Memoria: Memory, History, Education* 10 (July 2018): 6–15.

70. See, for example, testimony of Ne'omi Sneh, December 9, 1996, VHA 24739, seg. 95; testimony of Benjamin Shenker, June 17, 1998, VHA 42659, 80. For other reports about the sounds of the camp in that night, see testimony of Elisabeth Guttenberger, February 2, 1965, Frankfurt Auschwitz trial; in the documents of the trial, see trial day 135 (February 11, 1965), Fritz Bauer Institut and Staatliches Museum Auschwitz-Birkenau, *Der Auschwitz-Prozeß: Tonbandmitschnitte, Protokolle, Dokumente*, Digitale Bibliothek 101 (Berlin: Directmedia Publishing, 2004), DVD, 29136 (the DVD includes the trial documents); deposition of Karl Seefeld, January 5, 1960, HHStAW, fonds 461, no. 37638/23, 3838–3841; testimony of Jozef Piwko, Gorzów (from International Auschwitz Commitee), February 5, 1959, Bl. 498, HHStAW, fonds 461, no. 37638/4.

71. Ideas about the centrality of such images and impressions also inform some theories of memory practices among Romani populations. See Michael Stewart, "Remembering without Commemoration: The Mnemonics and Politics of Holocaust Memories among European Roma," *Journal of the Royal Anthropological Institute* 10, no. 3 (2004): 561–82.

72. Transnistria was a vast, new administrative unit comprised of multiple ghettos and forced labor sites, as well as two concentration camps where Romanians deported approximately 25,000 Roma and 150,000 Jews. Transnistria also contained Jews who had lived there before the war. On the memories of various Jewish memory communities of the killings in the area, see Jeffrey Veidlinger, *In the Shadow of the Shtetl: Small-Town Jewish Life in Soviet Ukraine* (Bloomington: Indiana University Press, 2013), 186–231.

73. Yahad-in Unum 89Mo; see also Yahad-in Unum interviews 90M and 163RO. The latter interviewee relates that the queen dropped leaflets from a plane telling their guards not to shoot "Gypsies" because they play music.

74. The popular Queen Maria of Romania (1893–1927) had not been in power for ten years by the time Roma were deported and had been dead for two.

75. Michael Rajak and Zvi Rajak, *Khurbn Glubok* (Buenos Aires: Former Residents' Association in Argentina, 1956), 76–77, available in translation at www.jewishgen.org/Yizkor /Hlybokaye/Hlybokaye.html. On their testimony, see also Bartash, "The Romani Family," 32–33.

76. Testimony of Jacob Morden, December 9, 1996, VHA 23503. According to his account, the murderers then ordered local Poles and Russians to bury the dead and burn the wagons while they confiscated their animals. Morden was able to witness this only because he was passing as a non-Jewish Pole at the time. On the communal memories of Roma, remembering the murder of local Jews, see Bartash, "The Romani Family," 40–41.

77. See Amos Goldberg, "Rumor Culture among Warsaw Jews under Nazi Occupation: A World of Catastrophe Reenchanted," *Jewish Social Studies* 21, no. 3 (2016): 91–125; Isaiah

Kuperstein, "Rumors: A Socio-Historical Phenomenon in the Ghetto of Lodz," *The Polish Review* 18, no. 4 (January 1973): 63–83.

78. See, for example, testimony of Ewald Hanstein, December 16, 1997, VHA 40368, tape 4, on Romani prisoners learning information from Jews in labor commandos.

79. Szlamek took on the name Jakob Grojanowski or Yakub Grojnowski (depending on orthography) after escaping from Chełmno. His true identity remains unclear. He has been identified as either Szlamek Bajler or Winer. On the latter interpretation, see Patrick Montague, *Chelmno and the Holocaust: The History of Hitler's First Death Camp* (Chapel Hill: University of North Carolina Press, 2012), 241, note 13. On Ringelblum's archive, see Samuel D. Kassow, *Who Will Write Our History?: Emanuel Ringelblum, the Warsaw Ghetto, and the Oyneg Shabes Archive* (Bloomington: Indiana University Press, 2007).

80. "An Account by Szlamek," in *Chelmno Witnesses Speak*, ed. Lucja Pawlicka-Nowak (Konin, Poland: District Museum in Konin, 2004), 101–18.

81. On the use of the Grojanowski report, together with others in the underground, see Lea Prais, "'Jews from the World to Come': The First Testimonies of Escapees from Chełmno and Treblinka in the Warsaw Ghetto, 1942–1943," *Yad Vashem Studies* 42, no 1 (2014): 47–81; Krakowski, *Chelmno*, 68–80; Gordon J. Horwitz, *Ghettostadt: Lódz and the Making of a Nazi City* (Cambridge, MA: Belknap Press of Harvard University Press, 2008), 151–53. There is no indication that the Jewish underground reacted to sections on the murder of Roma in the Grojanowski report.

82. Deposition of Johann Weihs, October 19, 1966, FBI SuR.

83. Testimony of Maly Kohn, September 18, 1997, VHA 36613, 61–62.

84. The "Gypsy Family Camp" was adjacent to the Jewish men's camp on one side, and the Theresienstadt family camp with Jewish men, women, and children, on the other. There are several records of trade across the barriers that divided Romani and Jewish prisoners. See, for example, testimony of Bernard Rosenberg, June 29, 1967, FBI SuR, 435–39. Trade was easier in other locations, such as labor camps, where prisoners could move between sections. On such interactions between Romani and Jewish inmates in the German labor camp and copper mines in Bor (today's Serbia), see the testimony of Ratomir Jeremić, May 10, 1998, VHA 48252, tape 2.

85. Interview of Yehuda Bacon with the author, July 31, 2018.

86. For deals that did not go well, see testimony of Geroge Szegö, September 4, 1997, VHA 33258, seg. 29.

87. On economic motives in the Holocaust, see Götz Aly, *Hitler's Beneficiaries: Plunder, Race War, and the Nazi Welfare State* (New York: Metropolitan, 2007); Jan Tomasz Gross, *Neighbors: The Destruction of the Jewish Community in Jedwabne, Poland* (Princeton, NJ: Princeton University Press, 2001). While Roma tended to have less property, their expropriation and removal nevertheless benefited their neighbors and municipalities. See Florian Freund, Gerhard Baumgartner, and Harald Greifeneder, *Vermögensentzug, Restitution und Entschädigung der Roma und Sinti*, Veröffentlichungen der Österreichischen Historikerkommission: Vermögensentzug während der NS-Zeit sowie Rückstellungen und Entschädigungen seit 1945 in Österreich 23/2 (Vienna: Oldenbourg, 2004).

88. Testimony of Nina Michowski, September 25, 1996, VHA 20203, seg. 24.

89. Edward Kopówka and Laura Crago, "Siedlce," in *The United States Holocaust Memorial Museum Encyclopedia of Camps and Ghettos, 1933–1945*, ed. Geoffrey P. Megargee and Martin Dean, vol. 2 (Bloomington: Indiana University Press, 2012), 429.

90. Fings and Sparing, *Z. Zt. Zigeunerlager*, 69; deposition of Helen K., Göttingen, November 20, 1958, StAM, Staatsanwaltschaften 21837, 51–52; deposition of Robert W., Kiel, November 11, 1958, StAM, Staatsanwaltschaften 21837, 55–58. For an account of Romanies working next to Jews and living in their houses after deportation from a different ghetto (Włodzimierz), see Edward Dębicki, *Totenvogel: Erinnerungen*, trans. Karin Wolff (Berlin: Friedenauer Presse, 2018), 90–93.

91. Kopówka and Crago, "Siedlce," 430.

92. Eddie Weinstein, *Quenched Steel: The Story of an Escape from Treblinka* (Jerusalem: Yad Vashem, 2002), 110–13.

93. For a Romani account of this, see deposition of Robert Weiss, November 11, 1958, StAM, Staatsanwaltschaften 21837. To give Jews and Roma the appearance that they were not immediately threatened during the period of the new ghetto, the administration allowed them to trade with Polish peasants. It is thus also possible that the Romani prisoners Michowski saw could have bartered with these local peasants for the clothes they wore. See Kopówka and Crago, "Siedlce," 430.

94. "Account by Szlamek," 107.

95. The phrase "choiceless choices" comes from Lawrence L. Langer, *Versions of Survival: The Holocaust and the Human Spirit*, SUNY Series in Modern Jewish Literature and Culture (Albany, NY: SUNY Press, 1982), 72. On the difficulty of accounting for such choices in interviews touching on relative privilege under persecution, see Adam Brown, "Confronting 'Choiceless Choices' in Holocaust Videotestimonies: Judgement, 'Privileged' Jews, and the Role of the Interviewer," *Continuum* 24, no. 1 (February 2010): 79–90.

96. On Sinti and Roma building the tracks and maintaining them, see deposition of Bruno Stein, trial day 150, April 22, 1965, Tonbandmitschnitte des Auschwitz-Prozesses (1963–1965), https://www.auschwitz-prozess.de/zeugenaussagen/Stein-Bruno/; testimony of Alfred Blum, FBI SuR, 139–40; testimony of Ewald Klein, February 9, 1967, FBI SuR, 148–50; testimony of Paul Habedank, February 21, 1967, FBI SuR, 184–87; testimony of Bernard Dombrowski, March 9, 1967, FBI SuR, 237–40; testimony of Heinrich Leimberger, September 11, 1967, FBI SuR, 473–74. On work at the ramp and with valuables, see testimony of Oswald Dambrowski, January 25, 1967, FBI SuR, 114–15; deposition of Otto Johannes Ernst, FBI SuR, 135–38; deposition of Rudolf Böhmer, February 1, 1967, FBI SuR, 151–53; deposition of Ferdinand Koslowski, February 1, 1967, FBI SuR, 154–55 (Koslowski also says he was tasked with driving Jews who could not walk from the ramp to the gas chambers); deposition of Jakob Kreis, March 7, 1967, FBI SuR, 235–36; deposition of Bernard Dombrowski, March 9, 1967, FBI SuR, 237–40; deposition of Julius Lange, March 17, 1967, FBI SuR, 241–44; deposition of Heinrich Dewis, March 16, 1967, FBI SuR, 253–55; deposition of Ludwig Hoffmann, Aprril 12, 1967, FBI SuR, 288–91; deposition of Heinrich Wachler, April 19, 1967, SuR, 310–13; deposition of August Steinbach, April 14, 1967, 314–19; deposition of Josef Köhler, May 19, 1967, FBI SuR, 391–95. Romanies called this the *Rollwagenkommando*, but it appears in scholarship also as *Aufräumkommando an der Rampe* (cleanup commando at the ramp). On the commando, see Andrzej Strzelecki, "The Plunder of Victims and Their Corpses," in *Anatomy of the Auschwitz Death Camp*, ed. Israel Gutman and Michael Berenbaum (Bloomington: Indiana University Press, in association with the United States Holocaust Memorial Museum, 1994), 250. Jewish victims sometimes encountered Sinti and Roma with such deployment upon arrival. See, for example, testimony of Martin

Aaron [Aron], April 27, 1997, VHA 28325, seg. 13 and my analysis of this testimony in Ari Josko-wicz, "Separate Suffering, Shared Archives: Jewish and Romani Histories of Nazi Persecution," *History and Memory* 28, no. 1 (2016): 110–40.

97. Testimony of Anton van Velsen at König Trial on May 12, 1986, Staatsarchiv NRW, Geri-chte 158, no. 1485, 19.

98. See deposition Arie Fuks, July 8, 1966, FBI, FAP2 HA 101–02, 19130–19133; Sol P. [Pluda], Fortunoff Archive, HVT-2273. Pluda reports that this deployment allowed him better food ra-tions for a while and thus helped him survive.

99. Testimony of Walter Stanoski Winter, June 30, 1996, VHA 16486, tape 4, min 11:20–14:00; Walter Stanoski Winter, *Winter Zeit: Erinnerungen eines deutschen Sinto, der Auschwitz überlebt hat* (Hamburg: Ergebnisse, 1999) 67–68. Winter reports that the Nazis ended up gassing the Jews the next day. Many Jews deported to BIIe—in particular those from northern Transylvania—did survive, however.

100. On Jadów, see, Witold Mędykowski and Martin Dean, "Jadów," in *The United States Holocaust Memorial Museum Encyclopedia of Camps and Ghettos, 1933–1945,* ed. Geoffrey P. Mega-rgee, vol. 2 (Bloomington: Indiana University Press in association with the United States Ho-locaust Memorial Museum, 2009), 379–80.

101. A. Wolf Jasny, ed., *Sefer Yadov* (Jersualem: Encyclopaedia of the Jewish Diaspora, 1966), NYPL Digital Collections, https://digitalcollections.nypl.org/items/bc143e40-79a9-0133 -d9d6-00505686d14e, 247–48.

102. Ibid., 248.

103. "Fäkalien- und Leichenabfuhr," in Biebow, Getto-Verwaltung to Älteste der Juden, No-vember 12, 1941, USHMM, RG-15.083M, reel 35, 67–69 and subsequent correspondence held in this file.

104. Lucjan Dobroszycki, *The Chronicle of the Lodz Ghetto, 1941–1944* (New Haven, CT: Yale University Press, 1984), 107–8. In Lackenbach, a camp established exclusively for Roma and Sinti in the Austrian Burgenland, prisoners who died there were interred in the Jewish cemetery. However, by this time there were no more Jews left in the town to perform this labor. As in Łódź, the authorities assigned a separate area in the Jewish cemetery to deceased Roma. Franz Karall, "Erinnerungsbericht über Lackenbach," September 24, 1954, DÖW 19360/1; Klaus-Dieter Alicke, *Lexikon der jüdischen Gemeinden im deutschen Sprachraum,* vol. 2 (Gütersloh, Germany: Gütersloher Verlagshaus, 2008), www.jüdische-gemeinden.de/index.php/gemeinden/k-l/1138 -lackenbach-burgenland-oesterreich.

105. The same principle of using anyone who could be requisitioned for such work applied also to the burial of Roma. In Szczurowa, the Germans ordered local firefighters to bury the murdered Roma. See Jan Grabowski, *Hunt for the Jews: Betrayal and Murder in German-Occupied Poland* (Bloomington: Indiana University Press, 2013), 75.

106. On the trains and these decisions, see Radu Ioanid, "The Holocaust in Romania: The Iasi Pogrom of June 1941," *Contemporary European History* 2, no. 2 (1993): 139–40; Ioanid, *Ho-locaust in Romania,* 80–82.

107. Testimony of May 12, 2016 with a Lipovan man from Târgu Frumos, Yahad-in Unum, 167RO.

108. On the perception that killing was clean work but handling the dead dirty work, see Ancel, *History of the Holocaust,* 227. A priest and Jewish youth also allegedly paid Roma to dig out

a survivor whose screams they heard from the burial pits. See Ioanid, "The Holocaust in Romania," 140.

109. Gila Fatran, "Die Deportation der Juden aus der Slowakei 1944–1945," *Bohemia: A Journal of History and Civilisation in East Central Europe* 37, no. 1 (1996): 114–15.

110. For a Romani account of this, see the testimony of Imrich Daško and Pavlína Dašková, in Milena Hübschmannová, *"Po Židoch Cigáni": Svědectví Romů ze Slovenska, 1939–1945* (Prague: Triáda, 2005), 313.

111. Testimony of Olga Capek, June 27, 1996, VHA 16940, seg. 140–41.

112. Avraham Sutzkever, "Petro, the Gypsy," *Lider fun yam ha-moves: Fun Vilner geto, vald un yander* (Tel Aviv: Farlag Bergen-Belzen, 1968), 264–65. "Petro, the Gypsy" formed part of the cycle of poems *Geheymstodt* in this volume. The poems "Petro, the Gypsy" and "Taboren zigeiner" were published originally in the May-June 1948 issue of *Die Zukunft*; see Abraham Nowersztern, *Avrom Sutskever-bibliografye* (Tel Aviv: Yiśroel-bukh, 1976), 74–75. The child is not gendered in Yiddish. I decided to use the male form in my translation because this was also the gender of the young child Sutzkever lost in the ghetto. Sutzkever also reports in his diary how during his time in hiding he encountered one of his childhood friends, Khaim Gordon, whom Roma had taken in for his protection. His friend, according to the narrative, had encountered the group and its leader Fodor when the Roma were ordered to bury the murdered Jews. See Abraham Sutzkever, *From the Vilna Ghetto to Nuremberg: Memoir and Testimony*, trans. Justin D. Cammy (Montreal: McGill-Queen's University Press, 2021). 31–32.

113. Papusza was originally shunned by other Polska Roma for revealing information about the group to outsiders and because non-Roma used her poetry to support forced assimilation and the settlement policies of the postwar Polish state. On her life and work, see, among others, Klaus Michael Bogdal, *Europa erfindet die Zigeuner: Eine Geschichte von Faszination und Verachtung* (Berlin: Suhrkamp, 2011), 472–74.

114. Papusza, *Pieśni Papuszy (Papušakra gila)*, ed. Jerzy Ficowski (Wroclaw, Poland: Ossoliński, 1956). The fact that Papusza's poetry only reaches us through Ficowski's translation, with changes to meter, rhyme, and content, presents additional challenges in interpreting her work. See Emilia Kledzik, review of *Bronislawa Wajs-Papusza: Miedzy Biografia a Legenda*, by Magdalena Machowska, *Romani Studies* 30, no. 2 (October 2020): 267–73.

115. Other war-related poems include "Smutna pieśń" and "Gruzy wszystko przypominają." Papusza and Jerzy Ficowski, *Piesni mówione* (Łódź, Poland: Wydawn. Łódzkie, 1973), 34, 35. For oral history interviews with similar stories of a Romani woman saving a Jewish girl whose parents were killed in a massacre in 1941, see Bartash, "The Romani Family," 41.

116. Papusza, *Pieśni Papuszy*, 64, 66. I quote her poem in translation by Yala Korwin, titled "Tears of Blood: How We Suffered under the German Soldiers in Volhynia from 1943 to 1944," in Piotr Wawrzeniuk, "Papusza: The Story of a Polish Roma Poet," *Balticworlds*, May 12, 2015, 4–7, https://balticworlds.com/papusza/. See also Papusza, *Papuszas gesprochene Lieder*, trans. Karin Wolff, Poesievolle Nachbarschaft 1 (Frankfurt an der Oder, Germany: Kleist-Museum, 2011).

117. Papusza, "Tears of Blood."

118. See also the testimony of Anna Kwiatkowska, August 5, 1997, VHA 35577, seg. 51–53. Kwiatkowska, a Romani woman from Poland, reported on hiding together with a Jewish man and woman in the forest. In the testimony of Stefania Surmaj Górniak, May 8, 1998, VHA 45755, Górniak mentions that her family helped a Jewish woman who escaped from a camp.

119. On buying food from Roma in 1942, see Itzjok Perlow, *Sefer Radom* (Tel Aviv: Irgun yots'e Radom be-Yiśra'el, 1961), 311. Ludwik Doliński remembers smuggling and selling food to Jews in Tarnów. Testimony of Ludwik Doliński, February 5, 1998, VHA 44108, seg. 52–54, 80.

120. Hübschmannová, *"Po Židoch Cigáni."* The linguist and folklorist Mozes Heintschink has also suggested in an interview I conducted with him that Romani women often worked in Jewish households in Izmir (including his own wife). Author's interview with Mozes Heintschink, July 2, 2011.

121. Milena Hübschmannová, "Vztahy mezi Romy a Židy na východním Slovensku před druhou světovou válkou," *Romano džaniben*, no. 1–2 (2000): 17–23. A new project directed by Kateřina Čapková and Helena Sadílková, entitled "Genocide, Postwar Migration, and Social Mobility: Entangled Experiences of Roma and Jews" (2019–23) and funded by the Czech Science Foundation, promises to fundamentally revise our understanding of Romani-Jewish relations in these regions.

122. Romani witnesses reporting on their relations with Jews during the interwar era often emphasize business relations. See, for example, the influential memoir of Elena Lacková, a Romani woman who worked with fellow Roma as an administrator for the postwar communist administration, where she recounts the regular but fraught commercial ties her family had with a Jewish herb dealer in interwar eastern Slovakia. Elena Lacková, *A False Dawn: My Life as a Gypsy Woman in Slovakia*, ed. Milena Hübschmannová, trans. Carleton Bulkin (Paris and Hatfield, UK: Centre de recherches tsiganes and University of Hertfordshire Press, 1999), 38–39. For similar descriptions of relations in interwar Hungary in a fictional account that uses biographical elements, see Menyhért Lakatos, *The Color of Smoke: An Epic Novel of the Roma*, trans. Ann Major (Williamstown, MA: New Europe Books, 2015). Jewish witnesses also recount regular commercial interactions, including their memories of Romani groups coming to town at regular intervals to sell products, tell the future, repair pots, or restore mattresses. Author's interviews with Isaac Nehama and Paulette Nehama, November 14, 2012; author's interview with Henry Greenbaum, June 2, 2017. Much more rarely one finds examples of individual Jews who remember engaging with Roma outside of such transactional relations, such as that of the Slovak Jewish man who recalled playing with Romani children during summer vacations in the countryside and learning some Romani in the process. See George Feher, *Thoughts on the Holocaust* (n. p.: Feher Publishing, 2017), 191, note 83.

123. Rare cases of the opposite pattern appear as well. Sofija Komarov, a Romani survivor, reported in an interview that, during her internment in Sajmište concentration camp, her grandmother received bread from a Jewish woman for whom her grandmother had previously done housekeeping work. See testimony of Sofija Komarov, October 3, 1998, VHA 49142, tape 1.

124. Testimony of Elizabeth K., Fortunoff Archive, HVT-2565. See also the testimony of her sister Judith P., Fortunoff Archive, HVT-2548, which is more distanced but contains many of the same familial narratives related to "the Gypsy boy." Not all such attempts were successful. Pavle Dekić, who was imprisoned as a Rom in the Sajmište concentration camp in today's Serbia, reports how a Jewish woman for whom his mother had worked asked him to smuggle a letter out of the camp when he managed to get released. Threatened with the death of his family if such a letter was found, he reported that he destroyed it. See testimony of Pavle Dekić, October 7, 1998, VHA 49214.

125. See "Imari Hajrija," in The Righteous Among the Nations Database, Yad Vashem, https://righteous.yadvashem.org/?search=hajrija&searchType=righteous_only&language

=en&itemId=4015348&ind=0. She is alternatively also called Hajrija Imeri and Hajirija Mihaljić in the file. For the Righteous among the Nations file, see Yad Vashem, M.31.2/4939 and Ester Levi's interviews with Yad Vashem, O.3/4553 and O.33.C721. On the difficulties of moving beyond the identification of each other as nameless Gypsies and Jews even in such cases, see Ari Joskowicz, "Separate Suffering, Shared Archives."

126. Akten-Notiz, Amtsleiter Biebow, October 30, 1941, USHMM, RG-15.083M, file 110, 77.

127. Dobroszycki, *Chronicle of the Lodz Ghetto*, 82–83. On these various obligations, see the correspondence between Älteste der Juden, Kriminalpolizei, and Getto-Verwaltung, USHMM, RG-15.083M, reel 35, file 110.

128. See testimony of Karl Brozik, April 30, 1996, VHA 14055, seg. 66–67. The Romani section is often referred to both as a ghetto and a camp in the literature.

129. See testimony of Elizabeth Feldstein, July 22, 1996, VHA 17633, seg. 38–41 on her experience contracting typhus as a Jewish nurse in the Romani ghetto.

130. There are various testimonies from other camps regarding Jews sharing or not sharing food. In the case of Westerbork, Lau Mazirel, a Dutch Catholic lawyer, resistance fighter, and advocate for Romani rights, claimed that she asked the Jewish Council to distribute its food to the hundreds of Dutch Sinti and Roma who were interned there for several days in 1944 before their deportation to Auschwitz. By her account, the Jewish Council declined, leaving Mazirel disappointed and, perhaps unrealistically, bitter about the unwillingness of her contacts to give their scarce resources to their fellow deportees. Mazirel to B. A. Sijes, February 7, 1969, NIOD 475/3cI. In other places, Romani survivors note how they ate food prepared by Jews. See, for example, testimony of Ana Vasić, May 24, 1998, VHA 46890 on the camp Sajmište.

131. See, for example, testimony of Ludwik Doliński, February 5, 1998, VHA 44108, seg. 52–54, on avoiding Jewish and German guards in the Tarnów ghetto; testimony of Michael and Anna Böhmer about Jewish police beating them in Siedlce, in Josef Behringer and Adam Strauss, eds., *Flucht, Internierung, Deportation, Vernichtung: Hessische Sinti und Roma berichten über ihre Verfolgung während des Nationalsozialismus* (Seeheim, Germany: I-Verb, 2005), 101–2.

132. Jews were also kapos of Romani workers, although they do not appear prominently in Romani testimonies. See testimony of Aron Blum, November 7, 1995, VHA 5384, seg. 74–75, for a Jewish prisoner overseeing Roma working on sewage lines in Auschwitz-Birkenau.

133. For narratives of kapos identified as "Gypsies" by Jewish survivors, see testimony of David Abrams, November 4, 1997, VHA 35133 (on Gusen); testimony of Tsvi Barlev, February 4, 1998, VHA 40348, seg. 469, 507 (on Gusen); testimony of Gabor Altmann, March 10, 1997, VHA 26994 (on Melk); testimony of Werner Bab, April 15, 1997, VHA 29164, seg. 117 (on Melk). These interactions frequently came up in very early testimonies recorded by representatives of a Bucharest-based historical commission established by the Association of Jewish Refugees from Poland between January and June 1945. Nearly a dozen of the Jewish survivors of Birkenau interviewed immediately after liberation mentioned their encounters with Sinti kapos in their testimonies. The first of these statements is by Gabor Schwartz, February 23, 1945, USHMM RG-68.151M, 647/01.

134. See, among others, testimony of George Szegö, September 4, 1997, VHA 33258, seg. 23; testimony of Ned Aron, October 19, 1995, VHA 7724, seg. 112–13; testimony of Joel Berkovic, November 25, 1997, VHA 35685, seg. 86–96.

135. Testimony of Donald Krausz, October 29, 1995, VHA 5163; testimony of Donald Krausz, August 5–6, 1997, Yad Vashem, O.3/10835; Donald Krausz, "Child of the Concentration Camp"

(unpublished manuscript, November 20, 2013). Krausz emphasized that he was freely distributing his memoir and does not wish to retain copyright. I thank Gerhard Baumgartner for making a copy available to me.

136. Testimony of Donald Krausz, October 29, 1995, VHA 5163, seg. 144.

137. There are few studies of masculinity among Romani victims, whereas there is a rich literature on Jewish victims. See, for example, Maddy Carey, *Jewish Masculinity in the Holocaust: Between Destruction and Construction* (London: Bloomsbury Academic, 2017).

138. Elie Wiesel, *Un di velt hot geshvign* (Buenos Aires: Tsentral-farband fun Poylishe Yidn in Argentine, 1956), 34, 37, 38, https://babel.hathitrust.org/cgi/pt?id=mdp.39015019304735.

139. Elie Wiesel, *Night; Dawn; Day* (Northvale, NJ: Aronson, 1985), 48. For another postwar memoir dealing with these events, see M. A. Stern, *Dos kol fun blut: A megileh fun yomer un shoyder* (Brooklyn, NY: M. A. Stern, [1950s]), 53.

140. Wiesel, *Un di velt hot geshvign*, 81.

141. There were witnesses who emphasized that they were familiar with "Gypsies" in some way and that the kapos were merely doing what they had been ordered to do. See, for example, Michael R., Fortunoff Archive, HVT-2540.

142. Beendorf was a sub-camp of Neungamme.

143. Testimony of Eva S., Fortunoff Archive, HVT-2288. On other smaller such conflicts during transports, see Marlies G., Fortunoff Archive, HVT-2176.

Chapter Two: Surviving Postwar Reconstruction

1. See Leora Auslander, "Holocaust Lists and Inventories: Recording Death vs. Traces of Lived Lives," *Jewish Quarterly Review* 111, no. 3 (2021): 347–55.

2. Founded in 1944 as the Central Tracing Bureau, the organization received its current name in 1948. The International Commission of the Red Cross operated the institution between 1954 and 2012. On the International Tracing Service, see Dan Stone, "The Memory of the Archive: The International Tracing Service and the Construction of the Past as History," *Dapim: Studies on the Holocaust* 31, no. 2 (May 2017): 69–88; Bernd Joachim Zimmer, *International Tracing Service Arolsen: Von der Vermisstensuche zur Haftbescheinigung: Die Organisationsgeschichte eines "ungewollten Kindes" während der Besatzungszeit* (Bad Arolsen, Germany: Waldeckischer Geschichtsverein, 2011).

3. See USHMM, RG-17.007M, A/VIE/IKG/III/NAM/3/ file 3. All these lists were sent by the Action Committee—Aktionskommittee der wegen ihrer Abstammung Verfolgten, in German—to the Jewish Community (Israelitische Kultusgemeinde, IKG). The leadership of both institutions was nearly identical. Besides the separate list of "Gypsies" discussed below, individual Romani victims appeared on various lists.

4. The Action Committee of those Persecuted for their Descent (Aktionskomitee der wegen ihrer Abstammung Verfolgter), had originally been founded as the Action Committee of Jewish Camp Prisoners (Aktionskomitee der jüdischen KZler) as an independent organization on February 10, 1946. Four days later, the largest victim and resistance organization, the KZ-Verband, reacted by including Jews as victims of Nazism on their rolls. The Action Committee remained responsible for certifying Jews for eligibility once the state moved to centralize all such certificates in the KZ-Verband. See Brigitte Bailer, "Der KZ-Verband: Informationen zu

einer wesentlichen Quelle des Projektes der namentlichen Erfassung der Opfer der politischen Verfolgung," *DÖW Jahrbuch* (2007): 38. On the organization's conflicts with Jews, see Helga Embacher, *Neubeginn ohne Illusionen: Juden in Österreich nach 1945* (Vienna: Picus, 1995), 104–5. Even when a reorganized association included victims of racial persecution, the KZ-Verband continued to define itself as an organization representing the legacy of political resistance. See Franz Sobek, "Vom KZ-Verband zum Österreichischen Bundesverband ehemals politisch verfolgter Antifaschisten," *Mahnruf für Freiheit und Menschenrecht* 1, no. 1 (November 1946): 4–5.

5. "Liste der bei uns registrierten Zigeuner (17. Juli 1946)," Archive of the Israelitische Kultusgemeinde (IKG) Vienna, Bestand Wien, A/VIE/IKG/III/SOZ/1/4 [formerly A/VIE/IKG/III/NAM/3/3] (Loan Collection VWI). I am grateful to Susanne Uslu-Pauer of the IKG archive for suggesting that the IKG received these lists from the KZ-Verband. The dates listed in the KZ-Verband's membership files for individuals on these lists makes this the most likely scenario.

6. "Mitteilungen des Herrn Adolf Gussak über seinen Aufenthalt im KZ-Mauthausen, wo er als Zigeuner festgehalten wurde," January 1958, recorded by Emmi Moravitz, DÖW 03824; "Erlebnisse von Hermine Horwath," January 1958, recorded by Emmi Moravitz, DÖW 00118. See also the testimony of her sister, Kathi König (Horwath), "Mein Lebenslauf 1941–45," DÖW 00333. For more on Hermine Horwath, see TD file 324581, 6.3.3.2/93692190–93692192/ITS Digital Collection, Arolsen Archives, USHMM. On Adolf Gussak (also Hussak or Guszak), see TD file 302857, 6.3.3.2/93469127–93469131/ITS Digital Collection, Arolsen Archives, USHMM; 1.1.6.1 Dachau entry book/9909289/ITS Digital Collection, Arolsen Archives, USHMM; 1.1.26.1 Häftlingsliste Mauthausen/1288729/ITS Digital Collection, Arolsen Archives, USHMM; 1.1.26.3 Mauthausen prisoner file/1480628–1480633/ITS Digital Collection, Arolsen Archives, USHMM.

7. Florian Freund, Gerhard Baumgartner, and Harald Greifeneder, *Vermögensentzug, Restitution und Entschädigung der Roma und Sinti*, Veröffentlichungen der Österreichischen Historikerkommission: Vermögensentzug während der NS-Zeit sowie Rückstellungen und Entschädigungen seit 1945 in Österreich 23/2 (Vienna: Oldenbourg, 2004). Municipalities had also refused to register the title to many Romani-owned properties and structures in the first place.

8. "Mitteilungen des Herrn Adolf Gussak."

9. Elisabeth Schenk, "Nachbarn und Grenzen, Begegnungen und Konflikte: Zwei niederösterreichische Gemeinden an der March" (Master's thesis [Diplomarbeit], University of Vienna, 2008), 67.

10. USHMM, RG-17.037 KZ-Verband Wien, files 3659–3663.

11. Gerhard Baumgartner and Florian Freund, "Der Holocaust an den österreichischen Roma und Sinti," in *Zwischen Erziehung und Vernichtung: Zigeunerpolitik und Zigeunerforschung im Europa des 20. Jahrhunderts*, ed. Michael Zimmermann, Beiträge zur Geschichte der Deutschen Forschungsgemeinschaft 3 (Stuttgart: Steiner, 2007), 203–25. The case of Josef Stoyka-Adelsburg (also Stojka-Adelsburg and Adelsburg-Stoyka) is instructive. A Romani pastry chef who was imprisoned as a "Gypsy" in Flossenbürg, Stoyka-Adelsburg registered with the Action Committee on June 17, 1946, around the time the Gussak and Horwath families also went to the Action Committee's offices. A commission under Wilhelm Krell (IKG community councilor or Kultusvorstand, general secretary after April 1, 1947), Dr. Otto Wolken (IKG community councilor, Kultusvorstand), and Martha Dollhofer confirmed his eligibility for the Action Committee, but the central office challenged that assessment and an honor court eventually

removed his status as a victim of Nazism. See KZ-Verband Adelsburg-Stoyka, Josef, DÖW 20100/68. Other authorities also challenged the eligibility of members of the Horwath family for recognition and compensation. See the files relating to applications of Hermine Horwath's sister to Lower Austrian authorities, NÖLA-Opferfürsorgeakt Katharina Horvath [Horwath], DÖW 20900/1998. In a report from October 22, 1952, in this file, authorities decided not to note the names and addresses of witnesses who lived with Katharina Horwath, apparently because they were "Gypsies."

12. See Anja Reuss, "'Return to Normality?': The Struggle of Sinti and Roma Survivors to Rebuild a Life in Postwar Germany," in *Jewish and Romani Families in the Holocaust and Its Aftermath*, ed. Eliyana R. Adler and Kateřina Čapková (New Brunswick, NJ: Rutgers University Press, 2021), 141–55.

13. Ibid.

14. On the JDC during the Holocaust, see Oscar Handlin, *A Continuing Task: The American Jewish Joint Distribution Committee, 1914–1964* (New York: Random House, 1965); Yehuda Bauer, *American Jewry and the Holocaust: The American Jewish Joint Distribution Committee, 1939–1945* (Jerusalem: The Institute of Contemporary Jewry, Hebrew University, 1981). On postwar activities, focusing on France, see Maud S. Mandel, "Philanthropy or Cultural Imperialism? The Impact of American Jewish Aid in Post-Holocaust France," *Jewish Social Studies* 9, no. 1 (2002): 53–94. The JDC funded between 40 percent and 48 percent of the Vienna Jewish community's budget, covering mostly expenses for the food and necessities of impoverished survivors. See Israelitische Kultusgemeinde Wien, *Bericht des Präsidiums der Israelitischen Kultusgemeinde Wien über die Tätigkeit in den Jahren 1945 bis 1948* (Vienna: IKG, 1948).

15. On Jewish refugees in Austria, see Thomas Albrich, *Exodus durch Österreich: Die jüdischen Flüchtlinge 1945–1948* (Innsbruck, Austria: Haymon Verlag, 1987); Christine Oertel, *Juden auf der Flucht durch Austria: Jüdische Displaced Persons in der US-Besatzungszone Österreichs* (Vienna: Eichbauer, 1999). For these numbers see, Albrich, *Exodus*, 223. On Germany, see Atina Grossman and Tamar Lewinsky, "Part One: 1945–1949: Way Station," in *A History of Jews in Germany Since 1945: Politics, Culture, and Society*, ed. Michael Brenner (Bloomington: Indiana University Press, 2018), 57–59; Angelika Königseder, *Waiting for Hope: Jewish Displaced Persons in Post-World War II Germany* (Evanston, IL: Northwestern University Press, 2001), 5–6.

16. See Eliyana R. Adler, *Survival on the Margins: Polish Jewish Refugees in the Wartime Soviet Union* (Cambridge, MA: Harvard University Press, 2020), 238–78.

17. Atina Grossmann, *Jews, Germans, and Allies: Close Encounters in Occupied Germany* (Princeton, NJ: Princeton University Press, 2007).

18. Sergio DellaPergola, "Reflections on the Multinational Geography of Jews after World War II," in *Postwar Jewish Displacement and Rebirth, 1945–1967*, ed. Françoise Ouzan and Manfred Gerstenfeld (Leiden, Netherlands: Brill, 2014), 16. For a larger narrative of this shift, see also Bernard Wasserstein, *Vanishing Diaspora: The Jews in Europe since 1945* (Cambridge, MA: Harvard University Press, 1996).

19. On Romani postwar migration, see Ari Joskowicz, "Romani Refugees and the Postwar Order," *Journal of Contemporary History* 51, no. 4 (October 2016): 760–87. Roma did move in substantial numbers within newly reestablished states.

20. On expulsions, see Philipp Ther and Ana Siljak, eds., *Redrawing Nations: Ethnic Cleansing in East-Central Europe, 1944–1948* (Lanham, MD: Rowman & Littlefield, 2001); Jessica Reinisch

and Elizabeth White, eds., *The Disentanglement of Populations: Migration, Expulsion and Displacement in Post-War Europe, 1944–9* (Basingstoke, UK: Palgrave Macmillan, 2011); Keith Lowe, *Savage Continent: Europe in the Aftermath of World War II* (New York: St. Martin's Press, 2012), 212–29.

21. Celia Donert, *The Rights of the Roma: The Struggle for Citizenship in Postwar Czechoslovakia* (Cambridge: Cambridge University Press, 2017), 15.

22. See Helena Sadílková, "The Postwar Migration of Romani Families from Slovakia to the Bohemian Lands: A Complex Legacy of War and Genocide in Czechoslovakia," in *Jewish and Romani Families in the Holocaust and Its Aftermath*, ed. Eliyana R. Adler and Kateřina Čapková (New Brunswick, NJ: Rutgers University Press, 2021), 190–217.

23. Ibid., 48–83. See Michael Stewart, *The Time of the Gypsies* (Boulder, CO: Westview Press, 1997), 97–99, for a brief description of similar developments in Hungary. These policies took some inspiration from interwar Soviet models but did copy the emphasis on Romani cultural development characteristic of 1920s Bolshevik policies. See Brigid O'Keeffe, *New Soviet Gypsies: Nationality, Performance, and Selfhood in the Early Soviet Union* (Toronto: University of Toronto Press, 2013).

24. Donert, *The Rights of the Roma*, 113–14.

25. The historiography on Romani persecution in France thus frequently works with a different periodization: Denis Peschanski, *La France des camps: L'internement, 1938–1946*, La Suite Des Temps (Paris: Gallimard, 2002); Emmanuel Filhol, *La mémoire et l'oubli: L'internement des Tsiganes en France, 1940–1946*, Interface (Paris: Centre de recherches tsiganes, Harmattan, 2004); Denis Peschanski, "Zigeuner in Frankreich 1912–1969: Eine Periode durchgehender Stigmatisierung," in *Zwischen Erziehung und Vernichtung: Zigeunerpolitik und Zigeunerforschung im Europa des 20. Jahrhunderts*, ed. Michael Zimmermann, Beiträge zur Geschichte der Deutschen Forschungsgemeinschaft 3 (Stuttgart: Steiner, 2007), 268–77.

26. See Archives départmentales Indre-et-Loire, 30W82, USHMM, RG-43.096M, which covers the census of *nomades* for the years 1940–51.

27. On post-liberation violence against "nomades," see Lise Foisneau, *Les Nomades face à la guerre (1939–1946)*, in collaboration with Valentin Merlin (Paris: Klincksieck, 2022). In the French context, liberation could be complicated for Jews as well. In liberated parts of North Africa, French authorities decided once again to rescind the Crémieux Decree that had awarded Algerian Jews citizenship in 1870, essentially making them stateless between March 14 and October 20, 1943. See Daniel Schroeter, "Between Metropole and French North Africa: Vichy's anti-Semitic Legislation and Colonialism's Racial Hierarchies," in *The Holocaust and North Africa*, ed. Aomar Boum and Sarah Abrevaya Stein (Stanford, CA: Stanford University Press, 2019), 19–49.

28. Gilad Margalit, *Germany and Its Gypsies: A Post-Auschwitz Ordeal* (Madison: University of Wisconsin Press, 2002), 56–82.

29. Ibid., 64–66.

30. The 1924 law is §20 of the Reichsfürsorgepflichtverordnung (RSV); the 1926 law had the German title "Gesetz zur Bekämpfung von Zigeunern, Landfahrern und Arbeitsscheuen."

31. "Überstellungen von Häftlingen aus dem Konzentrationslager Dachau nach Wanderhof "Herzogsägmühle" bei Schongau und in das 'Arbeitshaus Rebdorf,'" July 20, 1936–January 17, 1938, 1.1.6./8057100/ITS Digital Collection, Arolsen Archives. The camp is also recognized in

Germany as a place of forced labor for women: www.bundesarchiv.de/zwangsarbeit/haftstaetten /index.php?action=2.2&tab=7&id=69.

32. On the continued use of the same laws against those suspected of shying away from re-munerated labor, see Sven Korzilius, *"Asoziale" und "Parasiten" im Recht der SBZ/DDR: Rand-gruppen im Sozialismus zwischen Repression und Ausgrenzung* (Cologne: Böhlau, 2005), 70–71.

33. For the Lithuanian DP camp Rebdorf (1945–49), see https://dpcampinventory.its-arolsen .org/uebersicht-zonen/amerikanische-zone/dp-camps/?tx_itssearch_itssearch[action]=list&tx _itssearch_itssearch[controller]=Its&tx_itssearch_itssearch[%40widget_0][currentPage]=74 &cHash=d7af88f5ccca92259c249544880e9040. The camp held a substantial number of DPs, with 1,157 inhabitants on October 31, 1947.

34. Folder 17 175–2, "Order of Mil. Gov. Revoking and Rescinding 'Law for Protection against Gypsies, Vagrants and Persons Unwilling to Work,'" OMGBY, Legislative Branch, box 70, Record Group 260—Records of U.S. Occupation Headquarters, World War II, National Archives at College Park, College Park, MD. The Federal Republic abolished the crucial §20 RSV only in 1956. Matthias Willing, *Das Bewahrungsgesetz (1918–1967): Eine rechtshistorische Studie zur Geschichte der deutschen Fürsorge* (Tübingen, Germany: Mohr Siebeck, 2003), 258.

35. The inmates do not show up in other files on Romani victims, nor as registered prisoners in a concentration camp or refugees in the International Tracing Service database.

36. See also Margalit, *Germany and Its Gypsies*, 64–65.

37. Bayerisches Staatministerium des Innern to Bayerische Staatskanzlei, Munich, Febru-ary 6, 1948, BayHSt StK 14739.

38. Bayerischer Ministerpräsident, Dr. Hans Ehard to Amt der Militärregierung für Bayern, Legal Division, Legislation Branch, Munich, March 1, 1948, BayHSt StK 14739.

39. Bayerischer Landtag, 1948, Drucksachen, 94, Beilage 786. In German: "Die Staatsregier-ung sei zu beauftragen, mit der Militärregierung umgehende Verhandlungen aufzunehmen, um auf dem schnellsten Wege Lagerobjekte freizubekommen (Dachau) zur Errichtung von Arb-eitslagern für asoziale Elemente."

40. Bayerische Staatskanzlei to Bayerisches Staatsministerium für Arbeit und soziale Für-sorge, February 25, 1948 and Bayerisches Staatsministerium für Arbeit und soziale Fürsorge to Bayerische Staatskanzlei, March 3, 1948, BayHSt StK 14739.

41. *Stenographischer Bericht über die Verhandlungen des Bayerischen Landtags*, Bayerischer Landtag, 45th session, January 16, 1948, 587–89.

42. On consumption in the history of twentieth-century Germany, see Konrad Hugo Ja-rausch and Michael Geyer, *Shattered Past: Reconstructing German Histories* (Princeton, NJ: Princeton University Press, 2003), 269–314; for a European perspective, see Pamela Ballinger, "Impossible Returns, Enduring Legacies: Recent Historiography of Displacement and the Re-construction of Europe after World War II," *Contemporary European History* 22, no. 1 (Febru-ary 2013): 127–38. The emphasis on the right to property is underlined by the fact that in Ger-many it was often easier for Romanies to gain restitution of lost property than compensation for suffering under Nazism. Julia von dem Knesebeck, *The Roma Struggle for Compensation in Post-War Germany* (Hatfield, UK: University of Hertfordshire Press, 2011), 21. On the some-times traditional image of workers sought out by employers and officials, see Mark Roseman, "The Organic Society and the Massenmenschen: Integrating Young Labour in the Ruhr Mines, 1945–58," in *West Germany under Construction: Politics, Society, and Culture in the Adenauer Era,*

ed. Robert G. Moeller (Ann Arbor: University of Michigan Press, 1997), 287–320. For an example of the state's emphasis on the integration of postwar ethnic German migrants through labor, see, for example, Theodor Oberländer, *The Expellees Are Working: Picture Report of Reconstruction Work Done by the Expellees in Bavaria* (Gräfelfing, Germany: Verlag für Planung und Aufbau, 1951).

43. See Gerard Daniel Cohen, *In War's Wake: Europe's Displaced Persons in the Postwar Order* (New York: Oxford University Press, 2012), 105–8.

44. See Joskowicz, "Romani Refugees"; Silvia Salvatici, "From Displaced Persons to Labourers: Allied Employment Policies in Post-War West Germany," in *The Disentanglement of Populations: Migration, Expulsion and Displacement in Post-War Europe, 1944–9*, ed. Jessica Reinisch and Elizabeth White (Basingstoke, UK: Palgrave Macmillan, 2011), 210–28.

45. International Refugee Organization, *Report of the Director-General to the General Council, 1 July 1948–30 June 1949* (Geneva: IRO 1949), 24.

46. On these general suspicions, see Silvia Salvatici, "'Help the People to Help Themselves': UNRRA Relief Workers and European Displaced Persons," *Journal of Refugee Studies* 25, no. 3 (2012): 428–51.

47. See Regula Ludi, *Reparations for Nazi Victims in Postwar Europe* (Cambridge: Cambridge University Press, 2012), 189; Pieter Lagrou, *The Legacy of Nazi Occupation: Patriotic Memory and National Recovery in Western Europe, 1945–1965* (Cambridge: Cambridge University Press, 1999); Constantin Goschler, *Schuld und Schulden: Die Politik der Wiedergutmachung für NS-Verfolgte seit 1945* (Göttingen: Wallstein, 2005); Christian Pross, *Wiedergutmachung: Der Kleinkrieg gegen die Opfer* (Frankfurt am Main: Athenäum, 1988).

48. On the US and reconstruction, see David W. Ellwood, *Rebuilding Europe: Western Europe, America, and Postwar Reconstruction* (London: Longman, 1992).

49. Ibid.

50. Anna Holian, *Between National Socialism and Soviet Communism: Displaced Persons in Postwar Germany* (Ann Arbor: University of Michigan Press, 2011), 186–210.

51. See chapter 4 on Nuremberg.

52. UNRRA, US Zone, Administrative Order No. 23, March 11, 1946, 6.1.2/8248692/ITS Digital Collection, Arolsen Archives, USHMM.

53. Annex to the Constitution of the International Refugee Organization, Section C paragraph 1; reprinted in Louise W. Holborn, *The International Refugee Organization: A Specialized Agency of the United Nations: Its History and Work, 1946–1952* (London: Oxford University Press, 1956), 575–91. None of the published decisions of IRO's review board offered any special provisions for "Gypsies"—or individuals who would be identified today by the ethnicized categories of Roma, Roma and Sinti, or Romanies. See IRO, *Manual for Eligibility Officers* (Arolsen, Germany: IRO, 1949). The organization updated the manual on several occasions. References here are to one of the final versions, published in two identical copies numbered 241 and 242.

54. Joskowicz, "Romani Refugees."

55. Preparatory Commission for the International Refugee Organization (PCIRO), Central Tracing Bureau, Revised Procedure for Registration and Processing of Records, October 13, 1947, Appendix IV, 6.1.1/82504655–82504657/ITS Digital Collection, Arolsen Archives, USHMM, shows that only Jews and Roma were included in lists of deportees if the destination camp was not known. For other similar uses, see PCIRO, Procedure for Completing Inventory

Cards, November 15, 1946, 6.1.1/82510878–82510881/ITS Digital Collection, Arolsen Archives, USHMM. The child registration branch rejected the term "Gypsies" except in the case of Germans, for whom the categories of Jew, Gypsy, and political persecutee coexisted. Child Search Branch Inter-Zonal Conference, July 21, 1949, 6.1.2/82488822–82488827/ITS Digital Collection, Arolsen Archives, USHMM; Arthur T. Cooper, US Zone Child Search Officer to Principal Child Search Officer IRO Area 4, July 21, 1949, 6.1.2/82490625/ITS Digital Collection, Arolsen Archives, USHMM.

56. See, for example, the DP files of the family Lora, 3.2.1.1/79425584–79425588/ITS Digital Collection, Arolsen Archives, USHMM. Based on this determination the family received 26 months of support from UNRRA. See CM1 of May 20, 1948, 3.2.1.1/79425591/ITS Digital Collection, Arolsen Archives, USHMM. The UNRRA files then became the property of the IRO and subsequently formed the bulk of postwar records held by the International Tracing Service.

57. These numbers are based on the digitized files in the Arolsen Archives, which have been transcribed and indexed for Germany and Italy. We can presume that more individuals who identified as Romani crossed the border but did not enter "Gypsy" in the relevant fields. Others might also have not been included in my tabulation due to mistakes in the transcription of forms and the entry of information into databases by ITS digitization teams.

58. Biography, 3.2.1.2/80327761/ITS Digital Collection, Arolsen Archives, USHMM; Record of Interview for Bruno Braidich, September 18, 3.2.1.2/195180327761/ITS Digital Collection, Arolsen Archives, USHMM.

59. For full information about the eligibility rates for Romani applicants from different countries, see Joskowicz, "Romani Refugees," 777.

60. Archives Nationales (AN), Paris, AJ43/457/56, Review Board Cases—'Economic' Czech Refugees [1949].

61. Joskowicz, "Romani Refugees."

62. O'Keeffe, *New Soviet Gypsies.*

63. Margalit, *Germany and Its Gypsies,* 78–80.

64. Questionnaire, November 21, 1949, 3.2.1.2/80390252/ITS Digital Collection, Arolsen Archives, USHMM. For an emphasis on Nazi persecution from IRO personnel, see also Bianco Hudorovich, Biographical Page, February 2, 1951, 3.2.1.2/80390160/ITS Digital Collection, Arolsen Archives, USHMM; Peppino Braidich, Biographical Page, April 20, 1951, 3.2.1.2/80327821/ITS Digital Collection, Arolsen Archives; Carlo Braidich, Biographical Page, April 20, 1951, 3.2.1.2/80327808/ITS Digital Collection, Arolsen Archives, USHMM; 3.2.1.2/80327761/ITS Digital Collection, Arolsen Archives, USHMM.

65. Questionnaire, November 17, 1949, 3.2.1.1/80390248/ITS Digital Collection, Arolsen Archive, USHMM; Nino Hudorovich, Biographical Page, April 19, 1951, 3.2.1.1/80390340/ITS Digital Collection, Arolsen Archives, USHMM.

66. Cohen, *In War's Wake.*

67. Cf. Mark Mazower, "The Strange Triumph of Human Rights, 1933–1950," *The Historical Journal* 47, no. 2 (2004), 379–98.

68. United Nations High Commissioner for Refugees (UNHCR), *Convention Relating to the Status of Refugees,* Article 1A(2) (1951). On the role of collective categories in the international definition of refugees, starting with agreements in the League of Nations, see Ivor C. Jackson, *The Refugee Concept in Group Situations* (Boston: Martinus Nijhoff, 1999).

69. Oswald Hertzberg to ITS, Bamberg, January 23, 1950, TD file 122005, 6.3.3.1/85847694/ ITS Digital Collection, Arolsen Archives.

70. On the paradoxes of the quest to overcome victimhood by claiming victim status, see Regula Ludi, "The Vectors of Postwar Victim Reparations: Relief, Redress and Memory Politics," *Journal of Contemporary History* 41, no. 3 (2006): 421–50.

71. See Königseder, *Waiting for Hope*; Grossmann, *Jews, Germans, and Allies*, with a particular focus on Berlin and Jews outside of DP camps.

72. On Romani refugees from Czechoslovakia and the Italian-Yugoslav borderlands in particular, see Joskowicz, "Romani Refugees," 760–87.

73. Karola Fings and Frank Sparing, "Das Zigeunerlager in Köln-Bickendorf 1935–1958," *1999: Zeitschrift für Sozialgeschichte des 20. und 21. Jahrhunderts* 6, no. 3 (1991): 34–35.

74. This version is in a handwritten biography within their CM1 file, 3.2.1.1/79094722/ITS Digital Collection, Arolsen Archives.

75. CM1 of November 24, 1947, 3.2.1.1/79094712/ITS Digital Collection, Arolsen Archives, USHMM. The registry office in Berlin, however, recorded their marriage in Berlin on August 9, 1934 and subsequently recorded also the birth of several of the children. See Landesarchiv Berlin, Personenstandsregister Heiratsregister, Laufende Nr. 148, Erstregister Nr. 348, retrieved on ancestry.com.

76. DP1 of October 5, 1946 for Jozef Freiwald, 3.2.1.1/79094710/ITS Digital Collection, Arolsen Archives, USHMM and DP1 of October 5, 1946 for Maria Freiwald, 3.2.1.1/79094711/ITS Digital Collection, Arolsen Archives, USHMM.

77. Bescheinigung, Gemeindeverwaltung Krondorf, September 30, 1949, 3.2.1.1/79094714/ ITS Digital Collection, Arolsen Archives, USHMM.

78. Legal Councellor, Amberg, to Area Welfare Office, September 26, 1949, 3.2.1.1/79094719/ ITS Digital Collection, Arolsen Archives, USHMM.

79. Social Service Sub-Area Amberg, Visit of October 12, 1949, 3.2.1.1/79094727/ITS Digital Collection, Arolsen Archives, USHMM.

80. Resettlement Status Slip, September 23, 1949, 3.2.1.1/79094723/ITS Digital Collection, Arolsen Archives, USHMM.

81. Kibbutz Ma'apilim was part of the left-wing Hashomer Hatzair movement. Zeev W. Mankowitz, *Life between Memory and Hope: The Survivors of the Holocaust in Occupied Germany* (New York: Cambridge University Press, 2002), 155.

82. GFH 4973, 77.

83. On the camp, see Hagit Lavsky, *New Beginnings: Holocaust Survivors in Bergen-Belsen and the British Zone in Germany, 1945–1950* (Detroit, MI: Wayne State University Press, 2002).

84. Oral History Interview with Klaus and Anita Schopper by Gabriele Tyrnauer, July 17, 1991, USHMM, RG-50.719.0001, https://collections.ushmm.org/search/catalog/irn86035.

85. Album from the Zeilsheim DP camp, GFH 124727, 147, 155. The first performance was by C. Zukerman as part of Jidisz Teater beim Kulturamt in Zeilsheim, Muzikalische Kleinkust-Forstelung [sic], "Wen lebn zol zein gelebt," October 31, 1946. The second of Folman's performances took place December 26–28, 1946.

86. Werner Bergmann, "Philipp Auerbach—Wiedergutmachung war 'nicht mit normalen Mitteln durchzusetzen,'" in *Engagierte Demokraten: Vergangenheitspolitik in kritischer Absicht*, ed. Claudia Fröhlich and Michael Kohlstruck (Münster, Germany: Westfälisches Dampfboot,

1999), 57–70; Wolfgang Kraushaar, "Die Affäre Auerbach: Zur Virulenz des Antisemitismus in den Gründerjahren der Bundesrepublik," *Menora: Jahrbuch für deutsch-jüdische Geschichte 6* (1995): 319–43; Wolfgang Kraushaar, "Die Auerbach-Affäre," in *Leben im Land der Täter: Juden im Nachkriegsdeutschland (1945–1952)*, ed. Julius H. Schoeps (Berlin: Jüdische Verlagsanstalt, 2001), 208–18; Hannes Ludyga, *Philipp Auerbach (1906–1952): "Staatskommissar für rassisch, religiös und politisch Verfolgte"* (Berlin: Berliner Wissenschafts-Verlag, 2005). Jews held similar positions as administrators heading offices dealing with victim compensation and support in two other large postwar German states: Marcel Frenkel in North Rhine-Westphalia and Curt Epstein in Hesse. Neither assumed Auerbach's prominent position in public life. Auerbach's case is also a common topic in German high school curricula, see Karl Bachsleitner, "Der Fall Philipp Auerbach: Ein Lehrstück aus den 50er Jahren," *Geschichte Lernen*, no. 119 (2007): 33–41.

87. The biographical information here comes from Ludyga, *Philipp Auerbach*.

88. Ibid., 24.

89. Ibid., 26–27.

90. Ibid., 26. On internment information see, Certificate of Imprisonment 1361/T-58552 and other documentation from the International Tracing Service, T/D 58552, 92176765–92176767, USHMM.

91. Ludyga, *Philipp Auerbach*, 32.

92. Ibid., 36.

93. Ibid., 37.

94. On such conflicts between Jewish DPs and German Jews, see Holian, *Between National Socialism and Soviet Communism*, 186–210.

95. Sebastian Conrad, *Auf der Suche nach der verlorenen Nation: Geschichtsschreibung in Westdeutschland und Japan, 1945–1960* (Göttingen: Vandenhoeck & Ruprecht, 1999), 183. Conrad points out that this may have been the first historical analysis in Germany of German resistance to Nazism.

96. Staatskommissar Auerbach, *Bericht des Staatskommisariats für rassich, religiös und politisch Verfolgte für die Militärregierung von Bayern [1948]*, BayHST, RG 260, OMGBY (13/141–1/1), [microfilm].

97. Auerbach to Polizeipräsidium, July 19, 1948, BayHSt, StK Auerbach, Vorläufige Nr. 016b; Auerbach to Miniclier, OMGBY, July 18, 1947, BayHSt, StK Auerbach, Vorläufige Nr. 002.

98. Generalanwalt Auerbach to Hammer in Augsburg, September 8, 1949, BayHSt, StK Auerbach, Vorläufige Nr. 033.

99. Philipp Auerbach, "Zum Problem der Zigeuner," *Mitteilungsblatt des Landesausschusses der politisch Verfolgten in Bayern*, July 1, 1949. For the original see Auerbach als Generalanwalt für die rassisch, religiös und politisch Verfolgten im Bayerischern Landesamt für Wiedergutmachung, May 24, 1949, BayHSt, StK Auerbach, Vorläufige Nr. 56c.

100. Auerbach's surprise at the guards' willingness to commit murder where they had previously committed sexual assault appears to be based on the false assumption that their forcing sex upon Romani women somehow involved a romantic relationship.

101. On "asocials," see Wolfgang Ayass, *"Asoziale" im Nationalsozialismus* (Stuttgart: Klett-Cotta, 1995).

102. Bayerisches Hilfswerk für die durch die Nürnberger Gesetze Betroffenen, Zweigstelle Mainfranken to Beauftragten des Staatskommissars beim Regierungspräsidenten Würzburg,

Würzburg, January 30, 1947, BayHSt, StK Auerbach, Vorläufige Nr. 016b; Ritzau to Auerbach, February 1,1947, BayHSt, StK Auerbach, Vorläufige Nr. 016b.

103. Bayerisches Hilfswerk für die von den Nürnberger Gesetzen Betroffenen to Zentralamt für Kriminalstatistik-Abteilung Zigeunerpolizei, z. Hd. Hr. Uschold, Munich, June 14, 1950, Leo-Baeck Institute, New York, William G. Niederland Collection, Series II, Box 2, folder 1.

104. Auerbach to Beauftragen Ernst Ritzau, February 6, 1947, BayHSt, StK Auerbach, Vorläufige Nr. 016b. On the Hilfswerk, see Margalit, *Germany and Its Gypsies*, 91.

105. Auerbach, "Zum Problem der Zigeuner," 2: ". . . zu versuchen ihnen mit Liebe zu begegnen, denn nur dadurch wird es möglich sein, aus den Überresten der verbliebenen Zigeuner vollwertige Mitglieder unserer menschlichen Gesellschaft zu machen. Wir haben dabei wohl zu unterscheiden zwischen jenen Zigeunern, die aus rassischen Gründen verfolgt waren und solchen, die nachweislich wegen asozialen Verhaltens inhaftiert wurden."

106. Auerbach to Miniclier, March 28, 1947 [English], March 27, 1947 [German], BayHSt, StK Auerbach, Vorläufige Nr. 002.

107. Margalit, *Germany and Its Gypsies*, 96–97.

108. Auerbach to Hugo Schwarz, December 21, 1946 and Auerbach to Beauftragter Hugo Schwarz and [stellvertr.] Staatskommissar Aster, March 24, 1947, BayHSt, StK Auerbach, Vorläufige Nr. 033.

109. Hugo Schwarz to Auerbach, December 2, 1946 and Auerbach to Hugo Schwarz, December 4, 1946, BayHSt, StK Auerbach, Vorläufige Nr. 033.

110. Auerbach to Miniclier, July 18, 1947 [English], July 16, 1947 [German], BayHSt, StK Auerbach, Vorläufige Nr. 002. Auerbach's translator often rendered his German letters into non-idiomatic English. This is the German original of Auerbach's memo: "Es muß verhindert werden, daß Bayern zu einem Asyl herumreisender Zigeuner wird, die glauben, weil sie hier der Betreuung unterstehen, ihre Tätigkeit nach hier verlegen zu können." Around the same time, Auerbach was willing to have his office care for Jews fleeing Czechoslovakia. Auerbach to OMGBY Public Welfare Branch, Mr. Hoven, June 23, 1947, BayHSt, StK Auerbach, Vorläufige Nr. 002.

111. Auerbach to Miniclier, February 26, 1947 [English], and February 25, 1947 [German], BayHSt, StK Auerbach, Vorläufige Nr. 002.

112. Ibid.

113. Sicherheitsdirektor Herrmann, Polizeipräsidium München to Staatskommissariat für rassisch, religiös und politisch Verfolgte, September 14, 1948, BayHSt, StK Auerbach, Vorläufige Nr. 016b.

114. Sicherheitsdirektor Herrmann, Polizeipräsidium München to Bayerisches Staatsministerium des Inneren, Staatskommissariat für rassisch, religiös und politisch Verfolgte, October 7, 1948, BayHSt, StK Auerbach, Vorläufige Nr. 016b. The apartment owner shows up in the ledgers of the Auschwitz "Gypsy camp" by name and birthdate.

115. Ibid.

116. Staatskommissar Auerbach to Polizeipräsidium, Chef der Schutzmannschaft, September 17, 1948, BayHSt, StK Auerbach, Vorläufige Nr. 016b.

117. The approach of the Austrian government is nicely summarized by the title quote of Robert Knight's collection of protocols on cabinet debates on restitution for Jews: "I am in favour of stringing things out." Robert Knight, *"Ich bin dafür, die Sache in die Länge zu ziehen": Die*

Wortprotokolle der österreichischen Bundesregierung von 1945 bis 1952 über die Entschädigung der Juden, 2nd ed. (Vienna: Böhlau, 2000).

118. On retribution, see István Deák, Jan Tomasz Gross, and Tony Judt, eds., *The Politics of Retribution in Europe: World War II and Its Aftermath* (Princeton, NJ: Princeton University Press, 2000).

119. On Langbein, see Brigitte Halbmayr, *Zeitlebens konsequent: Hermann Langbein, 1912–1995: Eine politische Biografie* (Vienna: Braumüller, 2012) and Katharina Stengel, *Hermann Langbein: Ein Auschwitz-Überlebender in den erinnerungspolitischen Konflikten der Nachkriegszeit* (Frankfurt am Main: Campus Verlag, 2012).

120. Hermann Langbein to Adolf Gussak, December 14, 1961, AT-OeStA/AVA Nachlässe NZN E/1797/3.

121. Adolf Gussak, February 1958, Wiener Library, 33–01 P-III-h-794. The Documentation Center of the Austrian Resistance (Dokumentationsarchiv des österreichischen Widerstandes) in Vienna kept a copy of the testimony, DÖW 03824. For an early use of the document, see, for example, Donald Kenrick and Grattan Puxon, *The Destiny of Europe's Gypsies*, Studies in the Dynamics of Persecution and Extermination, Columbus Centre (London: Chatto and Heinemann Educational for Sussex University Press, 1972), 95.

Chapter Three: Blank Pages: Early Documentation Efforts

1. Lemkin to Mr. Bettos, May 5, 1949, box 2, folder 1, Raphael Lemkin Collection, American Jewish Historical Society (AJHS) archives; Lemkin to Salvatore Parisi, February 17, 1950, and Lemkin to George J. Patuzza, February 17, 1950, box 2, folder 3, Raphael Lemkin Collection, AJHS. On these conflicts, see also Pamela Ballinger, *The World Refugees Made: Decolonization and the Foundations of Postwar Italy* (Ithaca, NY: Cornell University Press, 2020).

2. Raphael Lemkin, "Genocide as a Crime under International Law," *United Nations Bulletin* 4, no. 2 (January 1948): 70–71; Raphael Lemkin, "Genocide," *The American Scholar* 15, no. 2 (1946): 227–30.

3. Nuremberg Trial Proceedings, vol. 1, Indictment [1945]—Count Three, "War Crimes," International Military Tribunal (IMT), online at The Avalon Project, Yale University, https://avalon.law.yale.edu/imt/count3.asp.

4. Raphael Lemkin, *Axis Rule in Occupied Europe; Laws of Occupation, Analysis of Government, Proposals for Redress* (Washington, DC: Carnegie Endowment for International Peace, Division of International Law, 1944).

5. See the facts mentioned in Raphael Lemkin to Dora Yates, August 2, 1949, GLS XV, Special Collections and Archives, University of Liverpool.

6. Hélène to Lemkin, [1948], box 1, folder 10, Raphael Lemkin Collection, AJHS. In his autobiography, Raphael Lemkin describes Hélène as a worker for Radio France helping him with translations. See his *Totally Unofficial: The Autobiography of Raphael Lemkin*, ed. Donna-Lee Frieze (New Haven, CT: Yale University Press, 2013), 158.

7. I. Schneersohn to Lemkin, May 13, 1949, box 1, folder 7, Raphael Lemkin Collection, AJHS.

8. Raphael Lemkin to Dora Yates, August 2, 1949, GLS XV, University of Liverpool Archives.

9. Dora Yates to Lemkin, August 29, 1949, reel 1, box 11, Raphael Lemkin Papers, Manuscripts and Archives Division, New York Public Library (NYPL). Yates sent Lemkin two letters—the first of which is lost—but the second letter makes clear the limited scope of her response.

10. Raphael Lemkin Papers, NYPL, reel 3, 2–1.

11. On her biography, see Antony Kamm, "Yates, Dora Esther (1879–1974)," *Oxford Dictionary of National Biography* (Oxford: Oxford University Press, 2004); "Dora Yates," *The Palgrave Dictionary of Anglo-Jewish History*, ed. William D. Rubinstein, Michael Jolles, and Hilary L. Rubinstein (Basingstoke, UK: Palgrave Macmillan, 2011), 1046.

12. On the entangled genealogies of the Yates and Samuel families, see Stuart Montagu Samuel, *The History and Genealogy of the Jewish Families of Yates and Samuel of Liverpool*, ed. Lucien Wolf (London: [Mitchell and Hughes, Printers], 1901).

13. Chaim Bermant, *The Cousinhood* (New York: Macmillan, 1972); on the Yates and Samuel families of Liverpool in this group, see 199–200. On Dora's participation in gift exchanges for birthdays into her 30s, see Netta Rensburg to Herbert Louis Samuel, July 29, [1910], and Netta Rensburg to Herbert Louis Samuel, July 17, [1910], Parliamentary Archives, London, SAM/B/3.

14. Dora Esther Yates, *My Gypsy Days: Recollections of a Romani Rawnie* (London: Phoenix House, 1953), 15. Her mentor used similar language to describe his interest in the subject as an "obsession" and a form of madness triggered by the word "Gypsy." John Simpson, "Gypsy Language and Origin," *JGLS* 1, no. 1 (July 1907): 4–22.

15. On scholars' emphasis of the unknown origins of European Romanies into the twentieth century, long after linguists settled the question, see David Mayall, *Gypsy Identities, 1500–2000: From Egipcyans and Moon-Men to the Ethnic Romany* (London: Routledge, 2004).

16. Kamm, "Yates."

17. Deborah Epstein Nord, *Gypsies & the British Imagination, 1807–1930* (New York: Columbia University Press, 2006), 75, 125–27, 147.

18. Yates to Hamill, December 15, 1936, series 3, box 5, folder 81, Alfred E. Hamill Papers, Newberry Library.

19. Gil Anidjar, *Semites: Race, Religion, Literature* (Stanford, CA: Stanford University Press, 2008); Gil Anidjar, *The Jew, the Arab: A History of the Enemy*, Cultural Memory in the Present (Stanford, CA: Stanford University Press, 2003); Ivan Davidson Kalmar and Derek J. Penslar, eds., *Orientalism and the Jews* (Hanover, NH: University Press of New England, 2005); James Pasto, "Islam's 'Strange Secret Sharer': Orientalism, Judaism, and the Jewish Question," *Comparative Studies in Society and History* 40, no. 3 (1998): 437–74.

20. On theories of shared origins, see, for example, Samuel Roberts, *Parallel Miracles; Or, The Jews and the Gypsies* (London: J. Nisbet, 1830). Romani evangelicals also propose such theories sometimes in the twenty-first century: "The Jewish-Romani Connection: Are Gypsies Descendants of Tribe of Simeon?," *Ynetnews*, May 5, 2018, https://www.ynetnews.com/articles/0,7340,L-5248902,00.html.

21. Yates to Hamill, September 3, 1936, series 3, box 5, folder 81, Alfred E. Hamill papers, Newberry Library; Anthony Sampson, *The Scholar Gypsy: The Quest for a Family Secret* (London: Murray, 1997).

22. On the centrality of this ideology for the Gypsy Lore Society, see Nord, *Gypsies & the British Imagination*, 125–56. For a comprehensive critique of the tradition of Romani Studies as practiced by the Gypsy Lore Society, see Thomas A. Acton, "Scientific Racism, Popular Racism and the Discourse of the Gypsy Lore Society," *Ethnic and Racial Studies* 39, no. 7 (2016): 1187–1204.

23. Revealingly, Sutzkever invoked the group's extinction in 1936—long before the Nazis invaded the Soviet Union—in his poem "Gypsy Autumn." An "old Gypsy" tells his "Gypsy

band": "[D]ear brothers, I see how the end's coming near to our Gypsy race. We shall sink in abyss and expire." Abraham Sutzkever, "Gypsy Autumn" [1936], in *A. Sutzkever: Selected Poetry and Prose*, ed. Barbara Harshav and Benjamin Harshav (Berkeley: University of California Press, 1991), 67–68. I adjusted the spelling, putting "Gypsy" in uppercase. Considering Jewish traditions of viewing the current generation as potentially the last Jewish generation, Sutzkever also opens the possibility for identification to Jewish readers. See Simon Rawidowicz, "Israel: The Ever-Dying People," in *Israel, the Ever-Dying People, and Other Essays*, ed. Benjamin C. I. Ravid (Rutherford, NJ: Fairleigh Dickinson University Press, 1986), 53–63.

24. Yates to Hamill, May 26, 1941, series 3, box 5, folder 86, Alfred E. Hamill papers, Newberry Library.

25. Hamill bequeathed the hundreds of letters that Yates had sent to him to the Newberry library but felt compelled to leave a cautionary note attached to the file: "This one-sided correspondence should be destroyed or else allowed rest unread till 1967 [. . .] Old letters can be interesting IF THEY ARE OLD ENOUGH! Please do not, anyone, read this before 1967." Series 3, box 5, folder 78, Alfred E. Hamill Papers, Newberry Library.

26. Yates to Hamill, April 2, 1942, series 3, box 5, folder 87, Alfred E. Hamill Papers, Newberry Library.

27. Yates to Hamill, October 6, 1945, series 3, box 5, folder 90, Alfred E. Hamill Papers, Newberry Library.

28. For an early diagnosis of the relations between Romani rights and Black Power movements, see Thomas A. Acton, *Gypsy Politics and Social Change: The Development of Ethnic Ideology and Pressure Politics among British Gypsies from Victorian Reformism to Romany Nationalism*, International Library of Sociology (London and Boston: Routledge and Kegan Paul, 1974), 233–34.

29. See letters from Andrew Marchbin regarding George S. Yates, Ottawa, January 24, 1934, University of Liverpool Archives, DY/1/1/3. "Aid for The Russian Jews," *New York Times*, May 10, 1882. The fund had been founded at a protest meeting held on February 1, 1882 at Mansion House, the residence of the Lord Mayor of the City of London.

30. See Gypsy Lore Society Collections, University of Liverpool Archives, DY/2/2.

31. Tony Kushner, *The Holocaust and the Liberal Imagination: A Social and Cultural History* (Cambridge, MA: Blackwell, 1994), 52–53.

32. Yates to Hamill, March 10, 1944, folder 89, Alfred E. Hamill Papers, Newberry Library.

33. Acton, *Gypsy Politics and Social Change*, 121; Ilona Klimova-Alexander, "The Development and Institutionalization of Romani Representation and Administration. Part 2: Beginnings of Modern Institutionalization (Nineteenth Century–World War II)," *Nationalities Papers* 33, no. 2 (June 2005): 263.

34. William Lygon, 7th Earl Beauchamp, made the amendment in the name of Lord Frank Russel, who was the driving force behind this clause protecting Travellers. House of Lords, Debate, November 30, 1908, vol. 197, col. 1040, https://hansard.millbanksystems.com/lords /1908/nov/30/children-bill-1#S4V0197P0_19081130_HOL_72.

35. House of Commons, Debate, December 15, 1908, vol. 198, col. 1632, https://hansard .millbanksystems.com/commons/1908/dec/15/children-bill#S4V0198P0_19081215_HOC _#434.

36. There is also no evidence of such an intervention in Herbert Samuel's papers. See Parliamentary Archives, London, SAM/B/3, SAM/B/4, and SAM/B/12.

37. Yates to Hamill, August 28, 1942, folder 87, Alfred E. Hamill Papers, Newberry Library.

38. Yates to Hamill, December 18, 1942, folder 87, Alfred E. Hamill Papers, Newberry Library.

39. Yates to Hamill, March 4, 1943, folder 88, Alfred E. Hamill Papers, Newberry Library.

40. Yates to Hamill, April 9, 1943, folder 88, Alfred E. Hamill Papers, Newberry Library.

41. Dora E. Yates, "Hitler and the Gypsies: The Fate of Europe's Oldest Aryans," *Commentary Magazine*, November 1949, 455–59. Yates's article remained the main source of information for many writers. See, for example, "How the Gipsies were Persecuted," *Wiener Library Bulletin* 10, no. 1/2 (1956): 11.

42. Vanya Kochanowski, "Some Notes on the Gypsies of Latvia," *JGLS* 25, 3rd Series (1946): 34–39 and Vanya Kochanowski, "Some Notes on the Gypsies of Latvia: By One of the Survivors," *JGLS* 25, 3rd Series (1946): 112–16. Kochanowski also published as Vania de Gila-Kochanowski.

43. For a critical reading of this essay, see Nord, *Gypsies & the British Imagination*, 154–55. The original manuscript ends with the following plea: "May American Jews, then, whose brethren in Europe have shared the same terrible persecution as the Romani race, henceforth do their utmost to secure this personal freedom for the Gypsies!" See University of Liverpool Archives, GLS D2/7/6.

44. Frédéric Max, "Le sort des tsiganes dans les prisons et les camps de concentration de l'Allemagne hitlerienne" [The Fate of the Gypsies in Prisons and the Concentration Camps of Hitler's Germany], *JGLS* 25, 3rd Series (1946): 24–34; Matéo Maximoff, "Germany and the Gypsies: From the Gypsy's Point of View," *JGLS* 25, 3rd Series (1946): 104–8; Jan Molitor, "The Fate of a German Gypsy," *JGLS* 26 (1947): 48–52; G[eneviève] L'Huillier, "Reminiscences of the Gypsy Camp at Poitiers," *JGLS* 27, 3rd Series (1948): 36–40; Jerzy Ficowski, "The Polish Gypsies of To-day," trans. Józef Rotblat, *JGLS* 29, no 3–4 (July–October 1950): 92–102.

45. Yates to Hamill, March 7, 1941, folder 86, Alfred E. Hamill Papers, Newberry Library.

46. Max, "Le sort des tsiganes."

47. Max added linguistic information to his text, adapting his account to the expectations of the Gypsy Lore Society. It appears that he published the Romani song he recorded in Buchenwald in May 1944 as an ethnological exercise, not to illustrate anything particular about camp life.

48. Yates to Hamill, September 1, 1945, folder 90, Alfred E. Hamill Papers, Newberry Library.

49. Krista Hegburg and Yasar Abu Ghosh, "Introduction: Roma & Gadje," *Anthropology of East Europe Review* 25, no. 2 (2007): 5–11.

50. Yates to Hamil, February 8, 1946, folder 91, Alfred E. Hamill Papers, Newberry Library.

51. L'Huillier, "Reminiscences." On L'Huillier, see Henriette David, "Hommage à Mme l'Huillier," *Etudes tsiganes* 21, no. 1 (March 1975): 60.

52. It is a testament to the marginality of Romani studies that most of Lemkin's successors in scholarship on genocide would rather cite the article Dora Yates wrote on the Romani Holocaust for a Jewish magazine than those published in the field's main scholarly journal. This starts with Philip Friedman, "The Extermination of the Gypsies: A Nazi Genocide Operation Against an Aryan People," *Jewish Frontier* 18, no. 1 (January 1951): 11–14.

53. Dora Esther Yates, *A Book of Gypsy Folk-Tales* (London: Phoenix House, 1948).

54. The book was methodologically problematic in many other respects. Yates did not care about the origin of stories, proper attribution, or variants. For an evaluation of this aspect of her work, see Stewart Sanderson, "Dora Yates: 1879–1974," in *Women and Tradition: A Neglected Group of Folklorists*, ed. Carmen Blacker and Hilda Roderick Ellis Davidson (Durham, NC: Carolina Academic Press, 2001), 121–38.

55. On Boder's biography and for a thorough analysis of his postwar work, see Alan Charles Rosen, *The Wonder of Their Voices: The 1946 Holocaust Interviews of David Boder* (New York: Oxford University Press, 2010).

56. Boder had published on technical devices previously: David P. Boder, "Some New Electronic Devices for the Psychological Laboratory," *The American Journal of Psychology* 45, no. 1 (1933): 145–47; David P. Boder, "A Metascope and Diploscope," *The American Journal of Psychology* 47, no. 4 (1935): 688–90.

57. See "Project Notes," Voices of the Holocaust, https://voices.library.iit.edu/index.php /project_notes.

58. , Boder to Ambassador Henry Bonnet, July 26, 1945, box 1, folder 1, David P. Boder Papers, UCLA Library Special Collections.

59. Boder also spoke to Jewish students on the topic. Student Organization of the Hebrew Theological College in Chicago to Boder, June 21, 1945, box 1, folder 1, David P. Boder Papers, UCLA Library Special Collections.

60. Boder to Samuel A. Goldsmith, The Jewish Charities (Chicago), July 17, 1945, box 1, folder 1, David P. Boder Papers, UCLA Library Special Collections.

61. Jürgen Matthäus, "Displacing Memory: The Transformations of an Early Interview," in *Approaching an Auschwitz Survivor: Holocaust Testimony and Its Transformations*, ed. Jürgen Matthäus, The Oxford Oral History Series (New York: Oxford University Press, 2009), 53, 59.

62. Rachel Deblinger, "David P. Boder: Holocaust Memory in Displaced Persons Camps," in *After the Holocaust: Challenging the Myth of Silence*, ed. David Cesarani and Eric J. Sundquist (London: Routledge, 2012), 115–26.

63. Donald L. Niewyk, *Fresh Wounds: Early Narratives of Holocaust Survival* (Chapel Hill: University of North Carolina Press, 1998), 187.

64. Boder interview with Mendel Herskovitz, July 31, 1946, Voices of the Holocaust, https:// voices.iit.edu/interviewee?doc=herskovitzM.

65. Boder interview with Kalman Eisenberg, July 31, 1946, Voices of the Holocaust, https:// voices.iit.edu/interviewee?doc=eisenbergK.

66. Boder interview with Fela Nichthauser, August 1, 1946, Voices of the Holocaust, https:// voices.iit.edu/interviewee?doc=nichthauserF.

67. Boder interview with Israel Unikowski, August 2, 1946, Voices of the Holocaust, https:// voices.iit.edu/interviewee?doc=unikowskiI.

68. Boder interview with Anna Braun, September 20, 1946, Voices of the Holocaust, https:// voices.iit.edu/interviewee?doc=braunA.

69. Boder interview with Dr. Jacob Oleiski, August 20, 1946, Voices of the Holocaust, https://voices.iit.edu/interviewee?doc=oleiskiJ.

70. Matthäus, *Approaching an Auschwitz Survivor*.

71. Boder interview with Helen[e] Tichauer, Sep. 23, 1946, Voices of the Holocaust, https:// voices.iit.edu/interviewee?doc=tichauerH.

72. I follow Boder's translation of the interview, reprinted in the appendix of Matthäus, *Approaching an Auschwitz Survivor*, 165.

73. Ibid., 168. I changed the translation here slightly, combining Boder's and the new one from Matthäus.

74. My translation based on the recording. Ibid., 163, translates as "worthwhile people," which obscures the monetary meaning of the German *wertvoll*.

75. My translation is based on the Yiddish recording. Boder translates this as: "Dante was just a dog. They know it much better." Boder interview with Anna Kaletska, September 26, 1946, Voices of the Holocaust, https://voices.iit.edu/interviewee?doc=kaletskaA.

76. David Boder, "The Tale of Anna Kovitzka: A Logico-Systematic Analysis or an Essay in Experimental Reading," November 15, 1956, box 4, David P. Boder Papers, UCLA Library Special Collections. I cite the November 15, 1956 version of the article but correct typos based on earlier versions. Only a few words differ between each version. Boder emphasized that the survivors had brought up the topic: "[M]ention of 'burning' of the Gypsies was made spontaneously by several of my interviewees residing at present (1946) in different D.P. Camps."

77. Ibid.

78. David Boder, *I Did Not Interview the Dead* (Urbana: University of Illinois Press, 1949), 1–25. Boder also changed the interviewee's name to Kovitzka to protect his subject's privacy. See Rosen, *The Wonder of Their Voices*, 129.

79. David P. Boder, *Topical Autobiographies of Displaced People: Recorded Verbatim in Displaced Persons Camps with a Psychological and Anthropological Analysis*, 5 vols. (Chicago: Boder, 1950).

80. Niewyk, *Fresh Wounds*, 210. Niewyk is otherwise a pioneer in writing an integrated history of the Jewish and Romani Holocaust. See Donald L. Niewyk and Francis R. Nicosia, *The Columbia Guide to the Holocaust* (New York: Columbia University Press, 2000), which discusses both genocides together.

81. See Rosen, *The Wonder of Their Voices*.

82. Boder interview with George Kaldore, August 31, 1946, Voices of the Holocaust, hppts://voices.library.iit.edu/interview/kaldoreG?search_api_fulltext=George%20Kaldore.

83. Gertner mentioned his deportation to the "Gypsy camp," but Boder asked him to explain what that meant. Boder interview with Alexander Gertner, August 26, 1946, Voices of the Holocaust, https://voices.library.iit.edu/interview/gertnerA.

84. Ibid., min 34:20.

85. In *The Columbia Guide to the Holocaust*, which he wrote with the historian Francis Nicosia, Niewyk decided to discuss the genocides of "all European Jews and Gypsies" together. Niewyk and Nicosia, *The Columbia Guide to the Holocaust*, 3 et passim.

86. Niewyk, *Fresh Wounds*, 192, note 3.

87. Survivors also encountered Goldstein's superiors Yvonne Braem and Fernand Erauw, who signed the testimonies as witnesses.

88. On Belgian compensation law, see Pieter Lagrou, *The Legacy of Nazi Occupation: Patriotic Memory and National Recovery in Western Europe, 1945–1965* (Cambridge: Cambridge University Press, 1999), 47–58; Pieter Lagrou, "Victims of Genocide and National Memory: Belgium, France and the Netherlands 1945–1965," *Past & Present*, no. 154 (February 1997): 181–222.

89. Various judicial decisions also barred Belgian courts from pursuing crimes against non-Belgian citizens, most importantly the decision of the Belgian Court of Appeals (Cour de

Cassation) of July 4, 1949 regarding proceedings against member of the Sipo-SD in Charleroi. As a consequence, Belgian military prosecutors were not able to reconstruct the persecution of Jews as a theme in itself. See Nico Wouters, "The Belgian Trials (1945–1951)," in *Holocaust and Justice: Representation and Historiography of the Holocaust in Post-War Trials*, ed. David Bankier and Dan Michman (Jerusalem: Yad Vashem, 2010), 219–44, especially 237.

90. Ministère de la justice, Commision des crimes de guerre, *Les Crimes de guerre commis sous l'occupation de la Belgique, 1940–1945: La persécution antisémitique en Belgique* (Liège, Belgium: Georges Thone, 1947), 13–14.

91. The report merely notes that at first Belgian Jews were given the false hope that only foreign-born Jews would be deported. While this statement is accurate, it is also misleading. The report does not mention that most Jews in Belgium were foreign-born or non-citizens. Ibid., 27.

92. Estelle Goldstein, *D'hier et d'aujourd'hui: Souvenirs* (Brussels: Société générale d'éditions "Sodi," 1967), 17–23.

93. The details of Goldstein's wartime activities and postwar trials come from a file at Brussels-based CEGES (since renamed CegeSoma), which the Belgian Ministry of Social Affairs put together after an inquiry by CEGES's director, José Gotovitch, in 1997. The complete dossier is filed under AA1587/PC32. On the inquiry, see, along with this file, Ministère des affaires sociales, de la Santé publique et de l'Environnement, Direction Recherches, Documentation et Décès to José Gotovich, Directeur du CEGES, September 11, 1997, CegeSoma, AA1587/PC32.

94. On the final appeal, see within Goldstein's CEGES file: Dispositif, Ministère de la Reconstruction, Commission d'Appel d'Agréation des Prisonniers Politiques et Ayants droit, dossier 124.779/2530/2414, decision of February 16, 1951, CegeSoma, AA1587/PC32.

95. Lagrou, "Victims of Genocide," 198.

96. On the collections of these missions, see Patrick Nefors, *Inventaris van het archief van de Dienst voor de Oorlogsslachtoffers / Inventaire des archives du Service des Victimes de la Guerre* (Brussels: Ministerie van Sociale Zaken, Volksgezondheid en Leefmilieu Dienst voor de Oorlogsslachtoffers en het SOMA Studie- en Documentatiecentrum oorlog en hedendaagse maatschappij, 1997). Representing the ministry at the International Refugee Organization, Fernand Erauw also pushed for a more efficient organization of International Tracing Service efforts to assist in the indemnification of approximately 200,000 applicants for state support. See, IRO General Council, 4th Session, Summary Record of the 59th Meeting, Geneva, October 1, 1949, 6.1.1/82503727–82503731/ITS Digital Collection, Arolsen Archives, USHMM.

97. Questionnaire Lija Gancberg, CJDC/Mémorial de la Shoah, CCXXV-241. On the deportation of Belgian Romanies, see José Gotovitch, "Enkele gegevens betreffende de uitroeiing van de zigeuners uit België," *Bijdragen tot de Geschiedenis van de Tweede Wereldoorlog* 4 (1976): 153–73.

98. The first traces of a systematic reflection on Roma came only in 1959, when the authorities in the German state of Schleswig-Holstein began to reject Romani compensation claims for deportations to Poland in 1940. DG Oorlogsslachtoffers, binder 429, Landesentschaedigungsamt van Schleswig-Holstein.

99. One Jewish survivor not interviewed by the Goldstein commission had also written a memoir about her internment at Malines, which included detailed descriptions of her impressions of Romani prisoners. See Hélène Beer, *Salle 1* (Brussels: C. Dessart, 1946).

100. On these reports, see DG Oorlogsslachtoffers, binder 2762; Fernand Erauw to Director General Devos, September 5, 1951, binder 2762, folder 625, DG Oorlogsslachtoffers.

101. Laura Jockusch, *Collect and Record!: Jewish Holocaust Documentation in Early Postwar Europe* (New York: Oxford University Press, 2012).

102. Jochheim-Arnim reported that the Gestapo used the fact that he had stolen a bicycle during an earlier attempt to escape from Dachau as a pretext for his recategorization. The International Information Office set up by the US Army in Dachau after liberation confirmed the central elements in Jochheim-Arnim's account, including the change of his prisoner category. International Information Office for the former Concentration Camp Dachau, March 1, 1946, TD file 84265, 6.3.3.1/85025664/ITS Digital Collection, Arolsen Archives, USHMM. On the Information Office, see Harold Marcuse, *Legacies of Dachau: The Uses and Abuses of a Concentration Camp, 1933–2001* (Cambridge: Cambridge University Press, 2001), 65–66.

103. On Tauber's early effort, see Tauber to Jochheim-Armin, August 13, 1946, Stadtarchiv München, Polizeidirektion 830. On their attempts to represent different persecuted groups, see Jochheim-Armin to Otto Aster, Kommissar für politisch Verfolgte, Munich, May 29, 1946, Stadtarchiv München, Polizeidirektion 830.

104. For copies of the journal *Die Vergessenen: Halbmonatsschrift für Wahrheit und Recht aller ehemaligen Konzentrationäre und Naziopfer* and these efforts, see Stadtarchiv München, Polizeidirektion 828.

105. Jochheim-Armin, Interessengemeinschaft deutscher Zigeuner to Gerichtshof in Nürnberg [International Military Tribunal], n.d., Stadtarchiv München, Polizeidirektion 828. It is unclear why Jochheim-Armin speaks of himself as a Romani victim in these letters.

106. A brief account appears in Ludwig Eiber, *"Ich wusste es wird schlimm": Die Verfolgung der Sinti und Roma in München 1933–1945* (Munich: Buchendorfer Verlag, 1993), 126–28.

107. See, for example, Bescheid, Amt der burgenländischen Landesregierung, VIII-544/3–1949, Eisenstadt, September 9, 1949, DÖW 19360/3. On Lackenbach, see Erika Thurner, *National Socialism and Gypsies in Austria* (Tuscaloosa: University of Alabama Press, 1998), 42–101.

108. See "Suchdienst," *Der neue Mahnruf,* no. 12 (1949): 14 and "Suchdienst," *Der neue Mahnruf,* no. 14 (1950): 14; "Zigeunerschicksal im heutigen Österreich," *Der neue Mahnruf,* no. 4 (1949): 10; "Du fragst–wir antworten," *Der neue Mahnruf,* no 2 (1951): 10; "Kundgebung in Oberwart," *Der neue Mahnruf,* no. 10 (1954): 5; "Lager Lackenbach," *Der neue Mahnruf,* no. 7 (1955): 5.

109. Other Roma had limited success in their attempt to seek justice against their persecutors. A trial against a policeman who had publicly abused two Roma during their arrest received a mild sentence of six months in 1946 (when most convictions by special courts, *Volksgerichte,* tended to be harsher). Ursula Mindler, "'Die Zigeuner und die Juden sind seit der Gründung des Dritten Reiches untragbar': Das Südburgenland im Gau Steiermark und sein Umgang mit der NS-Vergangenheit nach 1945," in *NS-Herrschaft in der Steiermark: Positionen und Diskurse,* ed. Heimo Halbrainer, Gerald Lamprecht, and Ursula Mindler (Vienna: Böhlau, 2012), 136–38.

110. Susanne Urban, Sascha Feuchert, and Markus Roth, eds., *Fundstücke: Stimmen der Überlebenden des "Zigeunerlagers" Lackenbach* (Göttingen: Wallstein, 2014); Gerhard Baumgartner, "'Wann endlich wird dies himmelschreiende Unrecht an uns gut gemacht werden?' Frühe

Zeugnisse österreichischer Roma und Romnia zu ihrer Verfolgung während des Nationalsozialismus," in "Feinbilder," ed. Christine Schindler, *Jahrbuch, Dokumentationsarchiv des österreichischen Widerstandes* (2015): 43–80, https://www.doew.at/cms/download/dblcd/jb2015 _baumgartner.pdf.

Chapter Four: Asymmetrical Justice: Roma and Jews in the Courtroom

1. Matéo Maximoff, "Germany and the Gypsies: From the Gypsy's Point of View," *JGLS* 25 (1946), 106. On the background of the article and for a copy of the original piece, see Marie-Christine Hubert, "Calling for an Allied Court of Justice," RomArchive, 2017, https://www .romarchive.eu/en/collection/die-bestrafung-der-moerder-von-500000-sinti-and-roma/.

2. Ibid., 107. Similar invocations appear later in his essay: "[W]herever we [Gypsies] go we carry with us that element of mystery which intrigues the whole world."

3. Matéo Maximoff to Dora Yates, August 20, 1946, GLS XII, 41, University of Liverpool Archives.

4. Maximoff, "Germany and the Gypsies," 107. Writing from France, he also inserted Roma into the foundational myth of the French postwar state that declared Vichy an aberration and the resistance and deportees as the true embodiments of the nation. On the place of Jewish victimhood in the context of a French memorial culture dominated by images of the antifascist resistance fighter and deportee, see Philip Nord, *After the Deportation: Memory Battles in Postwar France*, Studies in the Social and Cultural History of Modern Warfare (Cambridge: Cambridge University Press 2020); Simon Perego, *Pleurons-les: Les Juifs de Paris et la commémoration de la Shoah (1944–1967)*, Époques (Ceyzérieu, France: Champ Vallon, 2020). Maximoff's invocation of the dichotomy between German perpetrators and French resistance had its limits, as the Romani author surely knew. French forces were instrumental in the persecution he and his family experienced in Gurs and Lannemezan. Ulrich Baumann, "From the Gypsy's Point of View: Politique et mémoire au travers de la vie et l'œuvre de Matéo Maximoff," *Études tsiganes* 60, no. 1 (2017): 115–33. On the various parties who contributed to the persecution of French *nomades*, see Denis Peschanski, *Les tsiganes en France: 1939–1946*, Histoire 20e Siècle (Paris: CNRS éditions, 1994); Emmanuel Filhol, ed., *La mémoire et l'oubli: L'internement des Tsiganes en France, 1940–1946*, Interface (Paris: Centre de recherches tsiganes, Harmattan, 2004); Emmanuel Filhol and Marie-Christine Hubert, *Les Tsiganes en France, un sort à part, 1939–1946* (Paris: Perrin, 2009); Shannon L. Fogg, "'They Are Undesirables': Local and National Responses to Gypsies during World War II," *French Historical Studies* 31, no. 2 (2008): 327–58; Lise Foisneau, *Les Nomades face à la guerre (1939–1946)*, in collaboration with Valentin Merlin (Paris: Klincksieck, 2022).

5. For a similar depiction, see Jan Yoors, *Crossing: A Journal of Survival and Resistance in World War II* (New York: Simon and Schuster, 1971).

6. See Karola Fings, "The Number of Victims," RomArchive, www.romarchive.eu/en/voices -of-the-victims/the-number-of-victims.

7. This meant lobbying first with the United Nations War Crimes Commission and subsequently with the politicians and administrators defining the jurisdiction of the international tribunal in Nuremberg. Boaz Cohen, "Dr. Jacob Robinson, the Institute of Jewish Affairs and the Elusive Jewish Voice in Nuremberg," in *Holocaust and Justice: Representation and*

Historiography of the Holocaust in Post-War Trials, ed. David Bankier and Dan Michman (Jerusalem and New York: Yad Vashem and Berghahn, 2010).

8. See James Loeffler, *Rooted Cosmopolitans: Jews and Human Rights in the Twentieth Century* (New Haven, CT: Yale University Press, 2018), 34–57 for Robinson's interwar and wartime work.

9. On the early WJC, see Zohar Segev, *The World Jewish Congress during the Holocaust: Between Activism and Restraint*, New Perspectives on Modern Jewish History 7 (Munich: De Gruyter Oldenbourg, 2014), 1–10; on Robinson, see Segev, *The World Jewish Congress*, 185–201.

10. The Soviet concept played a minor role in the description of crimes against Jews and Roma. In one of the revisions to the indictment, the Russians actively removed the murder of Poles and "Gypsies" from a draft. See Francine Hirsch, *Soviet Judgment at Nuremberg: A New History of the International Military Tribunal after World War II* (New York: Oxford University Press, 2020), 104, note 106.

11. Arieh J. Kochavi, *Prelude to Nuremberg: Allied War Crimes Policy and the Question of Punishment* (Chapel Hill: University of North Carolina Press, 1998), 138–71.

12. Lawrence Douglas, *The Memory of Judgment: Making Law and History in the Trials of the Holocaust* (New Haven, CT: Yale University Press, 2001), 53–56. This was largely a discussion on crimes against humanity as defined in charge 6(c) of the indictment.

13. Douglas, *The Memory of Judgment*, 15; Bloxham, *Genocide on Trial*, 20. The Soviet team supported the concept by the end of the trial, when they eventually realized that Count 1 would be important for a conviction. Hirsch, *Soviet Judgment*, 371.

14. Count 1, (D)3.(d) starts with: "Implementing their 'master race' policy, the conspirators joined in a program of relentless persecution of the Jews, designed to exterminate them." It is part of the section "The Acquiring of Totalitarian Control of Germany: Political." Nuremberg Indictment, IMT, online at The Avalon Project, Yale University, https://avalon.law.yale.edu/imt/count1.asp.

15. Kim Christian Priemel, *The Betrayal: The Nuremberg Trials and German Divergence* (Oxford: Oxford University Press, 2016), 119.

16. *Trial of the Major War Criminals before the International Military Tribunal, Nuremberg, 14 November 1945–1 October 1946*, vol. 2 [The Blue Series] (Nuremberg, Germany: International Military Tribunal, 1947), 118.

17. Ibid.

18. This ambivalence appears often where prosecutors elaborated in greater detail or with greater emphasis on the systematic murder of Jews. See, for example, the statements by major Walsh, who followed most of the talking points Robinson had previously passed on to investigators (primarily at OSS) but nevertheless, by legal necessity, regularly referred back to the notion that this might have served a larger Nazi plan for aggression. IMT, vol. 3, 518, [December 13, 1945], online at The Avalon Project, Yale University, https://avalon.law.yale.edu/imt/12-13-45.asp; continued on December 14, 1945: IMT, vol. 3, 550, online at The Avalon Project, Yale University, https://avalon.law.yale.edu/imt/12-14-45.asp.

19. Judgement, Section "The Law Relating to War Crimes and Crimes Against Humanity Section," IMT, vol. 1, 254, online at The Avalon Project, Yale University, https://avalon.law.yale.edu/imt/judlawre.asp.

20. *General Report to the Combined Staffs of the Office by Dr. Jacob Robinson on the Nuremberg Criminal Trial, December 6, 1945*, AJA, WJC C14/16, 1, available digitally through Truman

Library: www.trumanlibrary.gov/library/research-files/report-jacob-robinson-world-jewish
-congress?documentid=NA&pagenumber=1. The idea of a conspiracy did not have a single
origin, but Robinson was one source for the idea to insert the murder of the Jewish people as a
crime into the trial in this form. Mark Lewis, *The Birth of the New Justice: The Internationalization
of Crime and Punishment, 1919–1950* (New York: Oxford University Press, 2014), 167–73.

21. See Lewis, *Birth of the New Justice*, 156; Laura Jockusch, "Justice at Nuremberg? Jewish
Responses to Nazi War-Crime Trials in Allied-Occupied Germany," *Jewish Social Studies* 19, no. 1
(2012): 113.

22. Michael Marrus, "Jewish Lobby at Nuremberg: Jacob Robinson and the Institute of
Jewish Affairs, 1945–46," in *The Nuremberg Trials: International Criminal Law since 1945: 60th An-
niversary International Conference*, ed. Herbert R. Reginbogin and Christoph J. M. Safferling
(Munich: Saur, 2006), 65.

23. Jockusch, "Justice at Nuremberg?," 127–29.

24. Loeffler, *Rooted Cosmopolitans*, 129–31.

25. Nuremberg Indictment [1945], Count Four, IMT, online at The Avalon Project, Yale
University, https://avalon.law.yale.edu/imt/count4.asp.

26. Jonathan Bush, "Nuremberg and Beyond: Jacob Robinson, International Lawyer," *Loyola
of Los Angeles International and Comparative Law Review* 39, no. 259 (2017): 281.

27. When Jacob's Brother Nehemia took over the Institute for Jewish Affairs in 1947, he made
several proposals to the preparatory bodies working on the genocide convention that would
have made the agreement more aggressive in policing the preparation of genocide. Lewis, *The
Birth of the New Justice*, 206–11.

28. *General Report to the Combined Staffs of the Office by Dr. Jacob Robinson on the Nuremberg
Criminal Trial, December 6, 1945.* Jim Loeffler suggests based on the same letter that Robinson
was offended mainly by the juxtaposition between Jewish and Polish victims. It appears that his
aversion to seeing Jews equated with Roma was greater than his discomfort with Polish claims
to victim status.

29. See his notes on works by Dora Yates, Léon Poliakov, Joseph (Jacov) Tenenbaum, Raul
Hilberg, and Danuta Czech's "Chronologies of Auschwitz" in *Hefte von Auschwitz*, Jacob Robinson Collection, Yad Vashem, O.65, file 48.

30. "Minutes of the Office Committee Meeting," December 10, 1945, AJA, WJC-C14/16, 2–3,
www.trumanlibrary.gov/library/research-files/minutes-office-committee-meeting-world
-jewish-congress.

31. Jochheim-Armin, Interessengemeinschaft deutscher Zigeuner to Gerichtshof in Nürnberg [International Military Tribunal], n.d., Stadtarchiv München, Polizeidirektion 828.

32. *General Report to the Combined Staffs of the Office by Dr. Jacob Robinson on the Nuremberg
Criminal Trial, December 6, 1945,* 4.

33. For an excellent early assessment of this documentation's makeup, availability, and impact, see John Mendelsohn, "Trial by Document: The Use of Seized Records in the United
States Proceedings at Nuernberg," (PhD diss., University of Michigan, 1974).

34. We can see this in the acknowledgments to Gerald Reitlinger's *The Final Solution* (1953).
He thanks a Foreign Office librarian for access to "the only classified collection from these im-
mensely bulky materials which was available in England." Gerald Reitlinger, *The Final Solution:
The Attempt to Exterminate the Jews of Europe, 1939–1945* (New York: A. S. Barnes, 1961), xi. Other

institutions did have Nuremberg records and volumes as well, including the Wiener Library, which Reitlinger used extensively. They had received these materials in exchange for help with the trial preparation. See Nuremberg War Crimes Trial: Documents, Wiener Library, 1655. Yet, the point remains that scholars struggled to get access to these materials, in particular outside of major research centers.

35. Léon Poliakov, *Harvest of Hate: The Nazi Program for the Destruction of the Jews of Europe* (Syracuse, NY: Syracuse University Press, 1954), x.

36. Portschy's memorandum is listed as "9 Feb 1939 (NG 845)," cited by Poliakov, *Harvest of Hate*, 265; Philip Friedman, "The Extermination of the Gypsies: A Nazi Genocide Operation Again an Aryan People," *Jewish Frontier* 18, no. 1 (January 1951): 11–14.

37. Prosecution evidence document NO–5322, *Trials of War Criminals Before the Nuernberg Military Tribunals Under Control Council Law no. 10, Nurnberg, October 1946–April 1949*, vol. 4, 855–59. Joseph Tenenbaum, *Race and Reich: The Story of an Epoch* (New York: Twayne Publishers, 1956), 401; Friedman "Extermination of the Gypsies," 12, without citing his source; B. A. Sijes, *Vervolging van zigeuners in Nederland 1940–1945*, Monografieën—Rijksinstituut voor Oorlogsdocumentatie 13 (The Hague, Netherlands: Nijhoff, 1979), 44–45; Michael Zimmermann, *Rassenutopie und Genozid: Die nationalsozialistische "Lösung der Zigeunerfrage"* (Hamburg: Christians, 1996), 171. Himmler wanted these deportations to happen together with the removal of all German Jews after the deportations of Poles out of areas earmarked for German settlement had completed. War planning changed the timeline. Most historians did not dwell further on the inclusion of "Gypsies" in the discussions of short and long-term resettlement policies toward Jews and Poles at the meeting. See, for example, Christopher R. Browning, *The Path to Genocide: Essays on Launching the Final Solution* (Cambridge: Cambridge University Press, 1992), 13; Michael Marrus, ed., *The Nazi Holocaust: Historical Articles on the Destruction of European Jews*, vol. 2, *The Origins of the Holocaust* (Westport, CT: Meckler, 1989), 769.

38. Poliakov, *Harvest of Hate*, 265–66.

39. Bloxham, *Genocide on Trial*, 185–200.

40. The phrase "alibi of a nation" comes from Gerald Reitlinger, *The SS: Alibi of a Nation, 1922–1945* (London: Heinemann, 1956).

41. Douglas, *The Memory of Judgment*, 69.

42. Rudolf Höß, *Kommandant in Auschwitz: Autobiographische Aufzeichnungen*, ed. Martin Broszat (Stuttgart: Deutsche Verlags-Anstalt, 1958), 11. Joseph Tenenbaum not only used the memoir in his historical writings, he even wrote an article on the document in the influential journal *Jewish Social Studies*. The fact that German and other non-Jewish scholars perceive the text to be unknown tells us much about the divide between Holocaust Studies and Jewish history. See Joseph Tenenbaum, "Auschwitz in Retrospect: The Self-Portrait of Rudolf Hoess, Commander of Auschwitz," *Jewish Social Studies* 15, no. 3/4 (1953): 203–36.

43. For the first English translation, see Rudolf Höss, *Commandant of Auschwitz: The Autobiography of Rudolf Hoess*, trans. Constantine FitzGibbon (London: Weidenfeld and Nicolson, 1959).

44. Tadeusz Szymański, Danuta Szymańska, and Tadeusz Snieszko, "The 'Hospital' in the Family Camp for Gypsies in Auschwitz-Birkenau," in *Nazi Medicine: Doctors, Victims, and Medicine in Auschwitz*, by International Auschwitz Committee, vol. 3 (New York: Howard Fertig, 1986), 35–36; Guenter Lewy, *The Nazi Persecution of the Gypsies* (Oxford: Oxford University

Press, 2000), 288–89. Franz Calvelli-Adorno, "Die rassische Verfolgung der Zigeuner vor dem 1. März 1943," *Rechtsprechung zum Wiedergutmachungsrecht* 12, no. 12 (1961): 534 cited Höß's incorrect and misleading claim that murder was ordered in the summer of 1942. On Calvelli-Adorno's essay, see chapter 5.

45. Raphael Gross and Werner Renz, eds., *Der Frankfurter Auschwitz-Prozess (1963–1965): Kommentierte Quelleneition*, vol. 1 (Frankfurt am Main: Campus Verlag, 2013), 257–60.

46. Martin Holler, *Der nationalsozialistische Völkermord an den Roma in der besetzten Sowjetunion (1941–1944): Gutachten für das Dokumentations- und Kulturzentrum Deutscher Sinti und Roma* (Heidelberg: Dokumentations- und Kulturzentrum Deutscher Sinti und Roma, 2009), 80.

47. Other documents from this trial also dealt with the killing of Roma. See, for example, the affidavit of Heinz Hermann Schuberg on the killing of Roma in Simferopol. Document NO–3055, *Trials of War Criminals*, vol. 6, 207–9. For references to Ohlendorf's testimony, see, for example, Donald Kenrick and Grattan Puxon, *The Destiny of Europe's Gypsies*, Studies in the Dynamics of Persecution and Extermination, Columbus Centre (London: Chatto and Heinemann Educational for Sussex University Press, 1972), 143–45; Miriam Novitch, *Le génocide des tziganes sous le régime Nazi* (Paris: Comité pour l'érection du Monument en mémoire des Tziganes assassinés à Auschwitz, 1968), 20.

48. Hilary Earl has noted that Heath, assigned to this position by US chief prosecutor Ben Ferencz, was not up to the task of cross-examination and failed to highlight the accused's inconsistencies. See Hilary Camille Earl, *The Nuremberg SS-Einsatzgruppen Trial, 1945–1958: Atrocity, Law, and History* (Cambridge: Cambridge University Press, 2009), 201–2.

49. *Trials of War Criminals*, vol. 6, 286–87. I retained the lowercase spelling of "Gypsy" from the official protocols.

50. *Trials of War Criminals*, vol. 6, 415–16.

51. Oberstaatsanwalt bei dem LG Würzburg to Generalstaatsanwalt beim OLG Bamberg, Würzburg, April 16, 1953, BayHSt, MJu 23672.

52. Ibid. "Der Beschuldigte musste somit die Maßnahmen gegen die Zigeuner keineswegs als eine der vielen Stationen eines systematischen Vernichtungsfeldzuges ansehen, wie es bei den sich über Jahre erstreckenden und sich aus dem allgemein bekannten Programm der NSDAP ergebenden Maßnahmen gegen die jüdischen Mitbürger hätte der Fall sein können."

53. Oberstaatsanwaltschaft Würzburg to Maria H. with Verfügung zu 1 Js 5784/63, June 4, 1964, and Oberstaatsanwaltschaft Würzburg to Christan H., April 12, 1965, BArch 162/26043.

54. On the decision not to seek a conviction only based on documentary evidence, which would have been easily possible, see Gideon Hausner, *Justice in Jerusalem* (New York: Harper & Row, 1966).

55. Leora Bilsky, "The Eichmann Trial: Towards a Jurisprudence of Eyewitness Testimony of Atrocities," *Journal of International Criminal Justice* 12, no. 1 (March 2014): 27–57; Douglas, *The Memory of Judgment*, 97–182.

56. See, for example, David Cesarani, "Introduction," in *After Eichmann: Collective Memory and Holocaust Since 1961*, ed. David Cesarani (Hoboken, NJ: Taylor and Francis, 2013), 3, who describes how this trial "catalyzed consciousness and crystallized certain trends" in public awareness of the Holocaust, even if it did not outright invent them.

57. One exception might be the trial against Friedrich Sowa, the former chief of the German criminal police and chief of staff of the police in the Protectorate of Bohemia and Moravia in

Czechoslovakia in 1947. The trial did not receive the same attention as Eichmann's, however. Sowa received a life sentence that was later reduced. Celia Donert, *The Rights of the Roma: The Struggle for Citizenship in Postwar Czechoslovakia* (Cambridge: Cambridge University Press, 2017), 44–45.

58. Bet ha-mishpat ha-mehozi and Misrad ha-mishpatim, *The Trial of Adolf Eichmann: Record of Proceedings in the District Court of Jerusalem*, vol. 1 (Jerusalem: Trust for the Publication of the Proceedings of the Eichmann Trial, in cooperation with the Israel State Archives and Yad Vashem, the Holocaust Martyrs' and Heroes' Remembrance Authority, 1992), 7.

59. On the Israeli trials against Jewish ghetto administrators and camp functionary prisoners, see Dan Porat, *Bitter Reckoning: Israel Tries Holocaust Survivors as Nazi Collaborators* (Cambridge, MA: Belknap Press of Harvard University Press, 2019).

60. On the evolution of the law, see Dan Porat, "Changing Legal Perceptions of 'Nazi Collaborators' in Israel, 1950–1972," in *Jewish Honor Courts: Revenge, Retribution, and Reconciliation in Europe and Israel after the Holocaust*, ed. Gabriel Finder and Laura Jockusch (Detroit, MI: Wayne State University Press, 2015), 303–26.

61. Interview of July 6, 1960, in *Trial of Adolf Eichmann*, by Bet ha-mishpat ha-mehozi and Misrad ha-mishpatim, vol. 7, 976–77. On the deportations to the Ghetto Łódź, see Zimmermann, *Rassenutopie*, 223–29.

62. Bet ha-mishpat ha-mehozi and Misrad ha-mishpatim, *Trial of Adolf Eichmann*, vol. 7, 1662–63. The mentioned document was the later exhibit T/166; Eichmann's section at this point was called IV D 4.

63. Bet ha-mishpat ha-mehozi and Misrad ha-mishpatim, *Trial of Adolf Eichmann*, vol. 7, 1674.

64. Ibid.

65. Bet ha-mishpat ha-mehozi and Misrad ha-mishpatim, *Trial of Adolf Eichmann*, vol. 7, 1675.

66. I am using the spelling that Bejlin chose when he wrote his name in the Roman alphabet in correspondence with German courts. Israeli courts and contemporary sources transcribed his name from the Hebrew spelling as Aharon Beilin.

67. For his testimony, see "Transcript of the Official Shorthand Notes on 'The Trial of Josef Kramer and Forty Four Others,'" BergenBelsen, October 1, 1945, www.bergenbelsen.co.uk/pages/TrialTranscript/Trial_Day_013.html. See also summary of interview with Charles Sigismund Bendel, The National Archives, UK, WO 309/625, www.nationalarchives.gov.uk/education/resources/holocaust/gas-chambers-crematoria-birkenau/. Dora Yates was among those who found reports on the killings of Romanies in Auschwitz confirmed by Bendel. Dora E. Yates, "Hitler and the Gypsies: The Fate of Europe's Oldest Aryans," *Commentary Magazine*, November 1949, 455–59 cites Bendel's testimony as reported on October 2, 1945, in the *Daily Telegraph*. Historians usually rely instead on Bendel's testimony in the Nuremberg trials. Bendel's numbers are higher than current scholarship presumes but they are relatively close to today's estimates compared to other estimates at the time. While some newspapers reported on his brief comments on Romanies, most emphasized his much more elaborate statements on the systematic murder of Jews. See, for example, "Doctor Describes Routine of Gas Chambers," *The Guardian*, October 2, 1945, www.theguardian.com/century/1940-1949/Story/0,,127738,00.html.

68. Bet ha-mishpat ha-mehozi and Misrad ha-mishpatim, *Trial of Adolf Eichmann*, vol. 3, 1255–67 for Bejlin's full testimony. This testimony has been rarely noted in the rich scholarship

on Eichmann. Annette Wieviorka, *Le procès Eichmann* (Brussels: Editions Complexe, 1989), 91–92 briefly mentions Bejlin's testimony without much comment. Most historians of the Jewish Holocaust have not discussed Bejlin's testimony. See, for example, Deborah E. Lipstadt, *The Eichmann Trial* (New York: Schocken, 2011); Hanna Yablonka, *The State of Israel vs. Adolf Eichmann* (New York: Schocken, 2004). Bejlin's testimony was eclipsed in part because of events in the morning session of the same day, when Yehiel Dinur, widely known as the author KZnik, broke down in the witness stand. On Dinur's statement, see Bet ha-mishpat ha-mehozi and Misrad ha-mishpatim, *Trial of Adolf Eichmann,* vol. 3, 1237.

69. Bet ha-mishpat ha-mehozi and Misrad ha-mishpatim, *Trial of Adolf Eichmann,* vol. 3, 1259. Bejlin first spoke of September 1944 but corrected himself later. He also claimed the camp section was empty, although the camp was created already in February 1943. In his testimony in Frankfurt am Main a few years later, Bejlin said the camp was already functioning when he arrived. First Frankfurt Auschwitz trial, Strafsache gegen Mulka u.a., 4 Ks 2/63, Landgericht Frankfurt am Main, trial day 83, August 28, 1964, 20–21.

70. Bet ha-mishpat ha-mehozi and Misrad ha-mishpatim, *Trial of Adolf Eichmann,* vol. 3, 1262.

71. Bet ha-mishpat ha-mehozi and Misrad ha-mishpatim, *Trial of Adolf Eichmann,* vol 3, 1260.

72. Bet ha-mishpat ha-mehozi and Misrad ha-mishpatim, *Trial of Adolf Eichmann,* vol. 3, 1260–61. *Mishpat Adolph Eichmann,* vol. 2 (Jerusalem: State of Israel, Ministry of Justice and Yad Vashem, 2002–3 [5763]), 1062.

73. Judith Sternberg Newman, *In the Hell of Auschwitz: The Wartime Memoirs of Judith Sternberg Newman* (New York: Exposition Press, 1963), 60.

74. For other outside attributions of Blackness to Roma, see: Gilad Margalit, "'Großer Gott, ich danke Dir, daß Du kleine schwarze Kinder gemacht hast.' Der 'Zigeunerpastor' Georg Althaus," *WerkstattGeschichte,* no. 25 (2000): 59–73. Such portrayals must be distinguished from European Romanies' own assertions of their Blackness, which appear in two registers, both as a self-description relating to appearance among some communities and as a diagnosis of their position in society. Among the Romani writers and survivors mentioned in this book, the idea of Roma as darker than other Europeans appears in the poetry of Papusza, for example. "I too am a dark Gypsy," she writes in her "Tears of Blood." The concept of Blackness also appears in ethnonyms of Romani groups such as Kaale ("black" in Finish Romani). For an analysis of the complicated politics of ascriptions of Blackness in Romani contexts, see Alaina Lemon, "'What Are They Writing about Us Blacks?': Roma and 'Race' in Russia," *Anthropology of East Europe Review* 13, no. 2 (1995): 34–40.

75. Hermann Langbein sent the manuscript version of Sternberg's account to the prosecutors of the Frankfurt Auschwitz trials. HHStAW, fonds 461, no. 37638/24, 3957: Langbein, Comité International d'Auschwitz, to Oberstaatsanwalt Dr. Wolf, Vienna, January 17, 1960; HHStAW, fonds 461, no. 37638/24, 3958–4005, Judith Sternberg, "In der Hölle von Auschwitz: Mein Leben," 3999.

76. Bet ha-mishpat ha-mehozi and Misrad ha-mishpatim, *Trial of Adolf Eichmann,* vol. 3, 1260–61.

77. Hausner was particularly eager to limit discussions of Jewish functionary prisoners or Jewish councils. On Hausner and the Eichmann trial as a turning point in Israeli kapo trials, see Porat, *Bitter Reckoning,* 173–86.

78. I could not find other testimonies that would confirm Bejlin's unlikely claim in this regard. There are, however, other testimonies about Romani men arriving in Birkenau in their Wehrmacht uniform. See, Hermann Langbein, *People in Auschwitz*, trans. Harry Zohn (Chapel Hill: University of North Carolina Press, 2004), 27.

79. Bet ha-mishpat ha-mehozi and Misrad ha-mishpatim, *Trial of Adolf Eichmann*, vol. 3, 1260.

80. Yablonka, *The State of Israel vs. Adolf Eichmann*, 69.

81. Reitlinger, *The Final Solution*, 149. Reitlinger's claim derives from his unimaginative interpretation of Kristina Żywulska's postwar memoir *I Came Back* (London: D. Dobson, 1951). Żywulska described how German Romani children played being SS men and allegedly said that they were pretending to burn Jews. Żywulska, *I Came Back*, 193. Children reenacting horrible scenes, which we also know from Jewish children in ghettos, is not sufficient evidence that adults condoned the murder of Jews. Reitlinger's comments on the Romani genocide were generally flawed: he stated erroneously for example, that all inmates of Auschwitz's "Gypsy camp" had come from the Białystok region; Reitlinger, *The Final Solution*, 448.

82. Bejlin's testimony on this topic also made it into news reports. See, for example, Homer Bigart, "Survivors Tell Eichmann Court of Days of Agony at Auschwitz: Spectator Cries 'Murderer!' and Author Collapses on Stand as Nazi Terror Is Recounted in Grim Detail," *New York Times*, June 8, 1961; Homer Bigart, "Horror Nears Peak in Eichmann Trial," *The Globe and Mail*, June 8, 1961. The most important French documentation of the trial published under the auspices of the Centre de Documentation Juive Contemporaine also included Bejlin's testimony. Léon Poliakov, ed., *Le procès de Jérusalem: Jugement-documents* (Paris: Calmann-Lévy, 1963), 77–81.

83. On Nebe, see Ronald Rathert, *Verbrechen und Verschwörung: Arthur Nebe der Kripochef des Dritten Reiches* (Münster, Germany: Lit, 2001); Lewy, *Nazi Persecution*, 369–76.

84. For contemporary discussions of the court's legitimacy, see for example, Pierre Achille Papadatos, *The Eichmann Trial* (New York: F. A. Praeger, 1964).

85. Bet ha-mishpat ha-mehozi and Misrad ha-mishpatim, *Trial of Adolf Eichmann*, vol. 5, 2101. Moshe Pearlman, *The Capture and Trial of Adolf Eichmann* (London: Weidenfeld and Nicolson, 1963), 570, also quotes from this section at length.

86. Bet ha-mishpat ha-mehozi and Misrad ha-mishpatim, *Trial of Adolf Eichmann*, vol. 5, 2193, point 211 of the judgment.

87. Hannah Arendt, *Eichmann in Jerusalem: A Report on the Banality of Evil* (New York: Penguin, 1994), 188.

88. K. E. Fleming, "The Stereotyped 'Greek Jew' from Auschwitz-Birkenau to Israeli Pop Culture," *Journal of Modern Greek Studies* 25, no. 1 (2007): 17–40.

89. Yablonka, *The State of Israel vs. Adolf Eichmann*, 89–99.

90. Christian Hilbert, Eingabe, Würzburg, February 2, 1965, Ludwigsburg BArch 162/26043.

91. Claudia Fröhlich, "Die Gründung der 'Zentralen Stelle' in Ludwigsburg—Alibi oder Beginn einer systematischen justitiellen Aufarbeitung der NS-Vergangenheit?" in *Justiz und Nationalsozialismus—Kontinuität und Diskontinuität: Fachtagung in der Justizakademie des Landes NRW, Recklinghausen, am 19. und 20. November 2001*, ed. Gerhard Pauli and Thomas Vormbaum (Berlin: Berliner Wissenschafts-Verlag, 2003), 213–50.

92. §211 Strafgesetzbuch, cited here in the translation of Devin O. Pendas, *The Frankfurt Auschwitz Trial, 1963–1965: Genocide, History, and the Limits of the Law* (Cambridge: Cambridge University Press, 2006), 56.

93. For an analysis of the subjectivist assumptions and limitations created by these legal framings, see Pendas, *Frankfurt Auschwitz Trial*, 53–79.

94. Verfügung, Ludwigsburg, August 7, 1967, BArch 162/7919, Dienststelle des Reichskommissariats Ostland -Vernichtung von Sinti und Roma.

95. Constantin Goschler, *Wiedergutmachung: Westdeutschland und die Verfolgten des Nationalsozialismus 1945–1954* (Berlin: Oldenbourg, 2009), 87–89; Herbert Diercks, ed., *Ausgegrenzt: "Asoziale" und "Kriminelle" im nationalsozialistischen Lagersystem* (Bremen, Germany: Edition Temmen, 2009).

96. Prosecutors in Stuttgart, where the investigation was originally located, clashed early on with Rögner. They wanted access to the written material he had collected on the accused. When Rögner refused to cooperate, they had them confiscated by prison authorities. See Beschluß, Amtsgericht Bruchsal, September 17, 1958, HHStAW, fonds 461, no. 37638/3, 107.

97. On Rögner, see Pendas, *Frankfurt Auschwitz Trial*, 25–28. Not the prosecutor but the defense lawyer for another accused, Stefan Baretzki, asked for Rögner to be heard in court. See Fritz Bauer Institut and Staatliches Museum Auschwitz-Birkenau, *Der Auschwitz-Prozeß: Tonbandmitschnitte, Protokolle, Dokumente*, Digitale Bibliothek 101 (Berlin: Directmedia Publ., 2004), DVD, 172. Trial day 172 (July 1, 1965), in Fritz Bauer Institut and Staatliches Museum Auschwitz-Birkenau, *Der Auschwitz-Prozeß*, 35496.

98. Deposition of Adolf Röger, Hohenasperg, May 6, 1958, HHStAW, fonds 461, no. 37638/1, 10–16. Rebecca Wittmann, *Beyond Justice: The Auschwitz Trial* (Cambridge, MA: Harvard University Press, 2005), 55–58 offers a thorough account of Rögner's letter and his role in the early investigation. She skipped the references to "Gypsy" prisoners, however.

99. Hofmann was Lagerführer of BIIe.

100. On his activities in the "Gypsy camp," see the indictment in Raphael Gross and Werner Renz, eds., *Der Frankfurter Auschwitz-Prozess (1963–1965): Kommentierte Quellenedition*, vol. 1 (Frankfurt am Main: Campus Verlag, 2013), 398–400 and the judgment in Gross and Renz, *Der Frankfurter Auschwitz-Prozess*, vol 2, 837–38, 844. The court relied for this conviction largely on the statements of two political prisoners: the Dutch navy colonel Anton van Velsen and Karl Bracht.

101. See the section on the "Final Solution," in Gross and Renz, *Der Frankfurter Auschwitz-Prozess*, vol. 1, 234–42.

102. Wittmann, *Beyond Justice*, 3. For a critique of the volume's self-positioning against Jewish historians of the Holocaust, see Nicolas Berg, *The Holocaust and the West German Historians: Historical Interpretation and Autobiographical Memory* (Madison: University of Wisconsin Press, 2015), 170–74.

103. Buchheim had previously contributed an expert opinion to support the Jewish lawyer Kurt May of the United Restitution Organization in his efforts to change the compensation law for Roma. Hans Buchheim, "Die Zigeunerdeportation vom Mai 1940," in *Das Entschädigungsrecht für die Opfer der national-sozialistischen Verfolgung: Teilausgabe des Handbuchs der Wiedergutmachung in Deutschland*, ed. Marcel Frenkel (Koblenz, Germany: Humanitas, 1957), 136–41.

104. Gross and Renz, *Der Frankfurter Auschwitz-Prozess*, vol. 1, 169.

105. Gross and Renz, *Der Frankfurter Auschwitz-Prozess*, vol. 1, 257–60.

106. The indictment cited a section on the destruction of the "Gypsy camp" in August 1944 from Bejlin's two-day deposition, recorded by a prosecutor in Frankfurt am Main in 1962. Gross

and Renz, *Der Frankfurter Auschwitz-Prozess*, vol. 1, 260. Vernehmung Aron Bejlin, August 28, 1962, HHStAW, fonds 461, no. 37638/71, 13358–13369.

107. In the indictment, Romani witnesses are quoted in the sections on crimes against individuals, not in the historical section on the camp as a whole. Gross and Renz, *Der Frankfurter Auschwitz-Prozess*, vol. 1, 398–99.

108. The International Auschwitz Committee, which was dominated by former political prisoners, had first sought to promote a trial against one of Auschwitz's SS-doctors, Claus Clauberg, but he died in 1957 before he could be indicted. The trial unfolding from Rögner was in large part the result of their effort. See Katharina Stengel, *Hermann Langbein: Ein Auschwitz-Überlebender in den erinnerungspolitischen Konflikten der Nachkriegszeit* (Frankfurt am Main: Campus Verlag, 2012), 343–442.

109. On Diamanski, see Heiko Haumann, *Hermann Diamanski (1910–1976): Überleben in der Katastrophe: Eine deutsche Geschichte zwischen Auschwitz und Staatssicherheitsdienst* (Cologne: Böhlau, 2011). Diamanski was Lagerältester in BIIe.

110. See Langbein's correspondence with Julius Hodosi, Hermine Horwath, and many other Austrian Roma in AT-OeStA/AVA Nachlässe NZN E/1797/3. See also the separate binder AT-OeStA/AVA Nachlässe NZN E/1797/272 with work on "Sinti and Roma" as well as other letters on the subject throughout his papers.

111. On Langbein, see Stengel, *Hermann Langbein* and Brigitte Halbmayr, *Zeitlebens konsequent: Hermann Langbein, 1912–1995: Eine politische Biografie* (Vienna: Braumüller, 2012).

112. Stengel, *Hermann Langbein*, 280–342.

113. See, for example, Nehemia Robinson, World Jewish Congress, to StA Vogel, December 29, 1959, HHStAW, fonds 461, no. 37638/22, 3658.

114. Lucie Adelsberger, *Auschwitz, ein Tatsachenbericht: Das Vermächtnis der Opfer für uns Juden und für alle Menschen* (Berlin: Lettner-Verlag, 1956). In English, it appeared as Lucie Adelsberger, *Auschwitz: A Doctor's Story* (Boston: Northeastern University Press, 1995). The Central Office of the Ministries of Justice in Ludwigsburg sent the book to Frankfurt prosecutors early on. See Zentrale Stelle Ludwigsburg to Office of the Prosecutor in Frankfurt am Main, June 30, 1959, Ermittlungsverfahren gegen Beyer u.a., *Der Auschwitz-Prozeß*, disc 1, 1365.

115. Eva Reichmann to Langbein, April 26, 1957, AT-OeStA/AVA Nachlässe NZN E/1797/45; Langbein to Reichmann, May 8, 1957, AT-OeStA/AVA Nachlässe NZN E/1797/45.

116. Deposition of Lucie Adelsberger, New York, December 9, 1963, FBI, FAP2 HA 114–115, 21463–21467.

117. Bejlin briefly mentioned her in his testimony. Trial day 83, August 28, 1964, *Der Auschwitz-Prozeß*, disc 1, 16311.

118. Pendas, *Frankfurt Auschwitz Trial*.

119. Karola Fings, "Auschwitz and the Testimony of Sinti and Roma," RomArchive, accessed February 17, 2017, https://blog.romarchive.eu/?p=7336.

120. See testimony of Bruno Stein, trial day 150, April 22, 1965, Tonbandmitschnitte des Auschwitz-Prozesses (1963–1965), https://www.auschwitz-prozess.de/zeugenaussagen/Stein -Bruno/. Judge Hans Hofmeyer had made the mistake of suggesting to Stein in court that he might have known the SS doctor Franz Lucas from a roll call when he had read sterilization policies to prisoners. Stein confirmed Hofmeyer's leading question, only to have defenders disprove that Lucas had read the statement. None of this had anything to do with Stein's ability

to identify Lucas. Instead, the inept handling of the questions by the judge had rendered him an unreliable witness.

121. Testimony of Paul Morgenstern, trial day 66, July 16, 1964, Tonbandmitschnitte des Auschwitz-Prozesses (1963–1965), www.auschwitz-prozess.de/zeugenaussagen/Morgenstern -Paul/.

122. Testimony of Waldemar Schröder, trial day 64, July 10, 1964, Tonbandmitschnitte des Auschwitz-Prozesses (1963–1965), https://www.auschwitz-prozess.de/zeugenaussagen /Schroeder-Waldemar/; testimony of Max Friedrich, trial day 121, December 11, 1964, Tonband-mitschnitte des Auschwitz-Prozesses (1963–1965), https://www.auschwitz-prozess.de /zeugenaussagen/Friedrich-Max/. The officer is identified as Kriminalobermeister (Sergeant) Sauerwein. The court asked Friedrich to explain the details of the earlier police interrogation as part of their attempt to understand various irregularities in the depositions, including the similarity in some of the statements. A central question was whether both survivors had said that two members of their family had died during "Sport." It turned out that the two dead prisoners were only related to Friedrich at the time of their death but indirectly became relatives when Schröder married Friedrich's niece after the war.

123. Testimony of Max Friedrich, trial day 121, December 11, 1964, Tonbandmitschnitte des Auschwitz-Prozesses (1963–1965), https://www.auschwitz-prozess.de/zeugenaussagen /Friedrich-Max/. König was on trial from 1987 to 1991.

124. Ari Joskowicz, "The Age of the Witness and the Age of Surveillance: Romani Holocaust Testimony and the Perils of Digital Scholarship," *American Historical Review* 125, no. 4 (October 2020): 1205–31.

125. Among the exceptions, see the blog entry by Fings, "Auschwitz and the Testimony of Sinti and Roma." None of the major literature mentions the fact. See Pendas, *Frankfurt Auschwitz Trial* and Wittmann, *Beyond Justice*, for example. I also had several informal conversations with colleagues who wrote on the trial who were not aware of such testimony. The larger context of the trial also facilitated an investigation and trial in Cologne that dealt with police officers and "Gypsy experts" who prepared Romani deportations to Auschwitz. These proceedings, which did not lead to convictions, also received hardly any attention and have become the subject of scholarship only recently. See Ulrich Friedrich Opfermann, "Zum Umgang der deutschen Justiz mit an der Roma-Minderheit begangenen NS-Verbrechen nach 1945. Das Sammelverfahren zum 'Zigeunerkomplex' (1958–1970)," report for the Unabhängige Kommission Antiziganismus, Berlin, 2021, https://www.bmi.bund.de/SharedDocs/downloads/DE /veroeffentlichungen/themen/heimat-integration/antiziganismus/opfermann-nsg-verfahren.pdf ?__blob=publicationFile&v=2.

126. On Diamanski, see Haumann, *Hermann Diamanski*, 337–61 on his role in the Frankfurt Auschwitz-trial, without references to his testimony regarding the "Gypsy camp."

127. Beweisantrag der Verteidigung, November 11, 1988, Gerichte Rep. 158, no. 1460, 80–81, LA-NRW. See also Werner Renz, "Auschwitz vor Gericht: Anmerkungen zum Tonband-mitschnitt im 1. Frankfurter Auschwitz-Prozess," Tonbandmitschnitte des Auschwitz-Prozesses (1963–1965), September 2013, https://www.auschwitz-prozess.de/materialien/T_03_Der _Tonbandmitschnitt_des_Auschwitz-Prozesses.

128. Bürger knew of the tapes and had a good sense of their content because he had defended one of the accused at the Frankfurt Auschwitz trial.

129. OStA Röseler to Landgericht Schwurgericht Siegen, 28 November 28, 1988, Gerichte Rep. 158, no. 1460, 82–84, LA-NRW.

130. See Frankfurt Auschwitz trial, Testimonies and Recordings (1963–1965), www.auschwitz -prozess.de/.

131. See, for example, John Megel, "The Holocaust and the American Rom," in *Papers from the Sixth and and [sic] Seventh Annual Meetings, Gypsy Lore Society, North American Chapter*, ed. Joanne Grumet (New York: Gypsy Lore Society, 1986), 187–90.

132. *Lundi Matin* [Metz], April 10, 1961; "De Jérusalem à L'O.N.U.: Les Gitans," *Le Lorrain* [Metz], April 12, 1961. Clippings of both articles can be found in the folder "Doctrines racistes-persecutions nazies," box 11b "Genocide (Camps) Allemagne, Pologne, Europe," FNASAT, Paris.

133. Pendas, *Frankfurt Auschwitz Trial*, 266.

134. Elisabeth Guttenberger, "Das Zigeunerlager," in *Auschwitz: Zeugnisse und Berichte*, ed. H. G. Adler, Ella Lingens, and Hermann Langbein (Frankfurt am Main: Europäische Verlag-sanstalt, 1962), 159–62. On the volume, see Katharina Stengel, "Auschwitz zwischen Ost und West: Das Internationale Auschwitz-Komitee und die Entstehungsgeschichte des Sammel-bandes 'Auschwitz. Zeugnisse und Berichte,'" in *Opfer als Akteure: Interventionen ehemaliger NS-Verfolgter in der Nachkriegszeit*, ed. Katharina Stengel and Werner Konitzer, Jahrbuch zur Geschichte und Wirkung des Holocaust (Frankfurt am Main: Campus Verlag, 2008), 174–96.

135. Hermann Langbein, "Die braunen Jahre: Auschwitz," recorded March 21, 1962, played April 3 and April 10, 1962, AT-OeStA/AVA Nachlässe NZN E/1797/19. The Hessischer Rund-funk arranged this show.

136. Langbein, "Die braunen Jahre."

137. Ibid.

138. There had been previous trials of individuals responsible for preparing deportation in Germany. Most were not successful, while some led at least to partial convictions. The best-known is the 1948 trial initiated by a 1946 complaint by Romani survivors from Berleburg against eleven local officials. See Opfermann, "Zum Umgang der deutschen Justiz," 21–23; Ul-rich Friedrich Opfermann, "Genozid und Justiz: Schlussstrich als 'staatspolitische Zielsetzung,'" in *Zigeunerverfolgung im Rheinland und in Westfalen 1933–1945: Geschichte, Aufarbeitung und Erin-nerung*, ed. Karola Fings and Ulrich Friedrich Opfermann (Paderborn, Germany: Schöningh, 2012), 315–26.

139. See Michael J. Bazyler, *Holocaust Justice: The Battle for Restitution in America's Courts* (New York: New York University Press, 2003).

140. Ibid, 8–9. Swiss bank cases were consolidated into one suit: *In re Holocaust Victims Assets Litigation*.

141. The Settlement Agreement with Swiss banks "designated five categories of 'Victims or Targets of Nazi Persecution' eligible for compensation: Jewish, Roma, Jehovah's Witnesses, disabled and homosexual persons persecuted or targeted for persecution by the Nazi regime." See the official website: "Overview of Litigation and Settlement," *Swiss Banks Settlement: In re Holocaust Victims Assets Litigation*, https://www.swissbankclaims.com/Overview.aspx.html.

142. Elizabeth J. Cabraser, "Human Rights Violations as Mass Torts: Compensation as a Proxy for Justice in the United States Civil Litigation System," *Vanderbilt Law Review* 57, no. 6 (2004): 2230, citing the transcript of the Fairness Hearing of November 29, 1999.

143. On the commissions as a result of transnational Holocaust litigation, see Leora Bilsky, *The Holocaust, Corporations and the Law: Unfinished Business*, Law, Meaning, and Violence (Ann Arbor: University of Michigan Press, 2017), 131–41.

144. See International Commission on the Holocaust in Romania, *Final Report* (Iași, Romania: Polirom, 2004), especially chapter 8, "The Deportation of the Roma and their Treatment in Transnistria," 233–41, http://www.inshr-ew.ro/ro/files/Raport%20Final/Final_Report.pdf. Florian Freund, Gerhard Baumgartner, and Harald Greifeneder, *Vermögensentzug, Restitution und Entschädigung der Roma und Sinti*, Veröffentlichungen der Österreichischen Historikerkommission: Vermögensentzug während der NS-Zeit sowie Rückstellungen und Entschädigungen seit 1945 in Österreich 23/2 (Vienna: Oldenbourg, 2004).

145. The 2013 case was *Kiobel v. Royal Dutch Petroleum*. Bilsky, *The Holocaust, Corporations and the Law*, 1–3.

146. See, for example, the attempts of the Gypsy International Recognition and Compensation Action to sue IBM in Switzerland for profiting from Romani persecution through the sales of their devices to the Nazi regime via European subsidiaries. See Michael J. Bazyler and Amber L. Fitzgerald, "Trading with the Enemy: Holocaust Restitution, the United States Government, and American Industry," *Brooklyn Journal of International Law* 28, no. 3 (2002): 784–86.

147. Paul Erker, "Compensating the Rest of the World: Das Entschädigungsmanagement der International Organization for Migration (IOM)," in *Die Entschädigung von NS-Zwangsarbeit am Anfang des 21. Jahrhunderts*, ed. Constantin Goschler, vol. 2, *Transnationale Opferanwaltschaft: Das Auszahlungsprogramm und die internationalen Organisationen* (Göttingen: Wallstein Verlag, 2012), 80–196. Some of the most impressive illustrations of this failure appear in sociologist Michelle Kelso's film *Hidden Sorrows: The Persecution of Romanian Gypsies during the Holocaust* (2005), which shows her efforts to help Romani claimants in Romania to apply for these funds. See also Michelle Kelso, "Holocaust-Era Compensation and the Case of the Roma," *Studia Hebraica*, no. 8 (2008): 298–334; Associated Press, "Romanian Gypsies Wait for Slave-Labor Payment," *New York Times*, July 24, 2000. Other groups struggled with other issues including the challenges of having more than one reason for persecution. On the procedural challenges of the largest foundation established in the wake of these litigation efforts, see Constantin Goschler, ed., *Compensation in Practice: The Foundation 'Remembrance, Responsibility and Future' and the Legacy of Forced Labour during the Third Reich* (New York: Berghahn Books, 2017).

Chapter Five: Jewish Institutions and the Rise of Romani Holocaust Scholarship

1. Siegfried Fauck, Institut für Zeitgeschichte, to Zentralkomitee der Zigeuner in Frankfurt am Main, August 25, 1960, IfZ, MS 410.

2. Joseph Tenenbaum, *Race and Reich: The Story of an Epoch* (New York: Twayne Publishers, 1956); Dora E. Yates, "Hitler and the Gypsies: The Fate of Europe's Oldest Aryans," *Commentary Magazine*, November 1949, 455–59.

3. Léon Poliakov, *Harvest of Hate: The Nazi Program for the Destruction of the Jews of Europe* (Syracuse, NY: Syracuse University Press, 1954), 265–66.

4. Landesentschädigungsamt Schleswig-Holstein, Kiel, January 12, 1959, DG Oorlogsslachtoffers, Brussels, 429/154.434.

5. The authorities in Schleswig-Holstein had been at the forefront of attempts to deny such claims and had faced some challenges in appeals courts, in spite of previous landmark decisions confirming their rejection of such claims. See decision of Bundesgerichtshof May 6, 1959, IV ZR 290/59 Schleswig, *Rechtsprechung zum Wiedergutmachungsrecht*, no 8/9 (1959): 419.

6. Marie-Christine de Dorlodot to Bosmans, June 30, 1959 and report, DG Oorlogsslachtoffers, Brussels, 429/154.434. Dorlodot, as chief of the Belgian mission to the Bad Arolsen archives of the ITS, was one of the most prolific collectors of information for the Belgian government from the late 1940s on.

7. The file had a further scandalous history when the German historian Hellmut Auerbach used it as the basis for a 1981 expert opinion that challenged the claims of a Romani woman for compensation. She had been deported to Radom. Usually such opinions remain anonymous but, in this case, the claimant published it, undermining Auerbach's position. The document also appeared via Auerbach in the trial against Ernst August König in the late 1980s. Hellmut Auerbach to Landgericht Stuttgart, December 21, 1981, Gerichte Rep. 118, no. 2496, 2405–6, LA-NRW; Rundschreiben, LEA Schleswig-Holstein, Kiel, January 12, 1959, Gerichte Rep. 118, no. 2496, 2407–14, LA-NRW.

8. See Julia von dem Knesebeck, *The Roma Struggle for Compensation in Post-War Germany* (Hatfield, UK: University of Hertfordshire Press, 2011) on Romani struggles for redress and the concrete practice of compensation claim-making.

9. For an anthropological and autobiographical analysis of this process, see Susan Slyomovics, *How to Accept German Reparations*, Pennsylvania Studies in Human Rights (Philadelphia: University of Pennsylvania Press, 2014).

10. Individuals who resided in countries that had been occupied during the war also had much greater difficulty receiving compensation. As a result, 90 percent of all German compensation payments went to those who were either Germans or German residents at the time of their persecution, whereas only 10 percent went to everyone else. Funds did leave Germany, however. Indeed, 80 percent went to individuals who lived abroad, mostly in the United States and Israel, often destined for German citizens who had fled the country. Hans Günter Hockerts, "Die Entschädigung für NS-Verfolgte in West- und Osteuropa: Eine einführende Skizze," in *Grenzen der Wiedergutmachung: Die Entschädigung für NS-Verfolgte in West- und Osteuropa: 1945–2000*, ed. Hans Günter Hockerts, Claudia Moisel, and Tobias Winstel (Göttingen: Wallstein, 2007), 7–8, 25.

11. Bundesgesetz zur Entschädigung für Opfer der nationalsozialistischen Verfolgung (BEG), §1, www.gesetze-im-internet.de/beg/__1.html.

12. Urteil des BGH zu IV ZR 273/55, January 7, 1956, IfZ, MS 410, 291–305, reprinted in Bundesgerichtshof and Zentralrat Deutscher Sinti und Roma, *Doppeltes Unrecht—Eine späte Entschuldigung: Gemeinsames Symposium des Bundesgerichtshofs und des Zentralrats Deutscher Sinti und Roma zu den Urteilen vom 7. Januar 1956* (Karlsruhe, Germany: Bundesgerichtshof and Zentralrat Deutscher Sinti und Roma, 2016), 46–57, https://zentralrat.sintiundroma.de/doppeltes-unrecht-ein-spaete-entschuldigung/. For an analysis of the legal origins of the landmark cases, see Detlev Fischer, "Die Urteile des Bundesgerichtshofs vom 7. Januar 1956: Entscheidung, Vorgeschichte und Entwicklung," *Doppeltes Unrecht*, 25–40.

13. See Karola Fings, "Opferkonkurrenzen: Debatten um den Völkermord an den Sinti und Roma und neue Forschungsperspektiven," *S:I.M.O.N. Shoah: Intervention. Methods. Documentation* 2, no. 1 (2015): 79–101.

14. Hans Günter Hockerts, "Anwälte der Verfolgten: Die United Restitution Organization," in *Wiedergutmachung in der Bundesrepublik Deutschland*, ed. Ludolf Herbst and Constantin Goschler (Munich: R. Oldenbourg, 1989), 255.

15. "Kurt May" [obituary], *The Daily Telegraph*, June 1, 1992; "Kurt May" [obituary], *The Times*, June 3, 1992.

16. Franz Gumbert, "Obituary: Kurt May, Fighter for the Nazis' Victims," *The Guardian*, June 3, 1992; "Kurt May" [obituary], *The Independent*, June 3, 1992.

17. Norman Bentwich, *The United Restitution Organisation, 1948–1968: The Work of Restitution and Compensation for Victims of Nazi Oppression* (London: Vallentine Mitchell, 1968), 33.

18. Hockerts, "Anwälte der Verfolgten," 257.

19. §43 (1) 2 Bundesentschädigungsgesetz (BEG) of 1956.

20. On these efforts, see Hockerts, "Anwälte der Verfolgten." These volumes were also helpful for the parallel efforts of the Jewish Claims Conference. See Marilyn Henry, *Confronting the Perpetrators: A History of the Claims Conference* (London: Vallentine Mitchell, 2007), 36.

21. Hockerts, "Anwälte der Verfolgten," 263.

22. United Restitution Organization, *Judenverfolgung in Ungarn: Dokumentensammlung* (Frankfurt am Main,: URO, 1959); United Restitution Organization, *Dokumente über Methoden der Judenverfolgung im Ausland* (Frankfurt am Main: URO, 1959); United Restitution Organization, *Judenverfolgung in Italien, den italienisch besetzten Gebieten und in Nordafrika;* (Frankfurt am Main: URO, 1962); Bruno Fischer and United Restitution Organization, eds., *Dokumente über die Verantwortlichkeit des Reiches für die Judenmaßnahmen im besetzten und unbesetzten Frankreich, insbesondere auch in Algerien, Marokko, Tunis* (Frankfurt am Main: URO, 1959).

23. Hockerts, "Anwälte der Verfolgten," 269–70. Hockerts saw several letters in May's private archive while it was still with him. I could not locate this material in the holdings of the Frankfurt URO in the Central Archives of the History of the Jewish People (CAHJP) in Jerusalem, which received the collection. May also reported about judgments on Romani restitution in internal circulars. See Rundschreiben Nr. 071/57, URO Central Office to all URO offices, September 18, 1957 on Judgement BGH June 10, 1957, Az. IV ZR 150/57, Konrad Adenauer Stiftung, Nachlass Franz Böhm, I-200–005/4; Rundschreiben Nr. 143/58, March 12, 1958, folder 050a, CAHJP, URO Frankfurt, Administrative Akten.

24. Paul Kluke, "Vorwort, " *Gutachten des Instituts für Zeitgeschichte*, vol. 1 (Munich: Institut für Zeitgeschichte, 1958), 7. On the burden of these expert opinions and the politics behind them, see Mathew Turner, Tony Joel, and David Lowe, "'Between Politics and Scholarship': The First Decade of the Institut für Zeitgeschichte, 1949–1958," *European History Quarterly* 49, no. 2 (April 2019): 250–71.

25. On the role of the institute in legal proceedings, see Nicolas Berg, *The Holocaust and the West German Historians: Historical Interpretation and Autobiographical Memory* (Madison: University of Wisconsin Press, 2015), 161–62.

26. Hans Buchheim, "Die SS in der Verfassung des Dritten Reiches," *Vierteljahrshefte für Zeitgeschichte* 3, no. 2 (1955): 127–57.

27. Berg, *The Holocaust and the West German Historians*, 148.

28. Willi Winkler, "Institut für Zeitgeschichte: Altnazis waren dabei," *Süddeutsche*, April 2, 2018, www.sueddeutsche.de/kultur/institut-fuer-zeitgeschichte-alte-kameraden-1.3926474.

29. While Buchheim was by no means an apologist for the Nazi regime, he represented what Dirk Moses called an "integrative republicanism," which emphasized the positive aspects of Germany's cultural legacy. A. Dirk Moses, *German Intellectuals and the Nazi Past* (Cambridge: Cambridge University Press, 2007), 197–98.

30. Berg, *The Holocaust and the West German Historians*, chapter 3.

31. See, for example, Buchheim's request to help with estimates of Jewish victims and May's offer to connect him to Robinson. Hans Buchheim to Kurt May, April 15, 1958, IfZ, MS 410, 24.

32. Kurt May to Hans Buchheim, November 18, 1957, IfZ, MS 410, 306.

33. Hans Buchheim, "Die Zigeunerdeportation vom Mai 1940," in *Das Entschädigungsrecht für die Opfer der national-sozialistischen Verfolgung: Teilausgabe des Handbuchs der Wiedergutmachung in Deutschland*, ed. Marcel Frenkel (Koblenz, Germany: Humanitas, 1957), 136–41. Opponents of a more generous compensation for Sinti and Roma could make use of another article published by the lawyer Hans-Joachim Döring, who argued that "Gypsies," unlike Jews, were not treated as a racial threat, and that other motives had to be considered for the deportations of 1940. See Hans-Joachim Döring, "Die Motive der Zigeunerdeportation vom Mai 1940," *Vierteljahreshefte für Zeitgeschichte* 7, no. 4 (1959): 418–28. Döring tended to use police sources in his writings and wrote about Nazi persecutions from a criminological perspective. See Hans-Joachim Döring, *Die Zigeuner im nationalsozialistischen Staat*, Kriminologische Schriftenreihe 12 (Hamburg: Kriminalistik Verlag, 1964).

34. May also sent Buchheim's essay together with a voluminous file on the subject to Franz Böhm, an influential conservative politician who became a major advocate for compensation payments and reconciliation with Jews. See Nachlass Franz Böhm, Konrad Adenauer Stiftung, 01–200:005/4.

35. Georg D. Falk, *Entnazifizierung und Kontinuität: Der Wiederaufbau der hessischen Justiz am Beispiel des Oberlandesgerichts Frankfurt am Main* (Marburg, Germany: Historische Kommission für Hessen, 2017).

36. See decision, OLG Frankfurt am Main, May 2, 1961, 8 U 74/60, reprinted in *Rechtsprechung zum Wiedergutmachungsrecht* 12, no. 12 (1961), 544–46. Calvelli-Adorno was Senatspräsident of the second chamber of the Oberlandesgericht Frankfurt am Main; this position was later called Vorsitzender Richter am Oberlandesgericht. See Hockerts, "Anwälte der Verfolgten," 270, note 75 for May's correspondence with courts and some of the new decisions.

37. Franz Calvelli-Adorno, "Die Dokumentationsarbeit der URO," *Rechtsprechung zum Wiedergutmachungsrecht* 16 (1965): 198–99.

38. Franz Calvelli-Adorno, "Die rassische Verfolgung der Zigeuner vor dem 1. März 1943," *Rechtsprechung zum Wiedergutmachungsrecht* 12, no. 12 (1961): 529–37. Calvelli-Adorno cites Buchheim throughout. Footnote one explains that most documents exist in a copy in the URO archives.

39. Calvelli-Adorno, "Die Rassische Verfolgung," 536. Calvelli-Adorno also noted that the persecution of people who were "living like Gypsies" (*nach Zigeunerart lebende Personen*) mirrored the approach to "Jews and their friends" (*Juden und Judengenossen*). In both cases, the vagueness of categories allowed for the inclusion of additional groups.

40. BGH, December 18, 1963, *Rechtsprechung zum Wiedergutmachungsrecht*, no. 5 (1964), 209–11.

41. OLG Schleswig, November 4, 1964, *Rechtsprechung zum Wiedergutmachungsrecht*, no. 4 (1965) 165–66.

42. Knesebeck, *Roma Struggle*, 127. On this development, see also Arnold Lehmann-Richter, *Auf der Suche nach den Grenzen der Wiedergutmachung: Die Rechtsprechung zur Entschädigung für Opfer der nationalsozialistischen Verfolgung* (Berlin: Berliner Wissenschafts-Verlag, 2007), 252–57.

43. Zweites Gesetz zur Änderung des Bundesentschädigungsgesetzes (BEG-Schlußgesetz), Bundesministerium der Justiz, Art. IV, 1.2, (September 14, 1965 with further revisions August 30, 1971), www.gesetze-im-internet.de/begschlg/BJNR013150965.html.

44. Knesebeck, *Roma Struggle*, 127–29. The German parliament's research department also argues that the 1956 decision played no role anymore after the 1963 ruling. See "Verwendung des Rassebegriffs bei der Entschädigung von NS-Opfern," Ausarbeitung des Wissenschaftlichen Dienstes, Deutscher Bundestag, February 15, 2013, 7.

45. On Schwarz and the journal, see Hans Günter Hockerts, "Wiedergutmachung in Deutschland: Eine historische Bilanz 1945–2000," *Vierteljahrshefte für Zeitgeschichte* 49, no. 2 (April 2001): 197–98. C. H. Beck first sold *Rechtsprechung zum Wiedergutmachungsrecht* as a supplement to the *Neue Juristische Wochenschrift*, the most important legal publication in Germany, and then made it an independent periodical after 1957.

46. Aron Rodrigue, *French Jews, Turkish Jews: The Alliance Israélite Universelle and the Politics of Jewish Schooling in Turkey, 1860–1925* (Bloomington: Indiana University Press, 1990); Lisa Moses Leff, *Sacred Bonds of Solidarity: The Rise of Jewish Internationalism in Nineteenth-Century France*, Stanford Studies in Jewish History and Culture (Stanford, CA: Stanford University Press, 2006); Abigail Green, "Nationalism and the 'Jewish International': Religious Internationalism in Europe and the Middle East, c.1840–c.1880," *Comparative Studies in Society and History* 50, no. 2 (2008): 535–58; Jaclyn Granick, "Les associations juives à la Société des Nations, 1919–1929: L'accès sans l'influence," *Relations internationales*, no. 151 (2012): 103–14. Lisa Moses Leff and Nathan A. Kurz, "'Saving' the Jews of the Diaspora," in *The Oxford Handbook of the Jewish Diaspora*, ed. Hasia R. Diner (New York: Oxford University Press, 2021).

47. See Ronald W. Zweig, *German Reparations and the Jewish World: A History of the Claims Conference* (Boulder, CO: Westview Press, 1987), 128–46. On the history of the organization, see Henry, *Confronting the Perpetrators*.

48. Bentwich, *United Restitution Organisation*, 30.

49. Zweig, *German Reparations*, 129–32.

50. Boaz Cohen, *Israeli Holocaust Research: Birth and Evolution* (Abingdon, UK: Routledge, 2013), 46–54.

51. Bentwich, *The United Restitution Organisation*, 33–34. Private lawyers would ask for 15 percent or more.

52. They used the German term *Zigeunertum*, perhaps expressing what in Romani is called *romanipen* or *romanía*. See Matras, *The Romani Gypsies*, 16.

53. Satzung, Zentralkomitee der Zigeuner, BArch B122/15538, 161–62.

54. On the organization, see "Sie wollen keine Bürger zweiter Klasse sein: In Frankfurt wurde ein Zentralkomitee der Zigeuner für das gesamte Bundesgebiet gegründet," *Frankfurter Rundschau*, March 15, 1960; Präsident Heinrich Lübke, correspondence with Zentralkomitee der Zigeuner e.V., 1960, BArch B 122/4915. See also Yaron Matras, "The Development of the Romani Civil Rights Movement in Germany 1945–1996," in *Sinti and Roma: Gypsies in German-Speaking Society and Literature*, ed. Susan Tebbutt (New York: Berghahn Books, 1998), 49–63.

Another Sinti organization had preceded the 1970 one: the Verband rassisch verfolgter nicht-Juden (Association of Racially Persecuted Non-Jews), founded in 1956. It showed in its choice of name that the founders thought it unwise to present themselves as "Gypsies" or Sinti.

55. On the history of the organization, see Henry, *Confronting the Perpetrators*.

56. Vermerk, meeting with Zigeuner-Rechts-Mission, November 20, 1969, BArch, 122/15538.

57. Josef R. to Renate Meyer, November 11, 1969, BArch B122/15538, 169.

58. Zusammenkunft deutscher Sinti in Hildesheim am November 10, 1969, Protokoll, BArch B122/15538, 170–171.

59. Waldemar F. and Paul M. to President Heinemann, November 6, 1969, BArch B122/15538, 173–174.

60. Wilhelm Weiss to President Heinemann, November 3, 1969, BArch B122/15538, 189.

61. See correspondence of Bayerisches Staatsministerium des Inneren and Bayerisches Landeskriminalamt of May and June 1960, BayHSt Minn 92098.

62. Le Comité National d'Information et d'Action Sociale pour les 'gens du Voyage' et les personnes d'origine Nomade: Le problème des Tsiganes, Gitans, Yénitches; Les objectifs d'Action Sociale en leur faveur, July 1966, AN 19870256/3.

63. The full name is Comité National d'Information et d'Action Sociale pour les 'gens du Voyage' et les personnes d'origine Nomade.

64. Decisions of the Review Board of the PCIRO and IRO about appeals against rejected applications for aid, PCIRO decision of June 18, 1948, 3.2.1/81251044/ITS Digital Collection, Arolsen Archives.

65. See Jean-Pierre Liégeois, "Naissance du pouvoir tsigane," *Revue française de sociologie* 16, no. 3 (1975): 295–316. Liégeois wrote his analysis of Romani collective organization based on interviews he conducted from 1969 to 1972 for his doctoral dissertation.

66. See "The Statute and Regulations of the General Union of the Roma in Romania" [November 16, 1933] in *Roma Voices in History: A Sourcebook*, ed. Elena Marushiakova and Vesselin Popov (Leiden, Netherlands: Ferdinand Schöningh, 2021), 355–68. Lăzurică also became the founding president of the General Union in Romania. The constitution cites him as Voevod and also stipulates: "Under no circumstances will anyone be able to demand the removal of the active president." Marushiakova and Popov, *Roma Voices in History*, 365.

67. "L'indemnisation des victimes du nazisme," *La Voix mondiale tzigane* 4, no. 20 (September 1965): 7; "L'indemnisation des victimes du nazisme," *La Voix mondiale tzigane* 5, no. 27 (September 1966): 11.

68. Reports by Renseignements Généraux, the intelligence and surveillance branch of the French police, start in 1961. See María Sierra, "Creating Romanestan: A Place to Be a Gypsy in Post-Nazi Europe," *European History Quarterly* 49, no. 2 (2019): 275. To increase the pressure on the administration, intelligence reports also claimed in 1971 that the 100,000 "Gypsies" in France "demand respect"—"just like the Algerians responsible for the National Liberation Front (F.L.N.) branch in France 1956–60," thus portraying Romani activists as analogous to anticolonial groups that resorted to terror attacks within France. See "Vers une Intervention des tziganes sur la scène politique," Direction Centrale des renseignements genereaux, August 2, 1971, folder "Comité Internationale Tzigane," AN 19970156/3.

69. On his use of Zionist models for his ideas of Romanestan, see Sierra, "Creating Romanestan," 280–85.

70. Questions traitées avec M. Peyssard, October 28, 1964, folder "C.N.I.N.," Activité générale 1960–1971, AN 19870256/3. The request came from Henri Rey.

71. Questions traitées avec M. Peyssard, October 28, 1964, folder "C.N.I.N.," AN 19870256/3.

72. The missionary arm of the Catholic Church dealing with Roma was also concerned about the rise of Pentecostalism due to the "fierce hatred it infuses against the Catholic Church." Aumônerie Catholique des voyageurs tsiganes et gitans, L'Église catholique et les gitans (Romainville, France: Aumônerie nationale des gitans, 1969), 11.

73. Louis Peyssard to Pierre Join-Lambert, November 7, 1964, folder "C.N.I.N.," AN 19870256/3.

74. Jean-Paulin Niboyet, "Le décret-loi du 12 avril 1939 relatif aux associations," Travaux du Comité français de droit international privé 6, no. 1938 (1946): 53–56.

75. It was a decree-law, which the Frankfurt school theorist and émigré legal scholar Otto Kirchheimer associated with the slow breakdown of parliamentary rule in Europe. See, Otto Kirchheimer, "Decree Powers and Constitutional Law in France under the Third Republic," American Political Science Review 34, no. 6 (1940): 1104–23.

76. Niboyet, "Le décret-loi," 55.

77. Journal officiel, March 13, 1965, 2035.

78. Vanko Rouda established the association again in 1967 as the International Gypsy Committee (Comité Internationale Tsigane). It became a constitutive member of the International Romani Union, founded 1971.

79. The Institute for War Documentation (NIOD) commissioned Jacques or Jacob Presser to write a history of Jewish persecution in 1950 but it took the author 15 years to finish it. It thus appeared just after the Eichmann and Frankfurt Trials. J. Presser, Ondergang: De vervolging en verdelging van het Nederlandse jodendom, 1940–1945 (The Hague, Netherlands: Staatsuitgeverij, 1965). Presser worked with many victim testimonies, departing from earlier histories of Jewish persecution in the Netherlands.

80. Some of the diary collection work after the war is hard to classify according to categories of victims and bystanders. The Dutch government in exile had called for Dutch citizens to keep diaries of the German occupation (famously heeded by Anne Frank) and the NIOD continued the collection effort. See Arianne Baggerman and Rudolf Dekker, "Jacques Presser, Egodocuments and the Personal Turn in Historiography," European Journal of Life Writing 7 (August 2018): 90–110.

81. See Ruth Levitt, ed., Testimonies from "Kristallnacht" (London: Souvenir Press, 2015) and online at https://www.pogromnovember1938.co.uk/viewer/.

82. See Christine Schmidt, "'We Are All Witnesses': Eva Reichmann and the Wiener Library's Eyewitness Accounts Collection," in Agency and the Holocaust: Essays in Honor of Debórah Dwork, ed. Thomas Kühne and Mary Jane Rein, Palgrave Studies in the History of Genocide (Cham, Switzerland: Springer International Publishing, 2020), 123–40. On Reichmann, see also Monika Hübsch-Faust, "Eva Gabriele Reichmann, 1897–1998," The Encyclopedia of Jewish Women, Jewish Women's Archive, December 31, 1999, https://jwa.org/encyclopedia/article/reichmann-eva-grabriele; Kirsten Heinsohn, "Welche Aufgabe hat die Zeitgeschichte? Antworten von Eva G. Reichmann und Hans Rothfels," in Aus den Quellen: Beiträge zur deutsch-jüdischen Geschichte: Festschrift für Ina Lorenz zum 65. Geburtstag, ed. Ina Susanne Lorenz, Stefanie Schüler-Springorum, and Michael Studemund-Halévy (Munich: Dölling und Galitz,

2005), 378–87; Barbara Warnock, "Eva Reichmann," in *Verfolgen und Aufklären: Die erste Generation der Holocaustforschung / Crimes Uncovered: The First Generation of Holocaust Researchers,* ed. Hans-Christian Jasch and Stephan Lehnstaedt (Berlin: Metropol, 2019), 145–147; Nicolas Berg, *The Holocaust and the West German Historians: Historical Interpretation and Autobiographical Memory* (Madison: University of Wisconsin Press, 2015), 155–56.

83. Heinsohn, "Welche Aufgabe," 380.

84. Moravitz essentially wrote up these testimonies as her experience of encountering these survivors' stories. She tended toward a broad interpretation of the biographies she wanted to include, and Reichmann concurred. She was also willing to pay for interviews with members of the Slovenian minority in the Austrian province of Carinthia. Reichmann to Hermann Langbein, February 19, 1958, Nachlass Langbein, ÖStA, AVA, E/1797/34.

85. Eva Reichmann to Emmi Moravitz, October 2, 1957, Wiener Library, 3000/9/1/989; on payments, Reichmann to Moravitz, October 21, 1957, Wiener Library, 3000/9/1/989. Calculation of current value with an online tool of the Austrian National Bank: www.eurologisch.at /docroot/waehrungsrechner/#/. The Wiener Library intended to refrain from publishing these testimonies, unless the survivors gave permission in a second step. Bertha Cohn (for Reichmann) to Moravitz, March 10, 1958, Wiener Library, 3000/9/1/989. The accounts Moravitz collected also ended up in duplicate in Steinmetz's collection for the DÖW; see DÖW 19360/1. Some of these texts are reproduced in Gerhard Baumgartner, "'Wann endlich wird dies himmelschreiende Unrecht an uns gut gemacht werden?' Frühe Zeugnisse österreichischer Roma und Romnia zu ihrer Verfolgung während des Nationalsozialismus," in "Feinbilder," ed. Christine Schindler, *Jahrbuch, Dokumentationsarchiv des österreichischen Widerstandes* (2015): 43–80.

86. Schmidt, "'We are all Witnesses,'" 126.

87. Ibid., 130.

88. The third was the Austrian Rom Julius Hodosi whom Hermann Langbein had also invited to meetings of the International Auschwitz Committee where he spoke about the sterilizations of family members. Testimony of Julius Hodosi, 1957, Wiener Library, 1656/3/8/664. These connections came through Langbein, who did pioneering work in his attempt to integrate Roma and Sinti into international commemorative work. Langbein to Julius Hosodi, March 30, 1956, Nachlass Langbein, AT-OeStA/AVA Nachlässe NZN E/1797/3. See also Katharina Stengel, *Hermann Langbein: Ein Auschwitz-Überlebender in den erinnerungspolitischen Konflikten der Nachkriegszeit* (Frankfurt am Main: Campus Verlag, 2012), 165–66.

89. Eva Reichmann's husband, the lawyer Hans Reichmann, was also an advocate of Jewish responsibility toward Romani Holocaust documentation. Working for the London headquarters of the URO, he congratulated May on his success changing compensation practices for Roma. In the same letter, Hans Reichmann claimed that in 1945 he had already realized the need for legal redress for Roma when he assembled documents for the Nuremberg trials in the Wiener Library. See Hockerts, "Anwälte," 270–71.

90. See membership cards for Association France-URSS, 1944, 1945, and 1946, GFH 38956. One of the undated postwar cards lists Novitch as secretary of the association.

91. Fédération des sociétés juives de France, Attestation, January 26, 1945, GFH 38956. For some of the testimonies she collected, see "Témoignage recueilli après guerre par Miriam Novitch, de la Fédération des sociétés juives de France, concernant les massacres de Tarnow en

Pologne," CCXVI-75 and "Témoignage . . . concernant les camps de Tréblinka, Auschwitz et Belzec," CCXVI-76, CJDC/Mémorial de la Shoah.

92. Tom Segev, "The Makings of History: A Holocaust Obsession," *Haaretz*, July 10, 2008.

93. See Zvika Dror, *Masa Miryam: Sipur hayeha shel Miryam Novits'* (Lohamei HaGeta'ot, Israel: Bet lohame ha-getaot, 2008). Dror wrote her biography as a fellow member of the kibbutz.

94. For an interpretation for her place in scholarship, see Sharon Geva, "'To Collect the Tears of the Jewish People': The Story of Miriam Novitch," *Holocaust Studies* 21, no. 1–2 (2015): 73–92.

95. She acquired some in exchanges of duplicates with other archives. Among these archives were the Wiener Library and the NIOD, which employed some of the other protagonists of this chapter. For her early introduction to these archives, see de Jong to Alfred Wiener, October 22, 1952, Wiener Library, 3000/9/1/1149/64.

96. Miriam Novich [Novitch], "Jewish Partisans in Yugoslavia," in *Extermination and Resistance: Historical Records and Source Material*, ed. Zvi Sznerm, vol. 1 (Lohamei HaGeta'ot, Israel: Ghetto Fighters' House, 1958), 180–82.

97. Miriam Novitch, "Compte-rendu d'activité: Shlihouth en Europe, Septembre 1963—Décember 1964, Janvier 1965 et Plan pour 1965," 1965, GFH 32079reg. On the same trip, she also visited Frankfurt and allegedly wrote an article on "The Extermination of the Gypsies evoked at the Frankfurt Trial" for a Francophone Romani magazine. Novitch, "Compte-rendu d'activité," 6. Novitch cited her article as "L'extermination des Tziganes évoquée au procès de Francfort" in *Revue Gitane Mondiale* but I have been able to find no evidence of the existence of such a periodical.

98. On the latter, see, for example, Ota Kraus and Erich Kulka, *The Death Factory: Document on Auschwitz* [1946] (Oxford, UK: Pergamon Press, 1966), 202–5.

99. I am using the title of the most elaborate version of the essay, published as Miriam Novitch, *Le génocide des tziganes sous le régime Nazi* ([Paris?]: Comité pour l'érection du Monument en mémoire des Tziganes assassinés à Auschwitz, 1968).

100. Geva, "'To Collect the Tears of the Jewish People,'" 77; Novitch, *Le genocide des tziganes*, 11. Katzenelson did not speak of "Gypsies" in his poem.

101. Miriam Novitch, "Il genocidio degli Zigani sotto il regime nazista," *Quaderni del centro di studi sulla deportazione e l'internamento* 2 (1965): 31–61.

102. Novitch, "Le génocide des tziganes" [extract], *Revue de l'Association des médecins israélites de France*, no. 164 (March 1968). I could not find any trace in administrative files of the Committee for the Erection of a Monument in Memory of the Gypsies Murdered at Auschwitz, which appears as the publisher of the booklet.

103. Laura Jockusch, *Collect and Record!: Jewish Holocaust Documentation in Early Postwar Europe* (New York: Oxford University Press, 2012), chapter 2.

104. On Wiesenthal's biography, see Tom Segev, *Simon Wiesenthal: The Life and Legends* (New York: Doubleday, 2010).

105. Into the 1970s, labor Zionists found it convenient to attach their view of history to universal claims, arguing that they were building a new country in a progressive spirit that could serve as a beacon to others. Estelle Goldstein, who led the Belgian ministry commission that asked about Roma internees in the early 1950s, also wrote a book along those lines in 1961.

Estelle Goldstein, *Israël: Terre des contrastes* (Brussels: Pierre De Méyère, 1961). Camille Huysmans, the Belgian socialist politician and short-term prime minister, edited the series in which Goldstein's book appeared.

106. Segev, *Simon Wiesenthal*, 313–18.

107. Wiesenthal to Oberstaatsanwalt Schüle, Zentrale Stelle der Landesjustizverwaltungen (Ludwigsburg), June 18, 1965, VWI Archive, VWI.SWA.I.1, folder "Sinti und Roma 1."

108. The Ludwigsburg office did pass on the material to colleagues in Berlin where prosecutors were preparing a trial against members of the Reich Security Main Office; see Zentrale Stelle to Wiesenthal, June 28, 1965, VWI.SWA.I.1, folder "Sinti und Roma 1."

109. See, for example, "Nazi Records Describe Gypsies' Fate," *New York Times*, June 21, 1965.

110. Simon Wiesenthal, *The Murderers among Us: The Simon Wiesenthal Memoirs*, trans. Joseph Wechsberg (New York: McGraw-Hill, 1967), 238–42.

111. Ibid., 241.

112. Wiesenthal to Gesellschaft für bedrohte Völker, January 20, 1981, VWI.SWA.I.1, folder "Sinti und Roma 1."

113. B. A. Sijes, *Vervolging van zigeuners in Nederland 1940–1945*, Monografieën—Rijksinstituut voor Oorlogsdocumentatie 13 (The Hague, Netherlands: Nijhoff, 1979).

114. On the reluctance of his witnesses and the tensions he had with his students see, Richter Roegholt, *Ben Sijes: Een biografie* (The Hague, Netherlands: Sdu, 1988), 220–21. For his students' works, see Jan van Loenen, "De andere 'Endlösung': Het duits vervolgingsbeleid jegens de zigeuners in de periode 1933–1945: Een beijdrage aan de studie van het racisme" (Doctoral diss., University of Amsterdam, 1974); Annelies Visser, "Beeld en beleid: Woonwagenbewoners, zigeuners en de overheid, 1900 tot 1930" (Doctoral diss., University of Amsterdam, 1975).

115. On the biography of Steimetz, her work in the communist resistance in France, and her activities as a communist in postwar Austria, see Sonja Frank, ed., *Die drei Schwestern Selma, Berthe und Gundl, geb. Steinmetz: Frauen im Widerstand 1933–1945* (Vienna: Theodor Kramer Gesellschaft, 2021).

116. Selma Steinmetz, *Österreichs Zigeuner im NS-Staat* (Vienna: Europa-Verlag, 1966).

117. B. A. Sijes, *Ik vergat nog iets te vertellen* (Amsterdam: H.J.W. Becht, 1978), 40–41.

118. Arnon Lapid, "Goral Zoanei," *Ha-Daf Ha-Yarok* [Hebrew], April 23, 1985, 6.

119. Sijes to Wiesenthal, June 16, 1965, VWI.SWA.I.1, folder "Sinti und Roma 1."

120. Novitch to Dr. Mueller, September 24, 1980, GFH 32305.

121. See Michael Rothberg, *Multidirectional Memory: Remembering the Holocaust in the Age of Decolonization*, Cultural Memory in the Present (Stanford, CA: Stanford University Press, 2009).

122. On the human rights campaigns, see below on the Gesellschaft für bedrohte Völker. There was a minor interest in "Gypsies" among sociologists dealing with "deviance," but that field itself was short-lived. See, for example, Marcello Truzzi, ed., *The Subterranean Sociology Newsletter*, vol. 2, no. 1 (1968).

123. Steinmetz was a member of the communist party in Austria until 1968 and Sijes identified as a council communist during his adult life. See Barbara Kintaert, "Vertrieben und vergessen? Bibliothekarinnen in der Kinderfreunde- und Arbeiterbewegung," in *Österreichische Bibliothekarinnen auf der Flucht: Verfolgt, verdrängt, vergessen?*, ed. Ilse Erika Korotin (Vienna: Praesens, 2007), 169–212; Roegholt, *Ben Sijes*, 44–61; Frank, *Die drei Schwestern*, 70 mentions

that the letter announcing her withdrawal from the Austrian communist party was lost. A younger generation of Jewish authors who wrote about Romani Holocaust history were similarly socialized in the communist party. This includes Donald Kenrick and José Gotovitch, the latter of whom wrote the first study of the persecution of Roma in Belgium. José Gotovitch, "Enkele gegevens betreffende de uitroeiing van de zigeuners uit België," *Bijdragen tot de geschiedenis van de Tweede Wereldoorlog* 4 (1976): 153–73.

124. Donald Kenrick and Grattan Puxon, *The Destiny of Europe's Gypsies*, Studies in the Dynamics of Persecution and Extermination, Columbus Centre (London: Chatto and Heinemann Educational for Sussex University Press, 1972).

125. On Puxon's work, see Thomas Acton et al., "Pedagogies of Hope: The Gypsy Council and the National Gypsy Education Council," in *Hearing the Voice of the Gypsy, Roma and Traveller Communities: Inclusive Community Development*, ed. Andrew Ryder, Sarah Cemlyn, and Thomas Acton (Bristol, UK: Policy Press, 2014), 29–48. Puxon came from a well-off Anglo-Irish Huguenot family and was educated at the exclusive Westminster School in London. He started living with Travellers after moving to Ireland to avoid the draft in 1960.

126. Reimar Gilsenbach to D. S. Kenrick, October 3, 1967, Wiener Library, 611/3/3. Gilsenbach worked at the time at the radio station Berliner Welle and emphasized the need to talk to victims instead of reading only Nazi documents.

127. D. Kenrick and G. Puxon, *The Persecution of the Gypsies under the Nazis: An Interim Report*, prepared for the Institute of Contemporary History, London, July 1968, Wiener Library, 611/16.

128. See also: "Copy documents relating to the fate of gypsies in the occupied eastern territories," Wiener Library, 611/4/7 /1-/17, which came from YIVO in large parts.

129. They leaned especially on Novitch's earlier publication, which supplied them with facts on the persecution in concentration camps. See, Wiener Library, 611/5/6/29, 611/5/6/30, and 611/5/6/36. For Kenrick's account of their reliance on Novitch's pioneering work as an archivist, see Donald Kenrick's obituary for Novitch, "Miriam Novitch—Chronistin des Schicksals von Sinti und Roma," *Pogrom: Zeitschrift für bedrohte Völker* 21, no. 154 (August 1990): 66.

Chapter Six: The Path to Shared Romani-Jewish Remembrance after 1978

1. On the events and the conference, see the contributions to Anna Mirga-Kruszelnicka, Esteban Acuña, and Piotr Trojanski, eds., *Education for Remembrance of the Roma Genocide: Scholarship, Commemoration and the Role of Youth* (Kraków: Wydawnictwo Libron, Filip Lohner, 2015).

2. I would like to thank Sławomir Kapralski for translating the Polish speeches for me at the event.

3. This description is based on the author's participation in the events.

4. According to Gergely, the Romani organizers with whom she had worked intimately over the years, had invited her to take that role spontaneously to underline the prayer's interfaith character. Author's interview with Andi Gergely, August 10, 2014.

5. The conflicts around the Auschwitz memorial site were centrally about Jews and Poles. In this context, Romani concerns were merely footnotes. "The Yarnton Declaration of Jewish Intellectuals on the Future of Auschwitz," *European Judaism: A Journal for the New Europe* 23, no. 2

(1990): 43–45, mentions "Sinti and Rom" early on as other victims killed for their mere existence but does not discuss them further.

6. This shift happened at different paces in different contexts. On the general transformation of many memorials in those years, see Harold Marcuse, "Holocaust Memorials: The Emergence of a Genre," *American Historical Review* 115, no. 1 (2010): 53–89.

7. Helmut Walser Smith, *Germany: A Nation in Its Time: Before, During, and After Nationalism, 1500–2000* (New York: Liverlight, 2020), 446–47; Jacob S. Eder, *Holocaust Angst: The Federal Republic of Germany and American Holocaust Memory Since the 1970s* (New York: Oxford University Press, 2016), 17–19.

8. Peter Novick, *The Holocaust in American Life* (Boston: Houghton Mifflin, 1999), 146–69.

9. See Arlene Stein, *Reluctant Witnesses: Survivors, Their Children, and the Rise of the Holocaust Consciousness* (Oxford: Oxford University Press, 2014).

10. On the role of the television show in different contexts, see Jeffrey Shandler, *While America Watches: Televising the Holocaust* (New York: Oxford University Press, 1999), 155–78; Anton Kaes, "1979: The American Television Series Holocaust Is Shown in West Germany," in *Yale Companion to Jewish Writing and Thought in German Culture, 1096–1996*, ed. Sander L. Gilman and Jack Zipes (New Haven, CT: Yale University Press, 1997), 783–89; Novick, *The Holocaust in American Life*, 209–14; Jürgen Wilke, "Die Fernsehserie 'Holocaust' als Medienereignis," *Historical Social Research / Historische Sozialforschung* 30, no. 4 (114) (2005): 9–17; Emiliano Perra, "Narratives of Innocence and Victimhood: The Reception of the Miniseries Holocaust in Italy," *Holocaust and Genocide Studies* 22, no. 3 (2008): 411–40. On earlier TV productions in Germany that focused less on victims and more on resistance and everyday life in Germany, see Wulf Kansteiner, "Populäres Geschichtsfernsehen vor 'Holocaust': Die Darstellung des Nationalsozialismus und des Zweiten Weltkrieges in drei Erfolgssendungen des ZDF," *Historical Social Research / Historische Sozialforschung* 30, no. 4 (114) (2005): 53–73.

11. *Holocaust*, part 1, directed by Marvin J. Chomsky (NBC, 1978).

12. Before the screening and in coordination with NBC, the American Jewish Congress commissioned a viewer's guide that notes: "Green [the author of the script] aptly describes the Gypsies in Buchenwald. Actually, Gypsies were present at at least two other scenes portrayed in the script—the Warsaw Ghetto and Auschwitz." Written by a scholar at Spertus College in Chicago, the draft material also stated that up to 400,000 Roma might have died in killings by Einsatzgruppen and in extermination camps. See, Byron L. Sherwin "A General Educational Guide for NBC's Docu-Drama 'Holocaust': First Draft,"AJA, MS-603, box 85, folder 20. For an interview with a Romani survivor at the time of the series, see Katia D. Kaupp, "Quand Paprika raconte Auschwitz," *Le Nouvel Observateur*, April 9, 1979, 67–69.

13. Daniel Levy and Natan Sznaider, *The Holocaust and Memory in the Global Age* (Philadelphia, PA: Temple University Press, 2006), 134–62, express similar enthusiasm for the Americanization of the Holocaust, which they associate with the globalization and deterritorialization of Holocaust memory through popular culture.

14. Michael Berenbaum, "The Uniqueness and Universality of the Holocaust," in *A Mosaic of Victims: Non-Jews Persecuted and Murdered by the Nazis*, ed. Michael Berenbaum (New York: New York University Press, 1990), 23.

15. Shaul Magid, "The Holocaust and Jewish Identity in America: Memory, the Unique, and the Universal," *Jewish Social Studies* 18, no. 2 (2012): 100–135.

16. The conference was planned while Elie Wiesel chaired the USHMC but took place after his departure.

17. It should be added that Berenbaum was consistent in this approach even when he stopped speaking for the museum. In a foreword to the volume Erika Thurner, *National Socialism and Gypsies in Austria* (Tuscaloosa: University of Alabama Press, 1998), vii, Berenbaum explained the topic's relevance via the Jewish genocide, putting it in peculiar spatial terms as: "If Jews were at the center of the Nazi inferno, Roma and Sinti were their neighbors."

18. Gerhard Rüdiger, "'Jeder Stein ist ein Blutstropfen': Zigeuner in Auschwitz-Birkenau, Oświęcim-Brzezinka," in *In Auschwitz vergast, bis heute verfolgt: Zur Situation der Roma (Zigeuner) in Deutschland und Europa*, ed. Tilman Zülch, Rororo aktuell (Reinbek, Germany: Rowohlt, 1979), 135–46; Wolfgang Wippermann, *"Auserwählte Opfer?": Shoah und Porrajmos im Vergleich: Eine Kontroverse* (Berlin: Frank & Timme, 2005), 74.

19. This is the case in Auschwitz, which has a separate exhibit for Roma and Sinti. See Romani Rose, Frank Reuter, and Silvio Peritore, *The National Socialist Genocide of the Sinti and Roma: Catalogue of the Permanent Exhibition in the State Museum of Auschwitz* (Heidelberg: Dokumentations- und Kulturzentrum Deutscher Sinti und Roma, 2003).

20. Edward Tabor Linenthal, *Preserving Memory: The Struggle to Create America's Holocaust Museum* (New York: Columbia University Press, 2001), 240–42; Edward J. Boyer, "Gypsies Remember Holocaust, Want Role on Memorial Council," *Los Angeles Times*, June 26, 1984, C1.

21. Daniela Gress, "Protest und Erinnerung: Der Hungerstreik in Dachau 1980 und die Entstehung der Bürgerrechtsbewegung deutscher Sinti und Roma," in *Sinti und Roma: Der nationalsozialistische Völkermord in historischer und gesellschaftspolitischer Perspektive*, ed. Karola Fings and Sybille Steinbacher (Göttingen: Wallstein, 2021), 190–219.

22. The group produced 16 striped uniforms and 50 triangular insignia with the letter Z for "Zigeuner," which some activists also wore for a small memorial for Romani victims of Auschwitz in a Washington DC park before the protest. That day various Romani representatives also founded the US Romani Council in Washington and met staffers of various members of Congress. On the protest and the council, see Grattan Puxon, ed., "Gypsies: The Holocaust's forgotten victims," US Romani Council, n.d. [1984], Romani Archives and Documentation Center, University of Texas, Austin; untitled report by Grattan Puxon, n.d. [1984?], Bishopsgate Institute, Puxon/169.

23. Of the major papers, only the *Washington Post* reported on it in its local section (based on the ProQuest Historical Newspapers database): Lloyd Grove, "Lament of the Gypsies: 40 Years After Auschwitz, Petitioning for a Place," *Washington Post*, July 21, 1984, C1 and C4.

24. Marcia Feldman to Sigmund Strochlitz, April 11, 1986, USHMM IA 1997–014, folder 2.

25. Memorandum of Jonathan Bush to Micah H. Naftalin, April 9, 1984, Re: Status of P.R. Siege by Gypsy Groups, USHMM, IA 1997–014, folder 3.

26. Marcia Feldman to Sigmund Strochlitz, April 11, 1986, USHMM IA 1997–014, folder 2.

27. Ibid.

28. Meetings started February 20, 1986. See Memorandum from Marcia Feldman to Sigmund Strochlitz, February 24, 1986, USHMM IA 1997–014, box 77, folder "Gypsies." The May meeting included community leaders and activists (Ronald Lee, John Tene, Rita Caedi, John Marino, Gratton Puxton), Romani studies scholars (Bogumila Michalewicz, William Lockwood, Ruth Anderson, and Rena Gropper), and a lawyer representing Romani interests (Barry

Fischer). See Agenda for "Gypsy Leaders and Scholars," May 5, 1986, and handwritten note "5 May 86 Meeting w Gypsie reps," USHMM IA 2000.102, folder "Gypsies Exhibits/Projects."

29. Memo to Mark Talisman, May 6, 1986, USHMM IA 1997–014, folder 2.

30. Krista Hegburg, "'The Law Is Such as It Is': Reparations, 'Historical Reality,' and the Legal Order in the Czech Republic," in *Hidden Genocides: Power, Knowledge, Memory*, ed. Alexander Laban Hinton, Thomas LaPointe and Douglas Irvin-Erickson (New Brunswick, NJ: Rutgers University Press, 2013), 197. United States Holocaust Memorial Council, *Day of Remembrance: In Memory of the Gypsy Victims of Nazi Genocide: September 16, 1986* [sponsored by the USHMC in Association with the American Rom Community] (Washington DC: USHMC, 1986), 4–5, 11–13.

31. Programming Request for "Fate of the Gypsies during the Holocaust," 1987, USHMM IA 2000.102, box 15.

32. Linenthal, *Preserving Memory*, 245–46. James Marks had also written to submit himself as a candidate for the USHMC. Marks to Ronald Reagan, December 19, 1985, Bishopsgate Institute, Puxon/169.

33. "President Obama Announces More Key Administration Posts," White House Press Release, January 11, 2016, https://obamawhitehouse.archives.gov/the-press-office/2016/01/11/president-obama-announces-more-key-administration-posts?fbclid=IwAR1f-rO30zR-gvkzE1FBVASSM3duKlyeW2FgQ9MOEmApftvFv8KKcDToYLI.

34. See, for example, Ian Hancock, "Responses to the *Porrajmos* (The Romani Holocaust)," in *Is the Holocaust Unique?: Perspectives on Comparative Genocide*, ed. Alan S. Rosenbaum (Boulder, CO: Westview Press, 1995), 39–64.

35. See Nicolas J. Duquette, "Founders' Fortunes and Philanthropy: A History of the U.S. Charitable-Contribution Deduction," *Business History Review* 93, no. 3 (2019): 553–84.

36. See Lila Corwin Berman, "How Americans Give: The Financialization of American Jewish Philanthropy," *American Historical Review* 122, no. 5 (December 2017): 1459–89. The reliance on these dedicated funds also resonated with the Reagan administration's promotion of small government that persisted well into the 1990s. Lila Corwin Berman, *The American Jewish Philanthropic Complex: The History of a Multibillion-Dollar Institution* (Princeton, NJ: Princeton University Press, 2020), 139–63.

37. "An Act to Establish the United States Holocaust Memorial Council," Public Law 96–388, 96th Congress, H.R. 8081 (October 7, 1980), www.ushmm.org/information/about-the-museum/council/act-establishing-united-states-holocaust-memorial-council.

38. Katrin Pieper, *Die Musealisierung des Holocaust: Das Jüdische Museum Berlin und das U.S. Holocaust Memorial Museum in Washington D.C.: Ein Vergleich* (Cologne: Böhlau, 2006), 111.

39. Hancock to Tuttle, Office of Presidential Personnel, March 26, 1986, VWI.SWA.I.1, folder "Sinti und Roma 11."

40. Memorandum from Marcia Feldman (Director of Communications) to Sigmund Strochlitz, February 24, 1986, USHMM IA 1997–014, box 77, folder "Gypsies."

41. See also, Memorandum of Jonathan Bush to Micah H. Naftalin, April 9, 1984, Re: Status of P.R. Siege by Gypsy Groups, USHMM IA 1997–014, folder "Gypsies," which suggests a "fundraising . . . role" for "gypsy groups."

42. Exhibition Story Outline, Presented to the Content Committee, USHMM, May 11, 1988, USHMM IA 1997.017, box 4, folder 9.

43. Exhibition Story Outline: Presented to the Content Committee, May 11, 1988, USHMM IA 1997–017, box 4, folder 9, 3. The outline did not include any references to Roma. The only non-Jewish victims given any prominence are disabled people; see Exhibition Story Outline, 7.

44. See correspondence in USHMM IA 1998–011, folder "Roma (Gypsies)."

45. The President's Commission on the Holocaust, *Report to the President*, September 27, 1979, 10, www.ushmm.org/m/pdfs/20050707-pres-commission-79.pdf.

46. Minutes, Academic Committee Planning Group, May 2, 1989, USHMM IA 1997–016, box 1, folder 1.

47. Minutes, Informal meeting of the Academic Committee, June 22, 1989, USHMM IA 1997–016, box 1, folder 1. Gottschalk had invited member of the Academic Committee to Cincinnati from June 19 to June 26 for an informal meeting that would lead to the founding of a National Holocaust Research Center, but it seems from the minutes that other things were more urgent. Gottschalk to Academic Committee, May 18, 1989, USHMM IA 1997–016, box 1, folder 10.

48. Museum staff referred to these as records of the Extraordinary Investigation Commissions. "Types of Records to be Microfilmed in the Soviet Union," presented at Academic Committee meeting of June 22, 1989, USHMM IA 1997–016, box 1, folder 1. Committee members had a similar emphasis, see Informal Meeting of Academic Committee Members Regarding Archive Work in the USSR, February 1, 1990, USHMM IA 1997–016, box 1, folder 10.

49. Minutes, Academic Committee Meeting, October 5, 1993, USHMM IA 1997–106, box 1, folder 2.

50. Gottschalk wanted the museum to protest German policies of paying Romanian Roma who had come to Germany to return to Romania. See Academic Committee, Minutes, November 10, 1992, USHMM IA 1997–016, box 1, folder 16. Hilberg spoke of the persecution of Roma in rousing terms during a lecture for the USHMM on Sep. 21, 2000, www.ushmm.org/research/center/symposia/symposium/2000-09-21. He said, "If we want to build a world in which there is justice for all, where do we start? The answer is: The Roma."

51. Minutes, Academic Committee Meeting, July 8, 1991, USHMM IA 1997–016, box 1, folder 10, 2.

52. "Museum Announces Jack, Joseph and Morton Mandel Center for Advanced Holocaust Studies—United States Holocaust Memorial Museum," USHMM Press Release, March 12, 2014, accessed November 12, 2020, www.ushmm.org/information/press/press-releases/museum-announces-mandel-center. The first public ad mentioning the Center for Advanced Holocaust Studies appeared in 1997; see *New York Times*, September 7, 1997, E9.

53. That first scholar was Christopher Browning (with a historian of fascism and a historian of science and Nazi medicine as backup candidates), preselected by the professional staff of the institute and then approved by the committee. Staff Recommendations for first J. B. and Maurice Shapiro Senior Scholar in Residence, June 9, 1993, and Minutes of Academic Committee, June 11, 1993, USHMM IA 1997–016, box 1, folder 13.

54. While some of the infrastructure came from federally appropriated funds, committee members determined early on that certain programs would be able to proceed with greater ease based on private monies since federal appropriations for new purposes required congressional approval. See Academic Committee Meeting, December 4, 1995, USHMM IA 1997–016, box 1, folder 17.

55. See, for example, Informal Meeting of Academic Committee Members, Regarding Archive Work in the USSR, February 12, 1990, USHMM IA 1997–016, box 1, folder 10; Academic

Committee, June 11, 1993, USHMM IA 1997–016, box 1, folder 13. Milton had publicly positioned herself as a defender of Romani claims for inclusion in the larger history of the Holocaust and had written her response to Yehuda Bauer on official USHMM paper: USHMM IA 2000.102, box 15, folder "Gypsies Exhibits/projects and related correspondence."

56. Milton to Isabel Fonseca, June 15, 1995, USHMM IA 2000.102, box 15, folder "Gypsies Exhibits/projects and related correspondence."

57. Selected records from various archives of Romania concerning Roma, USHMM, RG-25.050M. These copies, incorporated into the archive in 2008, were made possible through funding from the Conference on Jewish Material Claims Against Germany.

58. The sociologist and former fellow Michelle Kelso donated some of her own interviews to the museum; see USHMM, RG-50.421.

59. See Erika Schlager, "Policy and Practice: A Case Study of U.S. Foreign Policy Regarding the Situation of Roma in Europe," in *Realizing Roma Rights*, ed. Jacqueline Bhabha, Andrzej Mirga, and Margareta Matache (Philadelphia: University of Pennsylvania Press, 2017), 59–75.

60. USHMM IA 2007.084, folder 44.

61. Miles Lerman, USHMC, to Janusz Ziolkowski and Jacek Starosciak, February 26, 1992, USHMM IA 2007.084, folder 44.

62. On the resolution, see Miles Lerman to Office of the President of Poland, Minister Andrzej Zakrzewski, Warsaw, May 30, 1992, USHMM IA 2007.084, folder 44.

63. Memorandum, "Points of Argument for your conversation with Wojciechowski" and Jeshajahu Weinberg to Grażyna Pawlak, March 31, 1992, USHMM IA, 2007.084, folder 44.

64. Jeffrey Shandler, *Holocaust Memory in the Digital Age: Survivors' Stories and New Media Practices* (Stanford, CA: Stanford University Press, 2017), 38–39.

65. Noah Shenker, *Reframing Holocaust Testimony* (Bloomington: Indiana University Press, 2015), 20–21; Eli N. Evans, *Striving to Make a Difference: The First Twenty Years*, President's Report (New York: Charles H. Revson Foundation, [1998]), https://revsonfoundation.org/files/2014/10/the_first_twenty_years_1978-1998.pdf.

66. Indeed, the Fortunoff Archive had a difficult relationship with the USHMM as a younger but more powerful archive that hoped to become a central depository for testimonies. On failed attempts to cooperate in the 1980s, see Jan Taubitz, *Holocaust Oral History und das lange Ende der Zeitzeugenschaft* (Göttingen: Wallstein Verlag, 2016), 103–5.

67. Gabrielle Tyrnauer, "Recording the Testimonies of Sinti Holocaust Survivors," in *Reflections on the Holocaust: Festschrift for Raul Hilberg on His Seventy-Fifth Birthday*, ed. Wolfgang Mieder and David Scrase (Burlington, VT: Center for Holocaust Studies at the University of Vermont, 2001), 223–37.

68. For an analysis of these testimonies, see Ari Joskowicz, "The Age of the Witness and the Age of Surveillance: Romani Holocaust Testimony and the Perils of Digital Scholarship," *American Historical Review* 125, no. 4 (October 2020): 1205–31.

69. See Shenker, *Reframing Holocaust Testimony*, 112–13. On the standardization of protocols for the collection, indexing, and inventorying of Shoah Foundation testimony, see Shandler, *Holocaust Memory*, 11–12.

70. This is true also for one of the main archives of material on Romani culture, history, and politics, which Ian Hancock founded at the University of Texas, Austin, where it remained until

2018. On the archive, see Mariana Sabino Salazar, "The Romani Archives and Documentation Center: A Migratory Archive?," *Critical Romani Studies* 3, no. 2 (2020): 104–11.

71. Romani Rose, "Vorwort an die Sinti," in *Sinti und Roma im ehemaligen KZ Bergen-Belsen am 27. Oktober 1979: Erste deutsche und europäische Gedenkkundgebung "In Auschwitz vergast, bis heute verfolgt": Eine Dokumentation der Gesellschaft für bedrohte Völker und des Verbands deutscher Sinti*, by Gesellschaft für bedrohte Völker and Verband deutscher Sinti, Reihe pogrom 76 (Göttingen: Die Gesellschaft, 1980), 15–18.

72. As the historian Charles Maier has argued, those who give priority to the narrative of the Holocaust (and, in his view, the Gulag) "have emerged with a profound distrust of transformative politics." The slogan "never again" implies that states could backslide into past atrocities but also that we are currently in a place where we have overcome the worst. Those who emphasize an "imperialist or neo-colonial narrative" of modern violence, by contrast, emphasize the need for fundamental change based on strong regulation, in Maier's account. Romani memory fits the latter pattern more than the former. Charles S. Maier, "Consigning the Twentieth Century to History: Alternative Narratives for the Modern Era," *American Historical Review* 105, no. 3 (2000): 807–31.

73. The rise in interest in Holocaust themes also facilitated greater foreign attention to the event. See, for example, "The Nazis' Forgotten Victims: Angry Gypsies are Pressing to Settle Old Scores," *Time*, November 19, 1979, 58.

74. Heinz Galinski, "Dieses Gedenken sei uns Mahnung zum Handeln," in *Sinti und Roma im ehemaligen KZ Bergen-Belsen*, 77–80. Like the Israeli ambassador 25 years later, Galinski had to excuse himself because the event happened on Shabbat and had his speech read for him instead.

75. Simone Veil, "Meine Anwesenheit bezeugt meine Solidarität gegenüber den Zigeunern," *Sinti und Roma im ehemaligen KZ Bergen-Belsen*, 50.

76. Ian Hancock invoked this image of mingled ashes also in his writings, see Ian Hancock, *The Pariah Syndrome: An Account of Gypsy Slavery and Persecution* (Ann Arbor: Karoma Publishers, 1987), 87. The Jewish-Romani Alliance, a small association founded in 1991 by Ian Hancock and Toby Sonneman, used a similar motto in its newsletter: "We died together" in English and Romani. On the organization, see "Romani-Jewish Alliance, 1991–1995," box 3, folder 19, Jewish Counter Culture Collection, I-504, American Jewish Historical Society.

77. Veil remained a dedicated friend of the Romani cause. Like Wiesenthal she used her stature and her experiences to intervene on behalf of Roma threatened with deportation. See Nicolas Sarkozy to Simone Veil, Paris, November 12, 2010, AN 688AP/361, Fonds Simone Veil, Roms d'Europe. See also the projects she hoped to see realized on the Romani genocide in "Historique Simone Veil et les Roms et projets futurs," AN 688AP/361.

78. Ernst Tugendhat, "Vorwort, " in *In Auschwitz vergast, bis heute verfolgt: Zur Situation der Roma (Zigeuner) in Deutschland und Europa*, ed. Tilman Zülch, Rororo aktuell (Reinbek, Germany: Rowohlt, 1979), 9–11.

79. Ibid., 10.

80. On the growth of the global movement for human rights in the 1970s, see Aryeh Neier, *The International Human Rights Movement: A History*, Human Rights and Crimes against Humanity (Princeton, NJ: Princeton University Press, 2012). In Germany, some of the theorists of human rights found its dehistoricized and abstract language a useful tool to articulate

the demands of German expellees from Eastern Europe. See Lora Wildenthal, *The Language of Human Rights in West Germany* (Philadelphia: University of Pennsylvania Press, 2013), 101–31.

81. Daniela Gress, "Geburtshelfer einer Bewegung? Die mediale Kampagne der Gesellschaft für bedrohte Völker für Bürgerrechte deutscher Sinti und Roma," in *Menschenrecht als Nachricht Medien, Öffentlichkeit und Moral seit dem 19. Jahrhundert*, ed. Birgit Hofmann (Frankfurt am Main: Campus Verlag, 2020), 288. US dollar equivalency is rounded down from values for 2019–22, based on the purchase parity chart of the German Bundesbank, "Kaufkraftäquivalente historischer Beträge in deutschen Währungen," https://bundesbank.de/resource/blob/615162 /3334800ed9b5dcc976da0e65034c4666/mL/kaufkraftaequivalente-historischer-betraege-in -deutschen-waehrungen-data.pdf.

82. Daniela Gress, "Memorandum des Verbandes Deutscher Sinti und der Romani-Union (1979)," *Quellen zur Geschichte der Menschenrechte*, ed. Arbeitskreis Menschenrechte im 20. Jahrhundert, September 2018, https://www.geschichte-menschenrechte.de/schluesseltexte /memorandum-verband-sinti-roma.

83. Gress, "Geburtshelfer einer Bewegung?," 288.

84. Sebastian Lotto-Kusche, "Spannungsfelder im Vorfeld der Anerkennung des Völkermords an den Sinti und Roma: Das Gespräch zwischen dem Zentralrat Deutscher Sinti und Roma und der Bundesregierung am 17. März 1982," in *Stigmatisierung, Marginalisierung, Verfolgung: Beiträge des 19. Workshops zur Geschichte und Gedächtnisgeschichte der nationalsozialistischen Konzentrationslager*, ed. Marco Brenneisen et al. (Berlin: Metropol, 2015), 224–44; Romani Rose, *Bürgerrechte für Sinti und Roma: Das Buch zum Rassismus in Deutschland* (Heidelberg: Zentralrat Deutscher Sinti und Roma, 1987), 99–102.

85. For a critique of Zülch's approach to Nazism, see Gilad Margalit, *Germany and Its Gypsies: A Post-Auschwitz Ordeal* (Madison: University of Wisconsin Press, 2002), 181–85.

86. See Quinn Slobodian, *Foreign Front: Third World Politics in Sixties West Germany*, Radical Perspectives (Durham, NC: Duke University Press, 2012).

87. Lasse Heerten, *The Biafran War and Postcolonial Humanitarianism: Spectacles of Suffering*, Human Rights in History (Cambridge: Cambridge University Press, 2017), 178, 184–85.

88. Ibid., 181. The emphasis on Jews was in part a result of the interaction between the New Left and foreign activists. On these interactions, see Christoph Kalter, *The Discovery of the Third World: Decolonization and the Rise of the New Left in France, c.1950–1976* (Cambridge: Cambridge University Press, 2016) and Slobodian, *Foreign Front.*

89. Lasse Heerten, "'A' As in Auschwitz, 'B' as in Biafra: The Nigerian Civil War, Visual Narratives of Genocide, and the Fragmented Universalization of the Holocaust," in *Humanitarian Photography: A History*, ed. Heide Fehrenbach and Davide Rodogno, Human Rights in History (Cambridge: Cambridge University Press, 2015), 249–74.

90. Amos Goldberg, "Ethics, Identity and Anti-Fundamental Fundamentalism: Holocaust Memory in the Global Age (a Cultural-Political Introduction)," in *Marking Evil: Holocaust Memory in the Global Age*, ed. Amos Goldberg and Haim Hazan (New York: Berghahn Books, 2015), 14. Hannah Arendt's *Origins of Totalitarianism* (1950) and W.E.B. Du Bois' short 1952 essay on the Warsaw Ghetto are among the best-known works in this category. Michael Rothberg, "W.E.B. DuBois in Warsaw: Holocaust Memory and the Color Line, 1949–1952," *Yale Journal of Criticism* 14, no. 1 (April 2001): 169–89.

91. Michael Rothberg, *Multidirectional Memory: Remembering the Holocaust in the Age of Decolonization*, Cultural Memory in the Present (Stanford, CA: Stanford University Press, 2009).

92. Israel was, for example, unwelcome at the Bandung Conference of nonaligned nations in 1955, the first large conference to present an Afro-Asian alliance against colonialism.

93. For a fascinating case study in the failure of outreach beyond these divisions, see Zach Levey, "The Rise and Decline of a Special Relationship: Israel and Ghana, 1957–1966," *African Studies Review* 46, no. 1 (2003): 155–77. Israel had identified with nonalignment and thus also had some affinity with other non-European nonaligned states in its early years. See, for example, Rotem Giladi, "Negotiating Identity: Israel, Apartheid, and the United Nations, 1949–1952," *The English Historical Review* 132, no. 559 (December 2017): 1440–72. For the debate within Jewish studies, see Derek Penslar's essay "Is Zionism a Colonial Movement?" and responses by Joshua Cole and Elisabeth F. Thompson in *Colonialism and the Jews*, ed. Ethan Katz, Lisa Moses Leff, and Maud Mandel (Bloomington: Indiana University Press, 2017), 275–340. On the counterimage of Israel as the result of an anticolonial struggle, see for example, Amy Kaplan, "Zionism as Anticolonialism: The Case of 'Exodus,'" *American Literary History* 25, no. 4 (2013): 870–95.

94. Incidentally, some states took a similar approach. In France, the office for social programs for migrants was in charge of so-called nomads and French Muslims from 1974 to 1975. See AN, 19870256/7 on department PSM3 within the Directorate for Population and Migration Affairs (Direction de la population et des migrations) in the Ministry of Social Affairs. The same scholar, the ethnologist Jean Servier, also submitted reports on both populations in the early 1970s.

95. Peter Vermeersch, *The Romani Movement: Minority Politics and Ethnic Mobilization in Contemporary Central Europe* (New York: Berghahn Books, 2006), 150–67.

96. Celia Donert, *The Rights of the Roma: The Struggle for Citizenship in Postwar Czechoslovakia* (Cambridge: Cambridge University Press, 2017), 236; Thomas Acton et al., "Pedagogies of Hope: The Gypsy Council and the National Gypsy Education Council," in *Hearing the Voice of the Gypsy, Roma and Traveller Communities: Inclusive Community Development*, ed. Andrew Ryder, Sarah Cemlyn, and Thomas Acton (Bristol, UK: Policy Press, 2014), 36. Due to the dissent of one committee member and the indifference of most others, the committee voted to strike that sentence. On the discussion, see Ilona Klímová-Alexander, *The Romani Voice in World Politics: The United Nations and Non-State Actors* (Aldershot, UK: Ashgate Publishing, 2005), 40–42.

97. On this larger relationship, see also Nidhi Trehan, "The Contentious Politics of the Indo-Romani Relationship: Reflections on the 'International Roma Conference and Cultural Festival' in New Delhi, February 2016 and Its Antecedents," *Indian Journal of Social Work* 78, no. 1 (January 2017): 11–26. On the flag, see Trehan, "The Contentious Politics," 12.

98. Acton, *Gypsy Politics*, 234.

99. There was nevertheless some cross-fertilization. US Jews took cues from the identity language of the Black Power movement: indeed, NBC *Holocaust* was designed to follow the success formula of ABC's *Roots* two years earlier. On these connections, see Marc Dollinger, *Black Power, Jewish Politics: Reinventing the Alliance in the 1960s*, Brandeis Series in American Jewish History, Culture, and Life (Waltham, MA: Brandeis University Press, 2018). On the transatlantic influences of the Black Civil Rights Movement in the US and German student

movements, see Martin Klimke, *The Other Alliance: Student Protest in West Germany and the United States in the Global Sixties*, America in the World (Princeton, NJ: Princeton University Press, 2010). On Israel and the influence of Black Panther politics and symbolism in Middle East politics, see, among others: Bryan Roby, *The Mizrahi Era of Rebellion: Israel's Forgotten Civil Rights Struggle 1948–1966* (Syracuse, NY: Syracuse University Press, 2015); Amir Goldstein, "Partial Establishment—Menachem Begin, Gahal and the Black Panthers," *Journal of Modern Jewish Studies* 17, no. 2 (2018): 236–51; Michael R. Fischbach, *Black Power and Palestine: Trans-national Countries of Color* (Stanford, CA: Stanford University Press, 2019); Nico Slate, *Black Power beyond Borders: The Global Dimensions of the Black Power Movement*, Contemporary Black History (New York: Palgrave Macmillan, 2012). For an attempt to think about Jewish and Palestinian histories of suffering together, see Bashir Bashir and Amos Goldberg, eds., *The Holocaust and the Nakba: A New Grammar of Trauma and History* (New York: Columbia University Press, 2018).

100. See, for example, Michael R. Fischbach, *The Movement and the Middle East: How the Arab-Israeli Conflict Divided the American Left* (Redwood City, CA: Stanford University Press, 2019); Paul Kelemen, *The British Left and Zionism: History of a Divorce* (Manchester, UK: Manchester University Press, 2018).

101. Kelemen, *The British Left and Zionism*, 177–180.

102. On the history of the organization and Jewish-Muslim relations, see Maud Mandel, *Muslims and Jews in France: History of a Conflict* (Princeton, NJ: Princeton University Press, 2014), 125–52; Ethan Katz, *The Burdens of Brotherhood: Jews and Muslims from North Africa to France* (Cambridge, MA: Harvard University Press, 2015), 302–7. For a take on the long-standing fissures that facilitated that break, see Johannes Heuman, "The Challenge of Minority Nationalism: Antiracism and Zionism in Postwar France," *French Historical Studies* 43, no. 3 (2020): 483–509. Eric Ghébali, an Algerian Jew and president of UEJF, became the new umbrella organization's secretary-general. Mandel, *Muslims and Jews*, 132. One of the original initiators, the former Trotskyite activist Julien Drey also descended from a Jewish family from the Algerian city of Oran.

103. Mandel, *Muslims and Jews*, 126.

104. See Peter Ullrich, *Die Linke, Israel und Palästina: Nahostdiskurse in Großbritannien und Deutschland* (Berlin: Dietz, 2008); Kelemen, *The British Left and Zionism*. On the history of British opposition to Zionism, see David Cesarani, "Anti-Zionism in Britain, 1922–2002: Continuities and Discontinuities," *The Journal of Israeli History* 25, no. 1 (2006): 131–60. Among the vast literature on criticism of Israel and antisemitism within the Left, see Christina Späti, *Die schweizerische Linke und Israel: Israelbegeisterung, Antizionismus und Antisemitismus zwischen 1967 und 1991* (Essen, Germany: Klartext, 2006); Margit Reiter, *Unter Antisemitismus-Verdacht: Die österreichische Linke und Israel nach der Shoah* (Innsbruck, Austria: Studien Verlag, 2001).

105. Dariusz Stola, "Anti-Zionism as a Multipurpose Policy Instrument: The Anti-Zionist Campaign in Poland, 1967–1968," *Journal of Israeli History* 25, no. 1 (2006): 175–201; Anat Plocker, *The Expulsion of Jews from Communist Poland: Memory Wars and Homeland Anxieties* (Bloomington: Indiana University Press, 2022).

106. See Donert, *The Rights of the Roma*, 198–99.

107. See, among others, Ljiljana Radonić, "From 'Double Genocide' to 'the New Jews': Holocaust, Genocide and Mass Violence in Post-Communist Memorial Museums," *Journal of*

Genocide Research 20, no. 4 (October 2018): 510–29; Jelena Subotić, *Yellow Star, Red Star: Holocaust Remembrance after Communism*, Cornell Scholarship Online (Ithaca, NY: Cornell University Press, 2019); John-Paul Himka and Joanna B. Michlic, eds., *Bringing the Dark Past to Light: The Reception of the Holocaust in Postcommunist Europe* (Lincoln: University of Nebraska Press, 2013). For the complicated consequences for the depiction of the Romani genocide in new museums created under pressure to meet European standards, see Ljiljana Radonić, "'People of Freedom and Unlimited Movement': Representations of Roma in Post-Communist Memorial Museums," *Social Inclusion* 3, no. 5 (September 2015): 64–77.

108. See, for example, the phenomenon of "virtual Jewish culture." Ruth Ellen Gruber, *Virtually Jewish: Reinventing Jewish Culture in Europe* (Berkeley: University of California Press, 2002).

109. Ronald Grigor Suny, "The Empire That Dared Not Speak Its Name: Making Nations in the Soviet State," *Current History* 116, no. 792 (2017): 251–57; James Mark and Péter Apor, "Socialism Goes Global: Decolonization and the Making of a New Culture of Internationalism in Socialist Hungary, 1956–1989," *Journal of Modern History* 87, no. 4 (2015): 852–91.

110. For a recent attempt to tie together the US civil rights movement and Romani rights, see Felix B. Chang and Sunnie T. Rucker-Chang, *Roma Rights and Civil Rights: A Transatlantic Comparison* (Cambridge: Cambridge University Press, 2020).

111. "About TernYpe," ternYpe International RomaYouth Network, accessed June 5, 2022, www.romayouth.com/about-ternype. On the centrality of these events, see Karolina Mirga and Jonathan Mack, "From Holocaust Remembrance to Youth Empowerment," in *Education for Remembrance of the Roma Genocide: Scholarship, Commemoration and the Role of Youth*, ed. Anna Mirga-Kruszelnicka, Esteban Acuña, and Piotr Trojanski (Kraków: Wydawnictwo Libron, Filip Lohner, 2015), 203–16.

112. For a critical analysis of tourism to sites connected to the Holocaust, including Auschwitz, see Daniel P. Reynolds, *Postcards from Auschwitz: Holocaust Tourism and the Meaning of Remembrance* (New York: New York University Press, 2018). This phenomenon is distinct from the commodification of Jewish and Romani culture in destinations that promote their traces, absence, or romanticized presence. See Monica Rüthers, *Juden und Zigeuner im europäischen Geschichtstheater: "Jewish Spaces", "Gypsy Spaces": Kazimierz und Saintes-Maries-de-la-Mer in der neuen Folklore Europas* (Bielefeld, Germany: Transcript, 2012); Melanie Smith and Anita Zatori, "The Political and Social Transformation of Roma and Jewish Communities through Tourism in Budapest," in *Transformational Tourism: Host Perspectives*, ed. Yvette Reisinger (Wallingford, UK: CAB International, 2015), 69–79.

113. Cited in Nadine Blumer, "Disentangling the Hierarchy of Victimhood: Commemorating Sinti and Roma and Jews in Germany's National Narrative," in *The Nazi Genocide of the Roma: Reassessment and Commemoration*, ed. Anton Weiss-Wendt (New York: Berghahn, 2013), 211.

114. On the history of the monument and the unexpected outcome of these efforts, see Nadine Blumer, "From Victim Hierarchies to Memorial Networks: Berlin's Holocaust Memorial to Sinti and Roma Victims of National Socialism" (PhD diss., University of Toronto, 2011) and Blumer, "Disentangling the Hierarchy."

115. "Terezín Initiative in Czech Republic does not want Romani names included in Shoah commemoration, director of its Institute disagrees," *Romea*, April 3, 2021, www.romea.cz/en /news/czech/terezin-initiative-in-czech-republic-does-not-want-romani-names-included-in -shoah-commemoration-director-of-its-institute. See also Renata Berkyová and Kateřina

Čapková, "Prague Forum for Romani Histories on the debate around reading the names of Romani victims," *Prague Forum on Romani Histories*, April 3, 2021, www.romanihistories.usd.cas .cz/forum-events/prague-forum-for-romani-histories-on-the-debate-around-reading-the -names-of-romani-victims/.

116. Guenter Lewy, *The Nazi Persecution of the Gypsies* (Oxford: Oxford University Press, 2000).

117. For a contrast between SOS Racisme and its more radical counterparts, see Thomas Martin, "Anti-Racism, Republicanism and the Sarkozy Years: SOS Racisme and the Mouvement des Indigènes de la république," in *France's Colonial Legacies: Memory, Identity and Narrative*, ed. Fiona Barclay (Cardiff, UK: University of Wales Press, 2013), 188–206.

118. Union des étudiants juifs de France, *Le Sionisme expliqué à nos potes* (Paris: La Martinière, 2003).

119. Complicating the history of FNASAT is its emergence from the intergovernmental committee whose key members used the power of the state to quash attempts at Romani self-organization in the 1960s.

120. "Ils offrent des poules, les poulets les embarquent," *L'Obs*, accessed May 5, 2021, www .nouvelobs.com/rue89/rue89-nos-vies-connectees/20100730.RUE7791/ils-offrent-des -poules-les-poulets-les-embarquent.html; "Roms: manifestation devant Beauvau, " *Le Figaro*, July 29, 2010.

121. "L'UEJF, avec SOS Racisme, la FNASAT (Fédération nationale d'associations de Tsiganes) et l'UFAT (Union française des Associations Tziganes) viennent 'rendre les poules,'" UEJF Press Release, August 28, 2010, https://uejf.org/2010/08/28/luejf-avec-sos-racisme-la-fnasat -federation-nationale-dassociations-de-tsiganes-et-lufat-union-francaise-des-associations -tziganes-viennent-rendre-les-poules/.

122. See *Pologne aller Retour*, directed by Anna Pitoun (Paris: Caravane Films, 2012), DVD. The film is not just celebratory but shows various conflicts among the participants about who should tell the Romani story.

123. See Michael Stewart, ed., *The Gypsy "Menace": Populism and the New Anti-Gypsy Politics* (London: Hurst & Co., 2012).

124. Author's interview with Rudolf Sarközi, July 10, 2012.

125. Similar funding sources also create similar pressures. On the role of philanthropies, in particular the Open Society Foundation, in encouraging an ethnic approach to Romani politics, see Douglas Neander Sambati, "Western Donors, Romani Organizations, and Uses of the Concept of Nation after 1989," *Critical Romani Studies* 3, no. 1 (December 2020): 26–45.

126. Author's interview with Sacha Reingewirtz, July 12, 2011.

127. In 2011, Reingewirtz and others were particularly concerned with the rhetoric of comedian Dieudonné M'bala M'bala who spent the previous decade invoking his postcolonial identity to promote Holocaust deniers and to make antisemitic jokes under the guise of antiracist satire. For an analysis and expression of that concern, see Michelle Mazel, "French Jewry and the Dieudonné Affair," *Jewish Political Studies Review* 26, no. 1/2 (2014): 70–78.

128. See Union des étudiants juifs de France, *Rwanda: Pour un dialogue des mémoires* (Paris: Albin Michel, 2007).

129. "Homepage," Europe of Diasporas, accessed May 15, 2021, http://www.europeofdiasporas .eu/, now defunct.

130. Open letter of EUJS and Phiren Amenca to President van der Leyen, President of the European Commission et al., announced August 6, 2020, https://drive.google.com/file/d/1Z qPu4sE2FZROEO3eSb2tQs5lAmIK2hl_/view.

131. "TernYpe—International Roma Youth Network," Facebook, https://facebook.com /www.ternype.eu/posts/3611319815553175.

132. "JSUD—Jüdische Studierendenunion Deutschland," Facebook, https://facebook.com /JSUDeutschland/posts/1902137053272875.

133. The inability of non-Romani activists to reflect on tacit prejudices and unequal resources is a broader problem in Romani NGO work. See Anna Daróczi, Kinga Kánya, Szilvia Rézműves, and Violeta Vajda, "Roma and Non-Roma Alliances for Political Empowerment: Experiences from Hungary," in *Dimensions of Antigypsyism in Europe*, ed. Ismael Cortés Gómez and Markus End (Brussels and Heidelberg: European Network Against Racism and Central Council of German Sinti and Roma, 2019), 333–52.

Conclusion: Stages of a Relationship

1. Some new Romani institutions fulfill part of the function of these institutions. One is the European Roma Institute for Arts and Culture (ERIAC), which also promotes awareness of Romani history. See "About ERIAC," ERIAC, https://eriac.org/about-eriac/. The second is RomArchive, a digital archive for Romani arts and cultures. RomArchive collects digital primary source material related to Romani history and has well-researched sections dealing, among other themes, with the "Roma Civil Rights Movement" and "Voices of the Victims." See "Curated Sections," RomArchive, https://www.romarchive.eu/en/sections/.

BIBLIOGRAPHY

Archives

American Jewish Archives, Cincinnati, OH
  MS-60: Raphael Lemkin Papers, 1942–1959
  MS-603: Rabbi Marc H. Tanenbaum Collection, 1945–1992
  MS-712: USHMM Committee Collection of Alfred Gottschalk, 1978–2000
  WJC C14–16: Institute of Jewish Affairs, Correspondence
American Jewish Historical Society, New York
  P-154: Raphael Lemkin Collection
  I-504: Jewish Counter Culture Collection
Archives Nationales, Paris
  19870256: Direction de la population et des migrations
  688AP: Fonds Simone Veil
  AJ43: Archive of the International Refugee Organization
Bayerisches Hauptstaatsarchiv, Munich
  Minn 92098: Bayerisches Staatsminiserium des Innern, Vereine
  MJu 23672: Ermittlungsverfahren Christian Blüm
  RG 260: OMGBY Office of the Military government, Bavaria, Microfiche
  StK 14739: Staatskanzlei, Arbeitsrecht
  Staatskommissar für rassisch, religiös und politisch Verfolgte (Auerbach)
Bishopsgate Institute, London
  Grattan Puxon Archive
Bundesarchiv, Koblenz, Germany
  B122/15538: Präsident Heinemann, Gespräche zu Situation der "Zigeuner"
  B189/3742: Lage der Zigeuner in der Bundesrepublik, 1961–1972
Bundesarchiv, Ludwigsburg, Germany
  B162/3231: Einzeltötungen von Sinti und Roma in dem vom Selbstschutz im Jahre
    1940 eingerichteten Arbeitslager Belzec / Distrikt Lublin
  B162/7348–7351: Tötung von Sinti und Roma in Hamburg in der Zeit von 1940 bis
    1945 durch Angehörige der dortigen Kriminalpolizeileitstelle
  B162/7919: Dienststelle des Reichskommissariats Ostland—Vernichtung von Sinti
    und Roma
  B162/26043: Ermittlungen StA Würzburg gegen Ch. Blüm

B162/28141: Ermittlungen StA Hamburg gegen G. Junge wegen der Beteiligung an der Deportation von etwa 1500 Sinti und Roma am 16.5.1940 von Hamburg nach Belzec

CegeSoma, formerly CEGES, Brussels

    AA 2112: Onderzoeksarchief vervolging van zigeuners

    AA1587/PC32: Dossier Estelle Goldstein

Central Archives for the History of the Jewish People, Jerusalem

    URO Frankfurt, Administrative Akten

Centre de documentation juive contemporaine/Mémorial de la Shoah, Paris

    CCXVI: Fédération des sociétés juives de France, Testimonies

    CCXXIV-CCXXV: Belgique, Ministère de la Reconstruction belge

David Boder Interviews, Voices of the Holocaust, https://voices.library.iit.edu

Directie-generaal Oorloogslachtoffers/ Direction générale Victimes de la Guerre (renamed Dienst Archief Oorlogsslachtoffers/Service Archives des Victimes de la Guerre), Brussels

    429/154.434: Landesentschaedigungsamt van Schleswig-Holstein, 1959

    429/J: Formulieren met vragenlijsten voor Joden die gedeporteerd waren geweest, 1951–1952

    2762: Rapport van Mevr Goldstein over de Jodendeportatie, c. 1953

Dokumentationsarchiv des österreichischen Widerstandes, Vienna

    19360: Steinmetz Collection on "Gypsies"

Fortunoff Visual History Archive, New Haven, CT

Fritz Bauer Institut, Frankfurt am Main

    FAP2 HA, 2: Frankfurter Auschwitz Prozess, Handakten Vernehmungsprotokolle Sinti und Roma (SuR)

Ghetto Fighters' House Archive, Kibbutz Lohamei HaGeta'ot, Israel

    5130reg: Trial against Ernst August König

    38956: Estate of Miriam Novitch: personal documents

    32078reg: History of Ghetto Fighters' House: European mission report, Miriam Novitch

    32079reg: History of Ghetto Fighters' House

    32305: Toldot, Collection of letters on Research on Gypsies

Leo-Baeck Institute, New York

    AR 7165: William G. Niederland Collection,

Hessisches Hauptstaatsarchiv Wiesbaden, Germany

    Fonds 461: Frankfurt-Auschwitz Prozess

Institut für Zeitgeschichte Munich

    MA-21: Behandlung der Zigeuner im Dritten Reich

ITS Digital Collection, Arolsen Archive, Bad Arolsen, Germany

Konrad Adenauer Stiftung, Archiv, Sankt Augustin, Germany

    Nachlass Franz Böhm

Landesarchiv Nordrhein-Westfalen, Duisburg, Germany

    Gerichte Rep. 118 and 158: Trial of Ernst August König

Médiathèque Matéo Maximoff, Le centre de ressources Fnasat-Gens du voyage/Études tsiganes, Paris

The National Archives, Kew, UK
    WO 309: Judge Advocate General's Office, British Army of the Rhine War Crimes
        Group
National Archives and Records Administration, College Park, MD
    RG 260: Box 70, OMGBY
NIOD Institute for War, Holocaust and Genocide Studies, Amsterdam
    263b: Zigeuners
    271d: Mannheimer, K. F.
    475: B. A Sijes Papers
Newberry Library, Chicago
    Alfred E. Hamill Papers, Series 3: Dora E. Yates
New York Public Library, Manuscripts and Archives Division
    Raphael Lemkin Papers
Österreichisches Staatsarchiv, Vienna
    AVA Nachlässe NZN E/1797: Hermann Langbein Papers
Parliamentary Archives, London
    SAM: Herbert Samuel Papers
Romani Archives and Documentation Center, University of Texas, Austin
Stadtarchiv München
    Polizeidirektion 828
    Polizeidirektion 830
UCLA Library Special Collections
    David P. Boder Collection
United States Holocaust Memorial Museum, Washington, DC
    Institutional Archive
    RG-15.079M: Underground archives of the Warsaw Ghetto
    RG-15.083M: The Elders of the Jews in the Łódź Ghetto
    RG-15.101M: Judenrat in Lublin
    RG-17.007M: Archive of the Jewish Community Vienna, Vienna Component
        Collection
    RG-17.037: KZ-Verband Wien
    RG-43.096M: Records from Departmental Archives Indre-et-Loire
    RG-50: Oral Histories
    RG-68.151M: Postwar testimonies and Jewish Social Mutual files
University of Liverpool, Special Collections and Archives
    DY: Dora Esther Yates Papers
    GLS: Gypsy Lore Society Archive
USC Shoah Foundation
    Visual History Archive
Vienna Wiesenthal Institute for Holocaust Studies
    Israelitische Kultusgemeinde Wien, Bestand Wien (loaned collection)
    VWI.SWA.I.1–5, Sinti und Roma
Wiener Library, London
    611: Material Relating to the Persecution of the Gypsies under the Nazis

1655: Nuremberg War Crimes Trial: Documents
3000/9: Correspondence of the Wiener Library
Eyewitness Accounts
Yad Vashem, Jerusalem
M.31: Righteous of the Nations Files
O.3: Testimonies
O.65: Jacob Robinson Collection
Yahad-in Unum, Paris
Video Collection

Interviews conducted by the author (selection)

Yehuda Bacon, July 31, 2018
Jane Braden-Golay, August 8, 2014
Emmerich Gärtner-Horvath, December 28, 2011
Petra Gelbart, May 1, 2013
Andi Gergely, August 10, 2014
Henry Greenbaum, June 2, 2017
Mozes Heintschink, July 2, 2011
Saniye Jasaroski, May 1, 2013
Dani Karavan, July 12, 2012
Isaac Nehama and Paulette Nehama, November 14, 2012
Rudolf Sarközi, July 9, 2012

Periodicals (selection)

*Die Vergessenen: Halbmonatsschrift für Wahrheit und Recht aller ehemaligen Konzentra-
tionäre und Naziopfer*
Der neue Mahnruf
Rechtsprechung zum Wiedergutmachungsrecht
Deutschland-Berichte der Sozialdemokratischen Partei Deutschlands (Sopade)
La Voix mondiale tzigane

Published Primary Sources

Works of historiography, sometimes discussed in this work as primary sources, are generally
listed under secondary literature.

"About TernYpe," ternYpe International RomaYouth Network, accessed June 5, 2022. www
.romayouth.com/about-ternype.
"An Act to Establish the United States Holocaust Memorial Council," Public Law 96–388,
96th Congress, H.R. 8081, October 7, 1980. www.ushmm.org/information/about-the
-museum/council/act-establishing-united-states-holocaust-memorial-council.
Adelsberger, Lucie. *Auschwitz: A Doctor's Story*. Boston: Northeastern University Press, 1995.

———. *Auschwitz, ein Tatsachenbericht: Das Vermächtnis der Opfer für uns Juden und für alle Menschen.* Berlin: Lettner-Verlag, 1956.

Adler, H. G., Hermann Langbein, and Ella Lingens, eds. *Auschwitz: Zeugnisse und Berichte.* Frankfurt am Main: Europäische Verlagsanstalt, 1962.

Auerbach, Philipp. "Zum Problem der Zigeuner." *Mitteilungsblatt des Landesausschusses der politisch Verfolgten in Bayern,* July 1, 1949.

Aumônerie Catholique des voyageurs tsiganes et gitans. *L'Église catholique et les gitans.* Romainville, France: Aumônerie nationale des gitans, 1969.

Beer, Hélène. *Salle 1.* Brussels: C. Dessart, 1946.

Behringer, Josef, and Adam Strauss, eds. *Flucht, Internierung, Deportation, Vernichtung: Hessische Sinti und Roma berichten über ihre Verfolgung während des Nationalsozialismus.* Seeheim, Germany: I-Verb, 2005.

Beregovski, M. *Yidishe folks-lider.* Kyiv: Melukhe-farlag far di natsyonale minderhaytn in U.S.S.R, 1938.

Bet ha-mishpat ha-mehozi and Misrad ha-mishpatim. *The Trial of Adolf Eichmann: Record of Proceedings in the District Court of Jerusalem.* 8 vols. Jerusalem: Trust for the Publication of the Proceedings of the Eichmann Trial, in cooperation with the Israel State Archives and Yad Vashem, the Holocaust Martyrs' and Heroes' Remembrance Authority, 1992.

Biletzky, Israel Ch. *Umru lider.* Tel Aviv: n.p., 1935.

Boder, David P. "A Metascope and Diploscope." *The American Journal of Psychology* 47, no. 4 (1935): 688–90.

———. "Some New Electronic Devices for the Psychological Laboratory." *The American Journal of Psychology* 45, no. 1 (1933): 145–47.

———. *Topical Autobiographies of Displaced People: Recorded Verbatim in Displaced Persons Camps with a Psychological and Anthropological Analysis.* 5 vols. Chicago: Boder, 1950.

———. *I Did Not Interview the Dead.* Urbana: The University of Illinois Press, 1949.

Boyer, Edward J. "Gypsies Remember Holocaust, Want Role on Memorial Council." *Los Angeles Times,* June 26, 1984, C1.

Buchheim, Hans. "Die SS in der Verfassung des Dritten Reiches." *Vierteljahrshefte für Zeitgeschichte* 3, no. 2 (1955): 127–57.

———. "Die Zigeunerdeportation vom Mai 1940." In *Das Entschädigungsrecht für die Opfer der national-sozialistischen Verfolgung: Teilausgabe des Handbuchs der Wiedergutmachung in Deutschland,* edited by Marcel Frenkel, 136–41. Koblenz, Germany: Humanitas, 1957.

Buchheim, Hans, Martin Broszat, Hans-Adolf Jacobsen, and Helmut Krausnick. *Anatomie des SS-Staates Gutachten des Instituts für Zeitschichte.* Olten, Switzerland: Walter, 1965.

Calvelli-Adorno, Franz. "Die Dokumentationsarbeit Der URO." *Rechtsprechung Zum Wiedergutmachungsrecht* 16 (1965): 198–99.

———. "Die rassische Verfolgung der Zigeuner vor dem 1. Marz 1943." *Rechtsprechung zum Wiedergutmachungsrecht,* no. 12 (1961): 529–37.

David, Henriette. "Hommage à Mme l'Huillier," *Etudes tsiganes* 21, no. 1 (March 1975): 60.

Döring, Hans-Joachim. "Die Motive der Zigeunerdeportation vom Mai 1940." *Vierteljahreshefte für Zeitgeschichte* 7, no. 4 (1959): 418–28.

———. *Die Zigeuner im nationalsozialistischen Staat.* Kriminologische Schriftenreihe 12. Hamburg: Kriminalistik Verlag, 1964.

Dubnov, Simon. *Velt-geshikhte fun Yidishn folk fun di eltste tsaytn biz tsu der hayntiker tsayt.* Vilnius: Yidisher visnshaftlekher institut, Historishe sektsye, 1938.

Ficowski, Jerzy. "The Polish Gypsies of To-Day." Translated by Józef Rotblat. *JGLS* 27, no. 3–4 (July–October 1950): 92–102.

Fischer, Bruno, and United Restitution Organization, eds. *Dokumente über die Verantwortlichkeit des Reiches für die Judenmaßnahmen im besetzten und unbesetzten Frankreich, insbesondere auch in Algerien, Marokko, Tunis.* Frankfurt am Main: URO, 1959.

Friedman, Philip. "The Extermination of the Gypsies: A Nazi Genocide Operation Against an Aryan People." *Jewish Frontier* 18, no. 1 (January 1951): 11–14.

Fritz Bauer Institut. "Tonbandmitschnitte des Auschwitz-Prozesses (1963–1965) [Frankfurt Auschwitz Trial, Testimonies and Recordings (1963–1965)]." Tonbandmitschnitte des Auschwitz-Prozesses (1963–1965), accessed June 16, 2022. www.auschwitz-prozess.de/.

Fritz Bauer Institut and Staatliches Museum Auschwitz-Birkenau. *Der Auschwitz-Prozeß: Tonbandmitschnitte, Protokolle, Dokumente.* Digitale Bibliothek 101. Berlin: Directmedia Publishing, 2004. DVD.

Gesellschaft für bedrohte Völker, and Verband deutscher Sinti. *Sinti und Roma im ehemaligen KZ Bergen-Belsen am 27. Oktober 1979: Erste deutsche und europäische Gedenkkundgebung "In Auschwitz vergast, bis heute verfolgt": Eine Dokumentation der Gesellschaft für bedrohte Völker und des Verbands deutscher Sinti.* Reihe pogrom 76. Göttingen: Die Gesellschaft, 1980.

"Gesetz zur Wiedergutmachung nationalsozialistischen Unrechts (Entschädigungsgesetz)" [August 10, 1949]. *Gesetz- und Verordnungsblatt für das Land Hessen,* August 18, 1949, no. 26–27.

Goldstein, Estelle. *D'hier et d'aujourd'hui: Souvenirs.* Brussels: Société générale d'éditions "Sodi," 1967.

———. *Israël: Terre des contrastes.* Brussels: Pierre De Méyère, 1961.

———. *Le Sionisme.* Brussels: L'Eglantine, 1933.

Gross, Raphael, and Werner Renz, eds. *Der Frankfurter Auschwitz-Prozess (1963–1965): Kommentierte Quellenedition.* 2 vols. Frankfurt am Main: Campus Verlag, 2013.

Grove, Lloyd. "Lament of the Gypsies: 40 Years After Auschwitz, Petitioning for a Place." *Washington Post,* July 21, 1984, C1 and C4.

Guttenberger, Elisabeth. "Das Zigeunerlager." In *Auschwitz: Zeugnisse und Berichte,* edited by H. G. Adler, Ella Lingens, and Hermann Langbein, 159–62. Frankfurt am Main, Germany: Europäische Verlagsanstalt, 1962.

Hausner, Gideon. *Justice in Jerusalem.* New York: Harper & Row, 1966.

Hillesum, Etty. *Etty: The Letters and Diaries of Etty Hillesum, 1941–1943.* Edited by Klaas A. D. Smelik. Translated by Arnold J. Pomerans. Grand Rapids, MI: William B. Eerdmans, 2002.

Höss, Rudolf. *Commandant of Auschwitz: The Autobiography of Rudolf Hoess.* Translated by Constantine FitzGibbon. London: Weidenfeld and Nicolson, 1959.

Höß, Rudolf. *Kommandant in Auschwitz: Autobiographische Aufzeichnungen.* Edited by Martin Broszat. Stuttgart: Deutsche Verlags-Anstalt, 1958.

"How the Gipsies were Persecuted." *Wiener Library Bulletin* 10, no.1/2 (1956): 11.

Institut für Zeitgeschichte. *Gutachten des Instituts für Zeitgeschichte.* Vol. 1. Munich: Institut für Zeitgeschichte, 1958.

International Refugee Organization. *Report of the Director-General to the General Council, 1 July 1948–30 June 1949.* Geneva: IRO, 1949.

International Tracing Service. *Catalogue of Camps and Prisons in Germany and German-Occupied Territories, Sept. 1st, 1939–May 8th, 1945.* Arolsen, Germany: International Tracing Service, 1949.

Israelitische Kultusgemeinde Wien. *Bericht des Präsidiums der Israelitischen Kultusgemeinde Wien über die Tätigkeit in den Jahren 1945 bis 1948.* Vienna: IKG, 1948.

Jasny, A. Wolf, ed. *Sefer Yadov.* Jersualem: The Encyclopaedia of the Jewish Diaspora, 1966. https://digitalcollections.nypl.org/items/bc143e40-79a9-0133-d9d6-00505686d14e.

Kaczerginski, Szmerke, ed. *Lider fun di geṭos un lagern.* New York: Tsiḳo, 1948.

Kaupp, Katia D. "Quand Paprika raconte Auschwitz." *Le Nouvel Observateur,* April 9, 1979, 67–69.

Kochanowski, Vanya. "Some Notes on the Gypsies of Latvia." *JGLS* 25, 3rd series (1946): 34–39.

———. "Some Notes on the Gypsies of Latvia: By One of the Survivors." *JGLS* 25, 3rd series (1946): 112–16.

Kraus, Ota, and Erich Kulka. *The Death Factory: Document on Auschwitz.* Oxford, UK: Pergamon Press, 1966.

Lacková, Elena. *A False Dawn: My Life as a Gypsy Woman in Slovakia.* Edited by Milena Hübschmannová. Translated by Carleton Bulkin. Paris and Hatfield, UK: Centre de recherches tsiganes and University of Hertfordshire Press, 1999.

Lakatos, Menyhért. *The Color of Smoke: An Epic Novel of the Roma.* Translated by Ann Major. Williamstown, MA: New Europe Books, 2015.

Langbein, Hermann. *Menschen in Auschwitz.* Vienna: Europaverlag, 1972.

Lapid, Arnon. "Goral Zoanei." *Ha-Daf Ha-Yarok,* 23 April 1985, 6.

Lemkin, Raphael. *Axis Rule in Occupied Europe; Laws of Occupation, Analysis of Government, Proposals for Redress.* Washington, DC: Carnegie Endowment for International Peace, Division of International Law, 1944.

———. "Genocide." *The American Scholar* 15, no. 2 (1946): 227–30.

———. "Genocide as a Crime under International Law." *United Nations Bulletin* 4, no. 2 (January 1948): 70–71.

L'Huillier, G[eneviève]. "Reminiscences of the Gypsy Camp at Poitiers." *JGLS* 27, 3rd series (1948): 36–40.

Levitt, Ruth, ed. *Testimonies from "Kristallnacht."* London: Souvenir Press, 2015.

Lis, Kalmen. *Kind un rind.* Warsaw: Shvalbn, 1936.

Max, Frédéric. "Le sort des tsiganes dans les prisons et les camps de concentration de l'Allemagne hitlerienne." *JGLS* 25, 3rd series (1946): 24–34

Maximoff, Matéo. "Germany and the Gypsies: From the Gypsy's Point of View." *JGLS* 25 (1946): 104–8.

Megel, John. "The Holocaust and the American Rom." In *Papers from the Sixth and and [Sic] Seventh Annual Meetings, Gypsy Lore Society, North American Chapter,* edited by Joanne Grumet, 187–90. New York: Gypsy Lore Society, 1986.

Metzker, Isaac. *Toli un Tobi.* New York: Matones, 1936.

Ministère de la justice, Commision des crimes de guerre. *Les Crimes de guerre commis sous l'occupation de la Belgique, 1940–1945: La persécution antisémitique en Belgique.* Liège, Belgium: Georges Thone, 1947.

Molitor, Jan. "The Fate of a German Gypsy." *JGLS* 26 (1947): 48–52.

Muzeum i Miejsce Pamięci w Bełżcu. "80th Anniversary of Extermination of Roma and Sinti in the Labour Camp in Bełżec—Bełżec." Muzeum i Miejsce Pamięci w Bełżcu, accessed November 6, 2020. www.belzec.eu/en/news/80th_anniversary_of_extermination/1363.

Nazi Conspiracy and Aggression. [The Red Series.] Washington, DC: United States Government Printing Office, 1946.

Newman, Judith Sternberg. *In the Hell of Auschwitz: The Wartime Memoirs of Judith Sternberg Newman.* New York: Exposition Press, 1963.

Niboyet, Jean-Paulin. "Le décret-loi du 12 avril 1939 relatif aux associations." *Travaux du Comité français de droit international privé* 6, no. 1938 (1946): 53–56.

Oberländer, Theodor. *The Expellees Are Working: Picture Report of Reconstruction Work Done by the Expellees in Bavaria.* Gräfelfing, Germany: Verlag für Planung und Aufbau, 1951.

Papadatos, Pierre Achille. *The Eichmann Trial.* New York: F. A. Praeger, 1964.

Papusza [Bronisława Wajs] and Jerzy Ficowski. *Pieśni Papuszy (Papušakra gila).* Wroclaw, Poland: Ossoliński, 1956.

Pearlman, Moshe. *The Capture and Trial of Adolf Eichmann.* London: Weidenfeld and Nicolson, 1963.

Perlow, Itzjok. *Sefer Radom.* Tel Aviv: Irgun yots'e Radom be-Yiśra'el, 1961.

Pinski, David. *Rayzebukh.* Warsaw: David Pinski bikher, 1938.

Pitoun, Anna, dir. *Pologne aller Retour.* Paris: Caravane Films, 2012. DVD.

Pliskin, David. *Vunderland lider un mayselekh.* Paris: Fraynt fun arbeter-kind, 1938.

Pohoryles, Yaniv. "The Jewish-Romani Connection: Are Gypsies Descendants of Tribe of Simeon?" *Ynetnews,* May 5, 2018. www.ynetnews.com/articles/0,7340,L-5248902,00.html.

"President Obama Announces More Key Administration Posts." White House Press Release, January 11, 2016. https://obamawhitehouse.archives.gov/the-press-office/2016/01/11/president-obama-announces-more-key-administration-posts?fbclid=IwAR1f-rO30zR-gvkzE1FBVASSM3duKlyeW2FgQ9MOEmApftvFv8KKcDToYLI.

Rajak, Michael and Zvi Rajak. *Khurbn Glubok.* Buenos Aires: Former Residents' Association in Argentina, 1956.

Reich, Tova. *My Holocaust.* New York: HarperCollins, 2007.

Roberts, Samuel. *Parallel Miracles; Or, The Jews and the Gypsies.* London: J. Nisbet, 1830.

Rose, Romani. "Vorwort an die Sinti." In *Sinti und Roma im ehemaligen KZ Bergen-Belsen am 27. Oktober 1979: Erste deutsche und europäische Gedenkkundgebung "In Auschwitz vergast, bis heute verfolgt": Eine Dokumentation der Gesellschaft für bedrohte Völker und des Verbands deutscher Sinti,* by Gesellschaft für bedrohte Völker and Verband deutscher Sinti. Reihe pogrom 76. Göttingen: Die Gesellschaft, 1980.

Rosenberg, Otto. *A Gypsy in Auschwitz.* London: London House, 1999.

Samuel, Stuart Montagu. *The History and Genealogy of the Jewish Families of Yates and Samuel of Liverpool.* Edited by Lucien Wolf. London: [Mitchell and Hughes, Printers], 1901.

Seltzer, David. *Besaraber Lider.* New York: Soroki, 1937.

Shindler, Eliezer. *In shtile farnakhtn: Mayselekh fun Mizreh un Mayrev.* Vilnius: Grinike beymelekh, 1937.

Sijes, B. A. *Ik vergat nog iets te vertellen.* Amsterdam: H.J.W. Becht, 1978.

Simpson, John. "Gypsy Language and Origin." *JGLS* 1, no. 1 (July 1907): 4–22.

Sobek, Franz. "Vom KZ-Verband zum Österreichischen Bundesverband ehemals politisch verfolgter Antifaschisten." *Mahnruf für Freiheit und Menschenrecht* 1, no. 1 (November 1946): 4–5.

Starkie, Walter. *In Sara's Tents*. London: John Murray, 1953.

Stenographischer Bericht über die Verhandlungen des Bayerischen Landtags. Bayerischer Landtag, 1946–. www.bayern.landtag.de/webangebot2/webangebot/protokolle;jsessionid=43A99 DBB75E51F099C8A3EAE5C1A0330?execution=e1s1.

Stern, M. A. *Dos kol fun blut: A megileh fun yomer un shoyder*. Brooklyn, NY: M. A. Stern, [1950s]. https://archive.org/details/nybc210375/mode/2up.

Sutzkever, Avraham [Avrom]. *Lider fun yam ha-moves: Fun Vilner geṭo, vald un vander*. Tel Aviv: Farlag Bergen-Belzen, 1968).

———. *A. Sutzkever: Selected Poetry and Prose*. Edited by Barbara Harshav and Benjamin Harshav. Berkeley: University of California Press, 1991.

"Terezín Initiative in Czech Republic does not want Romani names included in Shoah commemoration, director of its Institute disagrees." *Romea*, April 3, 2021. www.romea.cz/en /news/czech/terezin-initiative-in-czech-republic-does-not-want-romani-names-included -in-shoah-commemoration-director-of-its-institute.

"Transcript of the Official Shorthand Notes on 'The Trial of Josef Kramer and Forty Four Others.'" BergenBelsen, October 1, 1945. www.bergenbelsen.co.uk/pages/TrialTranscript /Trial_Contents.html.

Trial of the Major War Criminals before the International Military Tribunal, Nuremberg, 14 November 1945–1 October 1946. Vol 2. [The Blue Series.] Nuremberg, Germany: International Military Tribunal, 1947.

Union des étudiants juifs de France. *Le Sionisme expliqué à nos potes*. Paris: La Martinière, 2003.

Union des étudiants juifs de France. *Rwanda: Pour un dialogue des mémoires*. Paris: Albin Michel, 2007.

United Restitution Organization. *Dokumente über Methoden der Judenverfolgung im Ausland*. Frankfurt am Main: URO, 1959.

———. *Judenverfolgung in Italien, den italienisch besetzten Gebieten und in Nordafrika*. Frankfurt am Main: URO, 1962.

———. *Judenverfolgung in Ungarn: Dokumentensammlung*. Frankfurt am Main: URO, 1959.

United States Holocaust Memorial Council. *Day of Remembrance: In Memory of the Gypsy Victims of Nazi Genocide*. [Sponsored by the USHMC in Association with the American Rom Community.] Washington, DC: USHMC, 1986.

Vaserman, Shneur. *Shvebelekh: Kinder-lider un poemes*. Buenos Aires: Kultur-hoyz Mendele, 1938.

"Verwendung des Rassebegriffs bei der Entschädigung von NS-Opfern." Ausarbeitung des Wissenschaftlichen Dienstes, Deutscher Bundestag, February 15, 2013.

Volkzählung: Die Bevölkerung des Deutschen Reichs nach den Ergebnissen der Volkszählung 1933. Vol. 5, *Die Glaubensjuden im Deutschen Reich*. Berlin: Verlag für Sozialpolitik, Wirtschaft und Statistik, 1936.

Wiener, Meir. *Kolev Ashkenazi: Dertseylung*. Moscow: Farlag Emes, 1934.

Wiesel, Elie. *Night; Dawn; Day*. Northvale, NJ: Aronson, 1985.

———. *Un di velṭ hoṭ geshvign*. Buenos Aires: Tsenṭral-farband fun Poylishe Yidn in Argenṭine, 1956. https://babel.hathitrust.org/cgi/pt?id=mdp.39015019304735.

Wiesenthal, Simon. *The Murderers among Us: The Simon Wiesenthal Memoirs.* Translated by Joseph Wechsberg. New York: McGraw-Hill, 1967.

Yates, Dora E. "Hitler and the Gypsies: The Fate of Europe's Oldest Aryans." *Commentary Magazine,* November 1949, 455–59.

———. *A Book of Gypsy Folk-Tales.* London: Phoenix House, 1948.

———. *My Gypsy Days: Recollections of a Romani Rawnie.* London: Phoenix House, 1953.

Yoors, Jan. *Crossing: A Journal of Survival and Resistance in World War II.* New York: Simon and Schuster, 1971.

———. *The Gypsies.* New York: Simon and Schuster, 1967.

Zülch, Tilman, ed. *In Auschwitz vergast, bis heute verfolgt: Zur Situation der Roma (Zigeuner) in Deutschland und Europa.* Rororo aktuell. Reinbek, Germany: Rowohlt, 1979.

Zülch, Tilman, and K. Guercke. *Soll Biafra überleben?: Dokumente, Berichte, Analysen, Kommentare.* Berlin: Lettner, 1969.

Zülch, Tilman, and Gerhard Rüdiger, eds. "'Jeder Stein ist ein Blutstropfen': Zigeuner in Auschwitz-Birkenau, Oświęcim-Brzezinka." In *In Auschwitz vergast, bis heute verfolgt: Zur Situation der Roma (Zigeuner) in Deutschland und Europa,* edited by Tilman Zülch, 135–46. Rororo aktuell. Reinbek, Germany: Rowohlt, 1979.

Żywulska, Krystyna. *I Came Back.* London: D. Dobson, 1951.

Secondary Literature

Abakunova, Anna. "Extermination of the Roma in Transnistria during World War II: Construction of the Roma Collective Memory." In *The Burden of the Past: History, Memory, and Identity in Contemporary Ukraine,* edited by Anna Wylegała and Małgorzata Głowacka-Grajper, 206–28. Bloomington: Indiana University Press, 2020.

About, Ilsen, and Anna Abakunova. "The Genocide and Persecution of Roma and Sinti: Bibliography and Historiographical Review." International Holocaust Remembrance Alliance, March 2016.

"About ERIAC." ERIAC, accessed June 16, 2022. https://eriac.org/about-eriac/.

Achim, Viorel. "The Roma Organizations and their Relations with the Romanian Politics in the 1930s." In *Nouvelles Études d'Histoire.* Vol. 12, *Publiées à l'occasion du XXIe Congrès International des Sciences Historiques, Amsterdam, 2010,* edited by Dan Berindei, 85–102. Bucharest: Editura Academiei Române, 2010.

Acton, Thomas. "Modernity, Culture and 'Gypsies': Is There a Meta-Scientific Method for Understanding the Representation of 'Gypsies'? And do the Dutch Really Exist?" In *The Role of the Romanies: Images and Counter-Images of "Gypsies"/Romanies in European Cultures,* edited by Nicholas Saul and Susan Tebbutt, 98–116. Liverpool: Liverpool University Press, 2004.

Acton, Thomas A. "Scientific Racism, Popular Racism and the Discourse of the Gypsy Lore Society." *Ethnic and Racial Studies* 39, no. 7 (2016): 1187–1204.

Acton, Thomas, Peter Mercer, John Day, and Andrew Ryder. "Pedagogies of Hope: The Gypsy Council and the National Gypsy Education Council." In *Hearing the Voice of the Gypsy, Roma and Traveller Communities: Inclusive Community Development,* edited by Andrew Ryder, Sarah Cemlyn, and Thomas Acton, 29–48. Bristol, UK: Policy Press, 2014.

Adler, Eliyana R. *Survival on the Margins: Polish Jewish Refugees in the Wartime Soviet Union.* Cambridge, MA: Harvard University Press, 2020.

Adler, Eliyana R., and Kateřina Čapková, eds. *Jewish and Romani Families in the Holocaust and Its Aftermath.* New Brunswick, NJ: Rutgers University Press, 2021.

Albrich, Thomas. *Exodus durch Österreich: Die jüdischen Flüchtlinge 1945–1948.* Innsbruck, Austria: Haymon Verlag, 1987.

Alicke, Klaus-Dieter. *Lexikon der jüdischen Gemeinden im deutschen Sprachraum.* Vol. 2. Gütersloh, Germany: Gütersloher Verlagshaus, 2008.

Altgeld, Wolfgang. *Katholizismus, Protestantismus, Judentum: Über religiös begründete Gegensätze und nationalreligiöse Ideen in der Geschichte des deutschen Nationalismus.* Mainz, Germany: Matthias-Grünewald-Verlag, 1992.

Aly, Götz. *Hitler's Beneficiaries: Plunder, Race War, and the Nazi Welfare State.* New York: Metropolitan, 2007.

Ancel, Jean. *The History of the Holocaust in Romania.* Lincoln and Jerusalem: University of Nebraska Press and Yad Vashem, 2011.

Anidjar, Gil. *Semites: Race, Religion, Literature.* Stanford, CA: Stanford University Press, 2008.

Arendt, Hannah. *Eichmann in Jerusalem: A Report on the Banality of Evil.* New York: Penguin, 1994.

Auslander, Leora. "Holocaust Lists and Inventories: Recording Death vs. Traces of Lived Lives." *Jewish Quarterly Review* 111, no. 3 (2021): 347–55.

Ayass, Wolfgang. *"Asoziale" im Nationalsozialismus.* Stuttgart: Klett-Cotta, 1995.

Ayzman, Yudeh. *Mi-ma'amakim: Folkslider fun lagers un getos in Poyln.* Bucharest: Bibliotek hehaluts, 1945.

Bachsleitner, Karl. "Der Fall Philipp Auerbach: Ein Lehrstück aus den 50er Jahren." *Geschichte Lernen*, no. 119 (2007): 33–41.

Baggerman, Arianne, and Rudolf Dekker. "Jacques Presser, Egodocuments and the Personal Turn in Historiography." *European Journal of Life Writing* 7 (August 2018): 90–110.

Bailer, Brigitte. "Der KZ-Verband: Informationen zu einer wesentlichen Quelle des Projektes der namentlichen Erfassung der Opfer der politischen Verfolgung." *DÖW Jahrbuch* (2007): 36–49.

Ballinger, Pamela. "Impossible Returns, Enduring Legacies: Recent Historiography of Displacement and the Reconstruction of Europe after World War II." *Contemporary European History* 22, no. 1 (February 2013): 127–38.

———. *The World Refugees Made: Decolonization and the Foundations of Postwar Italy.* Ithaca, NY: Cornell University Press, 2020.

Baranowski, Julian. *The Gypsy Camp in Lodz, 1941–1942.* Łodz, Poland: Archiwum Państwowe w Łodzi & Bilbo, 2003.

Bársony, János, and Ágnes Daróczi. *Pharrajimos: The Fate of the Roma During the Holocaust.* New York: International Debate Education Association, 2007.

Bartash, Volha. "The Romani Family before and during the Holocaust: How Much Do We Know? An Ethnographic-Historical Study in the Belarusian-Lithuanian Border Region." In *Jewish and Romani Families in the Holocaust and Its Aftermath*, edited by Eliyana R. Adler and Kateřina Čapková, 17–41. New Brunswick, NJ: Rutgers University Press, 2021.

Bartov, Omer. *Mirrors of Destruction: War, Genocide, and Modern Identity.* Oxford: Oxford University Press, 2000.

Bashir, Bashir, and Amos Goldberg, eds. *The Holocaust and the Nakba: A New Grammar of Trauma and History*. New York: Columbia University Press, 2018.

Bauer, Yehuda. *American Jewry and the Holocaust: The American Jewish Joint Distribution Committee, 1939–1945*. Jerusalem: The Institute of Contemporary Jewry, Hebrew University, 1981.

———."'Es galt nicht der gleiche Befehl für beide': Eine Entgegnung auf Romani Roses Thesen zum Genozid an den europäischen Juden, Sinti und Roma." *Blätter für deutsche und internationale Politik* 43 (1998), 1380–86.

———. "Gypsies." In *Anatomy of the Auschwitz Death Camp*, edited by Yisrael Gutman and Michael Berenbaum, 441–55. Bloomington and Washington DC: Indiana University Press, published in association with the United States Holocaust Memorial Museum, 1994.

———. "Whose Holocaust?" *Midstream* 26, no. 9 (November 1980).

Bauer, Yehuda and Sybil Milton. "Correspondence: 'Gypsies and the Holocaust.'" *The History Teacher* 25, no. 4 (August 1992): 513–21.

Bauman, Zygmunt. *Modernity and the Holocaust*. Ithaca, NY: Cornell University Press, 1989.

Baumann, Ulrich. "From the Gypsy's Point of View: Politique et Mémoire au travers de la vie et l'œuvre de Matéo Maximoff." *Études tsiganes* 60, no. 1 (2017): 115–33.

Baumgartner, Gerhard. "'Wann endlich wird dies himmelschreiende Unrecht an uns gut gemacht werden?' Frühe Zeugnisse österreichischer Roma und Romnia zu ihrer Verfolgung während des Nationalsozialismus." In "Feinbilder," edited by Christine Schindler. *Jahrbuch, Dokumentationsarchiv des österreichischen Widerstandes* (2015): 43–80. www.doew.at/cms /download/dblcd/jb2015_baumgartner.pdf.

Baumgartner, Gerhard, and Florian Freund. "Der Holocaust an den österreichischen Roma und Sinti." In *Zwischen Erziehung und Vernichtung: Zigeunerpolitik und Zigeunerforschung im Europa des 20. Jahrhunderts*, edited by Michael Zimmermann, 203–25. Beiträge zur Geschichte der Deutschen Forschungsgemeinschaft 3. Stuttgart: Steiner, 2007.

Bazyler, Michael J. *Holocaust Justice: The Battle for Restitution in America's Courts*. New York: New York University Press, 2003.

Bazyler, Michael J., and Amber L. Fitzgerald. "Trading with the Enemy: Holocaust Restitution, the United States Government, and American Industry." *Brooklyn Journal of International Law* 28, no. 3 (2002): 683–810.

Beckerman, Michael. "The World According to the Roma." *The Cambridge History of World Music*, edited by Philip Bohlman. Cambridge: Cambridge University Press, 2013.

Bentwich, Norman. *The United Restitution Organisation, 1948–1968: The Work of Restitution and Compensation for Victims of Nazi Oppression*. London: Vallentine Mitchell, 1968.

Berenbaum, Michael, ed. *A Mosaic of Victims: Non-Jews Persecuted and Murdered by the Nazis*. ACLS Humanities EBook. New York: New York University Press, 1990.

———. "The Uniqueness and Universality of the Holocaust." In *A Mosaic of Victims: Non-Jews Persecuted and Murdered by the Nazis*, edited by Michael Berenbaum, 20–36. New York: New York University Press, 1990.

Berg, Nicolas. *The Holocaust and the West German Historians: Historical Interpretation and Autobiographical Memory*. Madison: University of Wisconsin Press, 2015.

Bergmann, Werner. "Philipp Auerbach—Wiedergutmachung war 'nicht mit normalen Mitteln durchzusetzen.'" In *Engagierte Demokraten: Vergangenheitspolitik in kritischer Absicht*, edited by Claudia Fröhlich and Michael Kohlstruck, 57–70. Münster, Germany: Westfälisches Dampfboot, 1999.

Berkyová, Renata. "Concept of the Porajmos as a Reflection of the Marginalization of Roma in Historiography." *Romea*, June 6, 2018. www.romea.cz/en/news/world/renata -berkyova-concept-of-the-porajmos-as-a-reflection-of-the-marginalization-of-roma-in -historiography.

Berman, Lila Corwin. "How Americans Give: The Financialization of American Jewish Philan- thropy." *American Historical Review* 122, no. 5 (December 2017): 1459–89.

———. *The American Jewish Philanthropic Complex: The History of a Multibillion-Dollar Institu- tion.* Princeton, NJ: Princeton University Press, 2020.

Bermant, Chaim. *The Cousinhood.* New York: Macmillan, 1972.

Bilsky, Leora. "The Eichmann Trial: Towards a Jurisprudence of Eyewitness Testimony of Atrocities." *Journal of International Criminal Justice* 12, no. 1 (March 2014): 27–57.

———. *The Holocaust, Corporations and the Law: Unfinished Business.* Law, Meaning, and Vio- lence. Ann Arbor: University of Michigan Press, 2017.

Black, Peter R. "Rehearsal for 'Reinhard'?: Odilo Globocnik and the Lublin Selbstschutz." *Cen- tral European History* 25, no. 2 (1992): 204–26.

Bloxham, Donald. *Genocide on Trial: The War Crimes Trials and the Formation of Holocaust His- tory and Memory.* Oxford: Oxford University Press, 2001.

Blumer, Nadine. "From Victim Hierarchies to Memorial Networks: Berlin's Holocaust Memo- rial to Sinti and Roma Victims of National Socialism." PhD diss., University of Toronto, 2011.

Boas, Jacob. *Boulevard Des Misères: The Story of Transit Camp Westerbork.* Hamden, CT: Archon, 1985.

Bogdal, Klaus Michael. *Europa erfindet die Zigeuner: Eine Geschichte von Faszination und Verach- tung.* Berlin: Suhrkamp, 2011.

Bradburn, Elizabeth. *Dr. Dora Esther Yates: An Appreciation.* Liverpool: University of Liverpool, 1975.

Brenner, Michael, Stefi Jersch-Wenzel, and Michael A. Meyer, eds. *German-Jewish History in Modern Times.* Vol. 2, *Emancipation and Acculturation.* New York: Columbia University Press, 1996.

Brittnacher, Hans Richard. *Leben auf der Grenze: Klischee und Faszination des Zigeunerbildes in Literatur und Kunst.* Göttingen: Wallstein, 2012.

Bronner, Stephen Eric. *A Rumor about the Jews: Reflections on Antisemitism and the Protocols of the Learned Elders of Zion.* New York: St. Martin's Press, 2000.

Brown, Adam. "Confronting 'Choiceless Choices' in Holocaust Videotestimonies: Judgement, 'Privileged' Jews, and the Role of the Interviewer." *Continuum* 24, no. 1 (February 2010): 79–90.

Browning, Christopher R. *Ordinary Men: Reserve Police Battalion 101 and the Final Solution in Poland.* New York: HarperCollins, 1992.

———. *The Path to Genocide: Essays on Launching the Final Solution.* Cambridge: Cambridge University Press, 1992.

Bundesgerichtshof and Zentralrat Deutscher Sinti und Roma. *Doppeltes Unrecht—Eine späte Entschuldigung: Gemeinsames Symposium des Bundesgerichtshofs und des Zentralrats Deutscher Sinti und Roma zu den Urteilen vom 7. Januar 1956: Vorträge gehalten am 17. Februar 2016 im*

Foyer der Bibliothek des Bundesgerichtshofs in Karlsruhe. Karlsruhe, Germany: Bundesgerichtshof and Zentralrat Deutscher Sinti und Roma, 2016.

Burleigh, Michael, and Wolfgang Wippermann. *The Racial State: Germany, 1933–1945*. Cambridge: Cambridge University Press, 1991.

Burns, Kathryn. *Into the Archive: Writing and Power in Colonial Peru*. Durham, NC: Duke University Press, 2010.

Bush, Johnathan. "Nuremberg and Beyond: Jacob Robinson, International Lawyer." *Loyola of Los Angeles International and Comparative Law Review* 39, no. 259 (2017): 259–86.

Cabraser, Elizabeth. "Human Rights Violations as Mass Torts: Compensation as a Proxy for Justice in the United States Civil Litigation System." *Vanderbilt Law Review* 57, no. 6 (2004): 2211–37.

"Calvelli-Adorno, Franz Wilhelm." Hessische Biografie, Landesgeschichtliches Informationssystem Hessen, November 1, 2016. www.lagis-hessen.de/de/subjects/rsrec/sn/bio/register/person/entry/reinhuber%252C%2Belisabeth%252C%2Bgeb.%2Bcalvelli-adorno.

Campos, Michelle U. *Ottoman Brothers: Muslims, Christians, and Jews in Early Twentieth-Century Palestine*. Stanford, CA: Stanford University Press, 2011.

Carey, Maddy. *Jewish Masculinity in the Holocaust: Between Destruction and Construction*. London: Bloomsbury Academic, 2017.

Cesarani, David, ed. *After Eichmann: Collective Memory and Holocaust Since 1961*. Hoboken, NJ: Taylor and Francis, 2013.

Chang, Felix B., and Sunnie T. Rucker-Chang. *Roma Rights and Civil Rights: A Transatlantic Comparison*. Cambridge: Cambridge University Press, 2020.

Chronakis, Paris Papamichos. "'We lived as Greeks, and we died as Greeks': Salonican Jews in Auschwitz and the Meanings of Nationhood." In *The Holocaust in Greece*, edited by Giorgos Antoniou and A. Dirk Moses, 157–80. Cambridge: Cambridge University Press, 2018.

Cohen, Boaz. "Dr. Jacob Robinson, the Institute of Jewish Affairs and the Elusive Jewish Voice in Nuremberg." In *Holocaust and Justice: Representation and Historiography of the Holocaust in Post-War Trials*, edited by David. Bankier and Dan Mikhman, 81–100. Jerusalem: Yad Vashem, 2010.

———. *Israeli Holocaust Research: Birth and Evolution*. Translated by Agnes Vazsonyi. Abingdon, UK: Routledge, 2013.

Cohen, Gerard Daniel. *In War's Wake: Europe's Displaced Persons in the Postwar Order*. New York: Oxford University Press, 2012.

Cohen, Julia Phillips author. *Becoming Ottomans: Sephardi Jews and Imperial Citizenship in the Modern Era*. Oxford: Oxford University Press, 2014.

Connelly, John. "Gypsies, Homosexuals, and Slavs." In *The Oxford Handbook of Holocaust Studies*, edited by Peter Hayes and John K. Roth, 274–92. Oxford: Oxford University Press, 2010.

Conrad, Sebastian. *Auf der Suche nach der verlorenen Nation: Geschichtsschreibung in Westdeutschland und Japan, 1945–1960*. Göttingen: Vandenhoeck & Ruprecht, 1999.

"Curated Sections." RomArchive, accessed June 16, 2022. https://www.romarchive.eu/en/sections/.

Daróczi, Anna, Kinga Kánya, Szilvia Rézmüves, and Violetta Vajda. "Roma and Non-Roma Alliances for Political Empowerment: Experiences from Hungary." In *Dimensions of Antigypsyism in Europe*, edited by Ismael Cortés Gómez and Markus End, 333–52. Brussels and

Heidelberg: European Network Against Racism and Central Council of German Sinti and Roma, 2019.

Deák, István, Jan Tomasz Gross, and Tony Judt, eds. *The Politics of Retribution in Europe: World War II and Its Aftermath*. Princeton, NJ: Princeton University Press, 2000.

Dębicki, Edward. *Totenvogel: Erinnerungen*. Translated by Karin Wolff. Berlin: Friedenauer Presse, 2018.

Deblinger, Rachel. "David P. Boder: Holocaust Memory in Displaced Persons Camps." In *After the Holocaust: Challenging the Myth of Silence*, edited by David Cesarani and Eric J. Sundquist, 115–26. London: Routledge, 2012.

DellaPergola, Sergio. "Reflections on the Multinational Geography of Jews after World War II." In *Postwar Jewish Displacement and Rebirth, 1945–1967*, edited by Françoise Ouzan and Manfred Gerstenfeld, 11–33. Leiden, Netherlands: Brill, 2014.

Desbois, Patrick. *The Holocaust by Bullets: A Priest's Journey to Uncover the Truth behind the Murder of 1.5 Million Jews*. New York: Palgrave Macmillan, 2008.

Dieckmann, Christoph. *Deutsche Besatzungspolitik in Litauen 1941–1944*. Göttingen: Wallstein, 2011.

Diercks, Herbert, ed. *Ausgegrenzt: "Asoziale" und "Kriminelle" im nationalsozialistischen Lagersystem*. Bremen, Germany: Edition Temmen, 2009.

Dlugoborski, Waclaw, ed. *Sinti und Roma im KL Auschwitz-Birkenau, 1943–44: Vor dem Hintergrund ihrer Verfolgung unter der Naziherrschaft*. Oświęcim, Poland: Staatliches Museum Auschwitz-Birkenau, 1998.

Dobroszycki, Lucjan. *The Chronicle of the Lodz Ghetto, 1941–1944*. New Haven, CT: Yale University Press, 1984.

Dollinger, Marc. *Black Power, Jewish Politics: Reinventing the Alliance in the 1960s*. Brandeis Series in American Jewish History, Culture, and Life. Waltham, MA: Brandeis University Press, 2018.

Donert, Celia. *The Rights of the Roma: The Struggle for Citizenship in Postwar Czechoslovakia*. Cambridge: Cambridge University Press, 2017.

Douglas, Lawrence. *The Memory of Judgment: Making Law and History in the Trials of the Holocaust*. New Haven, CT: Yale University Press, 2001.

Dror, Zvika. *Masa Miryam: sipur hayeha shel Miryam Novits'*. Lohamei HaGeta'ot, Israel: Bet lohame ha-getaot, 2008.

Duchein, Michel. "The History of European Archives and the Development of the Archival Profession in Europe." *The American Archivist* 55, no. 1 (1992): 14–25.

———. "Theoretical Principles and Practical Problems of *Respect Des Fonds* in Archival Science." *Archivaria* 160 (January 1983): 64–82.

Duquette, Nicolas J. "Founders' Fortunes and Philanthropy: A History of the U.S. Charitable-Contribution Deduction." *Business History Review* 93, no. 3 (2019): 553–84.

Dwork, Deborah, and R. J. van Pelt. *Auschwitz*. New York: Norton, 1996.

Earl, Hilary Camille. *The Nuremberg SS-Einsatzgruppen Trial, 1945–1958: Atrocity, Law, and History*. Cambridge: Cambridge University Press, 2009.

Eder, Jacob S. *Holocaust Angst: The Federal Republic of Germany and American Holocaust Memory Since the 1970s*. New York: Oxford University Press, 2016.

Ehrenburg, Ilya, and Vasily Grossman, eds. *The Complete Black Book of Russian Jewry*. Translated by David Patterson. New Brunswick, NJ: Transaction Publishers, 2002.

Eiber, Ludwig. *"Ich wusste es wird schlimm": Die Verfolgung der Sinti und Roma in München 1933–1945*. Munich: Buchendorfer, 1993.

Ellwood, David W. *Rebuilding Europe: Western Europe, America, and Postwar Reconstruction*. London: Longman, 1992.

Embacher, Helga. *Neubeginn ohne Illusionen: Juden in Österreich nach 1945*. Vienna: Picus, 1995.

Embacher, Helga, and Maria Ecker. "A Nation of Victims: How Austria Dealt with the Victims of the Authoritarian Ständestaat and National Socialism." In *The Politics of War Trauma: The Aftermath of World War II in Eleven European Countries*, edited by Jolande Withuis and Annet Mooij, 15–47. Studies of the Netherlands Institute for War Documentation 4. Amsterdam: Aksant, 2010.

Endelman, Todd M., and Tony Kushner, eds. *Disraeli's Jewishness*. Parkes-Wiener Series on Jewish Studies. London: Vallentine Mitchell, 2002.

Falk, Georg D. *Entnazifizierung und Kontinuität: Der Wiederaufbau der hessischen Justiz am Beispiel des Oberlandesgerichts Frankfurt am Main*. Marburg, Germany: Historische Kommission für Hessen, 2017.

Fassin, Didier. *Humanitarian Reason: A Moral History of the Present Times*. Berkeley: University of California Press, 2012.

Fater, Isaschar. *Yidishe muzik in Poyln tsvishn beyde velt-milhomes*. Tel Aviv: Velt-Federatsye fun Poylishe Yidn, 1970.

Fatran, Gila. "Die Deportation der Juden aus der Slowakei 1944–1945." *A Journal of History and Civilisation in East Central Europe* 37, no. 1 (1996): 98–119.

Feher, George. *Thoughts on the Holocaust*. n. p.: Feher Publishing, 2017.

Ficowski, Jerzy. *Cyganie na polskich drogach*. Kraków: Wydawn. Literackie, 1965.

——. *Cyganie Polscy Szkice Historyczno-Obyczajowe*. Warsaw: Panìstwowy Instytut Wydawniczy, 1953.

Filhol, Emmanuel, ed. *La mémoire et l'oubli: L'internement des Tsiganes en France, 1940–1946*. Interface. Paris: Centre de recherches tsiganes, Harmattan, 2004.

Filhol, Emmanuel, and Marie-Christine Hubert. *Les Tsiganes en France, un sort à part, 1939–1946*. Paris: Perrin, 2009.

Fings, Karola. "Auschwitz and the Testimony of Sinti and Roma." RomArchive, accessed February 17, 2017. https://blog.romarchive.eu/?p=7336.

——. "Nationalsozialistische Zwangslager für Sinti und Roma." In *Der Ort des Terrors: Geschichte der nationalsozialistischen Konzentrationslager*. Vol. 9, *Arbeitserziehungslager, Ghettos, Jugendschutzlager, Polizeihaftlager, Sonderlager, Zigeunerlager, Zwangsarbeiterlager*, edited by Wolfgang Benz, Barbara Distel, and Angelika Königseder, 192–217. Munich: C. H. Beck, 2009.

——. "The Number of Victims." RomArchive. www.romarchive.eu/en/voices-of-the-victims/the-number-of-victims/.

——. "Opferkonkurrenzen: Debatten um den Völkermord an den Sinti und Roma und neue Forschungsperspektiven." *S:I.M.O.N. Shoah: Intervention. Methods. Documentation* 2, no. 1 (2015): 79–101.

Fings, Karola, and Frank Sparing. "Das Zigeunerlager in Köln-Bickendorf 1935–1958." *1999: Zeitschrift für Sozialgeschichte des 20. und 21. Jahrhunderts* 6, no. 3 (1991): 11–40.

——. *Z. Zt. Zigeunerlager: Die Verfolgung der Düsseldorfer Sinti und Roma im Nationalsozialismus*. Cologne: Volksblatt Verlag, 1992.

Finkelstein, Norman G. *The Holocaust Industry: Reflections on the Exploitation of Jewish Suffering*. London: Verso, 2003.

Fischbach, Michael R. *Black Power and Palestine: Transnational Countries of Color*. Stanford, CA: Stanford University Press, 2020.

———. *The Movement and the Middle East: How the Arab-Israeli Conflict Divided the American Left*. Redwood City, CA: Stanford University Press, 2019.

Fishman, David E. *The Book Smugglers: Partisans, Poets, and the Race to Save Jewish Treasures from the Nazis*. Lebanon, NH: ForeEdge, an imprint of University Press of New England, 2017.

Fleming, K. E. [Katherine Elizabeth]. "The Stereotyped 'Greek Jew' from Auschwitz-Birkenau to Israeli Pop Culture." *Journal of Modern Greek Studies* 25, no. 1 (2007): 17–40.

Fogg, Shannon L. "'They Are Undesirables': Local and National Responses to Gypsies during World War II." *French Historical Studies* 31, no. 2 (2008): 327–58.

Foisneau, Lise. *Les Nomades face à la guerre (1939–1946)*. In collaboration with Valentin Merlin. Paris: Klincksieck, 2022.

Frank, Sonja, ed. *Die drei Schwestern Selma, Berthe und Gundl, geb. Steinmetz: Frauen im Widerstand 1933–1945*. Vienna: Theodor Kramer Gesellschaft, 2021.

Freund, Florian, Gerhard Baumgartner, and Harald Greifeneder. *Vermögensentzug, Restitution und Entschädigung der Roma und Sinti*. Veröffentlichungen der Österreichischen Historikerkommission: Vermögensentzug während der NS-Zeit sowie Rückstellungen und Entschädigungen seit 1945 in Österreich 23/2. Vienna: Oldenbourg, 2004.

Friedlander, Henry. "Step by Step: The Expansion of Murder, 1939–1941." *German Studies Review* 17, no. 3 (1994): 495–507.

———. *The Origins of Nazi Genocide: From Euthanasia to the Final Solution*. Chapel Hill: University of North Carolina Press, 1995.

Friedländer, Saul. *Nazi Germany and the Jews: The Years of Persecution, 1933–1939*. New York: HarperPerennial, 1998.

———, ed. *Probing the Limits of Representation: Nazism and the "Final Solution."* Cambridge, MA: Harvard University Press, 1992.

———. *Reflections of Nazism: An Essay on Kitsch and Death*. New York: Harper & Row, 1984.

Fritzsche, Peter. "The Archive." *History & Memory* 17, no. 1 (August 2005): 15–44.

Fröhlich, Claudia. "Die Gründung der 'Zentralen Stelle' in Ludwigsburg—Alibi oder Beginn einer systematischen justitiellen Aufarbeitung der NS-Vergangenheit?" In *Justiz und Nationalsozialismus—Kontinuität und Diskontinuität: Fachtagung in der Justizakademie des Landes NRW, Recklinghausen, am 19. und 20. November 2001*, edited by Gerhard Pauli and Thomas Vormbaum, 213–50. Berlin: Berliner Wissenschafts-Verlag, 2003.

Fuentes, Marisa J. *Dispossessed Lives: Enslaved Women, Violence, and the Archive*. Philadelphia: University of Pennsylvania Press, 2016.

Fulbrook, Mary. *Reckonings: Legacies of Nazi Persecution and the Quest for Justice*. New York: Oxford University Press, 2018.

Gebert, Konstaty. "Shoah and Porrajmos: Closely Connected, Yet Best Kept Separate." In *Beyond the Roma Holocaust: From Resistance to Mobilization*, edited by Thomas M. Buchsbaum and Slawomir Kapralski, 185–98. Kraków: Universitas, 2017.

Gerlach, Christian. *Extremely Violent Societies: Mass Violence in the Twentieth-Century World*. Cambridge: Cambridge University Press, 2010.

Giladi, Rotem. "Negotiating Identity: Israel, Apartheid, and the United Nations, 1949–1952." *The English Historical Review* 132, no. 559 (December 2017): 1440–72.

Gilman, Sander L. *The Jew's Body.* New York: Routledge, 1991.

Goldberg, Amos. "Ethics, Identity and Anti-Fundamental Fundamentalism: Holocaust Memory in the Global Age (a Cultural-Political Introduction)." In *Marking Evil: Holocaust Memory in the Global Age,* edited by Amos Goldberg and Haim Hazan, 3–29. New York: Berghahn Books, 2015.

———. "Rumor Culture among Warsaw Jews under Nazi Occupation: A World of Catastrophe Reenchanted." *Jewish Social Studies* 21, no. 3 (2016): 91–125.

Goldstein, Amir. "Partial Establishment—Menachem Begin, Gahal and the Black Panthers." *Journal of Modern Jewish Studies* 17, no. 2 (2018): 236–51.

Goschler, Constantin, ed. *Compensation in Practice: The Foundation "Remembrance, Responsibility and Future" and the Legacy of Forced Labour during the Third Reich.* New York: Berghahn Books, 2017.

———. *Schuld und Schulden: Die Politik der Wiedergutmachung für NS-Verfolgte seit 1945.* Göttingen: Wallstein, 2005.

———. *Wiedergutmachung: Westdeutschland und die Verfolgten des Nationalsozialismus 1945–1954.* Berlin: Oldenbourg Wissenschaftsverlag, 2009.

Goschler, Constantin, and Paul Erker, eds. "Compensating the Rest of the World: Das Entschädigungsmanagement der International Organization for Migration (IOM)." In *Die Entschädigung von NS-Zwangsarbeit am Anfang des 21. Jahrhunderts.* Vol. 2, *Transnationale Opferanwaltschaft: Das Auszahlungsprogramm und die internationalen Organisationen,* edited by Constantin Goschler, 80–196. Göttingen: Wallstein, 2012.

Gotovitch, José. "Enkele gegevens betreffende de uitroeiing van de zigeuners uit België." *Bijdragen tot de geschiedenis van de Tweede Wereldoorlog* 4 (1976): 153–73.

Grabowski, Jan. *Hunt for the Jews: Betrayal and Murder in German-Occupied Poland.* Bloomington: Indiana University Press, 2013.

Grandner, Margarete. "Staatsbürger und Ausländer: Zum Umgang Österreichs mit den jüdischen Flüchtlingen nach 1918." In *Asylland wider Willen: Flüchtlinge in Österreich im europäischen Kontext seit 1914,* edited by Gernot Heiss and Oliver Rathkolb, 60–85. Vienna: J & V Edition, 1995.

Granick, Jaclyn. "Les associations juives à la Société des Nations, 1919–1929: L'accès sans l'influence." *Relations internationales,* no. 151 (2012): 103–14.

Green, Abigail. "Nationalism and the 'Jewish International': Religious Internationalism in Europe and the Middle East, c.1840–c.1880." *Comparative Studies in Society and History* 50, no. 2 (2008): 535–58.

Gress, Daniela. "Geburtshelfer einer Bewegung? Die mediale Kampagne der Gesellschaft für bedrohte Völker für Bürgerrechte deutscher Sinti und Roma." In *Menschenrecht als Nachricht Medien, Öffentlichkeit und Moral seit dem 19. Jahrhundert,* edited by Birgit Hofmann, 267–306. Frankfurt am Main: Campus Verlag, 2020.

———. "Protest und Erinnerung: Der Hungerstreik in Dachau 1980 und die Entstehung der Bürgerrechtsbewegung deutscher Sinti und Roma." In *Sinti und Roma: Der nationalsozialistische Völkermord in historischer und gesellschaftspolitischer Perspektive,* edited by Karola Fings and Sybille Steinbacher, 190–219. Göttingen: Wallstein, 2021.

Gross, Jan Tomasz. *Neighbors: The Destruction of the Jewish Community in Jedwabne, Poland.* Princeton, NJ: Princeton University Press, 2001.

Grossmann, Atina. *Jews, Germans, and Allies: Close Encounters in Occupied Germany.* Princeton, NJ: Princeton University Press, 2007.

Grossman, Atina, and Tamar Lewinsky. "Part One: 1945–1949: Way Station." In *A History of Jews in Germany since 1945: Politics, Culture, and Society,* edited by Michael Brenner, translated by Kenneth Kronenberg, 55–144. Bloomington: Indiana University Press, 2018.

Gruber, Ruth Ellen. *Virtually Jewish: Reinventing Jewish Culture in Europe.* The S. Mark Taper Foundation Imprint in Jewish Studies. Berkeley: University of California Press, 2002.

Gruner, Wolf. *Öffentliche Wohlfahrt und Judenverfolgung: Wechselwirkungen lokaler und zentraler Politik im NS-Staat (1933–1942).* Munich: Oldenbourg, 2002.

Gutman, Israel, and Michael Berenbaum, eds. *Anatomy of the Auschwitz Death Camp.* Bloomington: Indiana University Press, published in association with the United States Holocaust Memorial Museum, 1994.

Hajnáczky, Tamás. "Trianon and Revisionist Gypsy Musicians." *Central European Political Science Review* 21, no. 81 (Fall 2020): 129–41.

Halbmayr, Brigitte. *Zeitlebens konsequent: Hermann Langbein, 1912–1995: Eine politische Biografie.* Vienna: Braumüller, 2012.

Hancock, Ian. *Danger! Educated Gypsy: Selected Essays.* Hatfield, UK: University of Hertfordshire Press, 2010.

———. "Elie Wiesel, Simon Wiesenthal, Romanies and the United States Holocaust Memorial Council." *The Holocaust in History and Memory* 4 (2011): 105–23.

———. *The Pariah Syndrome: An Account of Gypsy Slavery and Persecution.* Ann Arbor, MI: Karoma Publishers, 1987.

———. "Responses to the Porrajmos (The Romani Holocaust)." In *Is the Holocaust Unique?: Perspectives on Comparative Genocide,* edited by Alan S. Rosenbaum, 39–64. Boulder, CO: Westview Press, 2009.

———. *The Neglected Memory of the Romanies in the Holocaust /Porrajmos.* Edited by Jonathan C. Friedman. Routledge Handbooks Online. New York: Routledge, 2010.

Handlin, Oscar. *A Continuing Task: The American Jewish Joint Distribution Committee, 1914–1964.* New York: Random House, 1965.

Hanebrink, Paul A. *A Specter Haunting Europe: The Myth of Judeo-Bolshevism.* Cambridge, MA: Belknap Press of Harvard University Press, 2018.

Haumann, Heiko. *Die Akte Zilli Reichmann: Zur Geschichte der Sinti im 20. Jahrhundert.* Frankfurt am Main: S. Fischer Verlag, 2016.

———. *Hermann Diamanski (1910–1976): Überleben in der Katastrophe: Eine deutsche Geschichte zwischen Auschwitz und Staatssicherheitsdienst.* Cologne: Böhlau Verlag, 2011.

Heerten, Lasse. *The Biafran War and Postcolonial Humanitarianism: Spectacles of Suffering.* Human Rights in History. Cambridge: Cambridge University Press, 2017.

———. "'A' as in Auschwitz, 'B' as in Biafra: The Nigerian Civil War, Visual Narratives of Genocide, and the Fragmented Universalization of the Holocaust." In *Humanitarian Photography: A History,* edited by Heide Fehrenbach and Davide Rodogno, 249–74. Human Rights in History. Cambridge: Cambridge University Press, 2015.

Hegburg, Krista. "'The Law Is Such as It Is': Reparations, 'Historical Reality,' and the Legal Order in the Czech Republic." In *Hidden Genocides: Power, Knowledge, Memory*, edited by Alexander Laban Hinton, Thomas LaPointe, and Douglas Irvin-Erickson, 193–208. New Brunswick, NJ: Rutgers University Press, 2013.

Hegburg, Krista, and Yasar Abu Ghosh. "Introduction: Roma & Gadje." *Antrhopology of East Europe Review* 25, no. 2 (2007): 5–11.

Heinsohn, Kirsten. "Welche Aufgabe hat die Zeitgeschichte? Antworten von Eva G. Reichmann und Hans Rothfels." In *Aus den Quellen: Beiträge zur deutsch-jüdischen Geschichte: Festschrift für Ina Lorenz zum 65. Geburtstag*, edited by Ina Susanne Lorenz, Stefanie Schüler-Springorum, and Michael Studemund-Halévy, 378–87. Munich: Dölling und Galitz, 2005.

Henry, Marilyn. *Confronting the Perpetrators: A History of the Claims Conference*. London: Vallentine Mitchell, 2007.

Heuman, Johannes. "The Challenge of Minority Nationalism: Antiracism and Zionism in Postwar France." *French Historical Studies* 43, no. 3 (2020): 483–509.

Himka, John-Paul, and Joanna B. Michlic, eds. *Bringing the Dark Past to Light: The Reception of the Holocaust in Postcommunist Europe*. Lincoln: University of Nebraska Press, 2013.

Hirsch, Francine. *Soviet Judgment at Nuremberg: A New History of the International Military Tribunal after World War II*. New York: Oxford University Press, 2020.

Hockerts, Hans Günter. "Anwälte der Verfolgten: Die United Restitution Organization." In *Wiedergutmachung in der Bundesrepublik Deutschland*, edited by Ludolf Herbst and Constantin Goschler, 249–71. Munich: R. Oldenbourg, 1989.

———. "Die Entschädigung für NS-Verfolgte in West- und Osteuropa: Eine einführende Skizze." In *Grenzen der Wiedergutmachung: Die Entschädigung für NS-Verfolgte in West- und Osteuropa: 1945–2000*, edited by Hans Günter Hockerts, Claudia Moisel, and Tobias Winstel, 7–58. Göttingen: Wallstein, 2007.

———. "Wiedergutmachung in Deutschland: Eine historische Bilanz 1945–2000." *Vierteljahrshefte für Zeitgeschichte* 49, no. 2 (April 2001): 167–214.

Holborn, Louise W. *The International Refugee Organization: A Specialized Agency of the United Nations: Its History and Work, 1946–1952*. London: Oxford University Press, 1956.

Holian, Anna. *Between National Socialism and Soviet Communism: Displaced Persons in Postwar Germany*. Ann Arbor: University of Michigan Press, 2011.

Holler, Martin. *Der nationalsozialistische Völkermord an den Roma in der besetzten Sowjetunion (1941–1944)*. Heidelberg: Dokumentations- und Kulturzentrum Deutscher Sinti und Roma, 2009.

———. "The Nazi Persecution of Roma in Northwestern Russia: The Operational Area of the Army Group North, 1941–1944." In *The Nazi Genocide of the Roma: Reassessment and Commemoration*, edited by Anton Weiss-Wendt, 153–80. New York: Berghahn, 2013.

Holý, Dušan, and Ctibor Nečas. *Žalující píseň: O osudu Romů v nacistických koncentračních táborech*. Strážnice, Czech Republic: Ústav lidové kultury, 1993.

Horwitz, Gordon J. *Ghettostadt: Lódz and the Making of a Nazi City*. Cambridge, MA: Belknap Press of Harvard University Press, 2008.

Hubert, Marie-Christine. "Calling for an Allied Court of Justice." RomArchive, 2017. https://www.romarchive.eu/en/collection/die-bestrafung-der-moerder-von-500000-sinti-and-roma/.

Hübsch-Faust, Monika. "Eva Gabriele Reichmann, 1897–1998." *The Encyclopedia of Jewish Women,* Jewish Women's Archive, December 31, 1999. https://jwa.org/encyclopedia/article /reichmann-eva-grabriele.

Hübschmannová, Milena. *"Po Židoch Cigáni": Svědectví Romů ze Slovenska, 1939–1945.* Prague: Triáda, 2005.

———. "Vztahy mezi Romy a Židy na východním Slovensku před druhou světovou válkou." *Romano džaniben,* no. 1–2 (2000): 17–23.

Huonker, Thomas, and Regula Ludi. *Roma, Sinti und Jenische: Schweizerische Zigeunerpolitik zur Zeit des Nationalsozialismus: Beitrag zur Forschung.* Zürich, Switzerland: Chronos, 2001.

Illuzzi, Jennifer. *Gypsies in Germany and Italy, 1861–1914.* Basingstoke, UK: Palgrave Macmillan, 2014.

International Commission on the Holocaust in Romania. *Final Report.* Iaşi, Romania: Polirom, 2004. http://www.inshr-ew.ro/ro/files/Raport%20Final/Final_Report.pdf.

Ioanid, Radu. "The Holocaust in Romania: The Iasi Pogrom of June 1941." *Contemporary European History* 2, no. 2 (1993): 119–48.

Jackson, Ivor C. *The Refugee Concept in Group Situations.* Boston: Martinus Nijhoff, 1999.

Jarausch, Konrad Hugo, and Michael Geyer. *Shattered Past: Reconstructing German Histories.* Princeton, NJ: Princeton University Press, 2003.

Jasch, Hans-Christian, and Stephan Lehnstaedt, eds. *Verfolgen und Aufklären: Die erste Generation der Holocaustforschung / Crimes Uncovered: The First Generation of Holocaust Researchers.* Berlin: Metropol, 2019.

Jensen, Uffa. *Gebildete Doppelgänger: Bürgerliche Juden und Protestanten im 19. Jahrhundert.* Kritische Studien zur Geschichtswissenschaft 167. Göttingen: Vandenhoeck & Ruprecht, 2005.

Jockusch, Laura. *Collect and Record!: Jewish Holocaust Documentation in Early Postwar Europe.* New York: Oxford University Press, 2012.

———. "Justice at Nuremberg? Jewish Responses to Nazi War-Crime Trials in Allied-Occupied Germany." *Jewish Social Studies* 19, no. 1 (2012): 107–47.

Joskowicz, Ari. "Romani Refugees and the Postwar Order." *Journal of Contemporary History* 51, no. 4 (October 2016): 760–87.

———. "Separate Suffering, Shared Archives: Jewish and Romani Histories of Nazi Persecution." *History and Memory* 28, no. 1 (2016): 110–40.

———. "The Age of the Witness and the Age of Surveillance: Romani Holocaust Testimony and the Perils of Digital Scholarship." *American Historical Review* 125, no. 4 (October 2020): 1205–31.

Kaes, Anton. "1979: The American Television Series Holocaust Is Shown in West Germany." In *Yale Companion to Jewish Writing and Thought in German Culture, 1096–1996,* edited by Sander L. Gilman and Jack Zipes, 783–89. New Haven, CT: Yale University Press, 1997.

Kalisch, Shoshana, and Barbara Meister. *Yes, We Sang!: Songs of the Ghettos and Concentration Camps.* New York: Harper & Row, 1985.

Kalman, Julie. *Rethinking Antisemitism in Nineteenth-Century France.* New York: Cambridge University Press, 2010.

Kalmar, Ivan Davidson. "Benjamin Disraeli, Romantic Orientalist." *Comparative Studies in Society and History* 47, no. 2 (2005): 348–71.

Kalmar, Ivan Davidson, and Derek J. Penslar, eds. *Orientalism and the Jews.* Hanover, NH: University Press of New England, 2005.

Kalter, Christoph. *The Discovery of the Third World: Decolonization and the Rise of the New Left in France, c.1950–1976.* Cambridge: Cambridge University Press, 2016.

Kamm, Antony. "Yates, Dora Esther (1879–1974)." *Oxford Dictionary of National Biography.* Oxford: Oxford University Press, 2004.

Kansteiner, Wulf. "Populäres Geschichtsfernsehen vor 'Holocaust': Die Darstellung des Nationalsozialismus und des Zweiten Weltkrieges in drei Erfolgssendungen des ZDF." *Historical Social Research / Historische Sozialforschung* 30, no. 4 (114) (2005): 53–73.

Kaplan, Amy. "Zionism as Anticolonialism: The Case of 'Exodus.'" *American Literary History* 25, no. 4 (2013): 870–95.

Kapralski, Sławomir. "The Aftermath of the Roma Genocide from Implicit Memories to Commemoration." In *The Nazi Genocide of the Roma: Reassessment and Commemoration,* edited by Anton Weiss-Wendt, 229–51. New York: Berghahn, 2013.

Kapralski, Slawomir Martyniak. *Roma in Auschwitz.* Voices of Memory 7. Oświęcim, Poland: Auschwitz-Birkenau State Museum, 2011.

Karp, Jonathan, and Adam Sutcliffe, eds. *Philosemitism in History.* New York: Cambridge University Press, 2011.

Kassow, Samuel D. *Who Will Write Our History?: Emanuel Ringelblum, the Warsaw Ghetto, and the Oyneg Shabes Archive.* Bloomington: Indiana University Press, 2007.

Katz, Ethan. *The Burdens of Brotherhood: Jews and Muslims from North Africa to France.* Cambridge, MA: Harvard University Press, 2015.

Kelemen, Paul. *The British Left and Zionism: History of a Divorce.* Manchester, UK: Manchester University Press, 2018.

Kelso, Michelle, dir. *Hidden Sorrows: The Persecution of Romanian Gypsies during the Holocaust.* N.p.: In the Shadow Productions, 2005. YouTube video. https://www.youtube.com/watch?v=qQNhSQemCzo&t=1780s.

———. "Holocaust-Era Compensation and the Case of the Roma." *Studia Hebraica,* no. 8 (2008): 298–334.

———. "Romani Women and the Holocaust: Testimonies of Sexual Violence in Romanian-Controlled Transnistria." In *Women and Genocide: Gendered Experiences of Violence, Survival, and Resistance,* edited by JoAnn DiGeorgio-Lutz and Donna Gosbee, 37–72. Toronto: Women's Press, 2016. ProQuest. http://ebookcentral.proquest.com/lib/vand/detail.action?docID=6282125.

Kenrick, Donald. *Historical Dictionary of the Gypsies (Romanies).* Lanham, MD: Scarecrow Press, 1998.

———. "Miriam Novitch—Chronistin Des Schicksals von Sinti Und Roma." *Pogrom: Zeitschrift Für Bedrohte Völker* 21, no. 154 (August 1990): 66.

Kenrick, Donald, and Grattan Puxon. *The Destiny of Europe's Gypsies.* Studies in the Dynamics of Persecution and Extermination, Columbus Centre. London: Chatto and Heinemann Educational for Sussex University Press, 1972.

Kermish, Joseph. "Emmanuel Ringelblum's Notes, Hitherto Unpublished." *Yad Vashem Studies* 7 (1968): 173–83.

Kintaert, Barbara. "Vertrieben und vergessen? Bibliothekarinnen in der Kinderfreunde- und Arbeiterbewegung." In *Österreichische Bibliothekarinnen auf der Flucht: Verfolgt, verdrängt, vergessen?,* edited by Ilse Erika Korotin, 169–212. Biografia 4. Vienna: Praesens, 2007.

Kirchheimer, Otto. "Decree Powers and Constitutional Law in France under the Third Republic." *The American Political Science Review* 34, no. 6 (1940): 1104–23.

Klimke, Martin. *The Other Alliance: Student Protest in West Germany and the United States in the Global Sixties*. America in the World. Princeton, NJ: Princeton University Press, 2010.

Klímová-Alexander, Ilona. "Development and Institutionalisation of Romani Representation and Administration. Part 1." *Nationalities Papers* 32, no. 3 (September 2004): 599–629.

———. "The Development and Institutionalization of Romani Representation and Administration. Part 2: Beginnings of Modern Institutionalization (Nineteenth Century—World War II)." *Nationalities Papers* 33, no. 2 (June 2005): 155–210.

———. "The Development and Institutionalization of Romani Representation and Administration. Part 3a: From National Organizations to International Umbrellas (1945–1970)—Romani Mobilization at the National Level." *Nationalities Papers* 34, no. 5 (November 2006): 599–621.

———. "The Development and Institutionalization of Romani Representation and Administration. Part 3b: From National Organizations to International Umbrellas (1945–1970)—the International Level." *Nationalities Papers* 35, no. 4 (September 2007): 627–61.

———. "The Development and Institutionalization of Romani Representation and Administration. Part 3c: Religious, Governmental, and Non-Governmental Institutions (1945–1970)." *Nationalities Papers* 38, no. 1 (January 2010): 105.

Knesebeck, Julia von dem. *The Roma Struggle for Compensation in Post-War Germany*. Hatfield, UK: University of Hertfordshire Press, 2011.

Knight, Robert. *"Ich bin dafür, die Sache in die Länge zu ziehen": Die Wortprotokolle der österreichischen Bundesregierung von 1945 bis 1952 über die Entschädigung der Juden*. 2nd ed. Vienna: Böhlau, 2000.

Kochanowski, Jan. "Gypsies and the Problem of Their Acculturation." *Indo-Asian Culture* 14, no. 1 (January 1965): 21.

Kochavi, Arieh J. *Prelude to Nuremberg: Allied War Crimes Policy and the Question of Punishment*. Chapel Hill: University of North Carolina Press, 1998.

Königseder, Angelika. *Waiting for Hope: Jewish Displaced Persons in Post-World War II Germany*. Evanston, IL: Northwestern University Press, 2001.

Korb, Alexander Martin. *Im Schatten des Weltkriegs: Massengewalt der Ustaša gegen Serben, Juden und Roma in Kroatien 1941–1945*. Studien zur Gewaltgeschichte des 20. Jahrhunderts. Hamburg: Hamburger Edition, 2013.

Korzilius, Sven. *"Asoziale" und "Parasiten" im Recht der SBZ/DDR: Randgruppen im Sozialismus zwischen Repression und Ausgrenzung*. Cologne: Böhlau, 2005.

Krakowski, Shmuel. *Chełmno: A Small Village in Europe: The First Nazi Mass Extermination Camp*. Jerusalem: Yad Vashem, 2009.

Kraushaar, Wolfgang. "Die Affäre Auerbach: Zur Virulenz des Antisemitismus in den Gründerjahren der Bundesrepublik." *Menora: Jahrbuch für deutsch-jüdische Geschichte* 6 (1995): 319–43.

———. "Die Auerbach-Affäre." In *Leben im Land der Täter: Juden im Nachkriegsdeutschland (1945–1952)*, edited by Julius H. Schoeps, 208–18. Berlin: Jüdische Verlagsanstalt, 2001.

Kronauer, Ulrich. "Vom gemeinsamen Vorurteil gegenüber 'Juden, Zigeunern und derlei Gesindel' im 18. Jahrhundert." In *"Zigeuner" und Nation: Repräsentation—Inklusion—Exklusion*, edited by Herbert Uerlings and Iulia-Karin Patrut, 137–50. Frankfurt am Main: Peter Lang, 2008.

Krutikov, Mikhail. "Wiener, Meir." *YIVO Encyclopedia of Jews in Eastern Europe*, November 4, 2010. https://yivoencyclopedia.org/article.aspx/Wiener_Meir.

Kubica, Helena, and Piotr Setkiewicz. "The Last Stage of the Functioning of the Zigeunerlager in the Birkenau Camp (May–August 1944)." *Memoria: Memory, History, Education* 10 (July 2018): 6–15.

Kuperstein, Isaiah. "Rumors: A Socio-Historical Phenomenon in the Ghetto of Lodz." *The Polish Review* 18, no. 4 (January 1973): 63–83.

Kuwalek, Robert. *Das Vernichtungslager Belzec*. Translated by Steffen Hänschen. 2nd ed. Berlin: Metropol, 2014.

Kyuchukov, Hristo, Elena Marushiakova, and Vesslin Popov, eds. *Roma: Past, Present, Future*. Munich: Lincom, 2016.

Lagrou, Pieter. *The Legacy of Nazi Occupation: Patriotic Memory and National Recovery in Western Europe, 1945–1965*. Cambridge: Cambridge University Press, 1999.

———. "Victims of Genocide and National Memory: Belgium, France and the Netherlands 1945–1965." *Past & Present*, no. 154 (February 1997): 181–222.

Landes, Richard. "The Jews as Contested Ground in Postmodern Conspiracy Theory." *Jewish Political Studies Review* 19, no. 3/4 (2007): 9–34.

Langbein, Hermann. *People in Auschwitz*. Translated by Harry Zohn. Chapel Hill: University of North Carolina Press, 2004.

Langer, Lawrence L. *Versions of Survival: The Holocaust and the Human Spirit*. SUNY Series in Modern Jewish Literature and Culture. Albany, NY: SUNY Press, 1982.

Laqueur, Walter. *The Terrible Secret: An Investigation into the Suppression of Information about Hitler's "Final Solution."* London: Weidenfeld and Nicolson, 1980.

Lassner, Phyllis, and Lara Trubowitz, eds. *Antisemitism and Philosemitism in the Twentieth and Twenty-First Centuries: Representing Jews, Jewishness, and Modern Culture*. Newark: University of Delaware Press, 2008.

Lavsky, Hagit. *New Beginnings: Holocaust Survivors in Bergen-Belsen and the British Zone in Germany, 1945–1950*. Detroit, MI: Wayne State University Press, 2002.

Leff, Lisa Moses. *Sacred Bonds of Solidarity: The Rise of Jewish Internationalism in Nineteenth-Century France*. Stanford Studies in Jewish History and Culture. Stanford, CA: Stanford University Press, 2006.

———. *The Archive Thief: The Man Who Salvaged French Jewish History in the Wake of the Holocaust*. The Oxford Series on History and Archives. New York: Oxford University Press, 2015.

Leff, Lisa Moses, and Nathan A. Kurz. "'Saving' the Jews of the Diaspora." In *The Oxford Handbook of the Jewish Diaspora*, edited by Hasia R. Diner. New York: Oxford University Press, 2021.

Lehmann-Richter, Arnold. *Auf der Suche nach den Grenzen der Wiedergutmachung: Die Rechtsprechung zur Entschädigung für Opfer der nationalsozialistischen Verfolgung*. Berlin: Berliner Wissenschafts-Verlag, 2007.

Lemon, Alaina. *Between Two Fires: Gypsy Performance and Romani Memory from Pushkin to Post-Socialism*. Durham, NC: Duke University Press, 2000.

———. "'What Are They Writing about Us Blacks?' Roma and 'Race' in Russia." *Anthropology of East Europe Review* 13, no. 2 (1995): 34–40.

Levey, Zach. "The Rise and Decline of a Special Relationship: Israel and Ghana, 1957–1966." *African Studies Review* 46, no. 1 (2003): 155–77.

Levy, Daniel, and Natan Sznaider. *The Holocaust and Memory in the Global Age*. Translated by Assenka Oksiloff. Philadelphia, PA: Temple University Press, 2006.

Lewis, Mark. *The Birth of the New Justice: The Internationalization of Crime and Punishment, 1919–1950*. New York: Oxford University Press, 2014.

Lewy, Guenter. "Gypsies and Jews Under the Nazis." *Holocaust and Genocide Studies* 13, no. 3 (December 1999): 383–404.

———. *The Nazi Persecution of the Gypsies*. Oxford: Oxford University Press, 2000.

Lie, Siv B. *Django Generations: Hearing Ethnorace, Citizenship, and Jazz Manouche in France*. Chicago: University of Chicago Press, 2021.

Liégeois, Jean-Pierre. *Mutation tsigane: La révolution bohémienne*. L'Humanité complexe. Brussels: Editions Complexe, 1976.

———. "Naissance du pouvoir tsigane." *Revue française de sociologie* 16, no. 3 (July 1975): 295–316.

Linenthal, Edward Tabor. *Preserving Memory: The Struggle to Create America's Holocaust Museum*. New York: Columbia University Press, 2001.

Lockman, Zachary. "Railway Workers and Relational History: Arabs and Jews in British-Ruled Palestine." *Comparative Studies in Society and History* 35, no. 3 (1993): 601–27.

Loeffler, James. *Rooted Cosmopolitans: Jews and Human Rights in the Twentieth Century*. New Haven, CT: Yale University Press, 2018.

Lotto-Kusche, Sebastian. "'. . . Daß für sie die gewöhnlichen Rechtsbegriffe nicht gelten': Das NS-Zwangslager für 'Zigeuner' in Flensburg und dessen Wahrnehmung in der Stadtbevölkerung." *Demokratische Geschichte: Jahrbuch für Schleswig-Holstein* 28 (2018): 225–38.

———. "Politische Anerkennung der Sinti und Roma in der Bundesrepublik Deutschland: Eine Untersuchung anhand des Wandels in der Sprachpraxis staatlicher Stellen." In *Textuelle Historizität Interdisziplinäre Perspektiven auf das historische Apriori*, edited by Heidrun Kämper, Ingo H. Warnke, and Daniel Schmidt-Brücken, 247–60. Berlin: De Gruyter Mouton, 2016.

———. "Spannungsfelder im Vorfeld der Anerkennung des Völkermords an den Sinti und Roma: Das Gespräch zwischen dem Zentralrat Deutscher Sinti und Roma und der Bundesregierung am 17. März 1982." In *Stigmatisierung, Marginalisierung, Verfolgung: Beiträge des 19. Workshops zur Geschichte und Gedächtnisgeschichte der nationalsozialistischen Konzentrationslager*, edited by Marco Brenneisen, Christine Eckel, Laura Haendel, and Julia Pietsch, 224–44. Berlin: Metropol, 2015.

Lowe, Keith. *Savage Continent: Europe in the Aftermath of World War II*. New York: St. Martin's Press, 2012.

Lucassen, Leo. *Zigeuner: Die Geschichte eines polizeilichen Ordnungsbegriffes in Deutschland, 1700–1945*. Weimar, Germany: Böhlau, 1996.

Lucassen, Leo, Wim Willems, and Annemarie Cottaar. *Gypsies and Other Itinerant Groups: A Socio-Historical Approach*. New York: St. Martin's Press, 1998.

Ludi, Regula. *Reparations for Nazi Victims in Postwar Europe*. Cambridge: Cambridge University Press, 2012.

———. "The Vectors of Postwar Victim Reparations: Relief, Redress and Memory Politics." *Journal of Contemporary History* 41, no. 3 (2006): 421–50.

Ludyga, Hannes. *Philipp Auerbach (1906–1952): "Staatskommissar für rassisch, religiös und politisch Verfolgte."* Berlin: Berliner Wissenschafts-Verlag, 2005.

Lustig, Jason. *A Time to Gather: Archives and the Control of Jewish Culture.* The Oxford Series on History and Archives. New York: Oxford University Press, 2022.

Magid, Shaul. "The Holocaust and Jewish Identity in America: Memory, the Unique, and the Universal." *Jewish Social Studies* 18, no. 2 (2012): 100–135.

Maier, Charles S. "Consigning the Twentieth Century to History: Alternative Narratives for the Modern Era." *American Historical Review* 105, no. 3 (2000): 807–31.

Majtényi, György. "The Memory and Histography of Porrajmos: Making a Transnational National Site of Memory." *S:I.M.O.N. Shoah: Intervention. Methods. Documentation* 8, no. 1 (2021): 86–103.

Mandel, Maud. *Muslims and Jews in France: History of a Conflict.* Princeton, NJ: Princeton University Press, 2014.

———. "Philanthropy or Cultural Imperialism? The Impact of American Jewish Aid in Post-Holocaust France." *Jewish Social Studies* 9, no. 1 (2002): 53–94.

Mankowitz, Zeev W. *Life between Memory and Hope: The Survivors of the Holocaust in Occupied Germany.* New York: Cambridge University Press, 2002.

Marcuse, Harold. "Holocaust Memorials: The Emergence of a Genre." *American Historical Review* 115, no. 1 (2010): 53–89.

———. *Legacies of Dachau: The Uses and Abuses of a Concentration Camp, 1933–2001.* Cambridge: Cambridge University Press, 2001.

Margalit, Gilad. *Germany and Its Gypsies: A Post-Auschwitz Ordeal.* Madison: University of Wisconsin Press, 2002.

———. "'Großer Gott, ich danke Dir, daß Du kleine schwarze Kinder gemacht hast.' Der 'Zigeunerpastor'—Georg Althaus." *WerkstattGeschichte*, no. 25 (2000): 59–73.

Mark, James, and Péter Apor. "Socialism Goes Global: Decolonization and the Making of a New Culture of Internationalism in Socialist Hungary, 1956–1989." *The Journal of Modern History* 87, no. 4 (2015): 852–91.

Marrus, Michael. "Jewish Lobby at Nuremberg: Jacob Robinson and the Institute of Jewish Affairs, 1945–46." In *The Nuremberg Trials: International Criminal Law since 1945: 60th Anniversary International Conference*, edited by Reginbogin, Herbert R., and Christoph J. M. Safferling, 63–71. Munich: Saur, 2006.

Marrus, Michael Robert, ed. *The Nazi Holocaust: Historical Articles on the Destruction of European Jews.* Vol. 2, *The Origins of the Holocaust.* Westport, CT: Meckler, 1989.

Martin, Thomas. "Anti-Racism, Republicanism and the Sarkozy Years: SOS Racisme and the Mouvement des Indigènes de la République." In *France's Colonial Legacies: Memory, Identity and Narrative*, edited by Fiona Barclay, 188–206. Cardiff, UK: University of Wales Press, 2013.

Marushiakova, Elena, and Vesselin Popov. "Gypsy Guilds (Esnafs) on the Balkans." In *Roma: Past, Present, Future*, edited by Hristo Kyuchukov, Elena Marushiakova, and Vesslin Popov, 76–89. Munich: Lincom, 2016.

———. "Roma Labelling: Policy and Academia." *Slovenský Národopis* 66, no. 4 (2018): 385–418.

Matras, Yaron. "The Development of the Romani Civil Rights Movement in Germany 1945–1996." In *Sinti and Roma: Gypsies in German-Speaking Society and Literature*, edited by Susan Tebbutt, 49–63. New York: Berghahn Books, 1998.

Matthäus, Jürgen, ed. *Approaching an Auschwitz Survivor: Holocaust Testimony and Its Transformations*. The Oxford Oral History Series. New York: Oxford University Press, 2009.

———. "Displacing Memory: The Transformations of an Early Interview." In *Approaching an Auschwitz: Survivor Holocaust Testimony and Its Transformations*, edited by Jürgen Matthäus, 49–72. The Oxford Oral History Series. New York: Oxford University Press, 2009.

Mayall, David. *Gypsy Identities, 1500–2000: From Egipcyans and Moon-Men to the Ethnic Romany*. London: Routledge, 2004.

Mazel, Michelle. "French Jewry and the Dieudonné Affair." *Jewish Political Studies Review* 26, no. 1/2 (2014): 70–78.

Mazower, Mark. "The Strange Triumph of Human Rights, 1933–1950." *The Historical Journal* 47, no. 2 (2004): 379–98.

Mechanicus, Philip. "Journal: Camp de Westerbork 28 mai 1943–28 février 1944." Translated by Laetitia Decourt, Hinde Kaddour, and Gaby Velthuys. *Po&sie* 142, no. 4 (2012): 85–108.

Mędykowski, Witold Wojciech. "Forced Labor in the Labor Camps." In *Macht Arbeit Frei?: German Economic Policy and Forced Labor of Jews in the General Government, 1939–1943*, 134–80. Brighton, MA: Academic Studies Press, 2018.

Megargee, Geoffrey P., and Martin Dean, eds. *The United States Holocaust Memorial Museum Encyclopedia of Camps and Ghettos, 1933–1945*. Vol. 2. Bloomington: Indiana University Press in association with the United States Holocaust Memorial Museum, 2009. www.loc.gov /catdir/toc/ecip0826/2008037382.html.

Mendelsohn, Erza. *On Modern Jewish Politics*. New York: Oxford University Press, 1993.

Mendelsohn, John. "Trial by Document: The Use of Seized Records in the United States Proceedings at Nuernberg." PhD diss., University of Michigan, 1974.

Mirga-Kruszelnicka, Anna, Esteban Acuña, and Piotr Trojanski, eds. *Education for Remembrance of the Roma Genocide: Scholarship, Commemoration and the Role of Youth*. Kraków: Wydawnictwo Libron, Filip Lohner, 2015.

Mirga, Karolina and Jonathan Mack, "From Holocaust Remembrance to Youth Empowerment." In *Education for Remembrance of the Roma Genocide: Scholarship, Commemoration and the Role of Youth*, edited by Mirga-Kruszelnicka, Anna, Esteban Acuña, and Piotr Trojanski, 203–16. Kraków: Wydawnictwo Libron, Filip Lohner, 2015.

Mitchell, Robert E. *Human Geographies Within the Pale of Settlement: Order and Disorder During the Eighteenth and Nineteenth Centuries*. Cham, Switzerland: Springer International, 2019.

Montague, Patrick. *Chełmno and the Holocaust: The History of Hitler's First Death Camp*. Chapel Hill: University of North Carolina Press, 2012.

Moser, Jonny. *Nisko: Die ersten Judendeportationen*. Vienna: Edition Steinbauer, 2012.

Moses, A. Dirk. *German Intellectuals and the Nazi Past*. Cambridge: Cambridge University Press, 2007.

Mostowicz, Arnold. *With a Yellow Star and a Red Cross: A Doctor in the Łódz Ghetto*. London: Vallentine Mitchell, 2005.

Nefors, Patrick. *Inventaris van het archief van de Dienst voor de Oorlogsslachtoffers / Inventaire des archives du Service des Victimes de la Guerre*. Brussels: Ministerie van Sociale Zaken, Volksgezondheid en Leefmilieu Dienst voor de Oorlogsslachtoffers en het SOMA Studie- en Documentatiecentrum oorlog en hedendaagse maatschappij, 1997.

Neier, Aryeh. *The International Human Rights Movement: A History*. Human Rights and Crimes against Humanity. Princeton, NJ: Princeton University Press, 2012.

Niewyk, Donald L. *Fresh Wounds: Early Narratives of Holocaust Survival*. Chapel Hill: University of North Carolina Press, 1998.

Niewyk, Donald, and Francis Nicosia. *The Columbia Guide to the Holocaust*. New York: Columbia University Press, 2003.

Nord, Deborah Epstein. *Gypsies & the British Imagination, 1807–1930*. New York: Columbia University Press, 2006.

Nord, Philip G. *After the Deportation: Memory Battles in Postwar France*. Studies in the Social and Cultural History of Modern Warfare. Cambridge: Cambridge University Press, 2020.

Novick, Peter. *The Holocaust in American Life*. Boston: Houghton Mifflin, 1999.

Novitch, Miriam. "Il genocidio degli Zigani sotto il regime nazista." *Quaderni del centro di studi sulla deportazione e l'internamento* 2 (1965): 31–61.

———. "Jewish Partisans in Yugoslavia." In *Extermination and Resistance: Historical Records and Source Material*. Vol. 1, edited by Zvi Szner, 180–82. Lohamei HaGeta'ot, Israel: Ghetto Fighters' House, 1958.

———. *Le génocide des tziganes sous le régime Nazi*. Paris: Comité pour l'érection du Monument en mémoire des Tziganes assassinés à Auschwitz, 1968.

Nowersztern, Abraham. *Avrom Sutskever-bibliografye*. Tel Aviv: Yiśroel-bukh, 1976.

Oertel, Christine. *Juden auf der Flucht durch Austria: Jüdische Displaced Persons in der US-Besatzungszone Österreichs*. Vienna: Eichbauer, 1999.

O'Keeffe, Brigid. *New Soviet Gypsies: Nationality, Performance, and Selfhood in the Early Soviet Union*. Toronto: University of Toronto Press, 2013.

Opfermann, Ulrich Friedrich. "Genozid und Justiz: Schlussstrich als 'staatspolitische Zielsetzung.'" In *Zigeunerverfolgung im Rheinland und in Westfalen 1933–1945: Geschichte, Aufarbeitung und Erinnerung*, edited by Karola Fings and Ulrich Friedrich Opfermann, 315–26. Paderborn, Germany: Schöningh, 2012.

———. "The Registration of Gypsies in National Socialism: Responsibility in a German Region." *Romani Studies* 11, no. 1 (2001): 25–52.

———. "Seye kein Ziegeuner, sondern kayserlicher Cornet": Sinti im 17. und 18. Jahrhundert: Eine Untersuchung anhand archivalischer Quellen. Berlin: Metropol, 2007.

———. "Zum Umgang der deutschen Justiz mit an der Roma-Minderheit begangenen NS-Verbrechen nach 1945. Das Sammelverfahren zum 'Zigeunerkomplex' (1958–1970)." Report for the Unabhängige Kommission Antiziganismus. Berlin 2021. https://www.bmi.bund.de/SharedDocs/downloads/DE/veroeffentlichungen/themen/heimat-integration/antiziganismus/opfermann-nsg-verfahren.pdf?__blob=publicationFile&v=2.

Pasto, James. "Islam's 'Strange Secret Sharer': Orientalism, Judaism, and the Jewish Question." *Comparative Studies in Society and History* 40, no. 3 (1998): 437–74.

Patrut, Iulia-Karin. *Phantasma Nation: "Zigeuner" und Juden als Grenzfiguren des "Deutschen" (1770–1920)*. Würzburg, Germany: Königshausen & Neumann, 2014.

Pawlicka-Nowak, Lucja, ed. *Chelmno Witnesses Speak*. Konin, Poland: District Museum in Konin, 2004.

Pendas, Devin O. *The Frankfurt Auschwitz Trial, 1963–1965: Genocide, History, and the Limits of the Law*. Cambridge: Cambridge University Press, 2006.

Pendas, Devin O., Mark Roseman, and Richard F. Wetzell, eds. *Beyond the Racial State: Rethinking Nazi Germany*. Cambridge: Cambridge University Press, 2017.

Penslar, Derek. "Is Zionism a Colonial Movement?" In *Colonialism and the Jews*, edited by Ethan Katz, Lisa Moses Leff, and Maud Mandel, 275–300. Bloomington: Indiana University Press, 2017.

Perego, Simon. *Pleurons-les: Les Juifs de Paris et la commémoration de la Shoah (1944–1967)*. Époques. Ceyzérieu, France: Champ Vallon, 2020.

Perra, Emiliano. "Narratives of Innocence and Victimhood: The Reception of the Miniseries Holocaust in Italy." *Holocaust and Genocide Studies* 22, no. 3 (2008): 411–40.

Peschanski, Denis. *La France des camps: L'internement, 1938–1946*. La Suite Des Temps. Paris: Gallimard, 2002.

———. *Les Tsiganes en France: 1939–1946*. Histoire 20e Siècle. Paris: CNRS éditions, 1994.

———. "Zigeuner in Frankreich 1912–1969: Eine Periode durchgehender Stigmatisierung." In *Zwischen Erziehung und Vernichtung: Zigeunerpolitik und Zigeunerforschung im Europa des 20. Jahrhunderts*, edited by Michael Zimmermann, 268–77. Beiträge zur Geschichte der Deutschen Forschungsgemeinschaft 3. Stuttgart: Steiner, 2007.

Petrie, Jon. "The Secular Word Holocaust: Scholarly Myths, History, and 20th Century Meanings." *Journal of Genocide Research* 2, no. 1 (March 2000): 31–63.

Picker, Giovanni. *Racial Cities: Governance and the Segregation of Romani People in Urban Europe*. London: Routledge, 2017.

Pientka, Patricia. *Das Zwangslager für Sinti und Roma in Berlin-Marzahn: Alltag, Verfolgung und Deportation*. Berlin: Metropol-Verlag, 2013.

Pieper, Katrin. *Die Musealisierung des Holocaust: Das Jüdische Museum Berlin und das U.S. Holocaust Memorial Museum in Washington D.C.: Ein Vergleich*. Cologne: Böhlau, 2006.

Piotrowska, Anna G. *Gypsy Music in European Culture: From the Late Eighteenth to the Early Twentieth Century*. Boston: Northeastern University Press, 2013.

Poliakov, Léon. *Harvest of Hate: The Nazi Program for the Destruction of the Jews of Europe*. Syracuse, NY: Syracuse University Press, 1954.

———, ed. *Le procès de Jérusalem: Jugement-documents*. Paris: Calmann-Lévy, 1963.

Pollin-Galay, Hannah. "Avrom Sutzkever's Art of Testimony: Witnessing with the Poet in the Wartime Soviet Union." *Jewish Social Studies* 21, no. 2 (2016): 1–34.

———. *Ecologies of Witnessing: Language, Place, and Holocaust Testimony*. New Haven, CT: Yale University Press, 2018.

Porat, Dan. *Bitter Reckoning: Israel Tries Holocaust Survivors as Nazi Collaborators*. Cambridge, MA: Belknap Press of Harvard University Press, 2019.

———. "Changing Legal Perceptions of 'Nazi Collaborators' in Israel, 1950–1972." In *Jewish Honor Courts: Revenge, Retribution, and Reconciliation in Europe and Israel after the Holocaust*, edited by Gabriel Finder and Laura Jockusch, 303–26. Detroit, MI: Wayne State University Press, 2015.

Presser, J. *Ondergang: De vervolging en verdelging van het Nederlandse jodendom, 1940–1945*. The Hague, Netherlands: Staatsuitgeverij, 1965.

Prais, Lea. "'Jews from the World to Come': The First Testimonies of Escapees from Chełmno and Treblinka in the Warsaw Ghetto, 1942–1943." *Yad Vashem Studies* 42, no 1 (2014): 47–81.

Priemel, Kim Christian. *The Betrayal: The Nuremberg Trials and German Divergence*. Oxford: Oxford University Press, 2016.

Pross, Christian. *Wiedergutmachung: Der Kleinkrieg gegen die Opfer.* Frankfurt am Main: Athenäum, 1988.

Putnam, Lara. "The Transnational and the Text-Searchable: Digitized Sources and the Shadows They Cast." *American Historical Review* 121, no. 2 (April 2016): 377–402.

Rabin, Dana Y. "Seeing Jews and Gypsies in 1753." *Cultural and Social History* 7, no. 1 (March 2010): 35–58.

Rabinovici, Doron. *Instanzen der Ohnmacht: Wien 1938–1945: Der Weg zum Judenrat.* Frankfurt am Main: Jüdischer Verlag, 2000.

Radonić, Ljiljana. "From 'Double Genocide' to 'the New Jews': Holocaust, Genocide and Mass Violence in Post-Communist Memorial Museums." *Journal of Genocide Research* 20, no. 4 (October 2018): 510–29.

———. "'People of Freedom and Unlimited Movement': Representations of Roma in Post-Communist Memorial Museums." *Social Inclusion* 3, no. 5 (September 2015): 64–77.

Rathert, Ronald. *Verbrechen und Verschwörung: Arthur Nebe der Kripochef des Dritten Reiches.* Münster, Germany: Lit, 2001.

Rawidowicz, Simon. "Israel: The Ever-Dying People." In *Israel, the Ever-Dying People, and Other Essays,* edited by Benjamin C. I. Ravid, 53–63. Rutherford, NJ: Fairleigh Dickinson University Press, 1986.

Reinisch, Jessica, and Elizabeth White, eds. *The Disentanglement of Populations: Migration, Expulsion and Displacement in Post-War Europe, 1944–9.* Basingstoke, UK: Palgrave Macmillan, 2011.

Reiter, Margit. *Unter Antisemitismus-Verdacht: Die österreichische Linke und Israel nach der Shoah.* Innsbruck, Austria: Studien Verlag, 2001.

Reitlinger, Gerald. *The Final Solution: The Attempt to Exterminate the Jews of Europe, 1939–1945.* New York: A. S. Barnes, 1961.

———. *The SS: Alibi of a Nation, 1922–1945.* London: Heinemann, 1956.

Renz, Werner. "Fritz Bauer Institut: Mitschnitte Prozessprotokolle." Tonbandmitschnitte des Auschwitz-Prozesses (1963–1965), September 2013. http://www.auschwitz-prozess.de/index .php?show=T%2003_Der%20Tonbandmitschnitt%20des%20Auschwitz-Prozesses.

Reuss, Anja. "'Return to Normality?': The Struggle of Sinti and Roma Survivors to Rebuild a Life in Postwar Germany." In *Jewish and Romani Families, in the Holocaust and Its Aftermath,* edited by Eliyana R. Adler and Kateřina Čapková, 141–55. New Brunswick, NJ: Rutgers University Press, 2021.

Reynolds, Daniel P. *Postcards from Auschwitz: Holocaust Tourism and the Meaning of Remembrance.* New York: New York University Press, 2018.

Rieger, Berndt. *Creator of Nazi Death Camps: The Life of Odilo Globocnik.* London: Vallentine Mitchell, 2007.

Roby, Bryan K. *The Mizrahi Era of Rebellion: Israel's Forgotten Civil Rights Struggle 1948–1966.* Syracuse: Syracuse University Press, 2015.

Rodrigue, Aron. *French Jews, Turkish Jews: The Alliance Israélite Universelle and the Politics of Jewish Schooling in Turkey, 1860–1925.* Bloomington: Indiana University Press, 1990.

Roegholt, Richter. *Ben Sijes: Een biografie.* The Hague, Netherlands: Sdu, 1988.

Rose, Romani. "'Für beide galt damals der gleiche Befehl': Eine Entgegnung auf Yehuda Bauers Thesen zum Genozid an den europäischen Juden, Sinti und Roma." *Blätter für deutsche und internationale Politik* 43 (1998), 467–72.

Rose, Romani, Frank Reuter, and Silvio Peritore. *The National Socialist Genocide of the Sinti and Roma: Catalogue of the Permanent Exhibition in the State Museum of Auschwitz.* Heidelberg: Dokumentations- und Kulturzentrum Deutscher Sinti und Roma, 2003.

Roseman, Mark. "The Organic Society and the Massenmenschen: Integrating Young Labor in the Ruhr Mines, 1945–48." In *West Germany under Construction: Politics, Society, and Culture in the Adenauer Era,* edited by Robert G. Moeller. Ann Arbor: University of Michigan Press, 1997.

Rosen, Alan Charles. *The Wonder of Their Voices: The 1946 Holocaust Interviews of David Boder.* New York: Oxford University Press, 2010.

Rosenbaum, Alan S., ed. *Is the Holocaust Unique?: Perspectives on Comparative Genocide.* 3rd ed. Boulder, CO: Westview Press, 2009.

Rosenberg, Clifford D. *Policing Paris: The Origins of Modern Immigration Control between the Wars.* Ithaca, NY: Cornell University Press, 2006.

Rosenfeld, Oskar. *In the Beginning Was the Ghetto: Notebooks from Lodz.* Evanston, IL: Northwestern University Press, 2002.

Rosenhaft, Eve. "A Photographer and His 'Victims' 1934–1964: Reconstructing a Shared Experience of the Romani Holocaust." In *The Role of the Romanies: Images and Counter-Images of "Gypsies"/Romanies in European Cultures,* edited by Nicholas Saul and Susan Tebbutt. Liverpool: Liverpool University Press, 2004.

———. "At Large in the 'Gray Zone': Narrating the Romani Holocaust." In *Unsettling History: Archiving and Narrating in Historiography,* edited by Sebastian Jobs and Alf Lüdke, 149–68. Frankfurt am Main: Campus Verlag, 2010.

———. "Blacks and Gypsies in Nazi Germany: The Limits of the 'Racial State.'" *History Workshop Journal* 72, no. 1 (2011): 161–70.

Roth, Joseph. *Juden auf Wanderschaft.* Berlin: Die Schmiede, 1927.

Rothberg, Michael. *Multidirectional Memory: Remembering the Holocaust in the Age of Decolonization.* Cultural Memory in the Present. Stanford, CA: Stanford University Press, 2009.

———. "W.E.B. DuBois in Warsaw: Holocaust Memory and the Color Line, 1949–1952." *The Yale Journal of Criticism* 14, no. 1 (April 2001): 169–89.

Rüthers, Monica. *Juden und Zigeuner im europäischen Geschichtstheater: "Jewish Spaces", "Gypsy Spaces": Kazimierz und Saintes-Maries-de-la-Mer in der neuen Folklore Europas.* Kultur und soziale Praxis. Bielefeld, Germany: Transcript, 2012.

Sadílková, Helena. "The Postwar Migration of Romani Families from Slovakia to the Bohemian Lands: A Complex Legacy of War and Genocide in Czechoslovakia." In *Jewish and Romani Families in the Holocaust and Its Aftermath,* edited by Eliyana R. Adler and Kateřina Čapková, 190–217. New Brunswick, NJ: Rutgers University Press, 2021.

Salazar, Mariana Sabino. "The Romani Archives and Documentation Center: A Migratory Archive?" *Critical Romani Studies* 3, no. 2 (2020): 104–11.

Salvatici, Silvia. "From Displaced Persons to Labourers: Allied Employment Policies in Post-War West Germany." In *The Disentanglement of Populations: Migration, Expulsion and Displacement in Post-War Europe, 1944–9,* edited by Jessica Reinisch and Elizabeth White, 210–28. Basingstoke, UK: Palgrave Macmillan, 2011.

———. "'Help the People to Help Themselves': UNRRA Relief Workers and European Displaced Persons." *Journal of Refugee Studies* 25, no. 3 (September 2012): 428–51.

Sambati, Douglas Neander. "Western Donors, Romani Organizations, and Uses of the Concept of Nation after 1989." *Critical Romani Studies* 3, no. 1 (December 2020): 26–45.

Sampson, Anthony. *The Scholar Gypsy: The Quest for a Family Secret.* London: Murray, 1997.

Sanderson, Stewart. "Dora Yates: 1879–1974." In *Women and Tradition: A Neglected Group of Folklorists,* edited by Carmen Blacker and Hilda Roderick Ellis Davidson, 121–38. Durham, NC: Carolina Academic Press, 2001.

Sarna, Jonathan. "The American Jewish Press." In *The Oxford Handbook of American Public Opinion and the Media,* edited by Robert Y. Shapiro and Lawrence R. Jacobs, 537–50. The Oxford Handbooks of American Politics. Oxford: Oxford University Press, 2011.

Saul, Nicholas. *Gypsies and Orientalism in German Literature and Anthropology of the Long Nineteenth Century.* London: Legenda/Modern Humanities Research Association and Maney Publishing, 2007.

Saul, Nicholas, and Susan Tebbutt, eds. *The Role of the Romanies: Images and Counter-Images of "Gypsies"/Romanies in European Cultures.* Liverpool: Liverpool University Press, 2004.

Schechter, Ronald. *Obstinate Hebrews: Representations of Jews in France, 1715–1815.* Studies on the History of Society and Culture 49. Berkeley: University of California Press, 2003.

Schenk, Elisabeth. "Nachbarn und Grenzen, Begegnungen und Konflikte: Zwei niederösterreichische Gemeinden an der March." Master's thesis [Diplomarbeit], University of Vienna, 2008.

Schlager, Erika. "Policy and Practice: A Case Study of U.S. Foreign Policy Regarding the Situation of Roma in Europe." In *Realizing Roma Rights,* edited by Jacqueline Bhabha, Andrzej Mirga, and Margareta Matache, 59–75. Philadelphia: University of Pennsylvania Press, 2017.

Schmidt, Christine. "'We Are All Witnesses': Eva Reichmann and the Wiener Library's Eyewitness Accounts Collection." In *Agency and the Holocaust: Essays in Honor of Debórah Dwork,* edited by Thomas Kühne and Mary Jane Rein, 123–40. Palgrave Studies in the History of Genocide. Cham, Switzerland: Springer International Publishing, 2020.

Schorske, Carl E. *Fin-de-Siècle Vienna: Politics and Culture.* New York: Vintage Books, 1981.

Schram, Laurence. "De Malines à Auschwitz: Déportation des Juifs et des Tsiganes du Nord de la France." *Tsafon* [Lille, France], no. 79 (2020): 75–96.

Schroeter, Daniel J. "Between Metropole and French North Africa: Vichy's Anti-Semitic Legislation and Colonialism's Racial Hierarchies." In *The Holocaust and North Africa,* edited by Aomar Boum and Sarah Abrevaya Stein, 19–49. Stanford, CA: Stanford University Press, 2019.

Schulman, Elias. *Yung Vilne 1929–1939.* New York: Getseltn, 1946.

Scott, James C. *The Art of Not Being Governed: An Anarchist History of Upland Southeast Asia.* Yale Agrarian Studies Series. New Haven, CT: Yale University Press, 2009.

Segev, Tom. "The Makings of History: A Holocaust Obsession." *Haaretz,* July 10, 2008.

———. *Simon Wiesenthal: The Life and Legends.* New York: Doubleday, 2010.

Segev, Zohar. *The World Jewish Congress during the Holocaust: Between Activism and Restraint.* New Perspectives on Modern Jewish History 7. Munich: De Gruyter Oldenbourg, 2014.

Shandler, Jeffrey. *Holocaust Memory in the Digital Age: Survivors' Stories and New Media Practices.* Stanford, CA: Stanford University Press, 2017.

———. *While America Watches: Televising the Holocaust.* New York: Oxford University Press, 1999.

Shenker, Noah. *Reframing Holocaust Testimony*. Bloomington: Indiana University Press, 2015.

Sierra, María. "Creating Romanestan: A Place to Be a Gypsy in Post-Nazi Europe." *European History Quarterly* 49, no. 2 (2019): 272–92.

Sijes, B. A. *Vervolging van zigeuners in Nederland 1940–1945*. Monografieën—Rijksinstituut voor Oorlogsdocumentatie 13. The Hague, Netherlands: Nijhoff, 1979.

Slate, Nico. *Black Power beyond Borders: The Global Dimensions of the Black Power Movement*. Contemporary Black History. New York: Palgrave Macmillan, 2012.

Slezkine, Yuri. *The Jewish Century*. Princeton, NJ: Princeton University Press, 2004.

Slobodian, Quinn. *Foreign Front: Third World Politics in Sixties West Germany*. Radical Perspectives. Durham, NC: Duke University Press, 2012.

Slyomovics, Susan. *How to Accept German Reparations*. Pennsylvania Studies in Human Rights. Philadelphia: University of Pennsylvania Press, 2014.

Smith, Helmut Walser. *Germany, a Nation in Its Time: Before, during, and after Nationalism, 1500–2000*. New York: Liveright Publishing Corporation, 2020.

Smith, Mark L. *The Yiddish Historians and the Struggle for a Jewish History of the Holocaust*. Detroit, MI: Wayne State University Press, 2019.

Smith, Melanie, and Anita Zatori. "The Political and Social Transformation of Roma and Jewish Communities through Tourism in Budapest." In *Transformational Tourism: Host Perspectives*, edited by Yvette Reisinger, 69–79. Wallingford, UK: CAB International, 2015.

Solonari, Vladimir. "Ethnic Cleansing or 'Crime Prevention'? Deportation of Romanian Roma." In *The Nazi Genocide of the Roma: Reassessment and Commemoration*, edited by Anton Weiss-Wendt, 96–119. New York: Berghahn, 2013.

Späti, Christina. *Die schweizerische Linke und Israel: Israelbegeisterung, Antizionismus und Antisemitismus zwischen 1967 und 1991*. Essen, Germany: Klartext, 2006.

Stampfer, Shaul. *Families, Rabbis and Education: Essays on Traditional Jewish Society in Eastern Europe*. London: Littman Library of Jewish Civilization, 2010.

State Museum of Auschwitz-Birkenau. *Memorial Book: The Gypsies at Auschwitz-Birkenau*. Munich: K. G. Saur, 1993.

Stauber, Roni and Raphael Vago. "The Politics of Memory: Jews and Roma Commemorate Their Persecution." In *The Roma: A Minority in Europe: Historical, Political and Social Perspectives*, edited by Roni Stauber and Raphael Vago, 117–33. Budapest: Central European University Press, 2007. https://books.openedition.org/ceup/1418.

Stein, Arlene. *Reluctant Witnesses: Survivors, Their Children, and the Rise of the Holocaust Consciousness*. Oxford: Oxford University Press, 2014.

Steinmetz, Selma. *Österreichs Zigeuner im NS-Staat*. Vienna: Europa-Verlag, 1966.

Stengel, Katharina. "Auschwitz zwischen Ost und West: Das Internationale Auschwitz-Komitee und die Entstehungsgeschichte des Sammelbandes 'Auschwitz. Zeugnisse und Berichte.'" In *Opfer als Akteure: Interventionen ehemaliger NS-Verfolgter in der Nachkriegszeit*, edited by Katharina Stengel and Werner Konitzer, 174–96. Jahrbuch zur Geschichte und Wirkung des Holocaust. Frankfurt am Main: Campus Verlag, 2008.

———. *Hermann Langbein: Ein Auschwitz-Überlebender in den erinnerungspolitischen Konflikten der Nachkriegszeit*. Frankfurt am Main: Campus Verlag, 2012.

Stengel, Katharina, and Werner Konitzer, eds. *Opfer als Akteure: Interventionen ehemaliger NS-Verfolgter in der Nachkriegszeit*. Jahrbuch zur Geschichte und Wirkung des Holocaust. Frankfurt am Main: Campus Verlag, 2008.

Stewart, Michael, ed. *The Gypsy "Menace": Populism and the New Anti-Gypsy Politics*. London: Hurst & Co., 2012.

———. "Remembering without Commemoration: The Mnemonics and Politics of Holocaust Memories among European Roma." *Journal of the Royal Anthropological Institute* 10, no. 3 (2004): 561–82.

———. *The Time of the Gypsies*. Boulder, CO: Westview Press, 1997.

Stola, Dariusz. "Anti-Zionism as a Multipurpose Policy Instrument: The Anti-Zionist Campaign in Poland, 1967–1968." *The Journal of Israeli History* 25, no. 1 (2006): 175–201.

Stoler, Ann Laura. *Along the Archival Grain: Epistemic Anxieties and Colonial Common Sense*. Princeton, NJ: Princeton University Press, 2009.

Stone, Dan. "The Memory of the Archive: The International Tracing Service and the Construction of the Past as History." *Dapim: Studies on the Holocaust* 31, no. 2 (May 2017): 69–88.

Strzelecki, Andrzej. "The Plunder of Victims and Their Corpses." In *Anatomy of the Auschwitz Death Camp*, edited by Israel Gutman and Michael Berenbaum, 246–66. Bloomington: Indiana University Press, published in association with the United States Holocaust Memorial Museum, 1994.

Subotić, Jelena. *Yellow Star, Red Star: Holocaust Remembrance after Communism*. Cornell Scholarship Online. Ithaca, NY: Cornell University Press, 2019.

Suny, Ronald Grigor. "The Empire That Dared Not Speak Its Name: Making Nations in the Soviet State." *Current History* 116, no. 792 (2017): 251–57.

Sutzkever, Abraham. *From the Vilna Ghetto to Nuremberg: Memoir and Testimony*. Translated by Justin D. Cammy. Montreal: McGill-Queen's University Press, 2021.

Szymański, Tadeusz, Danuta Szymańska, and Tadeusz Snieszko. "The 'Hospital' in the Family Camp for Gypsies in Auschwitz-Birkenau." In *Nazi Medicine: Doctors, Victims, and Medicine in Auschwitz*. Vol. 3, by International Auschwitz Committee, 1–45. New York: Howard Fertig, 1986.

Taubitz, Jan. *Holocaust Oral History und das lange Ende der Zeitzeugenschaft*. Göttingen: Wallstein Verlag, 2016.

Tenenbaum, Joseph. "Auschwitz in Retrospect: The Self-Portrait of Rudolf Hoess, Commander of Auschwitz." *Jewish Social Studies* 15, no. 3/4 (1953): 203–36.

———. *Race and Reich: The Story of an Epoch*. New York: Twayne Publishers, 1956.

"The Yarnton Declaration of Jewish Intellectuals on the Future of Auschwitz." *European Judaism: A Journal for the New Europe* 23, no. 2 (1990): 43–45.

Ther, Philipp, and Ana Siljak, eds. *Redrawing Nations: Ethnic Cleansing in East-Central Europe, 1944–1948*. Lanham, MD: Rowman & Littlefield, 2001.

Thurner, Erika. *National Socialism and Gypsies in Austria*. Tuscaloosa: University of Alabama Press, 1998.

Trehan, Nidhi. "The Contentious Politics of the Indo-Romani Relationship: Reflections on the 'International Roma Conference and Cultural Festival' in New Delhi, February 2016 and Its Antecedents." *The Indian Journal of Social Work* 78, no. 1 (January 2017): 11–26.

Tremlett, Annabel. "Making a Difference without Creating a Difference: Super-Diversity as a New Direction for Research on Roma Minorities." *Ethnicities* 14, no. 6 (December 2014): 830–48.

Trouillot, Michel Rolph. *Silencing the Past: Power and the Production of History*. Boston: Beacon Press, 1995.

Turner, Mathew, Tony Joel, and David Lowe. "'Between Politics and Scholarship': The First Decade of the Institut für Zeitgeschichte, 1949–1958." *European History Quarterly* 49, no. 2 (April 2019): 250–71.

Tyaglyy, Mikhail. "Nazi Occupation Policies and the Mass Murder of the Roma in Ukraine." In *The Nazi Genocide of the Roma: Reassessment and Commemoration*, edited by Anton Weiss-Wendt, 120–52. New York: Berghahn, 2013.

Tyrnauer, Gabrielle. "Recording the Testimonies of Sinti Holocaust Survivors." In *Reflections on the Holocaust: Festschrift for Raul Hilberg on His Seventy-Fifth Birthday*, edited by Wolfgang Mieder and David Scrase, 223–37. Burlington, VT: Center for Holocaust Studies at the University of Vermont, 2001.

Uerlings, Herbert, and Iulia-Karin Patrut, eds. *"Zigeuner" und Nation: Repräsentation—Inklusion—Exklusion*. Frankfurt am Main: Peter Lang, 2008.

Ullrich, Peter. *Die Linke, Israel und Palästina: Nahostdiskurse in Großbritannien und Deutschland*. Berlin: Dietz, 2008.

Urban, Susanne, Sascha Feuchert, and Markus Roth, eds. *Fundstücke: Stimmen der Überlebenden des "Zigeunerlagers" Lackenbach*. Göttingen: Wallstein, 2014.

Valman, Nadia. *The Jewess in Nineteenth-Century British Literary Culture*. Cambridge Studies in Nineteenth-Century Literature and Culture. Cambridge: Cambridge University Press, 2007.

van Baar, Huub. *The European Roma: Minority Representation, Memory and the Limits of Transnational Governmentality*. Amsterdam: F&N, 2011. www.huubvanbaar.nl/uploads/3/8/0/4/38045389/van_baar_2011_-_the_european_roma.pdf.

van Loenen, Jan. "De andere 'Endlösung': Het duits vervolgingsbeleid jegens de zigeuners in de periode 1933–1945: Een beijdrage aan de studie van het racisme." Doctoral diss., University of Amsterdam, 1974.

Veidlinger, Jeffrey. *In the Shadow of the Shtetl: Small-Town Jewish Life in Soviet Ukraine*. Bloomington: Indiana University Press, 2013.

Verdery, Katherine. *Secrets and Truths: Ethnography in the Archive of Romania's Secret Police*. Budapest: Central European University Press, 2014.

Vermeersch, Peter. *The Romani Movement: Minority Politics and Ethnic Mobilization in Contemporary Central Europe*. New York: Berghahn Books, 2006.

Visser, Annelies. "Beeld en beleid: Woonwagenbewoners, zigeuners en de overheid, 1900 tot 1930." Doctoral diss., University of Amsterdam, 1975.

Volkov, Shulamit. "Antisemitism as Cultural Code: Reflections on the History and the Historiography of Antisemitism in Imperial Germany." *Leo Baeck Institute Yearbook* 23 (1978): 25–46.

Wachsmann, Nikolaus. *KL: A History of the Nazi Concentration Camps*. London: Little, Brown, 2015.

Warnock, Barbara. "Eva Reichmann." In *Verfolgen und Aufklären: Die erste Generation der Holocaustforschung / Crimes Uncovered: The First Generation of Holocaust Researchers*, edited by Hans-Christian Jasch and Stephan Lehnstaedt, 145–47. Berlin: Metropol, 2019.

Wawrzeniuk, Piotr. "Papusza: The Story of a Polish Roma Poet." *Balticworlds*, May 12, 2015. https://balticworlds.com/papusza/.

Weinke, Annette. *Eine Gesellschaft ermittelt gegen sich selbst: Die Geschichte der Zentralen Stelle Ludwigsburg 1958—2008.* 2nd ed. Darmstadt, Germany: WBG, 2012.

Weinmann, Martin, and Anne Kaiser, eds. *Das Nationalsozialistische Lagersystem = (CCP).* Frankfurt am Main: Zweitausendeins, 1990.

Weinstein, Eddie. *Quenched Steel: The Story of an Escape from Treblinka.* Jerusalem: Yad Vashem, 2002.

Weiss-Wendt, Anton. "Introduction." In *The Nazi Genocide of the Roma: Reassessment and Commemoration*, edited by Anton Weiss-Wendt, 1–26. New York: Berghahn, 2013.

———, ed. *The Nazi Genocide of the Roma: Reassessment and Commemoration.* New York: Berghahn, 2013.

Weld, Kirsten. *Paper Cadavers: The Archives of Dictatorship in Guatemala.* Durham, NC: Duke University Press, 2014.

Werb, Bret. "Fourteen Shoah Songbooks." *Musica Judaica* 20 (2013): 39–116.

Werner, Michael, and Bénédicte Zimmermann. "Vergleich, Transfer, Verflechtung: Der Ansatz der *histoire croisée* und die Herausforderung des Transnationalen." *Geschichte und Gesellschaft* 28 (2002): 607–36.

Widmann, Peter. "The Campaign Against the Restless: Criminal Biology and the Stigmatization of the Gypsies, 1890–1960." In *The Roma: A Minority in Europe: Historical, Political and Social Perspectives*, edited by Roni Stauber and Raphael Vago, 19–30. Budapest: Central European University Press, 2007.

Wieviorka, Annette. *Le procès Eichmann.* Brussels: Editions Complexe, 1989.

———. *The Era of the Witness.* Ithaca, NY: Cornell University Press, 2006.

Wildenthal, Lora. *The Language of Human Rights in West Germany.* Philadelphia: University of Pennsylvania Press, 2013.

Wilke, Jürgen. "Die Fernsehserie 'Holocaust' als Medienereignis." *Historical Social Research / Historische Sozialforschung* 30, no. 4 (114) (2005): 9–17.

Willing, Matthias. *Das Bewahrungsgesetz (1918–1967): Eine rechtshistorische Studie zur Geschichte der deutschen Fürsorge.* Tübingen, Germany: Mohr Siebeck, 2003.

Winkler, Willi. "Institut für Zeitgeschichte: Altnazis waren dabei." *Süddeutsche*, April 2, 2018. www.sueddeutsche.de/kultur/institut-fuer-zeitgeschichte-alte-kameraden-1.3926474.

Winter, Walter Stanoski. *Winter Time: Memoirs of a German Sinto Who Survived Auschwitz.* Hatfield, UK: University of Hertfordshire Press, 2004.

———. *Winter Zeit: Erinnerungen Eines Deutschen Sinto, Der Auschwitz Überlebt Hat.* Hamburg: Ergebnisse, 1999.

Wippermann, Wolfgang. *"Auserwählte Opfer?": Shoah und Porrajmos im Vergleich: Eine Kontroverse.* Berlin: Frank & Timme, 2005.

———. *Wie die Zigeuner: Antisemitismus und Antiziganismus im Vergleich.* Antifa Edition. Berlin: Elefanten Press, 1997.

Wittmann, Rebecca. *Beyond Justice: The Auschwitz Trial.* Cambridge, MA: Harvard University Press, 2005.

Wouters, Nico. "The Belgian Trials (1945–1951)." In *Holocaust and Justice: Representation and Historiography of the Holocaust in Post-War Trials*, edited by David Bankier and Dan Michman, 219–44. Jerusalem: Yad Vashem, 2010.

Yablonka, Hanna. *The State of Israel vs. Adolf Eichmann.* New York: Schocken, 2004.

Zahova, Sofiya, Raluca Bianca Roman, and Aleksandar Marinov, eds. *Roma Writings: Romani Literature and Press in Central, South-Eastern and Eastern Europe from the 19th Century until World War II*. Paderborn, Germany: Brill Schöningh, 2021.

Zahra, Tara. "'Condemned to Rootlessness and Unable to Budge': Roma, Migration Panics, and Internment in the Habsburg Empire." *American Historical Review* 122, no. 3 (June 2017): 702–26.

Zelkowicz, Josef. *In Those Terrible Days: Writings from the Lodz Ghetto*. Jerusalem: Yad Vashem, 2002.

Zimmer, Bernd Joachim. *International Tracing Service Arolsen: Von der Vermisstensuche zur Haftbescheinigung: Die Organisationsgeschichte eines "ungewollten Kindes" während der Besatzungszeit*. Bad Arolsen, Germany: Waldeckischer Geschichtsverein, 2011.

Zimmermann, Michael. *Rassenutopie und Genozid: Die nationalsozialistische "Lösung der Zigeunerfrage."* Hamburg: Christians, 1996.

Zweig, Ronald W. *German Reparations and the Jewish World: A History of the Claims Conference*. Boulder, CO: Westview Press, 1987.

INDEX

Page numbers in italic refer to figures

A NOTE ON THE TYPE

This book has been composed in Arno, an Old-style serif typeface in the classic Venetian tradition, designed by Robert Slimbach at Adobe.